The First 100 Years

in the Americas

1917 - 2017

The Rev. R. John Brockmann, TSSF

1924—First symbol of the Third Order Secular of the American Congregation of Franciscans—cover art of *Bundle of Myrrh* Manual. The angel holds a shield with a *Tau* cross representing Christ's cross. Two arms cross the Tau: from the right, Christ's bare arm with the wound from the nail in front of Francis' clothed arm from the left with the mark of the stigmata. These arms create the *Conformity* (see page 13).

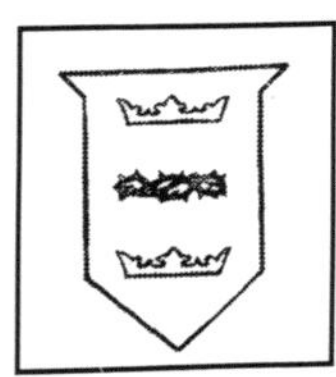

1929—"To the Crown of Thorns of the King of kings which (as the Third Order Shield on the cover of this book doth represent) was more to St. Louis and St. Elizabeth than their crowns of gold." Cover art of *Little Book of the Rule* (see pages 15, 33, and 44).

1984—MaryAnn Jackman creates the *Dancing Francis* as the Province of Americas' logo. Amongst many uses in the province, it was used in the masthead of the *Franciscan Times* from Winter 1999 to Winter 2016.

2002—Jacqui Belcher, Provincial Secretary, creates a triptych with three pieces of art for displays at diocesan conventions. Portions of the art of this triptych were also used on the homepage of the Province's website in 2005 & 2006 (see pages 231 & 232). The art on the cover is also part of this triptych.

ISBN-13: 978-1544813356
ISBN-10: 154481335x

Library of Congress Cataloging-in-Publication Data
Brockmann, R. John.
The First 100 Years in the Americas, 1917-2017 : The Third Order Society of St. Francis
Includes references and index.
ISBN-13: 978-1544813356
1. The Third Order Society of St. Francis, Province of the Americas, 1917-2017. 2. Anglican. Episcopalian. Religious Order. 3. Third Order Secular Franciscans. American Congregation of Franciscans. 4. TSSF Guardian. TSSF Provincial Minister. TSSF Minister General. 5. Justice, Peace & Integrity of Creation.

Acknowledgements

There are so many who knowingly or unknowingly have helped with this gigantic project. I apologize here and now if I have forgot to thank you personally: Br. ____for his hundreds of digitized pictures of the Orders of our Province; Br. Dunstan who in his 90's had a mind like a whip and was able to identify many of the people in these pictures. Clint and Weber and Kris who have helped post the TSSF archives up on the web from which so much of this is drawn. For the many I interviewed or emailed and who passed on their archival material: C. David Burt, Warren Tanghe, Mary Ann Jackman, Peter Funk, Kale King, Caroline Banks, E. Will Drake, Marie Webner, Judith Robinson, Lyndon Hutchinson-Housell, and Br. Robert Hugh.

For those who have help in the production itself of this book, most especially Tom Johnson who is not only an accomplished editor, but a good friend. For Anita Miner who has long been a friend and very helpful editor. For my editorial team: Alice Baird (the wiz with layout and design), Cathleen Reynolds, Verleah Kosloske, and Stuart Schlegel.

Online Historical Documents Easily Available to Complete Your Understanding of Our History

On the TSSF.org website, under the Resources tab, you will find complete copies of the material referenced in these pages: the early Formation booklets and letters (*Bundle of Myrrh* (1924), *Little Book of the Third Order Rule* (1929), *Third Order Manual* (1962), and *Formation Letters,* 1968-70, by Peter Funk); the 1925 Provincial Roster; *Tertiary Tidings* (London custodia newsletters from the Battle of Britain, 1938-1941); the *Information Sheet* complete run (1980-1998); the complete run of *Franciscans Canada* and its follow-up *THAW!*

Also you can find access to an indexed complete run of *Franciscan Times* (1971-2017) at the bottom of the homepage. Additionally, the website's video archives include: *A Day in the Life of* [Regional] *Convocations* (1995), five videos from the 1997 Provincial Convocation in New Orleans, and one from the Santa Barbara Convocation (2002).

When you see the name of a document in italics followed by an *, this indicates that that document in its entirety is reproduced in the online version of this book stored on the TSSF website (tssf.org) and located in the Resources pull-down menu. It is located in the same chapter as its callout here in this printed volume.

In the back of the book, **Discover More On TSSF.ORG,** there is also a chapter by chapter list of more to explore in the materials listed in TSSF.org

Each chapter concludes with a list of its references.

Imprimatur

Kenneth E. Norian, Minister General, Third Order, Society of Saint Francis, given on this feast day of the Annunciation, March 25th, 2017.

Introduction: What Kind of History is this History?

When one reviews what Francis of Assisi wrote, one is struck by how "unoriginal" most of his compositions were. Most were a pastiche of scripture and historical documents of the Church. Such an approach to composition reflected his humility, suggesting that there was nothing higher or truer than Scripture, so he would "write" with the words and phrases of this highest and truest language rather than the paltry inventions of his own creation.

This is a humble Franciscan history of Franciscans, and is thus, following the composition methods of our founder, a pastiche of a 100 years of voices in the Province of the Americas. Rather than comment upon papers or articles, the papers or articles are presented whole; so, in one fashion, this history is an **anthology** by many authors. Many gifted people over the last 100 years wrestled with many topics in the life of a tertiary, and the greatest acknowledgement we can pay to them is to read what they wrote. As 21st century Internet-experienced "readers", we are accustomed to a visual presentation of information. Thus you will find these pages filled with over 170 pictures, diagrams, and tables so that this history is also a **scrapbook** of what we looked like and who we were over the past 100 years. This history also has more **flesh and blood** stories written by those who experienced them rather than a comprehensive collection of facts.

We begin by looking at the big picture of the Province and its development over the last 100 years primarily using the most basic data in the annual directories, names and addresses. These directories were published sporadically in 1926, 1935, and 1948 until becoming regularized in the 1950s. One reason to look at such a "big picture" is because the specifics of the first 50 years of the Province are missing. Only the London and the New York Custodias ("Custodia" meant what we experience as "regional gatherings") left any record of their work and life prior to 1950. In fact, for the first 50 years of this Third Order Province, our only recorded notice appeared in the First Order's *Little Chronicle* newsletter.

The American Province's epoch year was 1968 when the independent Third Order Secular Order of Franciscans, American Congregation of Franciscans (TSF) joined with the British Third Order, Society of St. Francis (TSSF). Simultaneously with this union was the beginning of the independent existence of the Province of the Americas. Such a independent existence required governance (e.g. the creation of a Corporation and a Standing Committee with membership primarily drawn from tertiaries), record keeping in Chapter minutes, and the establishment of communication networks, notably the *Franciscan Newsletter/Times* and the *Information Sheet*. Much of the content of this book is drawn from these sources.

The first eight chapters of the book use the leaders of various eras to organize the historical information:

- Father Joseph was the leader of the Third Order Secular of Franciscans, American Congregation of Franciscans (TSF) from 1917 to 1966;

- Br. Paul was his successor from 1966 to 1968, and he along with the *Third Order Corporation* took TSF into TSSF;
- John Scott was the first tertiary Guardian from 1973-80;
- Kale King, second tertiary Guardian from 1980-81;
- Dee Dobson, third Guardian and first Minister Provincial from 1981-90;
- Alden Whitney, second Minister Provincial from 1990-96; and
- Anita Catron, third Minister Provincial from 1997 to 2002.

Then events of the Province became less easy to organize around single individuals, and so the next four chapters look at themes, projects, discussions or events that overlap the terms of individual Guardians or Ministers Provincial:

- the integration of Brazil's Order of St. Francis (OSF) and the Province of the Americas;
- the creation of the Safe Community and Conflict Resolution;
- our final act of independence from the First Order, the choosing of our own Bishop Protector;
- the evolution of the Justice, Peace, and the Integrity of Creation network (JPIC); and
- the Canadian story in our Province.

The next four chapters again organize events using the terms of the Ministers Provincial:

- Masud Ibn Syedullah, 2002-05;
- Ken Norian, 2005-11;
- John Brockmann, 2011-4; and
- Tom Johnson, 2014-

The final chapter finally returns to work that transcended any individual's term of office for it celebrates the work of the many authors of our Province. From Susan Pitchford's 2014 book, *The Sacred Gaze*; to spiritual anthropology in Stuart Schlegel's 1987 book, *Wisdom from a Rainforest,* to considerations of healthcare in William F. Haynes's 2010 book, *Is There a God in Health Care?*, tertiaries in the Province of the Americas have written many important books over a very long period of time.

For almost a 100 years this Province's tertiaries have worked to fulfill the Principle of Day 18: *In particular some of us accept the duty of contributing, through research and writing, to a better understanding of the church's mission in the world: the application of Christian principles to the use and distribution of wealth; questions concerning justice and peace; and of all other questions concerning the life of faith.*

Distribution of TSF 1926

HI
DC
State, Province, or Country Having at Least Five Percent of the Order
State with Some Presence (2 or more)
State with No Tertiaries

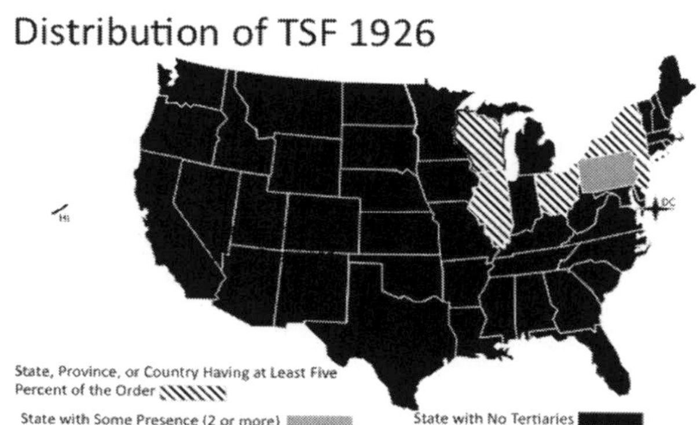

Distribution of of TSF 1935

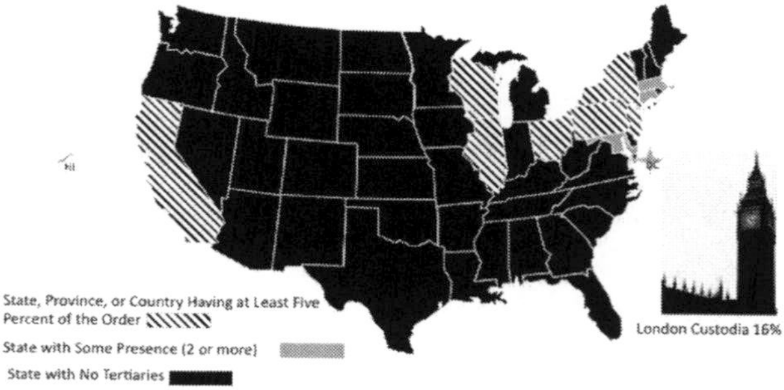

HI
State, Province, or Country Having at Least Five Percent of the Order
State with Some Presence (2 or more)
State with No Tertiaries
London Custodia 16%

Chapter 1: First the Long View— How the Province of the Americas Evolved

1926

The Third Order Secular of Franciscans, American Congregation of Franciscans (TSF) was founded in Cincinnati, Ohio in 1917, and in 1918, Father Joseph was invited by the Bishop of Fond du Lac Wisconsin to move to Merrill, Wisconsin where he then founded the First Order Brothers of the Province in 1919, the Second Order, the Poor Clares, in 1922, and professed the first tertiary, Mrs. Mary Humphrey, on June 8, 1923. A directory of the Province was not created until a reorganization of the Third Order in 1926, and thus it should not come as a surprise that the first center of tertiary activity of the 37 professed members and novices was centered in Wisconsin and Illinois (the "biretta belt"*). Other groups of Tertiaries gathered in New York/New Jersey/Pennsylvania. In his June 1925 Roster (posted on the TSSF website in *Historical Documents*), Father Joseph lamented that "a good many people apply to join the Order, enroll themselves as postulants and after a month or two cease reporting, and even some who have been clothed [a.k.a. "noviced"] cease reporting and so have to be dropped.... Apparently the monthly report is the hardest part of the Rule to keep, but it is by all means the most important, for few people will go on keeping the Rule without such constant spur, and, for most, the only contact the tertiary has with the Order is the monthly report."

1935

Nine years later in 1935, the Order doubled in its membership to 75, and moved its center of activity beyond Wisconsin, Illinois, New York, New Jersey, and Pennsylvania to California and London.

On June 15, 1928, Father Joseph moved the headquarters of the First Order to Mount Sinai, Long Island, in New York, and the Second Order Poor Clares also relocated to Maryhill in Mount Sinai.

By 1935 the membership had matured with nearly 80% of the members professed and only 10% novices and 10% postulants.

With the 1935 Directory one can begin to look at the longevity of those professed or in formation. For example, in the picture of a 1926 novicing ("clothing") with Father Joseph in the photo on page 15, one does not find the newly "clothed" Paul Everest's name on the roll of the next Directory in 1935. In fact, that Directory indicated that only 15% of those professed or noviced in 1926 continued in the Order (or had died while in the Order).

* *Expression for dioceses near the Great Lakes that were once characterized by Anglo-catholic practices. The term is derived from the fondness of some Anglo-catholic clergy for wearing biretta hats.*

Distribution of of TSF 1948

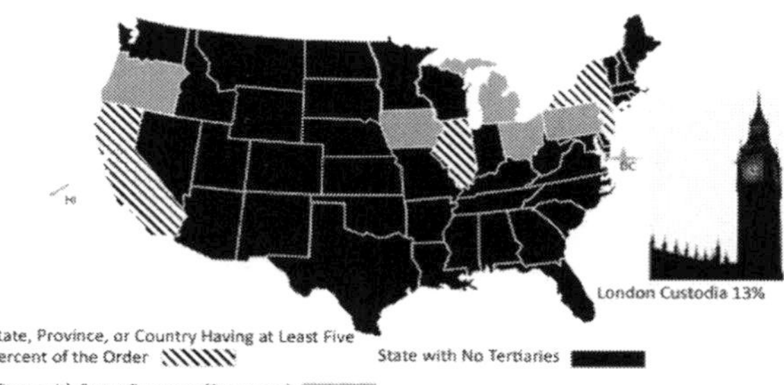

Distribution of of TSF 1955

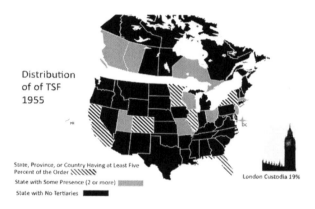

HI
DC
London Custodia 19%
State, Province, or Country Having at Least Five Percent of the Order
State with Some Presence (2 or more)
State with No Tertiaries

Distribution of of TSF 1960

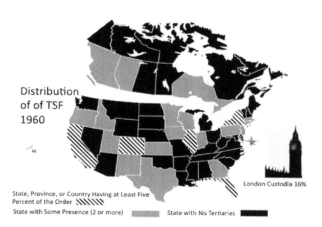

HI
DC
London Custodia 16%
State, Province, or Country Having at Least Five Percent of the Order
State with Some Presence (2 or more)
State with No Tertiaries

1948

Overall membership after WW II dropped 16% to 63. The distribution of the membership moved from concentrations in a few states and London now to a wider dispersion of members in six new states (indicated in gray): Iowa, Michigan, Indiana, Washington DC, Ohio, and Oregon. Also, for the first time, a place that was once a center of tertiary activity, Wisconsin, ceased to be a center of tertiary activity. The fact that the First and Second Orders had left Wisconsin in 1928 strongly suggests the reason for the diminished Third Order activity in Wisconsin.

Longevity of those professed or noviced was increasing with nearly 43% remaining from the 1926 directory—or 20 years in the Order—and from the 1935 directory—or at least 13 years in the the Order. So as of 1948, longevity of the members of the Order had dramatically increased.

1955

Seven years later, the Order grew by 120% to 148 professed and novices. The percentage of the Order's membership composed by the London Custodia also grew, and now tertiaries were gathering numbers in three provinces of Canada. Additionally, numbers of tertiaries were gathering in Colorado, Minnesota and Florida, while diminishing in New Jersey and Pennsylvania. Only New York and Illinois continue as populous centers of TSF from 1926 Directory, and California remains from the 1935 Directory. The Order was also becoming younger with a larger percentage of the Province being in formation as postulants and novices.

Longevity of those professed or noviced diminished to 31% remaining from the 1926 directory—or nearly 30 years in the Order—from the 1935 directory—or at least 20 years in the Order—and from the 1948 directory—or at least 7 years in the Order.

1960

Five years later, the Order basically remained steady at 146 professed and novices. No new centers of tertiary activity appear, but tertiaries vocations popped up in new states, especially in the South: Texas, New Mexico, and Georgia mark something new. The percentage of the Order composed by the London Custodia remained steady, as do the tertiaries gathering in three provinces of Canada. The Order continued the trend begun in 1955 of becoming younger with larger percentages of the Order being in formation as postulants and novices.

Longevity of those professed or noviced decreased to 17% remaining from the 1926 directory—or nearly 34 years in the Order—from the 1935 directory—or at least 25 years in the Order—from the 1948 directory—or at least 12 years in the Order.

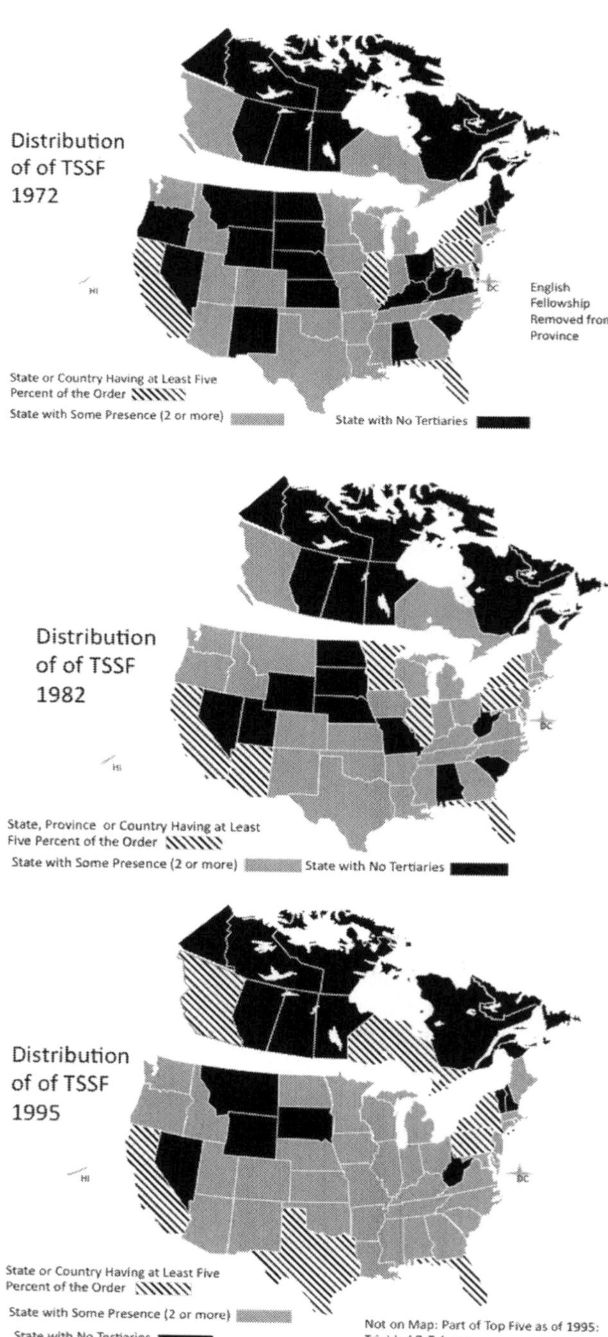

Distribution of of TSSF 1972
HI
DC
English Fellowship Removed from Province
State or Country Having at Least Five Percent of the Order
State with Some Presence (2 or more)
State with No Tertiaries
Distribution of of TSSF 1982
HI
DC
State, Province or Country Having at Least Five Percent of the Order
State with Some Presence (2 or more)
State with No Tertiaries
Distribution of of TSSF 1995
HI
DC
State or Country Having at Least Five Percent of the Order
State with Some Presence (2 or more)
State with No Tertiaries
Not on Map: Part of Top Five as of 1995: Trinidad & Tobago

1972

The Directory for 1968 has yet to be found, but it would show a tectonic shift in the Province, née Order, that will be discussed at length in Chapter 3. In 1967 the Third Order Secular of Franciscans, American Congregation of Franciscans, merged with The Third Order, Society of St. Francis, headquartered in England. As a consequence, the London Custodia of the American Congregation of Franciscans; 16% of the whole Third Order Secular of Franciscans, American Congregation of Franciscans disappeared (22) as well as 97 others both those professed and in formation in the Americas—119 in total. This was the largest exodus in the Order/Province's history.

By 1972, the new Province in the Americas had begun to lead a much more independent existence vis a vis the Province's First and Second Orders. There was a Third Order Provincial Chapter and a Provincial Guardian. The Province re-organized and increased to 219 professed members and novices. Such a dramatic increase continued for the next twenty years to the mid-1990s. No new centers of tertiary activity appear, but the spread of tertiaries to new states, especially again in the South: Oklahoma, Arkansas, Louisiana, Mississippi, Tennessee, and North Carolina; in the West: Arizona and Washington State, as well as the re-emergence in the Midwest: Missouri, Iowa, Minnesota, Wisconsin, Michigan, and Indiana mark something new. The Province quite dramatically reversed the trend begun in 1955 of becoming younger. In 1972 there seemed to be a dramatic fall in the numbers in formation to only 16% of all members and 84% of all members professed.

1982

The Province increased by 40% to 309 professed members and novices. A new center of tertiary activity appeared in Arizona, and the spread of tertiaries to new states becomes widespread now with only 10 states without any members. In 1982 the general trend in numbers in formation returns back to its earlier percentages with 51% of all members and 49% of all members professed. Including the recently deceased, 11% of the Province had been professed or noviced for at least 22 years.

1995

The Province experienced its largest increase of 117% to 672 professed members and novices. This was despite the fact of the second largest exodus in the Province in 1992-3 of 74 individuals. Since 1967, there had been no centers of tertiary activity outside the US and Canadian borders. However, with this Directory we find that there are new centers of tertiary activity where the First Order Brothers had traveled in Trinidad and Tobago.

In 1995 there was a dramatic fall in the numbers in formation to only 22% of all members with 78% of all members professed. These numbers and percentages remain fairly constant for the next couple of decades.

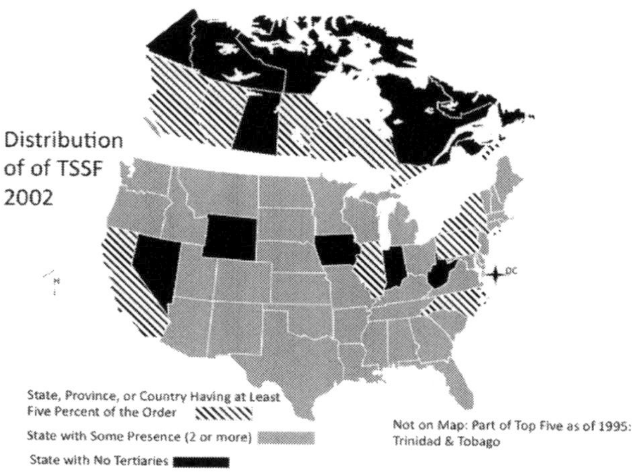

2002

The 2002 Directory indicates that the Province experienced the second decrease of its numbers since 1948—a drop of about 20% to 548 professed members and novices.

The 2002 Directory continued to show centers of tertiary activity outside the US and Canada, in Guyana, Trinidad, and Tobago. North Carolina also became a center of tertiary activity for the first time.

In 2002 there seemed to be steady state in formation (22% of all members) while 78% of all members were professed.

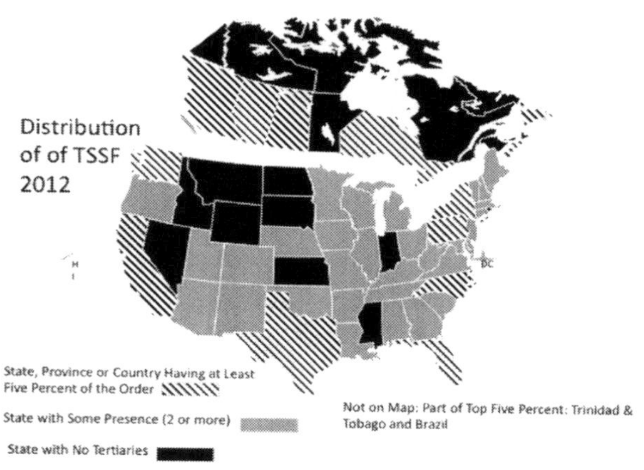

2012

The Province remained somewhat at a steady state, although there was a drop of 10 members to 538 professed members and novices.

The 2012 Directory continued to show centers of tertiary activity outside the US and Canada, in Trinidad and Tobago, Guyana, and now for the first time in Brazil. Washington State also became a center of tertiary activity for the first time. In 2012 there was little change in the proportion of membership in formation (19%) while 80% of all members were professed.

Three Exoduses Have Reformed the Character of the Province

Three times the Third Order in the Americas experienced a large (percentage) exodus of members. In 1919 Father Joseph made the Rule stricter when he reorganized the Third Order,and nearly half left. In 1968 when TSF became a TSSF province, nearly a third of the members left. And, in 1992-3, when the Province explicitly welcomed gay men and women, many conservatives left to found the Franciscan Order of the Divine Compassion (FODC)

Chapter Two: Father Joseph (Rev. Claude Crookston) Era 1917-1966

The First Religous Orders in the Episcopal Church

Henry VIII closed down all religious Orders in the mid-sixteenth century, and, only with the Oxford Movement in the 1830s, did the Anglican Church begin to recognize religious Orders. In the Episcopal Church in the United States, of those Orders which have continued, the first religious Order to be founded was the Community of St. Mary in 1865 (New York), followed by the Society of Saint John the Evangelist in 1870 (Boston), the Sisters of St. Margaret in 1873 (Boston), and the Community of Saint John Baptist in 1874 (New York). In 1884, the Order of the Holy Cross was founded in New York. Thus the centers of American religious Orders up to 1884 were Boston and New York. (Anson, Chapter VII, 1955)

However, in the 1880s, religious Orders began to be established in the American heartland: in 1882, in the Diocese of Fond du Lac in Wisconsin, Bishop Charles Grafton helped to establish the American Congregation of Saint Benedict (now The Benedictine Order of St John the Beloved), and, in 1898, the Community of the Transfiguration was established in the Cincinnati's West End in the parish of St. Luke's. The founder of the Community of the Transfiguration (C.T.), Eva Lee Matthews (Mother Eva Mary), was the sister of St. Luke's rector (The Rev. Paul Matthews). Bishop Boyd Vincent of the Diocese of Southern Ohio was intimately involved in their founding. (Anson, 1955, p. 563)

In the map on page 10, Figure A, St. Luke's Church is in the upper right corner, and one and half blocks away at 1711 Freeman Avenue, is Bethany House founded by Mother Eva Mary and the Community of the Transfiguration in 1898. Also in Figure A, at 1627 Freeman Street, is the House of Our Lady Help of Christians founded by the Rev. Claude Crookston in 1917.

Founding an Anglican Franciscan Order in the Americas

The religious Orders founded in the Episcopal Church in the United States from 1865 to 1898 were largely based on Benedictine principles and sensibilities. However, in 1898, Graymoor Friary in Garrison New York was the site of the first Franciscan foundation in the Episcopal Church. The Franciscan sisters and friars of the Order of the Atonement with Father Paul and Sister Lurana as their leaders created and publicized the *Week of Prayer for Christian Unity* (1908) that is still celebrated today. However, as part of their movement towards unity, this Episcopal Order advocated the primacy of the Roman pontiff. Such a position soon became untenable, and the whole Order with two friars, five sisters and ten tertiaries left the Episcopal Church in 1909 to transfer to the Roman Catholic Church. (This was the third U.S. religious Order to transfer to the Roman Catholic Church. (Anson, p. 547-8))

The Rev Claude Crookston - Fr Joseph, SSF

1909 Corporate Prayer

For the Founding of an American Franciscan Order

Blessed are the poor in Spirit: for theirs is the kingdom of heaven.

V. Francis poor and lowly enters heaven rich.

R. And is honored with the songs of heaven.

Grant, O Lord, to the American Church, many souls endued with the spirit of our Blessed Father Francis: and call them together under the Seraphic Rules, that the work Thou didst once begin in manifesting Thy glory in the lowly way may be continued in our generation.

Through Christ our Lord. Amen

Twenty miles further up the Hudson River, a Commissioned Lay Reader of the Diocese of New York, Claude Jansen Crookston, was probably familiar with Father Paul, Sister Lurana, and their foundation. Moreover, when the Franciscan Society of the Atonement left the Episcopal Church, and when some men and women in New York formed a group to pray for the re-formation of an Episcopal Franciscan Order, nineteen-year-old Claude Crookston emerged as a leader in the group.

From this time forward, young Claude Crookston seemed to have begun a single-minded quest to refound a Franciscan religious Order in the Episcopal Church. Yet, very much akin to St. Francis's 13th century mistakes and detours as he slowly came to understand his call to "Rebuild My Church," Claude Crookston had many 20th century mistakes and detours as he worked to establish a Franciscan religious Order in America.

His clerical mentor as a Commissioned Lay Reader in the Diocese of New York, the Rev. John Marshall Chew, arranged for Crookston to journey south to Uniontown, Kentucky where the Rev. Dr. Frederick Thompson, rector of Saint John's Episcopal Church, had a school for ministry postulants. From Uniontown, Crookston matriculated at the University of the South in Sewanee Tennessee where he completed his undergraduate degree in 1913. From Sewanee, Crookston went directly to General Theological Seminary back in New York. Somehow around this time, Crookston became an ordination candidate sponsored by the Missionary Diocese of Fond du Lac in Wisconsin where Bishop Grafton had earlier helped to establish the American Congregation of Saint Benedict. On behalf of the Bishop Weller, the then current Bishop of Fond du Lac, Crookston was ordained as deacon by a Pennsylvania bishop in St. Paul's Church, Overbrook, Pennsylvania (March 30, 1913).

Within months, Crookston journeyed out to Wisconsin and became the resident priest of Tomahawk, Wisconsin on June 13, 1913. (Jones, McVean and Others, 1924) Eight months later in February 1914, Crookston traveled to England to visit the Society of the Divine Compassion (SDC)—one of the few British religious Orders seeking to revive a Franciscan foundation—to see if they would take an American aspirant into their novitiate. The SDC declined. (Dunstan, p. 219)

Upon his return to the Diocese of Fond du Lac, Bishop Weller, Crookston's diocesan bishop, urged Crookston to join the Order of the Holy Cross or the Society of Saint John the Evangelist since Weller failed to see the need for a new community. Crookston, however, persisted in his vision of an episcopal Franciscan Order. (Williams, p. 154) Yet within the year, Crookston resigned his parish responsibilities in Tomahawk because of illness.

Leaving Wisconsin To See What Ohio and Tennessee Might Offer

At about the time that Crookston went on sick leave from his parish and the Diocese of Fond du Lac, his seminary roommate, Frank Gavin, was called as rector of St Luke's Church, Cincinnati. From this parish, the Community of the Transfiguration had been successfully founded seventeen years earlier. Crookston probably thought what better parish and diocese to launch a re-founding of Franciscan Orders in the US than here? So Crookston joined Gavin as an Assistant Rector that August. Within the year, however, Crookston received a letter of reprimand from Bishop Vincent of the Diocese of Southern Ohio concerning Crookston's Anglo-catholic practice of "reservation of the Sacrament." (Williams, p. 154) A strong objection to Reserving the Sacrament and a reprimand should have been expected from this "low church" bishop. (Krumm, 1989)

Crookston had begun his ministry as Assistant Minister at St. Luke's on August 1, 1915, left on October 4, 1915, only to resume his ministry as Assistant Minister on June 1, 1916. Thus there were eight months when he was gone from both his canonical diocese, Diocese of Fond du Lac, and from his duties in St. Luke's parish in Cincinnati. A hint of where he was and what he was up to appears in the record of the *84th Annual Convention of the Diocese of Tennessee* where it noted that Crookston led Morning Prayer for the Dioscean Convention in Chattanooga on May 11, 1916. Perhaps the Rev. William C. Robertson was responsible for bringing Crookston the 350 miles south to Chattanooga?

Both St. Luke's Church and 1627 Freeman Avenue, House of Our Lady Help of Christians were demolished.

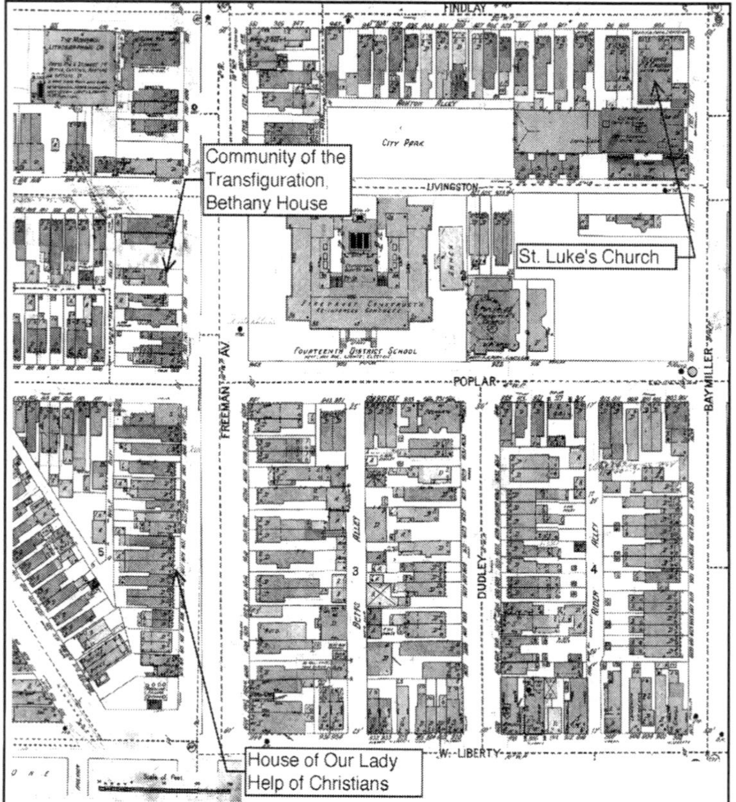

Figure A. Sanborn Insurance Maps of Cincinnati 204 and 205 (1904-1917)

The Rev. Robertson was called to Christ Church Chattanooga as their rector on December 8, 1900, and, in 1916, just at the time Crookston was absent from St. Luke's in Cincinnati, Robertson was in the process of helping Miss Jesse Tyler establish St. Gabriel's Convent. (Later in May 1918, Mother Mary Gabriel (the former Jesse Tyler) and Sister Mary Joseph would profess life vows at Christ Church, and found the Sisters of the Tabernacle. (Hamilton, 2015; Anson, p. 575) There is no record that Crookston was ever officially designated a clergy person associated with Christ Church Chattanooga, but he was probably there to both witness and aid Robertson in the creation of this new religious Order. With such firsthand experience of founding a religious Order, Crookston returned to his duties on June 1, 1916 as Assistant Rector at St. Luke's in Cincinnati.

Crookston's First Attempt at Founding Franciscan Orders

While St. Luke's Assistant Rector, on February 2, 1917, Rev. Crookston dedicated himself to a Franciscan vocation becoming Father Joseph. By that time, there were three other people in Cincinnati desiring to live a Franciscan life. They called upon a prayer group to keep a solemn novena as they sought guidance, and, even before the novena was finished, one of the women offered herself and a large sum of money for the creation of a convent if the Anglican

Franciscan life could be started immediately. Thus in May 1917, a house at 1627 Freeman Avenue was rented where three women began living a religious life. This "House of Our Lady, Help of Christians" was blessed on the Feast of the Sacred Heart, June 15, 1917. At this benediction all the men and women who later began the three Orders of St Francis were gathered together. By the end of 1917, 18 men and women had become novices in the 3rd Order Secular.

While all this was happening on Freeman Avenue, the Rev. Frank Gavin, Father Joseph's rector at St. Luke's, evidently sharing Crookston's sense of a call to a religious Order, left in November 1917 to enter the novitiate of Society of Saint John the Evangelist (SSJE) in Boston. That November Crookston began to look after Father Gavin's parish becoming its Rector-in-Charge only to leave the parish and Cincinnati two months later in January 1918 because he had suffered a heart attack. (Williams, p. 155)

The non-residential Third Order Secular was established by the time Father Joseph left Cincinnati, but Bishop Boyd Vincent of the Diocese of Southern Ohio did not support Father Joseph's attempt to form residential First and Second Orders. Why this happened is ambiguous. Bishop Vincent's opposition was partially the reaction of a Low Church bishop to High Church practices (Krumm), but only twenty years earlier Bishop Vincent had supported the establishment of the Community of the Transfiguration that grew out of the same parish. Thus his opposition to Crookston may also have been an instance of Bishop Vincent being wary of another Order attempting to establish itself only two blocks away from the diocese's established Community of the Transfiguration. (In the final chapter of this book, the Community of the Transfiguration reappears in the story of this Province as offering a home in 1976 to one of the Province's great healers and authors, Emily Gardiner Neal, who died there in 1989.)

Bishop Vincent had earlier tried to dissuade Mother Eva Mary from creating a religious Order in the diocese, but eventually relented. He probably relented because Mother Eva Mary was the sister of The Rev. Paul Matthews who was St. Luke's rector (1896-1906), then Dean of the Cathedral in Cincinnati (1906-1915), and finally Bishop of the Diocese of New Jersey (1915-1937). Mother Eva Mary was also the sister-in-law of Elsie Matthews of the Proctor (and Gamble) fortune that heavily endowed the diocese. Moreover, Mother Eva Mary's father had been a U.S. Senator from Ohio and member of the U.S. Supreme Court. Finally, in the negotiations, Mother Eva Mary had recognized Vincent's authority over her Order as her Diocesan Bishop.

Compare all of Mother Eva Mary's support with that of Crookston in 1917. He was only an Assistant Rector who was not cannonically-resident in the diocese, but who had already received a strong reprimand from Bishop Vincent. (Krumm, 1989) Moreover, there is no evidence that Father Joseph offered the same recognition of Bishop Vincent's authority over his Franciscan Orders.

The Respite and Re-focusing Offered by the SSJE

Crookston's "heart attack" in January 1918 may have been a physical manifestation of his spiritual exhaustion arising from his personal attempts to found Episcopal Franciscan Orders in the U.S. In any event, when Crookston left St. Luke's and the Diocese of Southern Ohio in January 1918, he followed his former seminary roommate, Frank Gavin, and spent eleven months with the Society of Saint John the Evangelist (SSJE) in Boston. (*Journal of the Annual Convention of the Diocese of Massachusetts*, 1918, p. 138; *Episcopal Year 1969*, p. 208) Father Joseph stayed at their Monastery of St. Mary and St. John probably to consult with Fr. Spence Burton about founding an Order since the American branch of SSJE had just gained independence from the British branch in 1914. He also probably came to experience life in a monastic community.

These months in 1918 were the first time that Father Joseph had lived in a friary, and his time here seems to have healed him physically and sharpened his sense of what an American religious Order entailed. In early 1919, Rev. Robertson of Chattanooga—who had finished the founding of the Sisters of the Tabernacle—invited Father Joseph to return to create a companion community of men. (Williams, p. 155) Father Joseph declined.

This Time The Founding Works

Very soon after Father Joseph's stay with the SSJE he reorganized the Third Order introducing a stricter Rule as part of the Poor Brethren of St. Francis of the American Congregation of Franciscans. (Only three novices transitioned to this new stricter Rule (later published in the 1924 *Bundle of Myrrh* manual). Many dropped out, though a number joined the First and Second Orders as they were organized.) Father Joseph returned to Diocese of Fond du Lac where he resumed his duties in Tomahawk (the parish he had left in 1915) along with the parish in Merrill in May 1919. (Jones, McVean and Others, 1924) About this same time the Order of the Holy Cross established a House in the Diocese at Ripon, and the Sisters of the Holy Nativity, established by Bishop Grafton, continued their work in the diocese.

Father Joseph was joined by one of the Cincinnati tertiaries from 1917, and, in the spring of 1919, by a priest. These three men began a community life and, on Holy Cross Day 1919, the Bishop received them as postulants, and the life of the First Order began.

Four years previously, the Bishop had been reticent to have Rev. Crookston found a religious Order, but by 1919 that had changed. Bishop Weller had come to believe that "he [Crooksaton] will do a blessed work among our people in a poor mission field where the Catholic religious can only be propagated through devotion and self-sacrifice of some earnest priest." (Williams, 154-5)

Forming the Life of the Third Order: 1919-1929

On September 14, 1919, Father Joseph reorganized the Third Order by introducing a stricter Rule. Only three novices transitioned to this new Rule (later printed in the 1924 *Bundle of Myrrh*, the first manual for the Third Order). Many dropped out; while a goodly number joined the First and Second Orders. As early as 1921, Father Joseph began work on the *Bundle of Myrrh*, and it was published by the brothers on their own Grace Dieu Press at Merrill, Wisconsin. (All these early manuals in their entirety are stored and downloadable in the *Historical Documents* section of the TSSF website.)

The *Bundle's* 66 pages were priced at fifty cents, and it was described in the *Little Chronicle* (1923): "This is the name of our Tertiaries's Manual, for Myrrh is bitter but a preservative, and the rules and counsels of this little book may sometimes be hard, but they will always give you health, sweetness, and peace at the last." Five hundred copies were printed, and, within two years, most were gone. The *Bundle* was an introductory brochure for parish tract racks, a detailed formation manual, and a collection of rites, rituals, and a *Devotional Calendar.*

The *Bundle* initial pages described the First and Second Orders and only on page 12 was the Third Order mentioned, and only on page 15 did the particulars of the Third Order commence.

A BUNDLE OF
MYRRH
MANUAL OF THE THIRD
ORDER

The first items devoted to the Third Order were the stages of formation (admission, postulancy, and noviate) as well as the form of profession. The use and parts of the "habit" were described in detail almost equal in length to the whole formation process.

Following these came the Rule (and Sacerdotal Rule for clerical members), the Examen on these Rules, and the Monthly Report on these Rules.

Four and a half pages were then devoted to laying out the *Credenda* (articles of belief akin to *The 39 Articles* of 1571 printed out in its entirety on page 14). The *Credenda* included some very "Roman Catholic teaching and practice" including some items in direct contradiction to the *The 39 Articles* of 1571 regarding Purgatory, the Immaculate Conception, the Assumption, and the intercession of the saints (although some wiggle-room in footnotes observed that these were "pious opinions").

Then came some 20 pages of Ceremonial: a Mass of St. Francis, the Clothing of a Postulant, the Admission of a Novice to Profession, and the Yearly Renewal of Profession Vows. The final 12 pages included the *Devotional Calendar*, various prayers, the Franciscan Crown Rosary, and various hymns.

The *Bundle of Myrrh* was the first attempt by Father Joseph and the Order to give shape and form to the burgeoning Third Order. Its Anglo-Catholic character was readily demonstrated not by its process of Formation, but also its *Credenda*, prayers, and ceremonials. Within three years, 1926, the Third Order of the Society had grown so considerably that one-on-one personal guidance by Father Joseph was no longer possible, and an organizational structure apart from Father Joseph had to be created. This he laid out in the *Pastoral Letter to Our Third Order* 1926*.

The Credenda of the Order of Saint Francis (OSF) and

the Third Order Society of St. Francis (TSF) 1921

1. *Belief that the Anglican provinces are part of the true Catholic Church and thus heirs to every teaching, devotion, and practice of the whole Church or any part of it.*
2. *Belief that the Holy Spirit guides the Church and guides her into all truth so that she is the divinely appointed witness to and teacher of revealed truth, with authority to demand the consent of faith from those who would live as her children.*
3. *Belief in the three Creeds (Apostles, Nicene, and Athanasian). The official documents of any particular part of the Catholic Church are to be interpreted by the Catholic Faith and not contrariwise (e.g., The Thirty Nine Articles).*
4. *Belief in the Holy Scriptures as interpreted by the whole Catholic Church and the consentient teaching of the Fathers.*
5. *Belief in the Seven Sacraments and the Sacrifice of the Mass.*
6. *Belief that there is an "Intermediate State"* [Purgatory] *and that the souls therein detained are holpen* [helped] *by the suffrages of the Faithful. Belief in the Invocation of Saints. Belief in the Immaculate Conception and the Assumption of the B.V.M. as Pious Opinions, i.e., not as dogmas imposed on us by Anglican authority, but as inferences from revelation which have been made and defended by great Theologians and Doctors of the Church.*
7. *Belief in the perfect Divinity, perfect Manhood and sinlessness of our Lord.*
8. *Acceptance of those things decreed at the Seven Ecumenical Councils.*

For many years, the Society of St. Francis has had a book called *The Book of Roots* (1975, 1978) with the latest version entitled titled *Walking in the Footsteps of Christ* (2003).

In addition to the early rules written by Francis and Clare for the three Orders in the 13th century, both versions of the *Book of Roots* have had only four items marking the modern roots of the Order. In 1978, the modern roots were the Principles of the First Order (pre-1966), and the Principles of the Third Order (post-1966) both from the English Society of St. Francis. In 2003, these two items were replaced by two older items: The Provisional Rule & Constitution, 1931/2 of the Brotherhood of St. Francis of Assisi and The Principles and Rule of Life of the Christa Prema Seva Sangha (1922-1934). All four documents chosen to represent the modern roots of the Order come from the roots of the Society in the English Church, and none from the American Church.

If the whole Third Order is to accurately know its modern roots, and particularly the Province of the Americas, Father Joseph's *Credenda* of the early 1920s needs to be reckoned with and included in any future version of a *Book of Roots*.

"The Clothing" (Novicing) of Paul Everest (1st on right with candle) January 28, 1925 at Merrill Wisconsin by Father Joseph (2nd from left). Everest exemplified Father Joseph's observation by being absent from the 1935 Directory.

In the year of our Lord, 1925, the 28th Day of January in the Chapel of the Franciscan Monastery, Merrill, Wis, I the undersigned gave the Habit of the Third Order of the Penitents of St. Francis to William Edward Everett, living in Medford, Wis, henceforth to be known as Brother Paul.
Signed: Fr. Joseph, OSF.

Written record of this "Clothing" signed by Father Joseph from the Annals.

Tertiaries from the late 1920s. All are wearing their habits (aprons) over black cassocks.

According to the Annals, an "older woman", Mrs. Mary Humphreys (Sr. Mary), was the first Third Order person to be professed June 8, 1923 in Merrill WI. She died six years later on June 13, 1929.

Father Joseph began preparing a new Third Order manual, *The Little Book of the Rule* in 1926, finally publishing it in 1929. It was again be printed by the brothers at their own Grace Dieu Press this time at their new home at Little Portion Friary in Mount Sinai, Long Island. (In 1928, Father Joseph had moved the headquarters of the First Order to Mount Sinai in New York and the Second Order Poor Clares also relocated to Mount Sinai. The Clares continued here until 2003 when the last Poor Clare in this Province died.)

An article in the *Little Chronicle* (#10, July 1925-6) noted that the primary impetus for so quickly revising a Third Order Manual was that the growth of the Third Order required statutes regarding governance much of which had been described in his 1926 pastoral letter. For example, a new rule was added: "In each place where there is a group of tertiaries there is to be a monthly fellowship meeting, and, at this time, a collection is taken up."

Also some of the customs of the Third Order needed more explanation. Moreover, the current form of the Third Order Rule in the *Bundle of Myrrh* was a revision of the one used by the Roman Catholic Church which was itself a revision of the ancient rule. Father Joseph wanted to work directly from Francis's original Rule and revise it.

The *Little Book of the Rule*, thus, rearranged content to fit the titles of the twelve chapters of Francis's original Rule. The language was, in places, made more explicit and less ambiguous, while "certain exhortations from sacred sources" were added to improve the beauty of the manual. Eventually the manual would be double the price of the *Bundle* when published in 1929, one dollar. By 1955, its supply had been exhausted.

After the *Pastoral Letter of 1926* and the second version of the Third Order Manual, *The Little Book of the Rule* (1929) that both grew out of its concern for a general organizational structure of the Third Order, it was nine years before there was any report on the effectiveness of these efforts. Such a report eventually appeared in the "Introductory Material" to the *1935 Roster of the Third Order**. In the first chapter's Geographic Distribution maps of 1926 and 1935, one can see the increase in the number of tertiaries in California and London, and that is reflected in the observations in this "Introductory Material." For example, the Director General, Father Joseph, overwhelmed by the growth of the Third Order to 86 members, wanted to stop any more disparate recruitment initiatives in order to focus recruitment in Cleveland, Chicago, Los Angeles, and London. Also implied in this "Introductory Material" is not only the strong hand of Father Joseph directing it, but the funds of the First and Second Order keeping it afloat.

Here is a report of a tertiary visiting Little Portion in 1929.

A Pilgrimage to a Modern La Verna

By Bro. Martin Joseph, Ob. S. F., a Visiting Tertiary, (reprinted from The Little Chronicle 9 (9) (June 1929)* (*An oblate, Third Order member who also takes an extra vow of chastity.)

As we arrived at Port Jefferson and alighted from the train grey-garbed friar who was none other than the genial Brother Andrew greeted us with true Franciscan cordiality. No doubt many of our tertiaries are familiar with him, in name only, through sending him their monthly reports, but he assured us he would like to know all the tertiaries more intimately by personal contact. It is to be hoped that many will take advantage of the opportunity to know him and the other members of the Community better by making a visit to Little Portion Friary at Mount Sinai on Long Island, New York. We are certain you will enjoy its hospitality and obtain an increase of faith to assist you along that path of perfection in Christ which was nobly trod by our Seraphic Father Francis.

Instead of having to walk the distance from the station to the friary as a pilgrim in the time of St. Francis might have done, we were conveyed in a motor car with a fleetness which no doubt would have caused a Franciscan of the 13th Century to think he was another Elijah going up into the starry abode, yet the bumps in the road every now and then made us realize that we still on terra firma

The red wooden cross and the sign "Little Portion" erected by the roadside informed us that we were at our destination. We drove into the grounds and Father Superior and other brethren met us stepping from the vehicle. The

Original Building on Grounds at Little Portion

buildings, though not of the traditional monastic style, seemed very substantial and had an inviting appearance. Upon entering them we sensed atmosphere of spirituality, one of typical Franciscan expression. All was neatness, cleanliness and good taste, especially in the matter of the fine art of decoration. Nothing was overdone tawdry or too ornate either in the chapel or other parts of the house, and while a certain primitive roughness and incompleteness testifies to the reality of the poverty professed, the dignity of holy poverty in imitation of Him who had not where to lay His Sacred Head was everywhere manifest.

The work of modernizing and adapting the buildings to the needs of the community has gone ahead at a rapid pace. To date much has been accomplished for the comfort and convenience of the Brethren. Nevertheless much remains to be done to the buildings and grounds, and the Order still begs our prayers and alms. The chapel, of course, is the center from which radiate all the activities of the community, both spiritual and material. It is not very spacious but fulfills the need for orderly and dignified worship of God in the Mass and Divine Office. Plans from the very first have been under consideration for its enlargement and beautification, but its present state represents a limited pocketbook. The possibilities for a suitable monastic foundation at Mount Sinai, however, are unlimited. The brethren have been ingenious and economical in using here in their new location all the material, which they brought with them from Merrill, Wisconsin, and the stones, trees and buildings, which the new site afforded. In the chanting of the Offices, the usual monastic forms are observed with slight variations due to peculiar Franciscan customs.

The Poor Clares were never seen except at Mass, Vespers, and Benediction. Their convent is quite a little distance from the friary, and they lead their life of adoration and reparation with no contact with the friary, except in an official capacity in the purely spiritual and priestly administrations of the monastic chapel. The friary is so arranged that the nuns or other women visitors may enter and leave the friary chapel without passing through the friary proper. In the chapel they occupy a screened-off gallery, which they do not leave even to receive Holy Communion.

With the permission of Father Superior, and, in company with two of the friars, we paid the Sisters a visit, kneeling a few moments in prayer in their beautiful and well-appointed chapel where the intense "Labor of Love," namely, adoration and reparation to Our Lord in the Blessed Sacrament, is carried on. Thus they are not much seen by the world as their intention is to lead a life "hid with Christ in God." As they grow they may wish to develop more and more of the spirit of enclosure.

Little Portion under construction in late 1920s.

Next we inspected the convent garden seeing all the members of what Brother Anthony termed "the Sisters' Zoo." Here are the Muscovy ducks, a small flock of hens guarded by a pompous rooster, and a flock of little chicks, all of which you have read about in recent issues of *The Little Chronicle*. The friars also have a mascot in the form of a very affectionate Scotch terrier, which is allowed to visit the convent at any time without the superior's permission, which all other visitors must obtain before going to the Convent.

As we rambled around the acreage of the friary and saw what had been accomplished and the work it must have entailed, we wondered how it could have been done with the little time allotted to this type of work over and above the chanting of the Offices, cleaning, repairing, and enlarging the house, preparing meals, and the other manifold duties of monastic life. It must have been a laborious task to subdue this primeval wilderness of trees and heavy undergrowth. Truly the wilderness and waste places of this spot have been made to "blossom like the rose."

Another thought presented itself to our minds as we viewed this process of cosmos rapidly evolving out of chaos. In spirit we reverted to the establishment of the monastic foundations of the monks of ancient times in the isles of Lindisfarne and Iona. They had conditions far more discouraging than those at Little Portion. It is recorded that they lived in wattle huts composed of reeds and mud. We know the remainder of the story: how in spite of all these natural handicaps they were the most instrumental in converting our forebears to Christianity. In comparison with the hardships of these "prisoners of the Faith," the friars at Little Portion are living in a palace and their subjection to the soil is as naught. God has continued to bless his servants even to this latter time.

The Community is attempting to be self-supporting in so far as it is possible, and extensive plans have been formulated for the raising of garden and dairy produce. Of course, the religious are grateful for and needful always of receiving donations of canned goods, jellies, and other articles along with financial assistance. If all would send a little, there would be no great burden on any one individual.

Bishop's Consecration of Little Portion Including Statue of St. Francis.

There are many objects of ecclesiastical art and devotion in and around the friary worthy of description and study, but space will not permit us to enlarge upon them. They should be seen to be appreciated.

Enough to mention the unique statue in the chapel, and its replica in the garden, of the Blessed Virgin and Child, designed and executed by one of our religious and adapted as the distinctive symbol of Little Portion, and hence entitled "Our Lady of Little Portion."

When the time drew near for our departure from this house of prayer and praise we were loath to do so, for we had become enchanted with its hospitality. We felt Little Portion to be another "House of God and Gate of Heaven." As we said farewell to our hosts they expressed a desire that many more of the tertiaries of the New York and neighboring Custodias [*fellowships*] would pay them a visit in the near future, and we hope that many of them will avail themselves of this invitation and privilege. Words fail to express suitably our gratitude and indebtedness to the kindly members of the Community for the hospitality extended to us and the spiritual favors enjoyed during our sojourn with them. But our hearts were full of appreciation, and we shall continue to pray that through the intercession of Our Lady of Little Portion and St. Francis, God may shower His blessings upon them and all their endeavors in His name.

Fellowship and Custodia Meetings

To Father Joseph, *Fellowship* meetings were "the smallest group of organization within the province, and corresponds somewhat to the friary at Little Portion, just as the *Custodia* of twelve or more members within a region corresponds to a custodia within a province, and the province corresponds to the ordinary provincial organization of the Order of St. Francis. A fellowship must have at least three members, and it is never to be a parish organization." From early on, Father Joseph urged Custodias to meet." Here is a record of two of those custodia.

The New York Custodia 1925-6 (from the *Little Chronicle* #6)

The Second Sunday in Lent was an important date for our Third Order. At that time nine Postulants received the habit, one novice made his profession, and a priest-oblate made his first annual vows. This unusual service took place in the Church of the Transfiguration, Brooklyn, New York, and it was certainly a beautiful sight to see the sanctuary filled with kneeling tertiaries who were offering themselves in fresh dedication to God and receiving as a token thereof the little habit and the lighted candle.

Our tertiaries have become so numerous in and about New York City that they have expressed the desire for some fellowship with each other and a more developed organization than has hitherto been necessary. With this in view a meeting of our tertiaries in the vicinity of New York City was called for the Third Sunday in Lent at Corpus Christi Church in NYC. Unfortunately no priest was able to be present, but the mere meeting together as a body corporate made the Eastern tertiaries feel their solidarity and was, on their part, an act of zeal and loyalty for the cause. We congratulate the Eastern tertiaries on their earnestness and interest. In the meantime, it seemed wise to the Father Director of the

Third Order in conference with certain priests-tertiary to agree upon a tentative method of organization which can be tried out for a year in order to see how it works. This will give us an opportunity to correct any deficiencies.

1929-30 (from the *Little Chronicle* #7)

The New York Custodia, which began under the leadership of the Rev. William Nichols and owes much to his fostering care, is still going forward under the impetus it gained from his leadership. The meetings are held on the Third Thursday of each month. But, in April, the third Thursday was Maundy Thursday, for which reason the meeting was postponed to Easter Thursday. The meeting and the one of the previous month had the largest attendance in the history of the Custodia. After supper at Corpus Christi House and a few minutes of social conversation, the Veni Creator was sung and a short exposition of the Rule given. Then all proceeded to the church for recitation of the Office, the investure of a novice, and Benediction. Tertiaries within reach of NYC are invited to send their names to Miss Henrietta Boyd, 4555 Gosman Avenue, Woodside, LI, NY to receive notices of the meetings in NYC. Tertiaries visiting in the East ought to visit their brethren and sisters of the Third Order in their monthly meeting.

The London Custodia: 1935-1968

The London Custodia of the American Province existed for 32 years with as many as 30 members in the 1950s. When TSF and TSSF merged in 1968, most of the names and records of the London Custodia (Fellowship) vanish; only two were recorded as becoming members of TSSF European Province. The 1967 TSF Directory records that a majority in the Custodia had over ten years in the Order, and two had 32 years in the Order.

Mabel Julia Mary Pinco (Sr. Mary Francesca) was first person to be professed, and she helped to found the English Custodia as she explains in this 1941 letter.

> *You say you like to hear how our movement came into being and that you gather we have connections with the Episcopal church in America. We have more than that, we only exist as a Custodia of the Third Order of the American Congregation of Franciscans, and the way we, the English Custodia, came into existence was as follows. A complete Franciscan Congregation should have the three Orders: the Friars, the Poor Clares, and the Tertiaries, and the last may have both religious and seculars members, though not many Congregations in our Communion have both, I believe. I went out to America some years ago to join the Poor Clares, but my health broke down, and it was decided I ought not to remain in America. Under those circumstances, I had of course to give up the hope of being a Poor Clare, but the Fr. Minister* [Father Joseph] *sent me back to England as a Franciscan Oblate* [Third Order member who took an additional vow of celibacy], *with the understanding that I might do what I could to spread interest in our work. With the help of Fr. Morse-Boycott, a friend of many years, we were able to*

start our little Custodia, which is very small, and will I think always remain so, as naturally English people who are drawn to St. Francis prefer to join one of the English Congregations. (Lambeth Palace Library:TSSF/8/6, May 3, 1941)

In another letter, a novice, Jane Mary, who lived in the United States during World War II, wrote to explain her impressions of how the American Third Order was distinct from the English Third Order:

One big difference is that American Tertiaries are not allowed to report on money or almsgiving—that is considered to be part of the "Inner Rule." Paradoxically enough, I find that it makes me more scrupulous in these things—rather like one's school days and being "put on one's honour." The other great difference is the wearing of a habit, and the taking of a religious name.... the Little Habit consists of a scapular, about four inches square, and a cord, with three knots—both of which are of obligation to be worn under the secular clothing, except under special dispensation. The Greater Habit is a black gown, with a long white scapular and cord, which holds it round the waist. This may not be worn except at Franciscan gatherings, and when visiting the friary, or otherwise when special permission is granted, but one has the privilege to be buried in it, if one wishes. (Lambeth Palace Library: TSSF/8/6),

For most of its existence, the English Custodia was consistently among the top five most populous regions of the American Order. In fact, whenever the *Little Chronicle* had a comment on organized custodias, the author would mention only New York, Los Angeles, and London (February #5, 1929-30). (Father Joseph traveled to England in 1933 and was a guest at a meeting of the English Custodia.) From 1935 to 1950, the Rev. Desmond Morse-Boycott directed the Custodia, but, in 1950, passed the leadership to the Rev. George Hall. The English Custodia consistently maintained very high levels of longevity or faithfulness. From 1935 to 1948, 66% remained faithful; from 1948 to 1955, 75% remained faithful; from 1955 to 1960, 70%; and from 1960 to the last records in 1967, 52% remained faithful.

In addition to the two letters above, a number of newsletters from the English Custodia, *Tertiary Tidings,* are preserved in the Lambeth Palace Library and Archives. Produced between 1938 and Spring 1941, these issues are not only the earliest custodia newsletters of the American Order, but they also capture the first-hand experience of Third Order Franciscans in the midst of war. (Complete copies of these six newsletters are available in the *Historical Documents* section of the TSSF website.) Although the newsletters were issued "under the authority of the Rev. Desmond Morse-Boycott" (Br. Anthony) and reviewed and approved by him as Father Provincial (Father Minister's [Father Joseph's] representative in England], however, most of the writing was done by Mabel Julia Mary Pinco.

As this *No. 3 Autumn Number* was written, the Sudetenland was taken by Nazi Germany between October 1 & 10, 1938:

St. Francis-tide dawns upon a troubled world. On every side the nations are aggressive, menacing, obsessed by fear which is the antithesis of love. Hatred is generally considered to be that, but surely fear is the creator of hatred and many other foul growths of our national life? But during the week of great anxiety, though which we have just passed, many must have been struck by the extraordinary appropriateness of the gospel appointed for Monday's Mass (Feast of St. Januarius and His Companions): "When ye shall hear of wars and rumours of wars, be not troubled, neither let thoughts arise in your hearts (thoughts of fear, distrust and discord). 'Nation shall rise against nation—but the end is not yet'. What that end may be none can say, but at least two salient facts seem emerging from the welter. First, that practically no civilized nation desires war, and secondly, that in England and doubtless in other countries also, there is an increasing belief in the power of prayer to control our destinies. The last is surely an immense spiritual gain, and I do beg all to do everything in your power to foster this spirit, both in yourselves and others."

As this *No. 6 Summer 1939* was published, a War Powers Act was approved by Parliament; the Royal Navy was put on a war footing; all leaves were cancelled; and the naval and coast defense reserves were called up:

"T.O.S.F." This strange unintelligible title came to my notice through one of our brothers at the C. A. Training College, and I was told it was a Third Order secular for men and women who, though not called to the monastic life, desired to carry out as far as they could the ideas of St. Francis in their daily life. So I prayerfully decided to offer myself for membership, being much inspired by the example of two members I knew personally. These two men seemed to remain quite undaunted by the sneers and rebuffs of people with adverse opinions; carrying on quietly in the true spirit of Franciscanism, fighting unweariedly in the battle against evil and striving always to draw men and women from the dark abyss of sin into that glorious Lovelight of the Sacred Heart of God. How could I resist such a wonderful call—the call which every Franciscan has received, the call which our Seraphic Father heard and obeyed. But the joy of that wonderful vocation cannot be complete unless we pass on that message of love to our fellow men. Such is the contest of the appeal made by the Editor in the Spring Number of Tertiary Tidings—that each Tertiary will make some effort to win souls to the fellowship of the League of the Sacred Heart. Our Franciscan Rule teaches us that we should be "in the world, but not of the world" and there is a divine inspiration in these words. An inspiration to t read the path which leads us at last to our goal—into the Presence and Love of the Sacred Heart of Our Blessed Redeemer.

As the *No. 11 Autumn 1940* "Foreword" was written by Rev. Desmond Morse-Boycott (Br. Anthony), Germany's Luftwaffe began bombing British civilian centers in the Battle of Britain. Thousands of pilots and aircrews engaged in battle in the skies above Britain, Germany, and the English Channel, each side losing more than 1,500 aircraft by the end of the year. Prime Minister Winston

Churchill, speaking of the British pilots said, "Never in the field of human conflict was so much owed by so many to so few." Rev. Desmond Morse-Boycott's St. Mary's of the Angels Song School was destroyed by fire (see picture on p. 27).

You will be glad to know that St. Mary-of-the-Angels Song School is still in being, despite its disastrous fire, and that a release of timber has been made by the Authorities, sufficient at least to roof the undamaged "Wing." We have a temporary lease of a house nearby the estate, and spend most of our nights all of a bunch in a sort of fortified coal-cellar. Our boys are serene and happy and daily defeat the nuisance-value of Mr. Schnickelgruber by learning history or singing Offices in their shelter. We sometimes get an early Mass in the small hours, in-between raids. In the midst of life we are in death, but get many laughs. I do not know if it is Franciscan mirth, but for some unknown reason all the family regard my clambering into an alleged bed on a table in the shelter as the evening's star turns. Certain "Angels" sleeping under it do not appreciate my suggestion that their shelter is thereby reinforced, and they make dark remarks about what may happen if the table collapses.

I ought to have told you that Schnickelgruber is Hitler's real name. I feel a comfortable assurance that no man with such a name can possibly "down" the British Empire. I have lately been talking with a rather pessimistic priest who says we are being punished for our national sins, and we are the most immoral nation in the world, and full of insincerity. Indeed we have previous sins of which to repent, but I told him that at any rate THIS was an attack by Berlin and Rome on Bethlehem; that we are not a nation that DELIGHTS in war; and that, without self-esteem, we could say that we had some of the human virtues without which God obviously can't get His world to work.

Our word is as good as our bond, even when it is to our great disadvantage (e.g., we are not using necessary ports in Eire; we went to the help of Poland, however ineffectually). Axis nations make treaties with the express intention of breaking them when it suits their purpose. We love freedom and fair-play. We do not machine-gun women and children. We are not embarking upon reprisals for the bombing of London. We know how to laugh. We acknowledge God by days of prayers.

It is a sinister fact that reputedly Catholic nations are arrayed against us: Italy, Austria, parts of Catholic Germany, and near-Catholic France. Spain will join our enemies actively just as soon as she thinks we are certain to lose. "Where the carcass is..."

General Franco, who I believe has since been blest by His Holiness the Pope, put Madrid through two years of the torment we are now experiencing ourselves. Most of us went on our ways indifferent. (The thought of how little I myself realized it, stabs me).

There must, therefore, be lonely souls in the Latin Communion who are looking for the coming of one with the spirit and power of St. Francis, an

Elisha to follow an Elijah, though sundered by the centuries. Meanwhile, to each of us in the Franciscan family is given one small lamp to be kindled and kept brightly burning. See to your one.

As *No. 12 Christmas 1941* was being written, on December 29-30, German aircraft blanketed incendiary bombs over London setting both banks of the Thames ablaze and killing almost 3,600 British civilians. December 29 saw the widespread destruction not just of civilian targets, but of great portions of London's cultural relics (the Old Bailey, Guildhall, and eight churches designed by Christopher Wren). Fifteen thousand separate fires were set by the bombs.

I must begin this new Issue of T.T. with an apology for its late appearance. As you know, we always try to get out the winter number in time to convey our Christmas greetings to you all, but this year both Fr. Antony and myself have had to change residence just before Christmas. Fr. Antony, having to remove a good deal more than just himself, finds it impossible to do more than send you his love and blessing through me, and leaves T.T. entirely in my hands for this issue. To Fr. Anthony's loving wishes I add my own praying that the New Year may bring you every blessing of the Sacred Heart, and may its close find us no longer in the midst of the horrors of war.

That is the thing we must all long and pray for, and yet we know there are worse things than even in its most horrible aspects we have seen it during the last few months. It is the forces of evil we have to fight, and we can sometimes only fight evil by suffering from it. Suffering is not in itself evil nay, it is forever redeemed and grown triumphant by the Cross. And if this blessed Christmastide is in so many homes overshadowed by that Cross, let us remember that the first Christmastide was only joyful for those few loving and simple souls who had eyes to see, and that the outward circumstances preceding the Birth of Jesus Christ were those of great hardship and difficulty. Mary and Joseph had terrible experience to go through before the ineffable joy of the, wondrous Birth. So on this first day of the New Year, though we know not what it may bring forth, let us thank God and take courage. Let us look forward with eager hope to the future; let us solemnly rededicate ourselves here and now to His service in whatever manner He may call us. So shall 1941 and every succeeding year we have to live be blest; so shall the mighty purpose of which even now we begin dimly to discern the working in the chaos which surrounds us find its echo in our own hears and enable us to fulfill our vocation to the end.

Mabel Julia Mary Pinco, Sister Mary Francesca, the first of the English Custodia to be professed and the editor of their newsletter, died five months after penning this issue of the *Tertiary Tidings* on May 10, 1942.

Desmond Lionel Morse-Boycott: Leader of London Custodia 1931-1950

From *The Little Chronicle* (December 1930-31)
"Our American tertiaries follow with interest any news of the London Custodia under the care of the Rev. Father Morse-Boycott. His plans to develop a choir

school in connection with St. Mary's Somers Town, seems to be working out gradually. Every tertiary should give him the support of constant prayer. It is to be hoped that all who can do so will buy his new book, *Ten Years in a London Slum*. This details the magnificent work being done there for God."

From "Official Chichester Cathedral Website"

Fr. Desmond, as he was known far and wide, served his first curacy at the Church of St. Mary's, Somers Town, which is situated in the King's Cross, Euston, area of London.

Rev. Desmond Morse-Boycott

In those days there was a terrible amount of real poverty, particularly within the parish in which Fr. Desmond served. He would venture out at night and mingle with young lads on street corners, many of whom he found playing cards and gambling. Often he put himself at physical risk trying to stop the gambling by the young and the more adult members of the population. The police in those days had hardly any success in stopping street gambling for there was little else for the men and youngsters to do. Fr. Desmond could be very persistent and persuasive, influencing the young and gaining the respect of the old. He encouraged some of the lads to partake of whatever food he could spare at the time. Coming as they did from poor homes where food was at a premium, such an offer was extremely popular. These boys eventually became the foundation of Fr. Desmond's choir and school.

After five years working in the parish, Fr. Desmond decided that the majority of the boys needed educating to a much higher standard. With this in mind, he resigned as curate at St. Mary's in order to found his school and, from then on, his life became one long struggle. His first home was "under the pavement" in Somers Town. This was where the school began and was called the St. Mary of the Angels Song School. Those boys who joined Fr. Desmond's school were given the opportunity to be educated and to be trained to sing in his choir. Because of Fr. Desmond's love of music, the boys were also encouraged to play various instruments under a professional tutor.

"The Boys Who Sang Like Angels"

UKAuthors.com 4/10/2013
What would you do to improve the lives of disadvantaged children from 1920s London?

Truth is much, much stranger than fiction. If you were a priest in a poverty-stricken area of London in the 1920s, how would you improve the lives of young boys living in slums? Father Desmond Morse-Boycott had his own solution.

Start a public school in a cellar. Turn them into choristers.

The Third Order of Saint Francis.
London Custody of the American
Congregation of Franciscans.

Saint Mary of the Angels.

This little pocket size, 4-fold booklet demonstrates how Father Morse-Boycott integrated his TSF life with his work with the St. Mary's choir boys. He adapted the TSF Rule and prayers to fit his elementary school pupils. For example, his boy's Franciscan Rule included

- *no smoking until 16*
- *to go to bed in good time*
- *to take care of clothes and*
- *to be chivalrous.*

Inside of booklet

A RULE OF LIFE.

1—To say my morning and evening prayers.

2—To say Grace before and after meals.

3—To deny myself something on Fridays and never, on that day, to go to the pictures or any entertainment, unless obliged to do so.

4—To refrain from smoking until I am sixteen, and thereafter to be moderate in the enjoyment of tobacco.

5—To make a private confession daily.

6—To confess before a Priest at least once a month.

7—To attend Mass at least twice on weekdays.

8—To make my Communion at least once a week.

9—To meditate daily (e.g., by spending a few minutes with my Bible, or Rosary, or at least by saying the Angelus).

10—To pray daily for others.

11—To give to God one-tenth of my pocket-money.

12—To avoid all quarrels. To be a peace-maker. To do at least one daily act of charity out of love for God, even though it be no more than to throw a crumb to a bird.

13—To plan each night when I shall get up the next morning, and to get up to it.

14—To go to bed in good time.

15—To be careful not to waste money, and to keep a strict account of what I have and spend.

16—To answer letters without delay.

17—To take care of clothes, and not to be in love with finery.

18—To be chivalrous and courteous.

19—To be careful in the friendships I enter into, lest they draw me away from God, or distract me in my work for Him.

Solemn Days for Franciscans.

April 16.—Solemnity of St. Francis.
May 25.—Translation of St. Francis.
July 16.—Canonization of St. Francis.
Sept. 17.—The Stigmata of St. Francis.
Oct. 3.—VIGIL OF ST. FRANCIS. (A day of Fasting.)
,, 4.—OUR SERAPHIC FATHER, ST. FRANCIS.
Dec. 12.—The Invention of St. Francis.

A Prayer.

O GOD, Who by the merits of blessed Francis dost increase Thy Church with a new offspring: grant, we beseech Thee, that after his pattern we may learn to despise all things earthly and ever to rejoice in the partaking of Thy heavenly bounty. Through Jesus Christ our Lord. Amen.

The priest and his wife had started by running a lad's club, first in their house, and then in a cellar in Somers Town, a poor area in central London. So far, so unremarkable. But then Morse-Boycott, in his account, casually explained that they had begged money to send a number of the boys to public schools.

Why? I doubt the board schools gave anything more than a basic education, but there were grammar schools and other institutions. I think the theory was that the boys would return during the holidays and spread new ideals gleaned on the playing fields of some select establishment.

1—A *postulant* must essay to keep the simple rule for at least three months, and furnish a monthly report to the Director, as do the Novices and Tertiaries. The postulancy is designed to shew the postulant whether he has a vocation (i.e. desire and fitness) for the life of the Third Order.

2—When the postulant is admitted to the *Noviciate*, he takes his first definite step in the Franciscan life. He is "clothed," being given the little Habit (a cord and a scapula), which must ever be worn, and a new name, by which he is known in the Order (selected in honour of a saint). He remains a Novice for at least a year and a day.

3—After that time, if he so desire, he may be admitted (at the discretion of the Director) to *profession*. This is not a taking of vows, nor does the profession bind one to observe the Rule (in this case the fuller Rule as set forth in the *Little Book of the Rule*) under pain of sin. But it fixes the Tertiary permanently as a member of the Franciscan family, and entitles him to the spiritual privileges thereof for eternity.

Wherefore none should be professed as Tertiaries without a deep desire for the honour, and a firm intention to observe the Franciscan Rule always.

At the profession the full Habit is granted, to be worn as the Director shall approve.

THE FRANCISCAN ROSARY. (The Crown of Our Lady's Joys)
1st Joy: Annunciation. 2nd: The Visitation. 3rd: The Nativity. 4th: Adoration of the Magi. 5th: The Finding in the Temple. 6th: The Resurrection. 7th: Crowning of Our Lady in Heaven.

After the seventh decade add two Aves to make 72 in all, the traditional age of Our Lady. Then a Pater and Ave for Church unity.

HYMN TO ST. FRANCIS, OUR SERAPHIC FATHER.

1 Blessed Francis, holy Father,
Now our hearts to thee we raise,
As we gather round thine altar,
Pouring forth our hymn of praise.
Bless thy children, holy Francis,
Who thy mighty help implore,
For in heaven thou remainest
Still the father of the poor.

2 By thy love, so deep and burning,
For thy Saviour crucified;
By the tokens which he gave thee
On thy hand, and feet, and side:
Bless thy children, holy Francis,
With those wounded hands of thine,
From thy glorious throne in heaven,
Where resplendently they shine.

3 Humble follower of Jesus,
Likened to him in thy birth,
From thy tender youth despising.
For his sake, the goods of earth.
Make us love the priceless virtue
By our hidden God esteemed:
Make it valued, holy Francis,
By the souls of the redeemed.

4 In thine own belov'd Assisi
Thou didst stir men's hearts to love,
Teaching them that holy penance
Was the road to heaven above.
Bless thy children, holy Francis,
Who thy mighty help implore,
For in heaven thou remainest
Still the father of the poor.

5 Teach us, also, dear St. Francis!
How to mourn for every sin;
May we walk in thy dear footsteps
Till the crown of life we win.
Bless thy children, holy Francis,
With these wounded hands of thine,
From thy glorious throne in heaven,
Where resplendently they shine.

Outside of booklet

Morse-Boycott and his choir boys rescuing books and material from their bombed-out school, 1940.

Not surprisingly, this sometimes failed. It was "a heavy risk." So he took the idea a step further. "Why not turn our underground Centre into a little Public School itself?"

And he did. The St. Mary's of the Angels Song School was founded in 1932, first as a day, and then as a residential, school. Morse-Boycott managed to raise enough money to keep it going, with himself in charge and his gallant wife as Matron. In a more relaxed age the fact that "My knowledge of school-mastering was nil" was not deemed relevant.

I can't help thinking this approach leaves a lot of poor people outside the school doors, such as females and those of us with voices like crows. But Father Desmond seems to have been committed and dedicated, and the school thrived. The boys leaned to sing like angels, and the choir became renowned, performing in cathedrals and churches throughout Britain, and touring Europe.

February 1950 and 1959 (From *The Little Chronicle)*

Father Morse-Boycott, by now famous for his founding in 1931 and directing the St. Mary's of the Angels Song School, had to give up his leadership of this Custodia of the American Province. The Little Chronicle went on to explain (in the February 1959 edition) that he started this school *"to take boys out of the London slums, give them an education, and make them into a well-trained choir which could be called upon at any time to provide proper music for Church services in any place. The school has cared for and helped into life 268 boys, 22 men have been helped into the priesthood, and 3 have become professional musicians. The choir has traveled 106,286 miles in its tours of professional work.*

CARICATURES OF THE AUTHOR. THAT ON THE LEFT IS BY SINCLAIR PHILLIPS AND THAT ON THE RIGHT BY SALLON.

Published Caricatures of Morse-Boycott

Morse-Boycott died died August 9, 1979. In addition to the *Ten Years* book, Father Morse-Boycott also wrote many other books with an emphasis on the Oxford Movement including: *The Secret Story of the Oxford Movement; Lead, Kindly Light; Studies of the Saints and Heros of the Oxford Movement; They Shine Like Stars; Pilgrimage of Song; The Great Crimes of the Bible; Fields of Yesterday; The Pilgrim's Way;* and *A Tapestry of Toil.*

H. Baxter Liebler: Tertiary Apostle to the Navajos (Professed 1926)

From the January 1980 Franciscan Times
After spending 25 years founding and building St. Savior's Church in Old Greenwich, Connecticut, Fr. Liebler came to Utah, where, in 1943, he fulfilled the dream of a lifetime by founding St. Christopher's Mission to the Navajo at Bluff Utah. He established St Christopher's Mission in a log-constructed cabin, and it became the first medical facility to treat tuberculosis and trachoma among the Navajo in Utah.

Another 25 years later, in 1966, he and three of his staff members retired together to a spot they named Hat Rock Valley Retreat Center saying that they were "retreatants from years of labor." At Hat Rock Valley Retreat Center, Fr. Liebier has continued his work with the Navajos.

When asked how he became a Franciscan in the first place, and how it has figured in his life, he sent this reply:

For a person who has not kept a diary, except for a few straggling weeks at a time, reminiscences are easy enough, but the fixing of dates is a difficult matter. When I am asked when I became a Tertiary of St. Francis, the answer does not come easily.

I do recall a deep devotion to St. Francis, our Blessed Father, from soon after my conversion to Jesus Christ, which was during my first year in college (1907-08). After I had been a priest for six or more years (I was made a priest on St. Francis' Day, 1914, by the Bishop's choice!) I read in some church papers about an effort to set up a Franciscan Order in the Episcopal Church. I noted that the founder was a classmate in seminary of a man who had been my classmate and roommate in college, and I asked him what he thought of the venture. I recall his precise words: "Anything that is associated with Claude Crookston is of God; fear it not!" Such words from a classmate are not to be taken lightly!

When I became rector of St. Paul's Church in Riverside, Connecticut, where I had been confirmed in 1908 and married in 1914, 1 invited Father Joseph to the parish to preach a mission, which he gladly did.

While he was staying with us, I asked him about the Third Order. He gave me an outline of the Rule. I asked if he would accept me as a postulant. He immediately said, "I'll enter you as a novice—you don't have to be a postulant"—which he proceeded to do.

Discussing the Rule with him, I found that I was already following a self-imposed Rule, which, except for the periodic reports, was the Rule for Tertiaries. He was delighted with this, and released me from the necessity of writing the periodic reports except when I felt I needed help.

Years later, having realized the poverty of my meditations, I asked him for advice. Foremost among his suggestions was to start writing them. This I did, and I still enjoy reading my Anima Christi, Meditations on the Prayer of St. Ignatius. It was published in 1925, and a copy is on my bookshelf within easy reach as I type!

While pastor of two shore lands parishes—Riverside and Sound Beach (now known as Old Greenwich)—I frequently took groups of parishioners to Little Portion, across the Long Island Sound in a borrowed motorboat, to the great edification and enjoyment of the people as well as the Friars!

Those days have gone, but I can still, as I near 90, say the Offices of the Seraphic Breviary, and pray especially for all who love and follow our Blessed Father Francis.

From “He Stood for Us Strongly: Father H. Baxter Liebler’s Mission to the Navajo” (McPherson,2012)

One Good Friday he took colored sands he had collected and created before the altar in the chapel a picture of the crucified Christ, Saint Mary, and Saint John in elongated form. While he drew this on the ground, he gave fragments of a sermon based on the Franciscan catechism and had Brother Michael and Helen Sturges sing appropriate hymns—all in good keeping with traditional Navajo ceremonialism. At one point in the service he covered the sun with black sand to represent the darkness that spread across the land at Christ’s death. Many Navajo people were impressed that a white man would think to create such images.

But they were even more impressed with what they considered the results. Over the next twenty-four hours clouds started to build, and, within two days, heavy, soaking rains pelted southeastern Utah, breaking a lengthy dry spell. Word spread that Father Liebler had strong prayers that could bring moisture to the land through his sand paintings, and had similar powers to heal the sick. The People talked about this event for years to come.

He obtained from a priest-friend a set of carved figures for a nativity scene. Mary, Joseph, and Jesus were dressed in Navajo clothing and hairstyles, but the wise men wore full war bonnets as Comanches, since everyone knew Comanches came from the East. Father Liebler believed it was one of his most successful efforts to bring home the real meaning of Christmas.

Another friend made a three-foot plaster statue of Saint Mary dressed as a Navajo woman and carrying Jesus in a cradleboard. This was placed in the church and was known as “Our Lady of the Navajo" or “Madonna of the Navajo.”

Navajo mythology has a comparable deity, Changing Woman, who gave birth through supernatural means to twin boys. They, in turn, received powerful, sacred weapons used to destroy evil monsters inhabiting the world. Whether traditional Navajos made this connection between Christ’s birth and ministry and that of the Twins is unknown, but certainly the idea was not foreign to their beliefs.

As a pedagogical device, the statue served to teach of God’s involvement with the Navajos, a theme that found its way into the art done by children attending the mission school. The figure’s significance increased in 1964: it was one of the few objects that remained unscathed when the original log church burned. For Liebler, “The God of Truth was not going to let the Father of Lies have his

Madonna of the Navajo

way without some witness.. . She seemed to declare to all who would listen, Here I stand. Were I not the Mother of God, you would have no Redeemer."

Navajos were impressed that "while he [Liebler] is singing, he places something in your mouth, that "it [the host] is holy," and that "the holiness remains in you." The singing and accompanying ritual appeared similar to the actions associated with the use of corn pollen in traditional ceremonies. One man explained that the sacrament was called "jish," or the medicine bundle used by chanters: "The Holy One set this for us, and this is the ceremony that is to be done. The one who has become a priest will perform this ceremony."

From His Most Famous book, *Boil My Heart for Me* (1969)

It will be recalled that in establishing St. Christopher's Mission, I had had some preconceived ideas that at that time received but little sympathy from official headquarters. These ideas had to do chiefly with a respect for native culture that would indicate a method of presentation of the Gospel, not as a contradiction but as a fulfillment of what the Indians, by their own and their ancestors' meditations and reasoning, had found to be a satisfactory way of life; and furthermore, a presenting of the Catholic religion as being the fullness of the Christian revelation, and as being the true religion of the Episcopal church, even though by the traditions of men much of it has been obscured and "made of none effect."

Indians who had been untouched by the man-made traditions would, I thought, have no mental or spiritual block that would require us to "go slow" in our evangelistic work. It was for this reason that I had sought, and been given, a hitherto untouched area in Utah, that I might not be required to undermine another man's work, or even to build upon it. Now, imagine my amazement to find that by far the greater number of those missionaries at this Conference, judging from their self-introductions, were definitely on the St. Christopher road. Where twenty years before I had found Morning or Evening Prayer and sermon, with a monthly communion service, the normal spiritual fare in the Sioux country, now Eucharistic worship with emphasis on both sacrifice and popular participation had come into its own. Absolution and other sacraments, long-laid aside, were being revived; the clergy were acting and talking and being treated like the priests they really were. Similarly the old idea that Christianity must first make a clean sweep of what had gone before so that it could set itself down, as it were, in a vacuum had given place to the policy on which the English church had been built fourteen centuries before.

Prayer After Mass

H. Baxter Liebler

The Rev. Harold Baxter Liebler, senior tertiary died November 21, 1982. He was professed for 56 years.

Jesus Christ, young man chief
God's son being
now your offering I've made–smoke I've made.
Today your child I became
          –today your grandchild I became
Just to me you say, I'll do
          your commandments I will follow
just as I pray to you, you do it–watch over me.
As my defence [sic] stand thou
          –for my defence [sic] stretch out thy hand
                    in my defence [sic] plead thou.
From wood stream to me be peace
          grass from under to me be peace
                    from breeze courses to me be peace
          from passing rains to me be peace
                    from passing thunder to me be peace
Just by me dew let fall
          just by me pollen let form.
Before me peace–behind me peace
          long life walking may I be
                    –after peace may I be.
          Peace has returned
                    —peace has returned.   (May, 2003)

Third Order Manual of the American Congregation of Franciscans (1962)

The third and final manual *Third Order Manual of the American Congregation of Franciscans* was published in 1962. On page 3, it had this description:

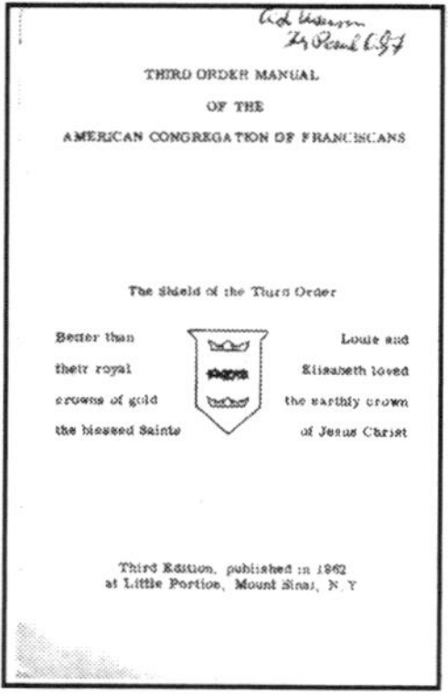

THIRD ORDER MANUAL
OF THE
AMERICAN CONGREGATION OF FRANCISCANS

The Shield of the Third Order

Better than their royal crowns of gold the blessed Saints

Louis and Elisabeth loved the earthly crown of Jesus Christ

Third Edition, published in 1962
at Little Portion, Mount Sinai, N. Y

The third edition attempts to emulate the devotional brevity of the former (Bundle of Myrrh), rather than the didactic amplitude of the latter (The Little Book of the Rule), with the result that informative or devotional material easily available from other sources is not included. It is assumed that all who need such material are likely to be already in possession of it, inasmuch as those who seek our Third Order will normally be those whose convictions have matured by virtue of their instruction in and practice of the Catholic Religion within the American Episcopal Church or some other part of the Anglican Communion. It should be noted, however, that the former Manuals may be used, if convenient, except for those points changed in the Rule.

From the "Preface" to the 1962 *Third Order Directory*

My Dear Brothers & Sisters of our Third Order:

Your names are often mentioned before God at Little Portion, for we pray for you daily. And of course you are remembered at the Convent and at St. Francis Seraphicus House, Avon Park, Florida. The friars and nuns of our Order need your prayers too. In their name I earnestly ask you for them, Help us daily.

I commend to you especially:

1. Our Mission Sisters in England *[three 3rd Order members of the London Custodia known as the Mission Sisters of the Charity of St. Francis SCSF],* for their growth in holiness, numbers and good works.

2. Our friars and nuns in the U. S. that God will give us a constant increase in vocations realized.

3. The hope of our Sisters to finance much needed repairs on a portion of the Convent which can't be used until these are accomplished (new roof, enlarged heating system, dividing some large rooms into several smaller ones, and the like).

4. That one of our tertiaries may get your hearty support and that of many Church people in the establishment of a first class nursing home for Episcopalians near St. Francis Seraphicus House, Avon Park, Florida, to be owned by our Third Order and chaplained by our friars. This is so that our sick people, especially aged folk, may have Church and sacramental privileges. Plans are afoot.

By way of introduction, look up the name "Hoffman" in this Roster. His wife is one of us also (a member of the Confraternity of St. Francis) and is a nurse, registered in NY., NJ., and Florida and presently helping to run a nursing home.

They are willing to give their life savings to establish this work for God, and ask no more than their livelihood from it, in the hope that eventually it could be completely manned by tertiaries. I am hoping that if I live to be old and infirm, as was Br. Giles, I won't have to be sent to a county institution as was he, but that I may be cared for in a Church institution like this. What about you? And what about members of other Religious Orders?

Whenever you think of this matter say a tiny prayer: "O Christ, arise, help us! Holy Mary, St. Joseph, St. Francis, St. Clare, St. Anthony, St. Louis, St. Elizabeth, help us by your prayers in heaven."

The nursing home plan in Florida was never fulfilled. However, the Hoffman's (Alvah and Anna) played key roles in the next Chapter when they steered the Province towards independence during the transition time of the Third Order Corporation.

St. Francis Seraphicus House, Avon Park, Florida L-R: Father Joseph, Br. Anthony, and Br. Paul Kenworthy

Father Joseph (Claude Crookston) died March 7, 1979 at Little Portion Friary.

Recollections of the Father Joseph Era: Marie Webner, May Alice White, The Rt. Rev. Minister General Michael Fisher, SSF, C. David Burt , Claire Lintzel, and Lucy Pierce

Marie Webner (Professed 1953) (from *Franciscan Times Easter 1992)*

On February 14, 1953, I made my profession in the Third Order at the pro-cathedral in Regina, Saskatchewan. Dean Noel received my vow and pledge on behalf of the Order. I don't remember anyone else being there, but my firstborn, Mary, was kicking lustily in the womb, but she would not be born for another six weeks.

It was a lonely business being a Franciscan back then. I had started my postulancy and novitiate in Washington, D.C. where the only tertiary I knew was the rector of St. James' Episcopal Church on Capitol Hill. Father Planck was an Anglo-Catholic of the old school; I never had any doubt that his life was prayer.

I met my first friar when Brother Charles SSF visited the Diocese of Qu'Appelle (southern Saskatchewan). He stayed with us at the vicarage and was enchanted with Mary, who, even at the age of two years, delighted in fun and laughter. She was equally at home with a Franciscan friar, the Bishop of Durham (who happened to grace the vicarage living room for an hour one day), the farmers, and the mechanics. Inside the womb or out, she had caught something of the Franciscan spirit. So eventually did her younger brother and sister.

In the 1960s, when I lived in Washington, D.C., I started making yearly retreats with the Poor Clares. From the beginning, I always felt welcome and at home with them. By that time, I had three children and no husband. Retreats were a foretaste of heaven. A silent breakfast was a far greater privilege than a banquet could possibly have been.

On my very first retreat, Sister Mary Catherine arranged for me to meet Father Joseph, the founder of the American Franciscan Orders. I climbed the hill to the friary somewhat nervously and was ushered into the little parlor to the right of the main entrance. Father Joseph was cordial and obviously relieved to find I was not going to be tearful or hysterical. I recognized and enjoyed his relief. It was true that my husband had left me and that I had suddenly become a single parent, but hysterical I was not. We walked a bit on the grounds and talked about my husband. Father Joseph was the only person I knew who took for granted my continuing concern for my husband. I loved him for that.

Once when I was staying at the Poor Clares' guesthouse, three brothers walked by on the road while a group of as were playing croquet. They were invited to join us but responded (very seriously), "We are not allowed to play games with young ladies."

In 1971 I moved to Tucson, Arizona. At first, I was teaching at Tuller School, where Father Joseph was staying in a cottage on the grounds. It was a privilege to visit with him, but an even greater privilege to conspire with Mary Ann Jackman and Brother Luke to get him back to the Order he had founded. The last time I saw Father Joseph was at Little Portion where he died in the heart of his community.

Mary Alice White (Professed 1961) (from *Franciscan Times 2003)*

Scapular: 1. A sleeveless outer garment falling from the shoulders worn as part of a monk's habit. 2. Two small pieces of cloth joined by strings, worn on the chest and back under the clothes by some Roman Catholics (and Anglicans) as a token of religious devotion.

The second meaning of 'scapular' was my first introduction in the fifties to the Order of St. Francis. I was on Altar Guild at the old St. Mary's Episcopal Church in Denver with Alice Trout. As we worked, I noticed she had a string attached to her bra strap. "What is that?" I asked. She pulled on the string and brought forth a tiny square of gray cloth. "It means," she explained, "that I'm a member of the Third Order of St. Francis." Inquiring further I found that the Tertiaries met once a month at St. Mary's or in some other church or more often in someone's home.

"How great that you are reminded of St. Francis, not just Sundays but every day through your scapular," I said rather liking that strange word and peculiar practice.

I began to attend the monthly meetings where Father James Mote of St. Mary's and Father Justin Van Lopik of St. Andrew's were members. Our meetings consisted of reading one chapter from *The Little Book of the Rule* and meditating thereon. *The Little Book of the Rule* observed "Would you know St. Francis? Read his rule. Would you know his rule? Study his life."

In those days we all abided by the rule as laid down in the *Little Book* and did not venture to make up our own rule. That was thought at that time to be presumptuous. I remember the eighth rule was to do one act of charity every day even though it be no more than to throw a crumb to a bird. I do not know for sure, but I should think our precepts in making a rule today are based on those in *The Little Book.*

We always had refreshments and always collected an offering for the Third Order because as far as I know, no one made a pledge of money in those days.

By the way, once we were professed, we did indeed wear a gray scapular, as in the first definition above, and a knotted white rope around the waist when we attended meetings. Once we had car trouble on the way to a meeting, and Fr. Mote remarked should someone see us they would think we were on the way to a masquerade.

But I'm getting ahead of myself. I must have attended meetings for several years before I thought seriously of becoming a novice. Why did it take me so long? I suppose it was a serious commitment and one I didn't want to enter into lightly. But finally in 1959, I did indeed become a novice. In those days, when we were professed, we took the name of a saint as our name within the Order. I chose the name of Sister Magdalene Claire at my profession on October 2, 1961 at St. Andrew's Church and Marjorie Nevels, mother of one of our priests, became Sister Mary Dominica. We were received with much ceremony and, of course, it was a momentous occasion for us both.

In those days, we reported directly to the brothers at Little Portion. I remember Father Hugh answered one of my reports as follows:

Dear Sister Magdalene Claire:

Thank you for your report and note. Please say the 84th psalm as penance for the reported infractions of the regulations.

God bless your striving to obtain the great virtue of Humility, which is basic in the development of the Life of Christian Perfection. (Note: Alas I'm still striving!) I think it is a good idea to have a checklist and to mark it at the close of each day. The Lord grant you His peace!

Faithfully yours in Him,

Fr Hugh, O.S.F

By the way, the monthly report of Tertiaries was formidable to say the least. In 1968 at the urging of Peter Funk, I became a novice mistress. That's what it was called at that time. In other words, novices reported to me, and I answered them. It had become too much for the brothers to do this work of direction as our numbers increased. This was a fruitful if fairly arduous job since I taught full time, and had three teens at home. In 1971, I asked to be relieved of this responsibility when my husband died in March of that year, and I went through a very stressful period. I do not know the date of Br. Robert Hugh's arrival from England and the merging of our Order into the English Society of St. Francis. I only know that there came a renaissance within the Order.

Other brothers, of course, came. I believe actually it was 1960 that I first met Br. Robert when he visited Denver. He told a small group of us what the brothers did in England as well as at Little Portion. Now that I think back upon it, I believe that his enthusiasm and knowledge of the brothers' work is what really inspired me to become a full-fledged tertiary in the first place. He then and now means so much to the Order and has influenced hundreds of people, I'm sure, to become Third Order people.

Another beautiful occasion was getting to meet and know Father Joseph a bit. He had been living in Orlando, Florida, and my friend, Marie Thompson, valued him very much. He came to Denver and stayed with Marie for a while. Once I was driving him to Marie's house in North Denver when he suddenly asked if I had read the book, *The Naked Ape*. I think it had not been long published, but he must have been in his early eighties at this time, and had a remarkable capacity for keeping up on books and other matters too, of course.

The Rt. Rev. Minister General Michael Fisher, SSF (From *For the Time Being* (1993))

I first met him in 1957, after my time at Brown University, Rhode Island. I had supposed that it would be polite and right to stay in their Friary on Long Island and went there for rest and recuperation. It was quite an experience. Father Joseph belonged to the old school and was a man of great integrity and quite uncompromising Anglican Catholicity—not least in all the outward observances of the religious life as he understood it. His relentless praying reminded me forcibly of Fr. Algy; they were much of the same stock, though he hadn't quite the same sense of humour. I thought it was right for me to go to him for Confession. It was a formidable business. The Chapel had traditional confessional boxes and, to me, Father Joseph's style seemed somewhat inquisitorial. Perhaps I deserved or needed it. I certainly felt I'd been put through the wringer, and vowed I'd never expose myself to the experience again.

Joseph and the brothers were courteous and generous on that occasion. They also made it clear that there could be no possible hope of S.S.F. and O.S.F. getting together.

C. David Burt (Professed 1966) Ordained Priest by Rt. Rev. Anson Phelps Stokes, Bishop of Massachusetts, May 24, 1968

C. David Burt (personal letter to the author)

A number of years later when OSF and SSF had merged, there was a jubilee celebration for Father Joseph in a church in New York. My wife and I went. Father Joseph was still allowed to wear his gray habit, and he was still called Father Joseph, O.S.F. He gave a sermon in which he pointed out that the word "catholic" was being misinterpreted as meaning "universal". He said it comes from the Greek "kata holos" which means "according to the whole." So the "Catholic" religion means the whole truth, not just selected truths. "Sounds different doesn't it?" he said.

So I saw that in the midst of the post Vatican II ferment, the changes in the prayerbook, and the merger between the Society of Saint Francis and the OSF, the man who had insisted on the *Credenda* for the American Congregation of Franciscans was still sticking to his guns.

Finally when I visited him on his death bed at Little Portion, I asked him what he thought of the ordination of women. He rose up in his bed and said as clearly as he could. "Well, it is heresy, and it will destroy the church."

Claire Lintzel (Professed 1961) *(Franciscan Times Summer 2011)*

After much discernment and prayer, still favoring Francis, I applied to the Third Order. This required my rector's recommendation and consent from my husband who was aware of my intentions and agreed to my vocation. Thus I had the opportunity to move through postulancy and novitiate. Fr. Hugh (a priest from the Netherlands Old Catholic Church) had gone to England during WWII, became a Franciscan, and later, was transferred to the US. He was delightful, playful, and an extraordinary scholar. He guided me in to the study of the saints, some history, legends, and a joyful awareness of living a Franciscan life in our secular society. He was quite elderly yet astute, and possessed a gift of understanding via mail of what I needed to do and how to manage it all within busy family life. His comments were given directly with a lighthearted style that penetrated the minutiae of my daily responsibilities. After two years as a postulant, I took vows at Little Portion and became a novice. The family was growing toward four children when I was life-professed in 1961.

The Founding Father, Father Joseph, came [to Little Portion] with a couple of friars. He was austere, tall with a straight back, and he emanated authority without pretense. His large eyes were aware of everything, but he said very little. The others carried the conversation and he remained very focused in manner and attitude. In short, he was quite formidable, and I simply did not force interaction with him. He had a very powerful presence in spite of saying so little.

Lucy Pierce (Professed 1946) (*Franciscan Times Fall 1998)*

My husband was the first one interested in the Third Order, and we started off together in it. He later became a Priest Associate of the Holy Cross, but I stayed on in the Third Order I think by the tenacity of the Holy Spirit. I knew that I wanted some framework to carry me through life, to keep me from ever getting lost, to keep me in the Faith. As I look back over the years, I'm somewhat amazed that I'm still here.

I've never had much contact with other Franciscans. In the early days, under the American Order of St. Francis, I reported to the First Order Priests. It was a numerical sort of report—how many times omitted grace before, after meal, morning, evening prayers, meditation, etc.

The reply contained a penance and counsel. I still have a few of the letters that were especially helpful. I don't remember much about the change from OSF to SSF, but I knew enough about the English Franciscans to welcome the change and to be glad to be part of a worldwide Order.

I once went to a retreat once conducted by Father Joseph, and I knew Fr. Vivian Peterson who helped the First Order get started. One of the Sisters of St. Helena, who I knew at school, was in the early Cincinnati Third Order group. I also knew Fr. Baxter Liebler who worked with the Native Americans in Utah, and the peripatetic bishop, Br. John Charles.

Most of the time I have been an isolated tertiary busy with children, or with teaching school. There were times I kept a minimum rule not very well, and hoped that some day I would do better.

I have received a great deal from TSSF and other tertiaries, and from OSF and SSF. I am grateful to have lived for so many years as part of the world-wide and ages-old Franciscan Order.

It's hard to look back over 50 years and come up with anything special. There's too much—the ups and downs, the good, the bad, the ugly, and the mountaintop beautiful. The rather surprising thing is that it really is always a journey. There is never a feeling of having arrived. I always feel that I know a bit more now than I did before.

At the moment, I am impressed with the literalness of St. Francis: the way he seemed to take every reading, every occasion in simple concrete terms. This is what it says; this is what it means. That's a great way, it seems to me, to look at psalms, lessons, and prayers. I stop and look closely at phrase in a collect. I try to look at gospel readings without a lifetime of familiarity. I stop and really immerse myself in an idea such as "in whom we live and move and have our being." Peter said that Jesus walked on water—there wasn't a sandbar. The water didn't suddenly freeze. That's what it says. That's what it means.

There are some commonsense rules to go with literalness: not taking things, for example, out of context, and being aware of cultural and linguistic analysis, that's for another time. Right now, I'm just trying to take a fresh, close look at old truths. It's a simple idea, and that's about where I am at the moment.

References

A Book of Roots: Source Documents for the Living Tradition of the Society of Saint Francis, 1975, 1978.

Anson, Peter F. *The Call of the Cloister: Religious Communities and Kindred Bodies in the Anglican Communion.* London: S.P.C.K, 1955.

Dunstan, Petå. *This Poor Sort: A History of the European Province of the Society of St Francis*. London: Darton Longman & Todd, 1997.

Fisher, Michael. *For the Time Being: A Memoir*. Leominster: Gracewing, 1993.

Hamilton, Chuck. *A Brief History of Christ Church, From its Founding in 1901 Up to the Present as of Spring 2015*. http://s3.amazonaws.com/dfc_attachments/public/ documents/3206501/History_of_Christ_Church_by_Chuck_Hamilton.pdf.

Jones, McVean and Others. *History of Lincoln, Oneida, and Vilas Counties Wisconsin*. Minneapolis: H.C. Cooper, Jr. & Co, 1924.

Krumm, The Rt Rev. John McGill, *Flowing like a River.* Cincinnati: Christian Forward Movement, 1989.

Liebler, H B. *Boil My Heart for Me*. New York: Exposition Press, 1969.

Long, Grady M., Notes Toward a History of Christ Church Parish 1900-1960. http://s3.amazonaws.com/dfc_attachments/public/documents/3155988/Notes_Toward_a_History_of_Christ_Church_Parish_1900-1960.pdf.

May, Majorie, *The Highly Adaptable Gospel: A Journey Through the Life of H. Baxter Liebler.* Chicago, Il: Dv polymedia, 2003

McPherson Robert S. Dinéjí Na`nitin: Navajo Traditional Teachings and History. Boulder, CO: University Press of Colorado, 2012.

Walking in the Footsteps of Christ: The Historical Documents of the Society of Saint Francis. Dorchester, Dorset: Society of St Francis, 2003

Williams, Barrie. *Franciscan Revival in the Anglican Communion.* London: Darton, Longman & Todd Ltd; 1982.

Chapter 3: Br. Paul & the Third Order Corporation 1966-73

How The Third Order Secular of the American Congregation of Franciscans, TSF, Became the American Province of the Society of St. Francis, TSSF in 1967

The Third Order Secular of the American Congregation of Franciscans, TSF, began, as we have seen, in 1917 in Cincinnati. By 1935, it had 75 members. The Third Order of St. Francis in England, TSSF, began when Father Algy and Dorothy Swayne met at her Club in Central London, where they adapted the Rule of Christa Seva Sangha (CSS, a Christian Ashram, started in 1920-22) for the new Franciscan Third Order, which came into being in June 1931. It took another six years before the CSS in St Ives and Brotherhood of Saint Francis of Assisi (BSFA) finally agreed to a merger, and the Society of St Francis was formed. In 1937, TSSF began its life, with Fr Algy as Father Guardian and Dorothy Swayne as Assistant Guardian of the Third Order and Senior Novice Mistress. The Constitution of the Third Order was worked out by him and Dorothy, together with Fr. Charles (the Chaplain-General) during the war. By 1949 there were about three hundred tertiaries. (Mumford (2011 & 2014); Beach (2000 & 2011); Williams, (1982)) (See also Swayne *Prayerbook*; *Meditation Book*.)

We Could Have Joined Together in the 1930s through the Auspices of Vida Scudder

Six days after the Feast of St. Francis, in *Holy Women, Holy Men (2010)*, you will find the feast day of Vida Scudder who lived a Franciscan life in the Christian Social Gospel movement (1890-1930). Scudder was a professed Companion and the Formation Director for many decades of an all-women Order, Companions of the Holy Cross (CHS), whose motherhouse is Adelynrood north of Boston. Scudder published both a novel about the early Franciscan movement, *Brother John: A Tale of the First Franciscans* (1927), and *The Franciscan Adventure: A Study in the First Hundred Years of the Order of St. Francis of Assisi* (1931). There is evidence in the Adelynrood archives that Scudder tried to steer CHS into joining the TSF of Father Joseph in the 1930s. This did not happen, but she did orchestrate an Institute of Franciscan Studies in 1933 at Adelynrood. (*On Journey*, pp. 339-42) As she described it

> *Eighty picked people were in attendance: Professor Booth's Franciscan seminar; diverse other academic folks; clergy from half a dozen communions, social workers, and naturally many companions.... We found that... a surprising number of groups, sometimes unknown to one another, scattered over many countries, are organized in the name of the saint and seek to embody his spirit.... I rejoiced to know Father Joseph and his brothers in our own American Church... Other connections with India came through the interesting group then active, the Christa Seva Sangha; they published every year a Franciscan number of their review to which I contributed an account of the Institute.*

Scudder knew Franciscanism intimately and lived Franciscanism extraordinarily. She could have been the link uniting our founder, Father Joseph and TSF, and the British/Indian Christa Seva Sangha movement that gave birth to TSSF.

The Situation in 1967

(much of the following is from Peta Dunstan (1997), pp. 219-24)
We've seen how in 1957 Father Joseph OSF made it clear to The Rt. Rev. Minister General Michael Fisher, SSF, that there could be no possible hope of O.S.F. and S.S.F. ever merging. Similarly, ten years later, Father Minister David, who succeeded Michael as SSF Minister General, objected to any mergers because he saw that OSF directed by Father Joseph's somewhat inflexible vision of community life, was resulting in few professions and a community that was aging and being reduced by deaths. With Br. Paul Kenworthy succeeding Father Joseph as Father Vicar (or assistant superior) of OSF in 1962, there were soon some more life professions and more brothers in the novitiate and formation, but the Order with a total of ten life-professed members could not be self-sustaining for much longer. In 1967, Br. Paul was elected as Minister General of OSF, and Father Joseph retired to Tucson. Br. Paul moved to begin negotiations for a merger and, by October 1967, the merger of OSF and SSF was accomplished. As indicated by the fact that the American OSF brothers changed into brown habits from their traditional grey habits on the first Sunday in Lent 1968, the American Congregation of Franciscans became one of several provinces in the Society of St. Francis (joining the European, Australia provinces), and thus the mores and traditions of SSF became the norm of the united Orders.

Since TSF and TSSF were governed by their First Orders, decisions of the First Orders had immediate impact on the Third Orders; there is no evidence that the First Orders consulted with the American Third Order concerning this merger. The mores and traditions of the British TSSF became the norm of the American TSF, and the scale of those who would be affected in TSF was larger by a number of degrees than the OSF First Order of ten life-professed members; TSF had 146 professed members with 24, 16% of its total members, in the London Custodia. (TSSF had 396 members.)

When John Scott, our first Provincial Guardian, wrote "The American Third Order Today" for *The Franciscan Revival in the Anglican Communion* (1982), Scott wrote this about the merger: "The transition to the Principles derived from the Christa Seva Sangha was not easy for many, and some members withdrew; the *Credenda* and the wearing of habits seemed to be so very basic to their beliefs and practices in the Order of St. Francis...From the time of the consolidation [to 1981] virtually ninety percent of the present 400 Third Order members...have entered its ranks." This was the largest exodus in the history of the province—119 members listed in the Directory left.* With Father Joseph distancing himself from the unification process by remaining in Tucson, TSF members saw this as a reason to be hostile to the process. For a time the situation was difficult. Minister General David wrote in November 1967 of how younger American friars had been verbally attacked at a Healing Mission by a tertiary for "their desertion" of the American Church, of the Clares and of the Third Order, an experience that shook them badly. Peta Dunstan observed in her book (1997) that "*had unity not been achieved so swiftly, the strength of the tertiary opposition, once mobilized, might have prevented the union.*" [See page 86-7]

What TSF Had To Give Up in the Merger

TSF as an Order had to give up many important traditional elements to become a province of TSSF. Gone were the habit, religious names given at profession, the optional vow of celibacy taken by professed members who became Oblates, a sense of a motherhouse at Little Portion Friary, and the *Credenda* signed by each at profession. (See this chapter's **Afterword** on the Franciscan Order of the Divine Compassion (FODC) that re-instituted most of these aspects in 1990s.) All subsequent narratives of the nativity of the Third Order (exemplified by *Walking in the Footsteps of Christ* (2003)) began with the British/Indian Christa Seva Sangha experience rather than the prior decades of experience in the United States. All Province of the Americas formation materials, prior to the 2016 edition, reflect this blindness to the first 50 years of American experience prior to the merger.

Fifty-four life professed members of TSF in North America (men, women, priests, oblates, a number of married professed couples, 37 in Formation across 19 states, Australia, and Canada) and nearly all of the London Custodia left the Order. (Of the 24 professed members in the London Custodia only two transferred to the European Province of TSSF.) Most of the 119 left because of a difference in tone between TSF and TSSF: both were centered on reaching Christ by following Francis; and both were led to express their Franciscanism through service to the world. However, the Anglo-Catholic tradition carried on by Father Joseph had always been a big attractor for the members of TSF.

In the amalgamation, with so much given up, two unique items were retained in the Province of America: the requirement to read a Daily Office, and the sacrament of penance (e.g. confession) was normative. As of 2013, there were some additional minor differences in the Province of the Americas Formation in the Americas requires monthly reporting for two and a half years not quarterly reporting as in the other provinces; the requirement of the Province of the Americas that ALL professed members be in parishes in communion with the See of Canterbury has led to the creation of an Order of Ecumenical Franciscans, the Order of Lutheran Franciscans, and the Order of Old Catholic Franciscans.

---

*This was determined by comparing the names of members in the TSF's 1967 Directory with the names that appear in the 1969 to 1976 TSSF American Province directories, as well as with the (British) *SSF Third Order Intercession and Address List 1970-1*. Names were also compared to the lists of deceased in all these directories.

With the transition from TSF to TSSF, a world of habits and ceremony ended. Here are some pictures of this lost world—the "veiling" (profession) of Anna Hoffman on March 27, 1966.

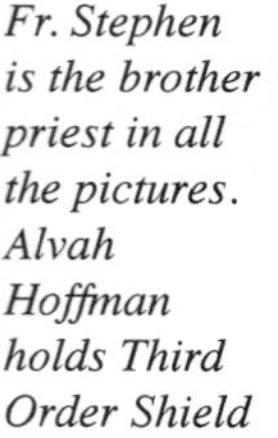

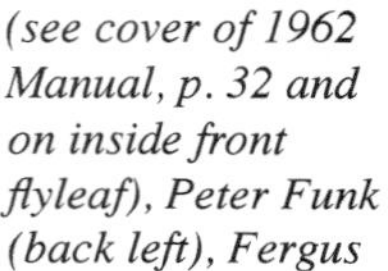

Fr. Stephen is the brother priest in all the pictures. Alvah Hoffman holds Third Order Shield (see cover of 1962 Manual, p. 32 and on inside front flyleaf), Peter Funk (back left), Fergus Fulford (3rd from lt), Ed Warner (4th from left in the back row), Leslie Hewett (5th from left in the back row), Anna Hoffman (front row right).

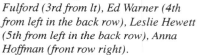

Anna Hoffman at the August 1968 Franciscan Festival after the merger of TSF and TSSF—She no longer wears a veil or habit.

Nurturing a New Third Order in this Province, 1967

Br. Paul, Minister General of the American Congregation of Franciscans, paved the way for union with the European Province of TSSF by appointing a Third Order Corporation. This Corporation included: Dr. G. Alvah Hoffman as President and his wife Anna as the Secretary General. The other officers included: Chaplain General, Br. Paul, Vice President, the Rev. Father Fergus M. Fulford and Treasurer, Mona Hull. John M. Scott was listed as Assistant Chaplain General and Peter Funk was the Novice Master.

Organizational Meeting to Launch the American Province of TSSF, April 25, 1968 at Little Portion Friary.

Those attending included: C. David Burt (Mass), Rev. Fergus Fulford (NJ), Alvah and Anna Hoffman (NJ), Mona Hull (MA), Rev. Hendrik Koning (PA), Rev. Robert Samuelson (TX), Rev. John Scott (PA), Rev. Edward Warner (Kansas City, MO), Catherine Welton (Montana), Rev. Robert Woodfield (CA), Rev. David Kennedy (Miami, FL), Bishop Charles Gaskell (Wisonsin), Justin Van Lopnik (Denver, CO), Rev. Gusweiller (NY). Among other action, Chapter voted for the Hoffmans to continue to serve on the Corporation. (along with Fulford, and Hull). Chapter then wrote to the English tertiaries to note that they had accepted their Rule with Amendments to their Constitution as of October 6, 1967.

At this meeting, Br. Paul explained that all aspirants must write to the Chaplain General, Br. Paul, for the introductory literature; submit three copies of their Rule for approval and only then will it be sent onto the Novice Master or Novice Mistress. Moreover the Chaplain General would be the person who would approve all novicing and professions. When the Professed rewrite their Rules as a preliminary to renewing their vows, copies are to be sent to the Chaplain General for comment and editing.

Also at this meeting, former 1st Order brother, the Rev. Robert Goode (a.k.a. "Gooch") was made an "itinerant tertiary" whose job was to visit the isolated tertiaries in the middle and southwest of the country. He explained that "some of these tertiaries had never had any direct contact with another tertiary." The importance of his work could be seen from the fact that one eighth of the budget was dedicated to this work—a little less than was gifted to the 1st Order.

First Chapter Meeting April 25, 1968 bottom row: Br. David (Minister General SSF), Mona Hull, John Scott, Hendrik Koning. back row: Anna Hoffman, Edward Warner, Alvah Hoffman, Br. Paul, C. David Burt, Catherine Welton, Robert Woodfield, David Kennedy, and Robert W. Samuelson. (Notice the lack of habits for all tertiaries.)

Anna Hoffman's May 1969 report as General Secretary

Our first year as a Corporation has been a most enlightening one. As Secretary General and Novice Mistress during this time it has brought closeness with our Tertiaries scattered throughout this large country. Little has been known about the activities in which our Tertiaries participate. In our own Fellowship we have two Tertiaries that are active all of the time. One does beautiful embroidery and has made many sets or vestments for some of our Missions; the other sees that all who belong to the Confraternity of the Blessed Sacrament receive their little Manuals of Intercessions four times a year.

There are lone Tertiaries who help with children and give their time to day nurseries, drive the infirm and sit with the lonely. There are those who have adopted children and opened their homes to the needy, and the homeless. Many do secretarial and other works for their parishes filling in as organists, and offering their time at our many camps during summers.

Our Florida Tertiaries have organized their own Fellowship under the direction of Fr. David Kennedy. This was done in February of this year. Our Chicago Fel1owship under the direction or Fr. Caskell admitted three Novices at the May meeting. One of our lone Tertiaries drove 400 hundred miles to be present at that meeting. Our Tertiaries on the West Coast are all active in some sort of charitable work. [Ed. *A letter from her husband in March of this year notes that there are active Fellowships in Washington DC, Chicago, Florida, and California. There was also a fellowship or "Custodium" in Denver.*] A great many of our lone Tertiaries belong to Prayer and Bible Study groups in other churches than their own. Being Novice Mistress has been a most enjoyable and interesting task. It has brought a closeness that otherwise I would never had known. A family, a Franciscan family, can be and is a most interesting family.

From Br. Robert Hugh, SSF

(Franciscan Times Fall 2012)
Br. Paul was the newly elected Minister of OSF. Father Joseph, the OSF founder, had by then been Minister. On Fr. Hugh's death, Br. Paul himself assumed the role of Chaplain to the Third Order, and it was Paul's vision for the Third Order that initiated and made possible the major changes in the Third Order's understanding of its own identity and vocation as a self-governing religious Order in its own right, with its own minister and administration, its own chaplain and provision of pastoral care, and its own formation team. It took a full decade to achieve all this. When Br. Luke became Minister Provincial SSF in 1970 he asked me to succeed Br. Paul as Third Order Chaplain, and I served as Chaplain for four years (1970-74). I took it as my goal to work myself out of a job, and thus I largely spent my time visiting tertiary fellowships and individuals to share and discuss this new vision. (Our tertiaries numbered about 200, and so I was able to visit personally with all but about five, I believe.) Br. Mark Francis succeeded me, and he was the last Friar Chaplain to the Third Order.

Today we take it for granted that the Third Order provides all its own leadership, and but, when I began as TSSF Chaplain, all inquiries, applications, and requests for profession, came through the Chaplain's office. Peter Funk's series of formation letters were well under way and every few months I had a lovely visit with Peter and Mary at Lambertville (New Jersey) where we looked at his latest offerings. If a newsletter were to go out, it was because the I as Chaplain wrote it, cut the stencil, turned the crank on the Gestetner duplicating machine, and mailed it.

"Touched by God: Reflections on a Franciscan Quest"

Peter Funk (1st Men's Formation Director, Author of 1st Formation Letters)
In one way or another, we are touched by God; through associations with people, through our readings, seeing, hearing, interior listening, and by our feelings. Often I reflect in astonishment that, through God's graciousness, I am where I am, from being an agnostic, perhaps even a deist. As a combat Marine in World War II in the South Pacific, I came home troubled and melancholic. In the war I lost not only a brother whom I loved, but also many friends.

Settling into civilian life, my wife Mary and I believed in the importance of setting an example for our children. Consequently, I went to church and served in various capacities. God touched me. An important event for me happened when I met Paul Moore, the future Bishop of New York and future Bishop Protector of the Society of St. Francis. A group of us from our church went to the torn-apart inner city of Jersey City to help refurbish the young priest's rectory and church. Paul had been a combat marine. We had something important in common.

Through Paul, I met Father Joseph of the Poor Brethren of St. Francis of the American Congregation of Franciscans (Greyfriars). My first session with Father Joseph intrigued me. I knew only a bit about St. Francis and was totally unaware of a Franciscan Order in the Episcopal Church. The headquarters, Little Portion Friary and the convent of the Poor Clares, were located on twenty acres donated by Br. Stephen's family in Mount Sinai, Long Island.

Through Paul I also met a young priest, Kim Myers. At one point he and Paul courageously stepped between two violent gangs, preventing a bloody battle. I wrote an article about this for *Faith Today*. Later Kim became Bishop of California and Regional Protector of the Society of St. Francis.

Innumerable people, either in depth or fleetingly, as well as my studies became the various touches of God. In the 1950s I founded and published *Faith Today* magazine. A pioneering effort, it became one of the first truly ecumenical publications and the only religious magazine sold at major newsstands. We had superb international writers, but due to a lack of financing, I ceased publication of *Faith Today*. With seven children to support, I took a job as a sales manager of a mutual fund, while writing novels in whatever time was left over. (He wrote three, and one was made into a movie.)

Peter in the TSF Habit: black cassock, grey apron, cincture with three knots, and skullcap.

During this time I experienced a growing yearning to "know God." My weekly church activities did not fulfill me in whatever I sensed I lacked. An interior odyssey developed into a search for the heart of God–a desire that's difficult to express for it comes from a source deeper than words. It is an instinctive longing to merge your life with God so totally that you will be made "one body with Christ, that he may dwell in us and we in him." So often such words slip past us, and we really do not understand their possibilities. I didn't know that I was in search of the Society of St. Francis. In 1961 I mulled over a possible story that might be written around Little Portion. I called Father Joseph and arranged a weekend visit. Following a business luncheon in New York—my luncheon companion thought my adventure sounded weird—I drove to Long Island.

As I drove, somehow I sensed a sharpening awareness that this weekend would have a profound, life-changing effect. In what way? I didn't know. I worried. Felt a chill. Then it seemed as if a strange magnetic force began misdirecting me. Inexplicably I made wrong turns. Became lost. Finally arrived in Port Jefferson, a few minutes drive from Little Portion. *[Ed. Compare this trip in 1961 to the story of a similar visit to Little Portion in 1929 on page 16.]* Expected at the Friary by 5:30, I decided they wouldn't miss me, and so I ate supper in town. I recall driving into the circular driveway. Lengthening evening shadows mystically encircled the white building and the railed bell tower with the tall cross. The time was a little after seven. Parking the car, I sighed. Climbing the steps to the front door, I pulled at the bell.

The door opened. A slender brother in a gray habit greeted me. "I'm Vladimir. I'm the Guest Master. We waited for you for supper." No sense of reproof lay in his words, only a kind of sadness and wondering. Franciscan courtesy highlighted my discourtesy. How thoughtless of me! I'd given no thought to their schedule and my obligation to be on time. I made profuse apologies.

"Father Joseph would like to talk to you. He's injured his leg and so he stays in his office where he listens to the services." Vladimir led the way. Impressions: A sturdy figure lying in bed. White hair and thick white eyebrows. Strongly handsome face with prominent finely shaped nose. Brown eyes search me, not severely but wanting to know me. I found humor and kindliness reflected in them.

Peter Teaching a TSF Formation Class.

Father Joseph was a scholar of the Anglican Church and may have influenced the revision of the Prayer Book we use today. Singlehandedly he created the *Anglican Breviary* (1955) and *The People's Missal* (1961) based on similar Roman Catholic texts. It was an enormous and magnificent undertaking. As Father Joseph explained, the Prayer Book Offices cannot be celebrated if one stuck to the *1929 Book of Common Prayer* in the sense of doing no more that what is ordered. "In other words, the Prayer Book Rite must be treated as an apocapated (shortened) liturgy, for that is precisely what it is in the 1929 BCP." The *Breviary* and the *Missal* corrected this shortcoming.

He dismissed my apologies for my rudeness with a gracious wave of his hand. We reviewed our first meeting, and he questioned what I had in mind. After talking a while, he suggested that Vladimir show me to my room. At nine o'clock I'd attend Compline. Vladimir would be with me. At the time I didn't know that Office, since it's not in the *1929 Book of Common Prayer.* That evening, Br. Vladimir accompanied me to the Visitor's Gallery. Below us, the brothers faced one another, their quiet voices filling the chapel. I felt a sense of peace. When the Office ended, the room was darkened abruptly, and the brothers pulled the hoods of their habits over their heads. "Put out the light," Vladimir whispered urgently. Since this was my first time, I had no idea of the customary practice, and, in my zeal, I nearly yanked the cord from the ceiling. The "Great Silence" began.

My room was a narrow cell. A bed with a cross over it, desk, bureau, and chair comprised the furnishings. That night I dreamt I'd died and could see myself in the coffin. Suddenly I sprang out of it. It was such a wondrous dream of new birth, and I knew that all would be well, even the huge debt I'd incurred with publishing *Faith Today.*

The following day I met many of the brothers Mary and I later learned to treasure as friends. Those who were there at the time included: Stephen, Leo, Dunstan, Mark Francis, Luke, Lawrence, and Paul. I also came to know the redoubtable Reverend Mother Mary Catherine of the Poor Clares.

I used the library, asked questions and cherished the periods of silence throughout the day and during meals. We celebrated the traditional seven Offices of Matins, Lauds, Prime, Terce, Sext, Nones combined with Vespers, and finally Compline. Generally silence was kept until about 10 a. m. (Today at the friary the routine is different and simplified; silence is kept after Compline until breakfast is completed, and four Offices from the Prayer Book are offered.)

Emerging from the overarching quiet of the Friary into my loving, rollicking, noisy family of seven children was like plunging into the wild maelstrom of the New York subway at commuting time. I felt immediately guilty knowing how much Mary would have enjoyed my experience; that would come later. I kept in touch, and learned about the Third Order. Without joining, I experimented with its Rule of Life. During this period I came under heavy stress. With the demanding job as a mutual fund sales manager I traveled half of my time around the country as well as trying to be a full-time writer, getting to bed late and up at 4 a.m. plus running a kind of farm. I felt dissatisfied in my work for I wanted more time to write. Even though I began to be successful in my writing, I didn't feel confident enough to go full time. Writing is a hazardous way for most people to earn a living, especially when supporting a large family.

Peter wrote three semi-fictional novels about large families, (one was made into a 1963 movie with Debbie Reynolds and Cliff Robertson); one book on spiritual topics; and nine books working from his continuing Reader's Digest series, "Word Power."

The apparently safe approach became the hazardous one. In 1965 I was diagnosed with terminal intestinal cancer, following which I'd acquired a violent case of hepatitis C from a transfusion. God had to give me a hard push to get me back on my path of life. The mutual fund company summarily fired me when it learned of my illness. Mary said "Good! Now you can get to your writing."

I became a postulant in the Third Order, reporting to Fr. Stephen who was in charge of the Third Order Formation [*Ed. See picture on page 44*], and I was professed in 1967. At that time New Jersey had a Fellowship with about seven or eight of us including Ed Warner who now lives in Georgia and Claudia Gammon who is still in New Jersey. Later we met with John Scott's lively group in Philadelphia.

As hard as it is to believe now, in those days we tertiaries took religious names. Ed Warner, for example, was Fr. Polycarp John. I was Peter Bernard: Peter for the disciple and Bernard for Bernard of Clairvaux whom I admired. Underneath our clothing we all wore small scapulars and, when we put them on each morning, we recited Francis's prayer, "Here O Lord in this church…"

At our meetings we wore a black cassock, a large gray scapula over the cassock and a gray yarmulka. However, as some people began "playing games" at being religious, these unnecessary outer symbols were quite correctly dumped. In 1968 the American Grayfriars merged with the world-wide Anglican Society of St. Francis with its roots in India. We became the American Province. Now whether priest, deacon or lay brother, all were called Brother or Sister. To help restructure our province, a group of First Order brothers and Third Order members gathered. The invaluable John Scott and others represented the tertiaries. [*Ed. This is the International Third Order Chapter that met at Hillfield Friary in England May 25-7, 1973. It is described later in this Chapter.]* In contrast to the Roman Church, the Third Order would eventually grow to have its own Minister Provincial and Novice Directors (later Formation Directors) rather than be under the aegis of the First Order. [*Ed. See Dee Dobson's chapter for further comment on the SFO/OFS development modeled on our Formation program.]*

At that time Br. Paul, the first Minister Provincial, suggested I become the Novice Director. As Director I wrote 30 formation letters outlining the different elements of the Franciscan life of a tertiary. These letters would be given to the postulants and novices each month during the 30 months of regular reporting to a counselor. [*Ed. These have all been gathered and are available on the TSSF website in Historical Documents*.]

About this time, the inimitable Br. Robert Hugh, Novice Director of the First Order, happily brust into Mary's and my life. Either, he visited us on our farm, or I would travel to Little Portion. He was my constant and always loving guide. For us he exemplified the Franciscan way of life. Eventually overwhelmed by the many formation reports I received, the Order decided to add counselors. Marie Webner became the first one. She was an indefatigably valuable help, having many good ideas.

The Order Grew.

Many people helped in different ways. What would we have done without Helen Webb, who not only played the piano at our Chapter and other meetings, but also acted as Secretary to the Third Order. In addition she typed, proofed, and offered suggestions on my formation letters. Dee Dobson played an essential role in shaping our Order's destiny.

Sometimes the friary would send us young First Order brothers not yet professed who needed some motherly love, of which Mary has in abundance. We remember one 18 year-old who spent the weekend in bed reading comics. We had delightful visits with Joel and Jeremy and worried about them when they left the Order. They seemed so vulnerable. Stephen visited us, and I put him to work helping to cultivate our Christmas tree farm. I nicknamed him Mighty Magoo, and he'd burst out in stuttering, happy laughter when I'd call out to him: "Hey, Mighty Magoo, are you feeding enough manure to those young trees?"

I remember so well the English Brother Geoffrey and his radiant smile and sound advice. As the Minister General he visited us one weekend with Br. Philip, his secretary, and Robert Hugh when we discussed Third Order matters. He suggested that a person cannot travel when burdened down with things. Mary and I felt overburdened then, and we still do. Geoffrey's helpful booklet, *The Way of St Francis,* is still available and given to each new postulant as part of *The Basics*. Yes, the Society of St. Francis has changed. But the change is outward only. Its inner essence remains the same. The Society of St. Francis has done much to help shape Mary's (who also was professed) and my life as we continue to search for God within and without.

("Touched by God: Reflections on a Franciscan Quest" by Peter Funk, Spring 1999, *Franciscan Times*) ***Peter died September 19, 2016.***

Forty Years Later A Commentary on Peter Funks' Formation Letters

Susan Pitchford (Franciscan Times, Advent 2013) [*Ed. Susan Pitchford and her books are featured in Chapter 16 of this book.]*

I suppose most of us in the Third Order are here because at some point we were charmed, or challenged, or changed, by Francis of Assisi. We recognized something of the Divine in him—his passion, his commitment, his joy—and we wanted to bring some of that spirit into our own lives. Unlike Elisha, I don't have the chutzpah to ask for a "double portion" of my mentor's spirit, though I do hope that if I hang around Francis and Franciscans, some of it will rub off on me. But moving from "charmed" to "changed" is a process, and a challenging one at that. Without a rigorous formation process, we'd be stuck forever splashing around the birdbath. And I've never seen a deep end to a birdbath.

The formation process is critical, and the "Formation Letters" have been a critical part of that process since the first version was written by Peter Funk, who was professed in 1967 and wrote the Formation Letters between 1968 and 1970.

There's so much that could be said about the twenty-two letters that make up the original document, but I'd like to focus on three things that stand out to me: As I've already suggested, the letters are *wise*, but they're also *passionate*, and they're *challenging*. For each of these characteristics I can only give a couple examples.

Wisdom

The wisdom in Peter's letters is apparent from the very beginning. *Letter 1*, "How to Write a Rule," anticipates the spiritual newbie's tendency to legalism, and cautions against scrupulosity. "You are not to fuss excessively," he says, sounding like an exceptionally wise great aunt. Lapses are normal, and when they occur, they are "only faults, not sins. Don't get bogged down by them." Peter points out the paradox of spiritual discipline: living under a rule of life is liberating, because it "helps to bring you into God's presence more consistently." It's about deepening one's spiritual awareness, not setting up a list of obligations, and it's in that attentive abiding in God that we find freedom.

One place where we find some of Peter's wisest counsel is *Letter 13*, "The Dry Period," in which he explains the sources and meanings of spiritual aridity. He acknowledges that spiritual dry spells can come for all kinds of reasons, but emphasizes that they are not necessarily a bad sign: "The dry periods that come from God have a purpose, and if we can understand that they are part of our overall spiritual growth and not simply a hiatus, we can use them creatively." Thus he manages to say in thirty-four words what took me two hundred pages in *God in the Dark*. Don't rely on your feelings, he says; feelings can be deceptive. Dry periods are largely about learning to trust in God when you *can't* feel his presence. We do that by holding fast to the Rule, and letting it carry us over the dry parts. Having summarized the teaching of John of the Cross in a couple of paragraphs, Peter concludes that the goal is "understanding the darkness as being light. It is to give up a lesser faith that we may acquire a greater one." How I wish I could have read that letter fifteen years ago.

Passion

Probably the most striking thing to me about these original Letters is how they communicate Peter Funk's deep passion for God. Thank God for that; how terrible it would be to be drawn to the Third Order by Francis' passion, only to be subjected to formation materials that were cold and distant, spiritually frozen over. Peter himself observes in *Letter 5* ("Four Pillars") that Francis' free choice of poverty and hardship only makes sense when we see that "Francis was a man truly in love." A great love redefines sacrifices as natural and joyful, but for many of us, the love of a spiritual giant like Francis can be more intimidating than inspiring. Peter has wisdom for us here, too: Start by loving other people. And *pray* for a deep, wide, consuming love for God. If we follow this advice, we'll have the two Great Commandments covered. Besides, this is such a great place for prayer to begin. If I had to pick one prayer out of the innumerable requests people make of God as "Most Likely To Be Granted," the prayer for a greater love would be my choice every time.

It's in the Letters on prayer that Peter's own passionate love for God is most evident. Listen to his advice on how to avoid worrying about whether you're "doing it right":

> *[T]oo many people have thought it depended on technique, that one had to be proficient in some kind of method. How wrong they are. Prayer is not a matter of technique ... Prayer is an exchange of love.*

When I read that, I did a little mental fist-pump and thought, *Yes*. It's not about getting stuff, even spiritual stuff; it's about allowing God in, allowing God close. Again and again Peter invites us to intimacy with God, and shows that intimacy involves a glorious, almost shocking mutuality. Even our confession is an exchange of love: "[W]e respond to His forgiving love with our penitential love" (*Letter 11*, "Forgive Us Our Sins"). This exchange reaches its pinnacle in the Eucharist: "At the Communion we give ourselves to Christ as he gives himself to us, so that we may go forth in union with him." Here's another paradox: In the Eucharist the soul communes intimately with God, and yet "[t]he Eucharist ought never to be thought of as a completely individual act." We receive the Body of Christ *as* the Body of Christ, and not as little isolated cells.

Challenge

Christians have sometimes tried to evangelize by pretending that following Christ is easy and fun, downplaying that bit about carrying the cross. These Letters do not make that mistake. There's an entire Letter on "Fasting," which was so tough to read I had to put it down and make myself a snack. He acknowledges that Francis found pledging himself to a community to be a mixed blessing, and we likely will too:

> *Community is a risk ... We cannot escape community. We can, however, go through life slithering and sliding in and out of different communities, avoiding responsibility and avoiding the commitment of total dedication.*

These are not the words of someone trying to make it look easy. But throughout these letters, there's a steady tension between challenge and support. You can see this in Peter's advice on how to "pray without ceasing": he makes a case for the Jesus Prayer, and then acknowledges that it's "easy to begin, and easy to forget." He advises people to begin slowly and realistically, and to be patient with themselves, returning to it anew when they forget. "Keep trying. It's worth every ounce of effort."

Peter also takes on a subject I wrestled with in my book *Following Francis (2006)*: "But I'm not poor … How then can I call myself a follower of St. Francis?" (*Letter 4*, "Poverty"). He admits that family obligations can prevent a person from renouncing their possessions. But whereas I reached that point and called it a day, Peter challenges us to ask ourselves what we'd do if no one were dependent on us; would we be willing to give it all away then? At this point, I'm ready for another snack. Or possibly a drink.

I can't resist one more example of how Peter challenges us. In the Letter on aridity, he quotes Thomas Merton: "The sacrifices that are not chosen are often of greater value than those we select for ourselves." Oh, how willingly I'd carry the cross if only I could design it myself. I'd like a nice light one, maybe Styrofoam, with plenty of padding where it would rest on my shoulder. Whereas the cross I've actually been given is, you could say, a righteous pain in the backside. But the commitment Francis modeled for us takes the cross of God's choosing, not our own. I'm like the spouse who says, "No, I won't get a job and help with the bills. But look, I made you a pie!" Peter is too realistic to downplay the cost of following Christ. But he, too, is a man in love. And because of that, he knows that whatever the price, it will be well worth it.

Treasures New and Old

One of the things John asked me to consider in this review is whether the original letters seemed at all "dated"; how well do they wear their forty-five years? There are the sorts of wrinkles you'd expect, like the gender assumptions: "A busy doctor does his [intercessions] for 15 minutes or so during noon. A mother and housewife finds that in the evening just prior to taking her bath works best for her." Some of the ways in which the Letters show their age are just funny: In Letter 5 Peter identifies love of God, simplicity of living, humility and trust in God as the "Four Pillars of Prayer," and offers the mnemonic: Lucky Strike Has Tobacco. We might make a different choice today; still, I won't be forgetting that soon.

Peter uses the terms "religious life" and "religious community" frequently in the Letters. He takes the notion of being a religious in the world very seriously, too seriously to want to see it degenerate into a game of dress-up.

When I entered formation in the Third Order twelve years ago, the Formation Letters—along with the sisters and brothers in my fellowship who taught them to me and lived by them—showed me what this life is about. The Letters have been expanded considerably since Peter's original efforts, of course, and some careful subsequent editing has removed the repetition and created a tighter organization. It's important to have those newer chapters about the history and structure of the Order as well as the Three Aims and Ways of Service, the Three

Notes, and my special favorites, the chapters on contemplation and action.

But Peter's Letters are the core. Reading them reminded me why I'm here—why, in spite of the long list of reasons why Francis probably wouldn't recognize me as one of his own, I am still hanging onto this community, hoping to be formed by it into something Francis might recognize. Lots of people admire Francis, of course, and are inspired by his life and charism. But it's another thing to incarnate that charism. This is what we are called to, and it doesn't come easily, though it is the way of "perfect joy."

So thank you, Peter; my skullcap's off to you. I know you didn't do it alone: I see a lot of Br. Robert Hugh, Thomas Merton and others cited here. But the gift you gave us in these Formation Letters has carried forth the work of Christ and of Francis in ways you can never know, this side of heaven. I know I speak for our brothers and sisters when I tell you how much that gift is treasured.

TSSF Second Chapter, May 6-8 1971 at Little Portion
At a meeting of the Pastoral Officers, the earlier officers were supplemented by the two Asst. Novice Mistresses, Marie Webner and Anna B. Hoffman, and two Asst. Novice Masters, Fr. Robert Goode and Fr. David Burt. Dr. G. A. Hoffman resigned as President because of health reasons [*Ed. He died five years later in 1976*], and, in August, his wife Anna resigned as General Secretary of the Province [*She died in 1981*].

At the November 8, 1972 meeting, most of the roles and leadership remained in place but a discussion of the "draft Principles and Constitution" occurred which indicated that the worldwide TSSF organization was working on universal Principles and a Constitution from which the American Province would draw its own.

An International Third Order Chapter was called by Br. Geoffrey, Minister General SSF, to meet at Hillfield Friary in England on May 25-7, 1973 to consider revised drafts of the Principles, and the Constitution. (John Scott, Peter Funk, and Marie Hayes were nominated as delegates by the Corporation; John Scott was elected to go with Chapter approving his election in May 1973.) To prepare for the International Chapter, a number of individuals were asked to write position papers on various subjects: C. David Burt—How may we best understand the Third Order today as indeed as an Order? What are those things which constitute an Order? What is the nature of our Profession and Vow? In what sense is the Third Order a Community?* Judith Robinson—What is contemporary Franciscan spirituality? What do the traditional terms like Poverty/Chastity/Obedience or Humility/Love/Joy mean for Tertiaries today?* John Scott—What should be the public stance of the Third Order today in its witness and outreach to an alien world that is increasingly secular and post-Christian?*

This is a VERY small photo that was hard to make out of TSSF Second Chapter. (Little Chronicle, June 1971) Those who have been identified include in the front row left to right: (1) Robert (Gooch) Goode (2) Terence Mainardi (Friar Novice) (3) Warren Tanghe (4) (5) Anna and Josephine Keer (6) Helen Webb (7) Anna Hoffman (8)Alvah Hoffman (9) Kale King (10) Peter Funk (11) Br. Robert Hugh (12) C. David Burt (13) John Scott (14) Marie Webner (15) David Kennedy (16) Hendrik Koning (17) Robert Woodfield.

Chapter May 1973—A Turning Point and the End of the Third Order Corporation (?)

When Br. Robert Hugh was reappointed as Friar Chaplain to the Third Order, American Province during Chapter, he explained that the office of Friar Chaplain had become more pastoral and less administrative (Minutes of the 3rd Order Chapter, May 1973). Thus Br. Robert Hugh proposed that a Third Order member be elected to handle the administrative aspects of the Province. In response, Chapter voted to give such a Third Order administrative officer the title of Guardian, and Chapter then elected John Scott to be this new Guardian. (These decisions seemed to be getting ahead of the process of creating a provincial organization since the Provincial Statues defining offices, terms, roles, etc. had yet to be created. Chapter asked Chapter member Warren Tanghe to draft such a document for review and approval at Chapter 1974.)

With the creation and election of a Provincial Guardian (renamed *Minister Provincial* in 1986), the priority and pragmatic governing role of the Third Order Cooperation ended. However, the Third Order Cooperation lives on symbolically today at each annual Chapter meeting in an odd, concluding ritual. (You can also find "Corporation members and officers" listed in each annual *Directory* just before Provincial Officers are listed; the Officers of the Corporation and the Officers of the Province are nearly identical.)

The odd, concluding ritual embodies the power of the Corporation over Chapter, and it proceeds as follows. Once all the regular work of Chapter is completed and a budget accepted for the coming year, the Minister Provincial as chair of the meeting calls for the temporary suspension of Chapter so that the budget may be presented to the Third Order Corporation for acceptance. Once the suspension of Chapter is approved, some members of Chapter are elected as Secretary, Vice President, and Treasurer while the Minister Provincial now becomes the President of the Corporation. The Corporation opens its meeting, and the budget created by Chapter is then presented to the Cooperation that votes for its acceptance. The Corporation then adjourns, and the Chapter meeting is reopened, and the budget finally approved.

Though there may be residual legal reasons for the continuing existence of a Third Order Corporation, they seem largely lost.

American Province at Hillfield Conference, 1973—1st International TSSF Conference: John Scott (circled at left back right), Br. Geoffrey, Minister General, SSF (center in photo)

Letters to His Friends

Brother Paul SSF

As he was dying, Brother Paul wrote a number of inspiring letters to friends. In 1980, the SSF published a booklet collecting many of these letters. Here is one.

This September I will be 74 years old. It has been a very happy life. It has been very fulfilling and rewarding. God has indeed been very good to me. I have enjoyed the sights and the sounds, the friends and the work. But the last few years I have begun to realize that this journey is a pilgrimage, and I long for journey's end.

When I was a boy away at school, it seemed the Christmas holidays would never come so I could join old friends and my loving family. And, oh the excitement and joy of the trip back home!

It seems to me that death is like going home for Christmas. God is our all-wise and ever-loving Father, and, to die, is to return home to his love. He is love. His love is a free unearnable gift and given for all time. It is true, of course, that he is also Judge,—but he is Judge and my Wise and Loving Father. I can trust his judgment as I trust his love. And this I know: he loves me!

In January I had an emergency prostate operation. It was cancerous, and the cancer has spread apparently to my whole bone structure and to one kidney. Where else it may be I do not know, and, frankly, I do not care. I am delighted because I can see not-too-far-ahead that journey's end for which I have waited. My bags are all packed, and Christmas is coming! Whatever time of year God calls me, I will be going home for Christmas. It will be a Merry Christmas.

Rejoice with me–and pray! **Br. Paul died December 27, 1979.**

Afterword. The Rev. John C. Vockler founded the Franciscan Order of the Divine Compassion (FODC) in 1991. FODC is closely aligned with *Forward in Faith North America*, a conservative Anglo-Catholic movement known for its opposition to the ordination of women as well as to liberal Anglican views of homosexuality. Their Bishop Protector, The Rt. Rev. Keith L. Ackerman, was professed in TSSF in 1971 (and released in 1992), and had experienced Father Joseph's TSF. Many of the terms and norms of TSF are replicated today in FODC; there is a FODC *Credenda*, the possibility of taking an extra vow of chastity to become an oblate, and religious names and habits are given.

References

Beach, Hugh. "History of of the Third Order: Some Snapshots " (2000) http://tssf.org.uk/wp-content/uploads/2010/08/history_of_the_third_order_winchester.pdf

___________. "Sixty Years in the Third Order" http://www.franciscans.org.uk/userfiles/pdf/Franciscan_January_2011/Articles/Sixty_years.pdf

Mumford, Denise. "Two Thousand Tertiaries Strong: the Development of TSSF from Small Beginnings." http://www.franciscans.org.uk/userfiles/pdf/Franciscan_January_2011/Articles/Two_thousand.pdf

____________. "'MARTHA' a life of Dorothy Swayne, lay founder of TSSF." February 2014, http://tssf.org.uk/wp-content/uploads/2014/10/Martha_8Jul.pdf

Dunstan, Petå. *This Poor Sort: A History of the European Province of the Society of St Francis*. London: Darton Longman & Todd, 1997.

Funk, Peter. *High Spirits*. Garden City, N.Y: Doubleday, 1983.

Holy Women, Holy Men: Celebrating the Saints. New York: Church Pub. Inc, 2010.

Scudder, Vida D. *Brother John: A Tale of the First Franciscans*. Boston: Little, Brown, and Co, 1927.

____________. *On Journey*. New York: E.P. Dutton & Co, 1937.

____________. *The Franciscan Adventure: A Study in the First Hundred Years of the Order of St. Francis of Assisi*. London: J.M. Dent and Sons, 1931.

Swayne, Dorothy. *Martha's Prayer Book* . London. Billing and Sons, Ltd., 1955.

______________. *Martha's Meditation Book* . London: Society for Promoting Christian Knowledge (SPCK), 1961.

The Anglican Breviary. Mount Sinai, N.Y: Frank Gavin Foundation, 1955.

The People's Anglican Missal in the American Edition: Containing the Liturgy from the Book of Common Prayer According to the Use of the Church in the United States of America : Together with Other Devotions and with Liturgical and Ceremonial Notes. Mt. Sinai, N.Y: Frank Gavin Liturgical Foundation, 1961.

Williams, Barrie. *Franciscan Revival in the Anglican Communion*. London: Darton, Longman & Todd Ltd; 1982.

Chapter 4: John Scott, First Provincial Guardian, 1973-1980

How Did You Come to be a Franciscan Tertiary?

Fr. Bill: Fr. Scott, would you tell us something about yourself and how you came to be a Franciscan tertiary?

Fr. Scott: Sure. My interest really began when I was around ten years old, back in 1939. I was given a book about St. Francis; I think it was titled *Book of Courage*. I became enamored by Francis immediately. I grew up on Long Island, not that far from the First Order Friary at Little Portion, but did not discover we had Franciscans in the Episcopal Church until my senior year of high school. In 1946 I began communicating with Little Portion. During my college years, I sometimes attended services at Little Portion. Visitors were kept separate from the friars then and they even brought us communion in the balcony. Father Joseph, founder of the First Order in the Episcopal Church, became my mentor. He truly was a father figure for me. He did keep rather tight control over the Third Order, so Dee Dobson was accurate in making her comparison with the 13th century office of First Order Visitor to the Third Order. I became a postulant to the Third Order during my senior year of college. The next year I entered Nashotah Seminary; I was a priest by age 25.

Fr. Bill: Dee tells me that the Rule under Father Joseph's direction was pretty rigorous.

Fr. Scott: I guess it was. We've heard about the seven Offices done daily by Louis and Elizabeth. I had to do six, but I was so comfortable with it that it seldom seemed a strain.

From "A Meeting of Franciscans: Part 3 of 3" by Bill Graham, *Franciscan Times*, Summer 1998.

1977 Chapter Picture at Little Portion (left to right)
(kneeling) Br. Luke (MP America SSF) Muriel Adey (Canada)
Dee Dobson, Helen Webb, Marie Webner, Br. Reginald
Sam Samuelson (Mexico), John Scott, Ken Cox (California)
Br. Jeffery (MG SSF), Kale King, Br. Mark Francis

An Era of Controversies: The Philadelphia Eleven (Women's Ordination July 1974 Philadelphia) and the Ordination of Gay Priests 1977

When John Scott was Guardian, the challenges were massive. It was not so much who he was as it was the times in which the Order existed as a religious organization, and he happened to be the Guardian. Probably never again would the Order face such challenges and assaults. John was very fortunate to have Rev. Robert Goode (nicknamed *Gooch*) as the Provincial Chaplain, for it is Gooch who offered these first two conciliatory letters seeking to bridge the varied political groups. The first was an open letter to the Order, and the second was a personal one.

> *I have offered to write to you out of concern for my brothers and sisters, who like myself are appalled by the agonies we are being asked to endure over the question of women priests. In discussions with other Chapter members I have pointed out that our problem is many-faceted. Scriptural authority, human sexuality, the received nature of the Faith, Catholic consensus, etc. are all involved. Our brothers and sisters represent just about all the possible positions in the Church, and we continue to be a "mixed bag" as an Order. This is a time for heroic charity, communication, and a lot of time on our knees.*
>
> *I still find as yet no reasonable and viable alternative to the Episcopal Church. There are already four splinter groups busily beating their own drums. Most of them seem more concerned about appearances and right-wing politics than the Gospel. None of them has the earthy, warm, embracing qualities I have come to look for in a truly Catholic atmosphere. Some of them sound <u>Jansenistic</u> and most of them have rather exotically derived episcopates, to say the least. The other legitimate Catholic Communions all require an assimilation of an ethnic tradition foreign to me. Having grown up in Irish Boston, I can say this also applies in some instances even still to the Roman Catholic Church.*
>
> *We also have to face the fact that discontented priests who feel they can command the allegiance of 100 or more persons are often very much aware that they are likely candidates for the episcopate of a splinter church.*
>
> *If you feel strongly enough, this might be a good time to reread some of the great heroes of the Oxford Movement. They operated in an atmosphere far more hostile than the present one. In addition, the clergy at least faced the possibility of civil penalties and imprisonment as well as ecclesiastical censure and deprivation. Our religious Orders themselves were born into what seemed an impossible situation. And remember, our Communion endured over three hundred years of prohibition of the religious life. Despite that, we still had our Little Giddings and our Nicolas Ferrars.*
>
> *Those of us who are considered conservative (odd, since I am a socialist and love the new Prayer Book) must ask ourselves how important the Franciscan*

life is. It is precisely that kind of life born in the spirit of the Passion and Franciscan penance, which may be the means of our healing. Do not abandon it lightly.

It is true that I cannot say, as I once could, that I will live and die a priest of this Church, though I may die trying. We Franciscans have been very adaptable and undaunted. After all, did we not go to the tents of the Sultan himself? Share your agony with me, or the Guardian, or another Chapter member. I even invite you to call me collect at __________if talking will help.

Let me also express to those of you who are concerned, my own feelings of confidence in the Chapter and its sense of fraternity and charity. At least in the Third Order, nobody is steamrolling anybody else. Those of you who read this who do not find any objection in what is going on should bear in mind that the problem is real and dangerous. These are my own personal feelings and opinions, and don't represent those of any official faction. Every strength and grace of our Franciscan training is called for in this difficult period. Let us not be found wanting.

With respect and love to all my Franciscan brothers and sisters.

Gooch+ (The. Rev. Robert Goode) Assistant Chaplain Member of Chapter

This next letter from Gooch discussed Bishop Paul Moore, who was the Bishop Protector for all three Orders, and was also an early advocate of women's ordination. Moreover, Bishop Moore was the first Episcopal bishop to ordain an openly gay person, Ellen Barrett, in 1977. In addition, the letter explains a seemingly harsh action taken by Chapter, which followed an element of Father Joseph's TSF that continued after the merger with TSSF: the requirement that ALL professed members in the American Province be in parishes in communion with the See of Canterbury.

February 2, 1978

Dear Sister,

Am writing you having just received your letter—so that you can get it from the horse's mouth. If people are looking for a scapegoat it would be very nice if they could lay all the troubles at our door. The First Order is as seriously divided as the rest of the Church. Though I am proud of the Brothers in that they have been very closed-mouth for unity's sake. So it is really hard to tell who is on what side of what issue. You should also know that some of us privately tried to arrange behind the scenes for Bishop Moore's connection with the Order to be severed. Since he is the Protector in other Provinces too, it would be too difficult and too upsetting to push this through several Chapters. So those of us who are opposed to his protectorship because of the association it gives us, must simply grin and bear it. Please understand that we are not all of one mind; except for this: "to make our Lord known and loved everywhere."

Chapter passed a conscience clause somewhat similar to the House of Bishop's, which is our way of recognizing that these troubles are not of our making, and we find ourselves in serious disagreement, just like everyone else. Since I represent the more conservative element in the Church and in the Third Order, I must in fairness say, that most of the Franciscans have been scrupulous in seeing that my viewpoint is expressed, accepting our differences and maintaining charity. To set the record straight; John Scott read an official statement that while he has an extensive ministry to the gay community, he has not performed any "marriages" and has not been asked to do so.

Now for our other problem. It is true that Chapter took the action you refer to [releasing those who were no longer in communion with the See of Canterbury]. But it is the context in which it was taken which is important to note and understand. When all is said and done about ecumenism it is an anomaly for people to be part of a Society when they cannot officially be in communion with us. Allowing for all the private opinions of Roman and Orthodox and the many instances when almost all of us have instituted an informal intercommunion, these persons who go ahead and do this are, in fact, being disobedient to the official positions of their Communion. You must understand the reason that some of these persons have gone to these other Communions is, in itself, schismatic. On the other hand, we are almost alone in the Episcopal Church (and vast sections of the Roman Church are wastelands in this regard) in standing for a traditional spiritual life. Consequently, all kinds of Protestant stray cats and dogs are attracted to us because they feel a void in their own Communion. Some of them are in a position where they cannot very well be in Communion with Canterbury or any other Bishop or give obedience outside their own Communions. In fact, I believe the interest is so great that we stand in danger of being overwhelmed enough to lose our identity in the very things which gives us our very strength, which attract people to us. We were trying to cope with the anomalies and doing fairly well, hence the Spirit that you refer to at convocation. But two things have come to pass since then, which we have had to deal with. One is that at Chapter we had to deal with people who as members of the Anglican Church of North America decided they were not in communion with us. What actually happened was that they have decided they can pick and choose which Diocese they are in communion with and each individual priest they are in communion with. For example one of them would attend my mass and not John Scott's, or would go to Fr. X's mass at the Convent but not genuflect to the Blessed Sacrament in the Brothers' Chapel. In short, and I am only referring to a small group of people, what some of these people wanted was the advantage of the facilities of TSSF and its structures, but the freedom to do spiteful things like this. While all this business does not affect a big portion of our Communion the troubles you describe at ______ and some of the others we have seen, made us realize the Episcopal Church, regardless of what divides us, must preserve her integrity. You must realize that this is a difficult time and, except for the non-juring clergy in the 17th century, we have never had a significant schism with valid orders.

I want you to understand that the spirit we did this in was not a spirit in which we tried to keep others outside the Society. In fact, it was quite the opposite. First, we were faced with the mess which now exists. Out of our discussions of that grew a realization that there is a hunger for the spiritual life everywhere in Christendom and that we are one of the few resources left equipped to serve that need. So we decided to see if we could approach the problem with our tradition of trying to be of service to man. We are opening the doors of the Society to all comers for the postulancy and novitiate (provided that is, they meet our usual standards of being truly serious). We will share all our resources of guidance and direction in training. One of the specific things we are doing through Dee Dobson is to make up a directory of Spiritual Directors, to share with not only the Society but anyone in the Episcopal Church or in the rest of Christendom who wants to use it. We are prepared to help people start up some kind of spiritual life in their own Communion even if it turns out not to be Franciscan. So you see we have not violated our spirit at all. We do recognize that there are those who cannot be in Communion with the See of Canterbury or whose legitimate obedience is to someone else; as in the case of a Lutheran minister who might be interested in what we have to offer. So what we are going to do is to train him in our usual way, give him the support of our fellowship during his postulancy and novitiate, and ask him to make his Profession to a person in his own Communion who would have the sympathy and authority to receive it. We will then extend our resources further to help this person set up a Franciscan or other type of group within his own Communion. What we have, in fact, done is far more outreaching than what we have ever before contemplated. This also allows us, however, to be able to say that there is such a thing as an Anglican, that there is a real and effective Anglican Communion, and some of our troubled conservative brethren very much need to know this right now. We are including the Anglican Church of North America in our offer of help, and we feel that when the heat of controversy dies we may be in an unusual position for helping to bring about a reunion—when that time comes, in God's mercy.

So as you suspected, the rumors are only half-truths and our ecumenical concerns are just as strong as they ever were. As to troubles in general, I can only say to you what my bishop says:

> *Christ's church is a given and divine thing, that is what it means to be High Church. It was instituted by Him, and it only ceases to be His church when He says so. If it was His church yesterday, it will be His church today and tomorrow. All the sinfulness of men, all the acts of General Convention, and all the wickedness of rumormongers not withstanding. He has overcome the world, but so few of us act like we really believe it.*

Rather than trying *"to arrange behind the scenes for Bishop Moore's connection with the Order to be severed,"* as Gooch wrote, John Scott wrote Bishop Moore a letter of support a year earlier enclosing a "pastoral letter" he had sent out to the whole Province.

March 30, 1977

Dear Bishop Moore:

Many of us have been sharing in some small degree the agony that has been placed upon you by the many criticisms you have received regarding the ordination of Ellen Barrett to the priesthood.

I would like to assure you that I believe you made what was clearly the right decision despite perhaps the inability to judge the depth of the critical response. Please hold firm and know that you have the prayers and support of many others.

I am enclosing a copy of a "Pastoral Letter," as it were which I have just mailed as Guardian to all of the members of the Third Order of the Society of St. Francis for the American Province. I hope that it will do some good in holding us firmly to the Gospel itself and the passion which is the heart of that.

Special Message, January 1978

The Rev. John N. Scott, Guardian

On January 9th a letter signed "Concerned Franciscans" under the letterhead of St. Mary 's Church, Denver, Colorado, was sent to all tertiaries on our May 1977 Address and Intercession List. Telephone calls I have received indicate considerable confusion. Let me try to clarify what is happening, inasmuch as some of you are not even aware of the convention of schismatic Episcopalians in St. Louis last September, which encouraged withdrawal from the Communion of the Episcopal Church, and elected our former tertiary, The Rev. James O. Mote (of St. Mary's Church, Denver) to be its bishop (Diocese of the Holy Trinity) when and if he could secure consecration. Some 30 congregations nationwide have formally withdrawn from the jurisdiction and communion of their dioceses and fellow Episcopalians.

The matter was discussed thoroughly at the annual Chapter meeting of the Third Order last November 11 and 12. While we understood the conscientious objections to the ordination of women (a subject on which we are certainly not all of a single mind) the matter of a schismatic withdrawal from the Communion and fellowship of the Episcopal Church and the Society of St. Francis–which, of course, is world-wide throughout the Anglican Communion–is a judgmental and presumptive step.

1. Chapter concluded that the Anglican Church of North America is a new denomination created by their withdrawal from us, and demonstrated and

articulated by Father C. David Burt, who attended part of the Chapter meeting. Therefore Chapter released him from vows, and assumed such was the intent also of Fr. Mote.

2. As the Society of St. Francis has sought to assist and guide members of churches not in the Anglican Communion, to establish the Franciscan life in their communions, so would we be willing to do for those in the Diocese of the Holy Trinity; but in no present sense could it be a Franciscan Order. Many persons live after a Franciscan style, though not within a Franciscan Order, and we rejoice in that.

3. The Franciscan life is expressed in three Orders in fellowship together. While the Third Order governs its own affairs, it is part of the whole Society of St. Francis–still very much part of the Episcopal Church and the Anglican Communion! (Those in communion with Canterbury are in communion with each other. There is no way to have parts not in communion with each other.)

4. Saint Francis himself always counseled loyalty to the Church, even when those exercising authority did not seem worthy, or when they differed from him. A case in point is that when a majority of the Friars Minor supported Brother Elias, St. Francis acquiesced even though he was disappointed in the compromise of the original Rule promoted by Elias. It also seems to me that Francis championed the depth and breadth of God's love for the whole creation. His penitence was at the failure to live like that, in himself and others. His penitence was not over points of doctrine, but the quality of life.

It is that love of simplicity, of hospitality, of humility, that we are called to live and to share. May that be manifest in this period of tension in the Episcopal Church and elsewhere in the Anglican Communion. Our ministry must be directed toward healing, reconciling, and peace-making.

Finally, there was this letter of April 1977 that illustrates John Scott at his most combative in defending the rights of minorities:

Because we do know each other, I feel free to say in response to your note to me and letter to Br. Luke that I am equally "shocked."

Nowhere do I say or suggest "approval for sodomy nor a desire to encourage it." That is a misrepresentation! I believe in sexual restraint and I recognize as well as you do that people can sin against one another by sexual exploitation and abuse, that that is equally applicable to homosexuals and heterosexuals, married and unmarried.

The question I want to ask you, and, one hard to do in a letter, is "Where are you coming from?" I can almost feel your flesh crawl as you talk figuratively at arm's length, about "the lesbian." [Ed. Ellen Barrett] *Is she not a human being, or is she like the leper of old, someone from whom you should flee?*

No, St. Francis did not love leprosy, but he took some risk when he embraced the leper, that he would, in fact, contribute to its spread.

I do believe it is a misnomer to call homosexuality a "lifestyle" (please notice I did not do so). That implies a choice or alternative. I do not believe the mystery of human personality, including sexual orientation, is a matter of choice. I have had six years of pastoral experience, counseling and study in depth, and I am able to say that the more about sexuality I know, the more I don't know too. What I am convinced of is that we heterosexuals and priests of the Episcopal Church have been practicing hypocrisy—condemning other persons (not acts) while reserving our "rights" as the heterosexual majority. Furthermore, many homosexuals have been confirmed or ordained, and forced to live a lie, and we have still been willing to accept their services and even praise them, if they have had the extraordinary grace of a W. H. Auden or a Benjamin Britten.

I pray, too, ______, for reforms amongst us, and a greater measure of the loving self-giving of St. Francis which turned the medieval world around. This world needs that too and your ramblings about TV, violence, and anything-for-a-price is something we agree on. I just ask that we stop beating and rejecting scapegoats. We have made some progress by not literally making them "faggots" any longer. The wonder is that they are still able to say in the face of the Church's persecution, "God loves me, too," and continue to pick up the crumbs that fall from the table.

International Beginnings in the Third Order

In addition to the explosion of new work that began in the John Scott era with formation, statutes, handling controversies, a very important area of work was the Province's international efforts. These came in two areas: the first two Interprovincial Ministers Meetings in 1973 and 1976, and the second was work in Trinidad and Tobago beginning in 1976.

1st Interprovincial Ministers Meeting (May 27th, 1973) Delegates John Scott & Brother Robert Hugh

The 1st Interprovincial Meeting took place in Hilfield Friary (the mother-house of the European Province), England (see photo on page 57). At the time there were three provinces, English, American, and Pacific. What would soon become the African and New Zealand Provinces were at this point part of the English and Pacific Provinces. A number of documents were created during the meeting including, a *Third Order Constitution,* which was approved and sent out to all Provincial Chapters for review and approval, and a revision of the "Rule of Life" was included in *The Manual*. Both are brief and contain what is necessary for the new common life of the provinces, while leaving the creation of specific statutes up to the Chapter of each province. In the "Rule" were two Anglo-Catholic liturgical practices of the American Province that were now included: the sacrament of Penance and the daily recitation of the Office.

Plans were made for the next Interprovincial Meeting in three years to consider another book common to all provinces, *A Book of Roots*. This book would include: the primitive Rules of the Three Orders, the Testament of St. Francis, and the Rule of the Christa Seva Sangha. Finally, a motion was made that one issue each year of *The Chronicle* (based in England) would include articles relevant for all provinces. John Scott wrote in the September 1973 *Franciscan Newsletter* that the single most important note about the meeting was the "remarkable common mind and direction" from Third Order representatives around the world in regards to the Third Order way of life and the organizational needs to support that way of life.

2nd Interprovincial Meeting, Third Order, Society of St. Francis, 1976

John Scott
This meeting, November 8-11, 1976, was held at the Bishop's Ranch Retreat in California under the call and leadership of SSF Minister General Br. Geoffrey.

Those present at the meeting were the three Provincial Friar Chaplains: Brother Edward of the European Province, Brother Mark Francis of the American Province, and Brother Reginald of the Pacific Province. In addition there were two representatives from each Province. New Zealand (with the Solomon Islands) and Australia (with Papua New Guinea) were expected to become separate Third Order provinces. In addition, Br. Geoffrey spoke for tertiary groups in Hong Kong, Singapore and Calcutta.

I stress all that for two reasons. First, in discussing the meaning of Franciscan life, especially the significance of poverty/simplicity, that diversification was very important. Second, power in this world resides in governments and the multi-national corporations. But, even in the powerlessness of those committed to the Gospel of Jesus Christ, communication, prayer and meals together for several days produce bonds and strengths that are not beholden to the "powers that be," but to the love of Christ. For peace and justice in this world, that is the route of ultimate vindication, together with hundreds and thousands of other such personal and group commitments to one another. It was clear to us that poverty, being the condition of so much of the Third World, means that Western understanding of that cannot be its meaning and appeal elsewhere. While we who live in the affluence of the United States, or New Zealand, for example, search for simplicity as an alternative to the consumer-oriented society; our brothers and sisters of the Third World need fundamental needs met, and some share of this world's goods, denied them by the power structures of this world.

For them, it is brotherhood, the simplicity of sharing across cultural and racial lines, that is the essential ingredient of Franciscan simplicity. When that begins to happen more and more, neither they nor we will continue to be blind to, and tolerate the injustices of the political and economic order. Because of the love of Christ manifest in brotherhood, we will be enabled to be God's agents for bringing Christ's Kingdom closer.

The Interprovincial Meeting adopted a common form for the Vow and Pledge of Profession in the Third Order and also a distinct (and we trust, unique) profession cross—a small crucifix in dull copper, designed by a New Zealand tertiary and executed there. Robert Fulton, on behalf of the New Zealand Province, offered to supply them for all the other Provinces for professions from now on. Almost all present looked with favor on the Tau Cross with Crossed Hands, which we have recently been using; but the distinctive and lovely design of our New Zealand tertiaries won us over. We did, however, endorse the smaller badge of the Tau with Crossed Hands as an external emblem for those who would like to wear one as a mark of identification.

It was also agreed that the *Third Order Manual, American Congregation* of 1962 be replaced by *The Manual*. *Part 1* of *The Manual* would be common to all provinces and printed centrally and *Part 2* would be specific to each province and its practices and be printed by each province. *Part 1* would contain:

The Way of St. Francis
The Constitution of the Society of St. Francis
The Constitution of the Third Order
The Rule of Life, and
The Form of Profession.

A *Devotional Calendar* for all provinces would always include: the Feasts of St. Clare on August 11, and St. Francis on October 4 as well as the day commemorating the Stigmata of St. Francis on September 17th, together with the Day of Penitence just prior to Palm Sunday.

Trinidad and Tobago Genesis

In 1974 Rt. Revd. Clive O. Abdulah, the Bishop of Trinidad and Tobago (T&T), issued an invitation to the First Order and the Robinson Family (Third Order members in the San Francisco Fellowship, see page 72) to come to Trinidad and Tobago to begin work recruiting and training members of the SSF First and Third Orders. Work began in 1975 and Brother Dunstan, whose signature is on most of the novicing and profession mandates, was absolutely crucial in its growth and success. Also in 1975, Chapter decided that a local Assistant Formation Director should be recruited to localize the formation process to fit the needs and background of those in Trinidad and Tobago.

	1976	1977	1978	1979
Postulants	2	4	3	6
Novices	1	3	5	5
Professed	1*	1*	1*	0
Total	**4**	**8**	**9**	**11**

*The Rev. Barry Coker was previously professed in the European Province, and he returned there in 1978.

Growth In Numbers in T&T

With the profession of Jacqueline Richards as the first Trinidadian to be professed, 1980 was the crowning year of growth followed quickly by two others. (Jackie was a nurse on the teaching staff of the Port of Spain General Hospital, and was one of the leaders of the charismatic movement in the Anglican Church in T&T.)

Jackie Richards wrote:

I first came into contact with the Franciscans in 1974, when Bro. Robert Hugh came to Trinidad & Tobago to conduct a Diocesan Mission. He was accompanied by Bros. Sebastian (now deceased) and Don. At that time I was a member of the Fellowship of St. Augustine. We were also Associates of the Companions of Jesus The Good Shepherd (C.J.G.S.). The Mother House was in West Ogwell, Surrey, England. Around this time the last of the three houses in the Caribbean which was run by the Sisters of the C.J.G.S. was in the process of being closed.

The Associates were given the option by our Chaplain to either become the Associates of the Sisters of St. Margaret (Boston, USA) or Third Order Members of the S.S.F. I chose the latter, since there was a First Order presence here in Trinidad & Tobago.

I became a Postulant in 1976. Bro. Dunstan was then my Spiritual Director. He was also Convener/ Area Chaplain. He walked me through my Formation until I was Professed on December 15th, 1979. By the time I was Professed, other persons showed interest, and the North Fellowship was formed. As the First Order S.S.F brothers changed residence and worked in other parishes throughout Trinidad and Tobago, the number of Tertiaries and Associates increased thereby forming the Southern and Tobago Fellowship as well.

In the early 1980s I was Area Chaplain/Spiritual Director and Convener. In the Mid 80's until mid 1990s, I attended Chapter regularly at Little Portion.

TSSF Provincial Chaplains

From 1917 until 1978 (five years after John Scott became Guardian) the First Order Brothers were the Provincial Friar Chaplains of the Third Order receiving applications from aspirants and granting permission for novicing as well as for profession. Most of the Ministers General of OSF were the TSF Provincial Chaplains: Father Joseph, Brother Paul, Brothers Hugh (both the OSF and SSF, 1970-74, brothers of the same name), and concluding in 1974-1978 with Brother Mark Francis SSF. (Yet even in 1978, when Br. Mark Francis became the "Provincial's Visitor to the Third Order," he still was "responsible for the oversight of the life of fellowships and other Third Order groups, and for supervising the work of the other pastoral officers, including the Chaplain.")

Eleven Third Order Provincial Chaplains were/are members of the Third Order (yet nearly half were/are formerly First Order Brothers):

The Rev. Robert Goode (Gooch) had been Assistant Chaplain serving under Brs. Robert Hugh and Mark Francis since 1973. In 1978 he became the first TSSF Chaplain and served for seven years through the era of John Scott and halfway into the era of Dee Dobson (1985). He died in 1998.

Only two years after his profession, **The Rev. Masud Ibn Syedullah** was elected by Chapter as the second Provincial Chaplain but the first tertiary to serve as Chaplain, and he served one term from 1985 to 1988. Masud, of course, later became Minister Provincial of the Order in 2002, served one term, and was later elected to Chapter in 2013.

In 1988, **The Rev. Jack Stapleton,** a university chaplain from Newark, Delaware, was nominated and elected as the third Provincial Chaplain. However, he resigned as Chaplain within a week and asked to be released from his vows in the Third Order six years later in 1994.

The Rev. Alden Whitney functioned as the Interim Provincial Chaplain until the 1989 Chapter, at which time Assistant Provincial Chaplain **Marie Webner** was elected as Provincial Chaplain. The first woman to hold this office. One of the big projects she worked on as Chaplain was the creation and publication of the *TSSF Devotional Companion* in 1994. She served two terms (six years), but her reappointment for a third term, in 1994 was not ratified by Chapter. She subsequently asked for release of her vows from the Third Order, and became an Associate of the Society of St. Francis.

Since Deacon Webner's failure to be reappointed had not been anticipated, former **Minister Provincial Kale King** served as Interim Provincial Chaplain for a year until **The Rev. David Burgdorf**, former Assistant Chaplain, was elected as Provincial Chaplain, and he served from 1995 to 2000.

Assistant Chaplain **Julia Bergstrom**, the first laywoman Assistant Chaplain, was elected as Provincial Chaplain in 2000 and served two terms until 2006.

Barbara Leonard was the second laywoman to be elected Provincial Chaplain, serving two terms (2006 - 2012).

The Rev. Dominic George was elected by Chapter in 2012. Dominic George was the third TSSF chaplain who was a former First Order Brother (the others were Goode and Burgdorf).

The Rev. Rick Simpson was elected in 2015.

Convocations Invented

During the John Scott era, Chapter sponsored General Chapters to which all tertiaries were invited. The first was on the East Coast at Little Portion (1971), and the second was on the West Coast at Redwood City thirty miles north of San Francisco (1973). Both of these were held as adjuncts to the Standing Committee and Provincial Chapter meetings. Thirty-five members attended the Redwood City meeting ("one sixth of the whole membership," according to John Scott (5/25/1973)). The primary focus of the General Chapter meeting on the West Coast at Redwood City was a discussion of the three position papers by Burt, Robinson, and Scott (see p. 55).

In 1975, General Chapter evolved into Provincial Convocations that focused on the meeting of all tertiaries. The first of these was in the Midwest in Racine, Wisconsin (1975); the second was in Fayetteville, Arkansas (1977); and the third was in Miami, Florida (1979). These General Chapters (later called Provincial Convocations) were the only occasion for tertiaries to gather in groups outside of local Fellowship meetings since Regional Convocations were not developed until the Dee Dobson era. During Dee Dobson's time as Minister Provincial, Regional Convocations replaced Provincial Convocations. It wasn't until 1997 that both Provincial and Regional types of convocations would be held simultaneously, and Chapter was forced to redefine the definition of "convocation."

Racine Wisconsin General Chapter (1975)

The Racine Wisconsin General Chapter, like the Redwood City General Convocation, focused on a discussion of three position papers. This new set of papers* was written by E. Will Drake, Judith Robinson, and Michael Hollingshead.

E. Will Drake has been professed for over 45 years, and is currently the longest professed member in Canada. This 1975 paper may, in fact, be the first presentation by a Canadian at any TSSF meeting. When he wrote this paper, he was working for the Candian Government in the Northwest Territories.

About Judith Robinson

(Don Carlson From Franciscan Newsletter #2 1971*)*

In this city of Saint Francis lives an inspired and inspiring Franciscan. Her name is Judith. She is married and at present the mother of four children. Her husband, Jerry, teaches at San Francisco's Mission High School, a public school just around the corner from the original Franciscan Mission Dolores and within a stone's throw of San Damiano House. Their first two children are: Mark, 12 years old, preparing for independence at a Free School, and Rachel, 9, who is a beauty and already has convent fever. Two adopted children are Marya, age 3, half black and half Irish, and a one-and-a half-year old Mayan Indian, Rebecca. Very soon, they hope, their family will be increased to five with the completed adoption of an 8-year old Korean boy.

One of Judith's major contributions is the two nights each week that she (with the Diggers) gives to counseling our draft-troubled youth, of whom we have many here in San Francisco. It is comforting to know that these young men have someone like Judith to whom they can look for help, counsel and guidance. When the San Francisco Fellowship was formally organized, it consisted of five Tertiaries: two postulants, a novice and two professed. Judith was the novice, but was unanimously elected 'Directress-In-Waiting' since, according to The Manual, she could not yet be the director. This preceded her Profession by about one month. Her Profession was celebrated by all sorts and conditions of men: black, white, red and yellow; poor and rich; priests, laymen and friars; Catholics in obedience to both Canterbury and Rome, Protestants and agnostics; and her St. Bernard, named Gertrude.

I think of Judith as a franciscan Franciscan, for she is one who truly turns the noun into the adjective.

Postscript by Author

Judith presented position papers at the 1971 Little Portion and 1973 Redwood City Convocations. Judith first encountered TSF in its birthplace in Cincinnati, Ohio in the mid-60s, but found the members to be "stodgy,"and her work in the Civil Rights movement not embraced by Fellowship members. In 1967, she just happened to move to Haight Asbury in San Francisco in time to experience the fabled *Summer of Love.* Through her children's friends, she discovered MaryAnn Jackman who lived a few streets away, and together they created a Third Order existence. Anna Hoffman was Judith's Woman's Formation Director. When the First Order Brothers and Sisters came out to San Francisco, they found the ground already tilled by Judith and MaryAnn. The presence of the First Orders drew John Scott, Peter Funk and many other TSSFers out to visit culminating in the Redwood City Chapter of 1973.

Judith and her family were invited by the Bishop of Trinidad and Tobago to accompany the First Order Brothers in establishing the Third and First Orders in Trinidad. Judith and her husband reconnoitered Trinidad, but the lack of guaranteed housing and jobs prevented them from accompanying the Brothers and Sisters since by that time they had adopted three very young children.

I met with Judith in October 2014 in Tucson, Arizona. She left the Order in the 1980s, but not the Franciscan spirituality which today she endeavors to live out in as a 6th degree black belt Aikido sensei.

Fayetteville, Arkansas Provincial Convocation April 22-24, 1977

Carolyn Banks (reprinted from the Arkansas Churchman, Diocese of Arkansas)

Delegates of the Third Order of St. Francis, American Province, met for their first biennial Convocation ever to be held in the South on April 21-24 at Mt. Sequoyah in Fayetteville. Hosts for the meeting were the Third Order members and Franciscan Associates of St. Paul's parish, Fayetteville.

Br. Geoffrey, SSF Minister General, Wray Wilkes (newly professed), Br. Mark Francis (TSSF Chaplain), and John Scott (Guardian).

The Franciscan Order is the fastest growing religious Order in the Anglican Communion. Delegates who attended represented Franciscan groups throughout the United States, Canada, and Great Britain. The moderator of the meeting was Fr. John Scott, Guardian of the Third Order and Rector of St. Mary's Episcopal Church in Philadelphia, Pennsylvania.

The meeting was also attended by three Franciscan friars, Br. Mark Charles from San Francisco, Br. Mark Francis, Friar Chaplain of the Third Order from Long Island, New York, and Br. Geoffrey, Minister General of the Society of St. Francis. Br. Geoffrey gave the keynote address and chaired informal workshops during the meeting.

On Friday night, the delegates had High Mass at Martin Chapel, during which Dr. Wray Wilkes of Fayetteville made his profession. At the same time all previously professed delegates renewed their vows, and three Fayetteville postulants were welcomed by the Friar Chaplain.

Jane Ellen Traugott (Chapter member) observing a very surprised Ken Cox (Formation Co-Director).

Brother Geoffrey has his headquarters at a friary in Dorset, England. While serving as a missionary in New Guinea, he was elected Minister General of the Franciscans in 1967 and now travels throughout the world ministering to Anglican Franciscans in 22 nations throughout all the continents.

Miami Provincial Convocation April 22-24, 1979

From Franciscan Newsletter, Peg Shull

Convocation began for most of us on Wednesday afternoon, April 18, when many of us arrived at the Miami airport to be met, we knew not by whom. Dee Dobson, who organized the meeting, had described herself to me as short and stout. Because she had a big voice, I had expected a much larger person. At the meeting I had many such surprises. She said herself or her son would meet me. It turns out, she has three sons, two of whom are identical and drive an ancient school bus named *Blue Moose*. And, it was John Scott I saw first at the airport.

With him was Br. Luke, who wasn't supposed to be there at all but had caught an earlier plane, and who looks, friends, I'm not lying, like a slightly older version of Luke Skywalker in *Star Wars*.

We all gathered at the Dobsons' and moved to the Dominical Retreat House in time for supper. Folks who had driven and late plane arrivals were already there. For folks who have not met many of us, here are some impressions: Helen Webb has beautiful auburn hair and a gentle smile; Marie Webner is tall, thin and graceful, like a willow tree; "Gooch," that's Fr. Goode, laughs a lot, with depths of seriousness underneath; Peg Shull generally hides behind a camera or a dulcimer.

Here is the order of events: Wednesday night, we visited and sang. I played the dulcimer. Then we read Compline and the night people went back to visiting. We spent Thursday at Concept House in downtown Miami. Thursday night we heard a report from David Catron, our tertiary in Mexico, and from the Trinidad tertiaries. They spent the rest of the afternoon at the beach. Br. Geoffrey spoke Friday evening. Saturday morning, Hendrik (Hank) Koning spoke. On Saturday afternoon they all piled into the *Blue Moose* and went to the Everglades. (Mary Ellen could wax eloquent on that, but we had to meet the newsletter's deadline.) Something must have happened on Sunday, but no one reported it.

Outside the Blue Moose tour/school bus: (1) Jane Ellen Traugott, (2) Br. Geoffrey, Minister General, (3) Jackie Richards, (4) John Scott, (5) Marie Webner, (6) Helen Webb, (7) Fr. Robert Goode (Gooch), (8) Dee Dobson, (9) Br. Luke, (10) Br. Mark Francis Provincial Chaplain, (11) Fr. Jack Stapleton, (12) (kneeling) David Catron, (13) Barbara Kelly, amd (14) Jeanne Walker.

The thing I remember most happily of Convocation was small groups of people sitting in the common room, or on the lawn, and visiting. It felt like a family reunion.

Hero of the John Scott Era: Hugo Muller Served the Cree Indians in Far North Quebec

The Rev. Hugo Muller served in the far north Quebec amongst the Cree Indians. (He was professed on November 22, 1967, and died on November 3, 1985.) He published three books which tell of the white man's effects had upon the Indians in Quebec especially since the advent of the James Bay Hydroelectric Project: *For No One Knows Waswanipi: A Collection of Songs and Poems of the Inland Cree* (1973); *Why Don't You?: A Look at Attitudes Towards Indians (1975); Waswanipi: Songs of a Scattered People* (1976).

[Ed. Here is a 1974 article written about him and his work, and it includes a short speech of his from *Algoma Anglican*, 18 (1) January 1974, 1.]

The Rev. Hugo Muller, rector of All Saints in Noranda Quebec, is also the author of a collection of songs and poems on the inland Cree Indian, under the title, *For No One Knows Waswasipi*. In the foreword to this publication, Bishop Watton of Moosonee wrote:

> *The author, Hugo Muller, was not born a Canadian. He is a native of Holland, coming to Canada more than 20 years ago. His first contact with the native peoples of Canada took place as he worked for the Hudson Bay Company in Northern Quebec. He later studied theology and was ordained a priest.*
>
> *In this capacity, he has been in constant touch with the Cree people in Northern Quebec. The depth of his understanding and love of these people underlines everything he has written. He might be called a romanticist, an idealist, a cynic, but if these terms are applied, they are applied to a man who gives of himself and asks nothing in return.*

Here is what Father Hugo presented at the banquet.

> *The federal government has "offered up 2,000 Cree Indians on the altar of political expediency," according to the Rev. Hugo Muller. He said that the federal government is unwilling to step in on the side of the Indians in the James Bay dispute because of the delicate balance of power in the Parliament.*
>
> *A major bloc of the Liberal MP's come from Quebec, he noted, and the government does not want to risk this block for the sake of the Indians.*
>
> *The James Bay Project is a multi-billion dollar hydroelectric power development being undertaken by the Quebec government in Northwestern Quebec. He called for an immediate halt to the project, and said, "The only way to stop this madness is by injunction." The inland Cree Indians of the area are being discriminated against by the Quebec government by not being consulted about the project, he pointed out. "Quebec is struggling to have its culture and language retained in Canada, but Quebec is not so ready to let other people retain their culture and language. More than trees are being bulldozed!"*

The Rev. Hugo Muller, parish rector from Northwestern Quebec, spoke on the plight of the James Bay Indians on December 2, 1973.

> *I noted the action already being taken by the Anglican Church in James Bay, but called on parishioners to stir up public opinion and awareness concerning the project. I could get a million signatures for baby seals," he commented, "but where are a million signatures for baby Crees?"*
>
> *The temporary injunction, which was granted to the Indians, was halted five days later because it was overruled by a higher court. "Indians just don't win court cases," Fr. Muller claimed.*

"The Indians are not against the project per se; they simply want their aboriginal rights to the land, and they want to be consulted. The Indians are the logical ecological consultants; they know the area like the back of their hands, both in winter and the summer."

"Moreover, the Cree Indians will not benefit from the project. For a while, there will be construction jobs, but after that, only a few highly trained people are needed to monitor the consoles."

In concluding, Fr. Muller remarked, "One day the Quebec government came down in helicopters and started surveying. The Indians only knew what was happening by reading it in the newspapers. They were never consulted, and there was a complete disregard for their rights." [cf. John Dorman and the Guyanese Amerindians, page 94.]

Reviews of Two Books by Hugo Muller: *Why Don't You: A Look at Attitudes Towards Indians* (1975) and *Waswanipi: Songs of a Scattered People* (1976)

Josiah W. Noel (Dean of the Cathedral in Newfoundland)

Fr. Hugo Muller was a tertiary serving in the far north of Quebec amongst the Cree Indians. He was professed on November 22, 1967, and died on November 3, 1985. He published three books about his experiences with the Cree:

- *For No One Knows Waswanipi: A Collection of Songs and Poems on the Inland Cree* (1973);
- *Why Don't You?: A Look at Attitudes Towards Indians* (1975);
- *Waswanipi: Songs of a Scattered People* (1976), in which he tells of the effects the white man has had upon the Indians in Quebec, especially since the advent of the James Bay Hydroelectric Project.

Why Don't You is dedicated to "The Right Reverend J.A. Watton, 7th Bishop of Moosonee; who got me into this and the Cree people of Waswanipi, who made it so enjoyable." This is a study of western attitudes, a few questions and ideas that came to Fr. Muller through a number of incidents, which made him think. He disqualifies himself noting: he is not an expert in disclosing timely Indian studies as he "does not know the Indian," only some Indians; his experience is limited to the Inland Cree of North Western Quebec of the Mistassini and Waswanipi Bands; and thirdly, he has been associated with two institutions many consider arch-villains of Indian-White confrontation—the Company of Gentlemen Adventurers trading into Hudson's Bay and the Anglican Church of Canada.

The 116 pages of this booklet is presented in ten chapters with multiple subsections giving it an oral textbook approach to his thesis, "Why don't you… (become like the white man – "westerner" – whose way is best)." Fr. Muller considers these words statements rather than questions because they mask the westerners' approach to Indians:

Why don't you build yourself a decent house (is the westerners' way of saying), "You have no business living in a disgraceful shack;"

Why don't you get a job (is the westerners' way of saying) "Just sitting around enjoying yourself certainly makes it look as if Indians are lazy;"

Why don't you make yourself some money (is the westerners' way of saying) "Why should we keep paying for your relief."

Unlike the western approach to expect less civilized cultures to assimilate into western culture, the Indian approach is to accept differences. The Indian lets be. They do not bug with questions or disapprovals. If one does not ask, the Indian will not provide you with an answer. The book is a carefully constructed, insightful picture of how western culture has misunderstood the Inland Cree of northwestern Quebec and Indian culture in general.

Some areas of insight and discussion include: the government-supported program of Indian residential schools; a western philosophy of nature, land ownership and development evident in the acquisitive and aggressive tendency in the colonization of the Americas; the paternalism of the western mind to know what is best for indigenous people; and western practice of administering through paperwork. This book was an informative and accurate picture of the struggle of the Inland Cree of Northwestern Quebec, and how an indigenous nomadic people continue to suffer in the midst of a major resource development that would bring an end to their way of life.

Waswanipi: Songs of a Scattered People records the negative result of the 1950s, 60s and 70s great resource development in northwestern Quebec. The Inland Cree saw mines, roads, towns, and the James Bay hydro-project within a very short period of time. For Fr. Muller, one of the most disturbing questions is: "Why a civilization which has produced Leonardo da Vinci, a Shakespeare and a Beethoven, seems to destroy any other culture it comes into contact with." As a parish priest he saw the result for the Inland Cree every day. He felt he was witnessing one of the greatest cultural tragedies in Canadian history. He dedicated his book to the Cree people who enriched his life and whose resilience may yet triumph over the worst we are doing to it.

One of the rivers to be dammed.

Not being a musician, I read this as a collection of poetry with photos taken by Fr. Muller of the people who were the subjects of his songs. Waswanipi (light on water) was the Indian band in Fr. Muller's parish. He saw so much waste and destruction of human life that he was moved to record his personal reflections through poetry/song. It has the feel of a Psalter for it contains many laments for a suffering people. *Lilly* typically portrays his lament for little girls whose vulnerability will take them into adulthood and whose future is far from secure.

It is remarkable that in the middle of the book the poem/song, *Apology*, describes Fr. Muller's desire to apologize on behalf of Canadians, the province of Quebec, the Anglican Church of Canada, his ethnic origin and himself because the ruling of the court to cease and desist the James Bay project in favour of the Inland Cree was overturned in Appeals Court in favour of "the white man." Fr. Muller's work among the Cree was all the more complicated by his feelings, conscience and knowledge of the injustice served to an indigenous people. He pointed out in both books that this misunderstanding was inevitable because of the westerners' preconceived attitudes, knowledge and relationship towards indigenous people. Coupled with the westerner's motivation as a superior outside race moving in to take ownership of land for exclusive personal use, westerners have not taken time or interest to understand, respect or befriend indigenous people.

Watching geese flying from the east at sunrise one morning he was overcome with sorrow and joy. He came to himself in a profoundly Franciscan appreciation of creation and creatures – animal and metaphorically, human.

Clash of Cultures, (Hugo Muller)

His spirituality and appreciation for St. Francis helped him see beyond "western white culture's" desire to possess, to own, to exploit, and destroy to a more open appreciation of gracious beholding and thanksgiving. The poem contrasts the desire not to possess the geese with what "western white culture" ought to do in order to appreciate the freedom of indigenous people. The mining, roads and James Bay project have spelled disaster for indigenous people who were forced to adapt to western culture from a disenfranchised, uneducated, economically challenged position. Communication continues to be one of the biggest barriers because diction and comprehension in one cultural setting is not easily transferrable to another even when both cultures speak the same language. The settlement of North America by Europeans has been a disaster for indigenous people of North America.

Through snippets (snapshots), and poems (songs) in both books, Fr. Muller provides an interlocking picture puzzle of how attitudes have led to complex misunderstandings in day-to-day life. He uses the local example of the Cree with whom he lived and served as a parish priest to point out the numerous ways in which the clash of cultures continues.

As Canadians, Fr. Muller calls us to affirm Indian status, education, giving the land back to the Indians, encourage parks, forestry, communications and compensation with revenue sharing as a priority for consideration.

As Christians, we are called to affirm one another as equal in Christ, share in a broad understanding of the mission of the church, speak out, give leadership, and walk together with native peoples.

The Canadians of European descent who settled Canada and have interacted with indigenous people on behalf of federal and provincial governments and who are now seen as 'the white man' have much to consider and think about – how do we exploit the vast natural resources of Canada while honoring the rights of indigenous people?

As a Christian reading this book, I was reminded of two questions in the Baptismal Covenant in the *Book of Alternative Services*:

> *Will you seek and serve Christ in all persons loving your neighbor as yourself?*
>
> *Will you strive for justice and peace among all people and respect the dignity of every human being?*

I am also reminded of the Marks of Mission of the Anglican Communion:

> *To proclaim the Good News of the Kingdom*
> *To teach, baptize and nurture new believers*
> *To respond to human need by loving service*
> *To seek to transform unjust structures of society, to challenge violence of every kind and to pursue peace and reconciliation*
> *To strive to safeguard the integrity of creation and sustain and renew the life of the earth*

Reflecting upon the predicament of the Inland Cree and all indigenous people, I am reminded of the three latter Marks of Mission in how we respond to human need, transform unjust structure, and safeguard the integrity of creation.

I am grateful that on August 6, 1993, the Anglican Primate of Canada offered an apology to indigenous people for the church's role in the abuse suffered by children in church-run residential schools. The Anglican Church of Canada has been actively involved in The Truth and Reconciliation Commission following the indigenous residential schools crises, including the most recent one held in Winnipeg in March 2014. The Anglican Church of Canada affirms the desire for Indigenous Anglicans to establish an official self-governing national identity within the Anglican Church of Canada beginning with the 2007 appointment of a National Anglican Indigenous Bishop, Rt. Rev. Mark MacDonald TSSF (see page 183), as part of an unfolding process of self-transformation. The National Church affirms the presence and gifts of indigenous Anglicans and join in their struggle for justice. Fr. Muller's story of the Inland Cree of Northwestern Quebec is part of the fabric of our Canadian story, which is full of joys and sorrows.

Construction Jumping-off-point. (Hugo Muller)

Waswanipi—Light on water.

I am hopeful that as Canadian Anglicans walk together with the Council of Indigenous Peoples and all people of Canada we can appreciate one another's lives as we strive to share the bounty of the earth with all people. The contribution Fr. Muller has made in these two books has helped weave a permanent place for these stories as part of our Franciscan and wider corporate memory. We are grateful for his life, witness and reflections.

Visitation to Third Order Franciscans of the American Province in South America, March 7-14, 1980

John Scott's last big project as Guardian was to visit personally the members of the American Province in the Carribean and South America, and to survey the future promise of the Province and to offer a few final bits of advice.

The presence of the friars in Trinidad unquestionably was the catalyst for the response of persons in Trinidad and Guyana to vocations in the Third Order. There are two novices from Guyana for the First Order in residence at St. Anthony's Friary in Port-of-Spain, but there are twelve Third Order members in Trinidad. One is professed, and three novices are near profession. In Guyana, Father John Dorman, English missionary for a quarter century (see page 92), and Charles Roland, a catechist, are novices; two others are postulants and some fourteen others are making inquiry. That makes, relatively speaking, the two fastest growing areas in the American Province. The Ninth Province of the American Church consists of the twelve dioceses of the Episcopal Church in Spanish-speaking countries. In Colombia there are two very active novices; in Bogota, Father Jose Valenzuela and Mario Cuellar, plus a postulant, and other interested persons in Colombia and Ecuador. (David Catron is in Mexico and Roy Mellish is in Honduras.) It would seem as if the three district groups of persons in the three countries, Trinidad and Tobago, Guyana and Colombia are inspired and encouraged by the presence of the brothers in Trinidad, but two of the dioceses (Trinidad and Tobago, Guyana) are in the Province of the West Indies (not the Episcopal Church), and Colombia is in the Ninth Province of the Episcopal Church. While English is spoken in Trinidad and Guyana the two Third Order groups are very different; Spanish is the language of Colombia and the whole Ninth Province, and the diocese is in every respect like those of the Episcopal Church! Furthermore, mail and travel between Trinidad and Colombia is unusual.

What this leads to is the sense that while the brothers in Trinidad are nearest to those in South America, and can continue to be supportive, each Third Order group will have to develop on its own with supervision from the Chapter. I feel very much assured of the Third Order commitments of those whom I met and we should give encouragement to the development of their vocations.

I will make some specific comments about each of the three groups, but before doing so, I would like to express how deeply significant the visitation was as far as I am concerned. Letters just do not substitute for spending a few days in one another's company. Furthermore I believe very strongly that it is the cross cultural meetings of "little-people" like the Third Order that does much to strengthen ties of understanding and sharing among all people toward the goal of world peace and cooperation. As the guest and visitor I was received with unbounded hospitality and grace; I am very much humbled and grateful.

I have underscored the note of fellowship and hospitality among the Franciscan household; I personally experienced no unfriendly action by anyone, but I could not help but be aware of the great concern for security and worries about violence. In that respect we who live in United State's big cities find the same climate in South America; locks and bolts and continued citizens' warnings about being on the streets after dark. There is violence in Trinidad; I was asked to celebrate and preach the one Sunday I was there—in the parish in Port-of-Spain where the priest had been killed only nine days before in a fire-bombing of the rectory; the same Sunday the home of a cabinet minister was similarly attacked; injuries resulted, but no deaths. The oil boom has brought almost instant prosperity to Trinidad (an OPEC member), but less peace.

In Guyana the airport sign welcomes the visitor to the "Cooperative Republic of Guyana," but security is very tight. There must be more barking watchdogs in Georgetown than any place on earth. Some interesting contrasts: Father Dorman worries that the Marxist government censors make receiving mail and packages difficult for Christians. On the other hand, when I had no Guyanese money to pay the airport departure tax (having had an extraordinary visit between midnight and 7AM), a man stepped up offering to pay my tax, saying, "just say a prayer for me" when I offered the equivalent in TT or 135 dollars. He turned out to be a prominent citizen, an Anglican lawyer who was on his way to India to participate in a Full Gospel Christian Business Men's Association mission. Guyana may not welcome foreign missionaries, but one of its most well known men in public life was going out from the country as a Christian missionary (Lionel Luckhoo had been Mayor of Georgetown and Ambassador to England).

Living as I do on the campus of a major university one is always aware of economic and political disputes in the world. For instance, there has been a fairly widely supported boycott of Nestlé's products due to evidence that Nestlé promoted and sold infant formula to poor people in Third World countries who couldn't use it properly; malnutrition and death were reported. Trinidad's and Guyana's glistening Nestlé's distribution centers were visible; yet no one had heard of infant formula problems. What I did observe was that the only coffee available was Nestlé's powdered—at about double the US price. The absurdity seems compounded. Guyana, a poor country, under a presumably Marxist government, and a grower of coffee, appears to sell it all to a foreign corporation who processes it, and returns the powder to Guyana at exorbitant prices.

Bogota is the scene of hostages held at the Dominican embassy, but as a city of four to five million, growing in all directions, life goes on with only detours around the area cordoned off by the police. Colombia's history has been fraught with civil war, although the past twenty years have been among its longest period of internal peace; the crisis over the hostages threatens a new outbreak. Episcopalians are a tiny minority; the Third Order is both a link with more of the church, but also for persons sensitive to the dangers of oppression and civil strife around them as well as the jealousies that can arise within a small ecclesiastical body, Franciscan humility and joy is a source of strength.

Trinidad

Brother Dunstan met me at the airport Friday night March 7th, and on Saturday we drove several miles out of Port-of-Spain to the Diocesan Conference Center at Maraval, where I conducted a Quiet Day for about forty persons, including all the tertiaries (except Father Spencer), some associates, and a number of interested people. The conference center is an attractive contemporary building, which serves both as a church and meeting room with areas for expansion. Also on the property is an older building which, with renovations, will become the friary. The brothers are presently given the use of the rectory of All Saints Church in return for their assisting with pastoral duties. The Conference Center site will give them a place of their own and allow a wider ministry than at present, although the location of All Saints parish, their present center of activity, is more central to the bustling activities of Port-of-Spain.

Dunstan provides a warm, loving, and close oversight of the Third Order, which is much appreciated. The tertiaries are a well-educated and responsible group of mature persons active in their respective parishes. Jacqueline Richards, one of the four who attended the Miami Convocation last year, is now professed and three others are nearing profession. The Fellowship should soon be active in planning and preparing its own agenda, times of meeting, and encouraging aspirants. I had planned on visiting Father Spencer in San Fernando, Trinidad's second largest city, but the unexpected call from Georgetown took precedence. On Sunday I took the services in the morning at St. Margaret's Belmont and, in the evening, addressed a group of associates of religious Orders in a meeting at the Cathedral where I was welcomed by the Dean at Evensong. At midday, Brothers Dunstan and Michael and I were invited to dinner at the home of Jackie Richards and her family; not only is she a good instructor in Nursing at the University, but she is an avid gardener and cook, and, most happily for me, arranged the one thing I wanted to do as a visitor to Trinidad: visit the bird sanctuary for the spectacle of the flocks of scarlet ibises coming in just before sundown.

Just before making the boat trip through the bird sanctuary, I discovered that Father Dorman and four Amerindians had come to Georgetown from the interior expecting me! I hadn't even planned on going to Guyana because I could not see how there was time to travel to their homeland in the interior. With a speed

I don't think I could have accomplished in the United States, in less than an hour, I arranged a roundtrip ticket for that night to be back the next morning to go on to Colombia, and received the necessary yellow fever shot for entrance to Guyana and return to Trinidad. From the bird sanctuary, with the great help of novice Dorothy Lockhart's driving, I made it to the airport for the plane to Georgetown.

Guyana

In most respects, both our Third Order groups in Trinidad and Colombia are very close in background and lifestyle to most of our members in the United States and Canada, but meeting John Dorman, Charles and Celian Roland (see pages 199-200) and Edwin and Theresa Lewis was both humbling and mind-boggling. I certainly don't believe I am worth a four-day walk through the jungle to get to an airstrip and then a bumpy plane ride to the capital. However, as mutual messengers of God's grace between very different worlds, we can all be very thankful. We spent the hours of midnight to 5 AM talking, praying, sharing a meal and celebrating the Eucharist together in the convent of the Anglican sisters in Georgetown.

John Dorman has been a missionary in Guyana for twenty-five years and is the best one can imagine that a missionary should be—strong, gentle, kind, and thoroughly identified with the Indian people of a vast area in which he travels. When Lionel Luckhoo asked me at the airport what I was doing in Guyana and I told him, he replied, "John Dorman is Guyana's saint." The questions are many; will the encroachments of the modern world allow the Amerindian cultures to survive? How can some of them be ordained? I was not the only reason for the visit to Georgetown. Charles and Edwin were meeting with the bishop to discuss preparation for ordination without their being shipped off to Codrington College on Barbados. Despite their English names, their lifestyle is very, very different. There is shyness although they read and speak English very well. The liturgy, Bible, and sacraments link us, and, in the mysterious ways of grace, so does St. Francis. At present John Dorman and John Bennett (another missionary whom I did not meet), the Rolands and another catechist, Winston Williams [*See page 96*], are novices. In addition, couples like the Lewises and other individuals have become postulants or expressed interest in doing so; a total of eighteen persons all together.

However, the eighteen persons are from five tribal groups and live in widely separated areas where travel is on foot or by canoe, and they often don't see each other for several months at a time. Letter writing is possible only with John Dorman, but we all agreed that if Chapter would provide some tape recorders, batteries and tapes, and fellowships in North America would make tapes of meetings and send it to them, they would listen and be willing to make a tape and send it back.

Furthermore, I was convinced that to really share our fellowship in the TSSF, someone would soon have to go and visit them where they live in the interior. To do so would require at least three months advance notice so that arrangements could be made. I assured them that Chapter would provide a visitor in November, if at all possible. To avoid the rainy season in summer is essential so that October to March are the best months for traveling. [Ed. It took until the Medical Mission in 2004 to finally accomplish this.]

Colombia

Dunstan had already planned to accompany me on the visit to Bogota because he had not met any of the novices there. Br. Desmond, Guardian of St. Anthony's Friary, Trinidad, had gone to Bogota last June and received Fr. Jose Valenzuela and Mario Cuellar as novices at the time of the consecration of Colombia's new bishop, The Rt. Rev. Bernardo Merino. My one misconnection occurred when our flight from Trinidad to Caracas was delayed and we taxied up to the terminal as our flight to Bogota took off. It meant spending a night there, but since I had not slept at all the night before, it felt good to go to bed early. We were unable to reach Bogota by telephone, but we left very early the next morning and arrived in Bogota by 9 AM.

Jose and Clarita Valenzuela received us at their charming apartment quite near the center of Bogota where Jose is professor of clinical psychology at the Pontifical Jesuit University and also teaches Protestant theology in the theological school of the University. We were soon joined by Mario Cuellar and so began two intense days of discussions, visits, meetings and a liturgy on Thursday night presided over by Bishop Merino and attended by some two dozen persons interested in the Third Order.

The Valenzueals hosted Br. Dunstan, and Bishop Merino very kindly hosted me at his home. Mario is in the catering business, and he and his wife invited another group to meet with Dunstan and me at a dinner meeting and Evensong at their home. Our hosts were much more proficient in English than we in Spanish, and Mario is an excellent on-the-spot interpreter; however, I did prepare a short sermon in Spanish for the liturgy. Mario visited the Miami Fellowship last fall after he had been to General Convention at Denver. Mario has an intense ministry with AA through both a large hospital and a halfway house. On Sundays, Jose is the vicar of the new mission congregation of San Miguel in one the burgeoning northern suburbs of Bogota. Br. Dunstan was to be the preacher there on Sunday the 16th, although I returned to the United States on the 14th.

Dunstan will continue to receive their novice reports, but, by this time next year, Jose and Mario will be ready for profession, and can continue as a Fellowship on their own. Thus the group in Bogota should be nearly self-sufficient. I do think that at least one of them should be included in the Interprovincial Chapter in England in 1981. There is good potential for growth not only in Colombia but also in Ecuador. Apparently the bishop there may need some assurance that we will not subvert his episcopal authority, but, if his fears can be allayed, some postulants may emerge. *The Way of St. Francis* has been so important in our Province that the next item most needed is a Spanish edition; Jose and Mario are preparing just such a translation. They already translated things like the report form. Here too before long a meeting should be arranged between the Colombians and our other two tertiaries in Latin America, Catron and Mellish. *La Carta Franciscana* is published by the Bogota' fellowship, and they have received the *Franciscan Times,* but they should also get copies of *The Little Chronicle* and *The Franciscan*.

Jose and Mario drove Dunstan and me to Zipaquira to visit the Salt Cathedral, half a mile under a mountain carved from a vast salt mine. Pre-Columbian Indians had developed the mine, and the purity of the salt attracted the Spanish to the high plateau where both Zipaquira and Bogota lie. The centuries-old mine continued working to the middle of the twentieth century when this Salt Cathedral was constructed. Its vastness, quiet and simple good taste stimulate and revive the spirit. We visited three shrine churches in Bogota's center, one built by friars in 1550, another a little later by the Third Order, and the third is a shrine for the national martyrs. Jose had informed and invited some of the local Roman Franciscans to our liturgy; just before the service I received a warm telegram of welcome from the Capuchins.

I almost hesitate to mention, but I was touched by the gift of a simple wooden cross (inch and a half) with a brass tau superimposed. It is being worn by the Bogota Fellowship, and would commend itself to us all had we not already accepted the gift of profession crosses from our New Zealand Third Order.

Conclusion

Our American Province seemed to be vast enough when we contemplated the whole United States and nearby Canada only seven years ago when we began to organize ourselves. In the last year we have seen a spurt of interest in Hawaii and, just recently, we have received new members in Alaska and Newfoundland. Now we are very much aware of the many new vocations that have arisen in South America. We may for a time longer continue to be this one vast Province, but soon, indigenous governance and life will have to become more important. However, the links we have found in our common response to Francis will continue to strengthen us all.

John Scott's Valedictory

In 1981, Barrie Williams asked John Scott for a description of the "The American Third Order Today" to be included in his book, *The Franciscan Revival in the Anglican Communion*. John wrote the following as his summation of his long work as a leader in the in the Order for nearly three decades:

> *From the time of the consolidation of the American Franciscans (Order of St. Francis) with the Society of St. Francis in 1967, virtually ninety percent of the present 400 Third Order members (professed, novices and*

postulants) of the American Province of the Third Order have entered its ranks. This extraordinary growth pattern has accompanied the assumption of responsibility for training, guidance and governance of the Third Order by its own members. The sense of belonging to the whole SSF has been strengthened, not diminished by less dependence upon the First Order direction of Third Order affairs.

In 1967 there were approximately 100 tertiaries, all of whom had entered the Third Order under the guidance and charismatic leadership of Father Joseph and had accepted the Post-Trent Credenda. The transition to the Principles derived from the Christa Seva Sangha was not easy for many, and some members withdrew; the Credenda and the wearing of habits seemed to be so very basic to their beliefs and practices in the Order of St. Francis. English tertiaries had not had the same experience except for the two dozen or so English tertiaries that followed Father Joseph. The English and American tertiaries of the Order of St. Francis had no contact, and the English group does seem to have been strongly called to community life in the manner of the numerous Roman Catholic Third Order Franciscan communities.

However, of the minority of present members of the American Province who antedate 1967, significant leadership was provided by Peter Funk in the development of a series of thirty letters on Franciscan spirituality which became the basis of postulant and novice training administered by the novice directors and counselors within the Third Order in the last dozen years. The first Guardian of the American Province was the Rector of St. Mary's Church, Hamilton Village on the University of Pennsylvania campus, John Scott (1973-80). In addition to several others who were among the first elected members of the Chapter, outstanding Franciscan witnesses in their lives and ministries (from the pre-1967 group) have been provided by priests such as H. Baxter Liebler, Hendrik B. Koning and James G. Jones, and lay members such as Marie Webner, Mona Hull, and Anna and Alvah Hoffman.

Father Liebler, now 92 years old, is also the American Province's longest professed tertiary (1926), founder of a mission among the Navajo Indians of Utah and Arizona, and still active there. Hendrik Koning, an electrical engineer by profession, has pioneered creative educational alternatives jointly sponsored by the Philadelphia School District, major businesses, and the teachers' union. Jim Jones is the dynamic and charismatic founder of Concept House in Miami, a residence and treatment center for former prisoners and addicts of all sorts. Marie Webner, an editor, has pioneered creative fellowship programs and inspired many to Franciscan vocations. Mona Hull, a scholar, has edited the papers of Sabatier that are in the custody of the Boston Public Library. The Hoffmans (before his early death) were planning a Franciscan-oriented Retirement and Nursing community.

The witness in many varied ways can be multiplied many times by the Third Order members who have entered since 1967 and who presently are the members of the Chapter, Novice Directors (Kenneth Cox and Glen-Ann Jicha, both laypersons), the Guardian (Dee Dobson) and the Chaplain (The Rev. Robert Goode). There are sixteen active fellowships meeting regularly in the United States, Canada, Trinidad, and Colombia. In addition, the fastest-growing membership in 1981 is among Amerindians in the remote outback of Guyana and the most promising Third Order community development is in the Yukon! In the latter wilderness, novices Llewellyn and Carol Johnson have built a retreat center on the Pelly River. In 1981, three convocations or conferences of Third Order members and their friends were held with the largest involving some sixty persons near New York in September. Intense sharing of people's spiritual journeys and witness to the Franciscan life characterized all these events.

From Chaplain Goode's ("Gooch") Letter to John Scott, July 15, 1980

We have so often been on different sides of some issues that I know I am not in danger of flattering you by this letter. However, I think someone should thank you on behalf of the whole Third Order.

Your leadership has helped us to survive as a community because it did not force or stifle. Many Chapter meetings found us taking very few votes because we grew into consensus. In a time of schism you respected the consciences of others enough to keep within our ranks those who need to disagree. You have been a peacemaker.

If you leave the office of Guardian with any mark upon us it would be your effort to keep the Gospel before us. Your concern for the poor and oppressed has colored every convocation and chapter as it colors your ministry at St. Mary's. You have proclaimed liberty to the captive.

Now that our mail has postmarks from Trinidad, Guyana, Alaska, Hawaii, Mexico, Columbia, etc., we can recognize your part in helping us to make our Lord known and loved everywhere.

One of your finest moments was the day you initiated and presided over our emptying the treasury of our surplus so that we might support the ministries of others. You kept us poor.

I can look for no better qualities than these in our next Guardian, nor can I think of higher praise to give you as a priest and as a Franciscan. God bless you!

John Scott died in the summer of 2006.

References

Muller, Hugo. *For No One Knows Waswanipi: A Collection of Songs and Poems on the Inland Cree*. Schumacher, Ont: J.A. Watton, Bishop of Moosonee, 1974.

———. *Waswanipi: Songs of a Scattered People*. Toronto: The Anglican Book Centre, 1976.

———. *Why Don't You?: A Look at Attitudes Towards Indians*. Place of publication not identified: publisher not identified, 1975.

The Book of Alternative Services of the Anglican Church of Canada. Toronto, Canada: Anglican Book Centre, 1985.

Williams, Barrie. *Franciscan Revival in the Anglican Communion.* London: Darton, Longman & Todd Ltd; 1982.

Chapter 5: Kale King, Provincial Guardian 1980-1

Biography

"Living the Gospel Now" Conference at Hillfield Friary, 1981. Left to Right: Dee Dobson; Br. Robert Hugh; Kale King; Archbishop Robert Runcie.

(part of a series of essays entitled My Franciscan Journey done by members of the Land of Sky Fellowship in 1993)

While in seminary–though having met no members of a religious community–I was being drawn to find an Order with whom I could associate in some fashion. I was looking for "Anglican" and "American," but I was also attracted to the kind itinerancy one finds in the life of Francis of Assisi. The stability of a Friary life was not really interesting. At the time the Order of the Poor Brethren of St. Francis (OSF), the Greyfriars, were very much rooted in Fr. Joseph's monastic life at the Friary of Little Portion, Long Island. I had inquired about some kind of association, but there was nothing attractive.

Just as my class was leaving seminary an underclassman told me about an English Order, the Society of St. Francis. In time I found their address, wrote to the then–Minister General, Br. Charles. He replied that since there were no SSF friars in North America, and thus there was no possibility for an SSF Third Order in North America. A couple of years later I discovered that there was a SSF friar in Canada due north of where l was serving. In writing to him I was sent a copy of the *Third Order Manual,* and I wrote my first rule at St. Francis-tide 1956. He suggested that my Rule be "tried for a year and report on it from time to time." However, by the time I sent off my first report, I discovered that he had already left the Society, and so I was "high and dry."

Three years later I wrote for the *American Third Order Manual* [*The Little Book of the Rule*]. It required assent to "Our *Credenda* as a treaty of peace and basis of the spiritual life." While I had no difficulty with most of it, several points put me off despite that they were to be taken as "pious opinions" rather than de fide. I did not follow through with the Third Order but, instead, became a Priest Associate. In early 1966 Br. Stephen OSF visited Idaho and assured me that the *Credenda* was no longer adhered to, and so I applied to be admitted as a postulant of the Third Order. The English Society was not completely out of the picture because I had met Brother Michael, SSF, when he led a week-long mission, at St. Stephen's and the Incarnation, Washington, D.C., in 1964. But, for the time being I had to be satisfied with this American Franciscan-ism. I was made novice by Br. Michael Thomas, a member of the same class as Br. Mark Francis, and I was given the name in religion of Boniface by Br. Paul, who directed the tertiaries. A year later Br. Paul succeeded Fr. Joseph OSF, the father founder, and my first formation director. The American and English Franciscan bodies merged to create a Franciscan body for the entire Anglican Communion.

The merger of the First Order brothers led to the merger of the Third Order, and its first gathering at Little Portion. At Br. Paul's invitation, I attended the 1970 chapter-in-the-making and was somehow appointed or elected to the body and was a member for the next ten years. I was even elected Guardian in 1979, but, a year and a half later, I resigned as the result of unrecognized stress and tension that grew out of serving the Church in Montana. However, I was fortunate, as Guardian, to attend the second Interprovincial Chapter, at Hilfield Friary in 1981—the Gospel Now Conference called by Br. Geoffrey SSF. I had also attended the 1976 Interprovincial Chapter at Bishop's Ranch in California, and met representatives from the African, New Zealand, Australian, and English provinces. All the association over the years with the many American friars, and, later, the English friars, thoroughly convinced me that this was a religious body I truly needed and wanted to associate with. The Gospel Now Conference affirmed that even more as we met with representatives of the First and Third Orders from around the world and considered how we might make the Gospel operative in our lives NOW.

I am richer in my spiritual life for having known personally Brothers Stephen, and Paul, Robert Hugh, David and Geoffrey, to some extent, Brother Michael, and, by correspondence, Father Joseph. I am richer for having shared the life of the Third Order with Peter Funk, my first Formation Director, John Scott and Dee Dobson, Guardians, Ken Cox and Alden Whitney, Formation Directors for Men, Robert "Gooch" Goode and Masud Ibn Syedullah, Provincial Chaplains, and a host of others on Chapter and throughout the Order. I am richer, for having become acquainted with the English Society's foundations in Brother Douglas and Brother Algy, and the American Order's by Father Joseph, and shared something of their vision for Franciscanism in the Anglican Communion.

Resignation as Minister Provincial, August 1981

Kale King

Please come to the next meeting of the Third Order Provincial Chapter, in Seattle, 9 -10 November 1981, and be prepared to elect a Guardian to complete the two years that remain of the present Guardian's term, in accordance with the Provincial Statutes, II D 6. It was pride that let me accept the nomination and that led me to think that I had the time, the equipment, and the assistance needed to carry out the functions of the office. I wanted to believe so much that I was being obedient. For some time, some of you have been aware that I have not been fulfilling the expectations of my Office. You were all too gracious in not speaking up. Those of you who have been praying that somehow it would all get straightened out for the good of the Order can now turn your attention to the election that lies ahead. The time has come to face reality.

I do hereby submit my resignation as Guardian of the Third Order of the Society of St, Francis, American Province, effective at the conclusion of the 1981 meeting of Chapter in Seattle.

I shall concentrate these last three months in bringing about the successful gathering of Chapter and Convocation and the 800th anniversary observance of Francis' birth. Only those actions that must be made before Chapter will be taken, I defer all others until the new Guardian can assume the leadership.

My deepest thanks to those of you who have given me encouragement and a great deal of support, I must admit that Brother Geoffrey is correct in questioning the holding of this office by one who is an isolated tertiary. At least this tertiary, who has been isolated from the beginning of postulancy, sees how being a part of a Fellowship would have made the office easier to fill,

The Chaplain should also plan to appoint another Area Chaplain for Idaho and Montana, and the Novice Director should plan to transfer those reporting to me to another counselor and remove my name from available counselors. After eleven years, I am tired. Chapter meetings and the one Convocation I could attend have been the only Franciscan fellowship I have had; my wife has had none except by telephone and letter. The annual gatherings will be missed, but it is time to go back to the ranks.

Response From John Scott August 30, 1981
Your letter of resignation arrived a few days ago. I will admit that I was feeling some concern that no special mailing had come for the Seattle meeting, but I was very glad that you did get to the Interprovincial meeting in England, and I was looking forward to hearing more about it. In the back of my mind I expected to get to Seattle, and perhaps it is more important now to make definite plans. Certainly no one is indispensable, but isolation and distances are problems for the individual as well as the Order.

What concerns me the most at the moment is you yourself. Guilt can be such a drag and enemy. Please do not feel that you have let anyone down. It is always a two-way street in the matter of support. I know that I felt like I had left you to grab the helm midway between chapter meetings and, by the time I got to the Ranch last year, realized that the transfer of leadership had been too abrupt and out of sequence—I felt guilty. Thank God the Lord can see it all and find ways to make up for our boners. But it is not only the matter of your feeling the necessity to step dawn. It is again you–and Amory—not feeling that the only option is to accept the isolation. As a matter of fact, you haven't entirely—Muriel and Lionel were with you for the big eruption last year, isn't that right? On the other hand, I know full well the feeling of being tired, and needing to let go of something, and nothing contributes to tiredness more than the frustration of not being able to deal with whatever situation the way it seems to demand....

Kale continued to provide leadership in TSSF as seen by his elections to Chapter and by taking on the emergency role of Interim Provincial Chaplain in 1994-5.

Seattle Provincial Convocation/Chapter November 9-10, 1981 (St. Thomas Center)

The Gospel Now was the convocation theme. Br. Robert Hugh and Sr. Cecelia both spoke in addition to the keynote speaker.

Br. Alan Barnabas (Province of Australia), Keynote Speaker.

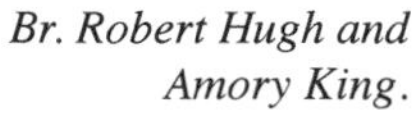

Br. Robert Hugh and Amory King.

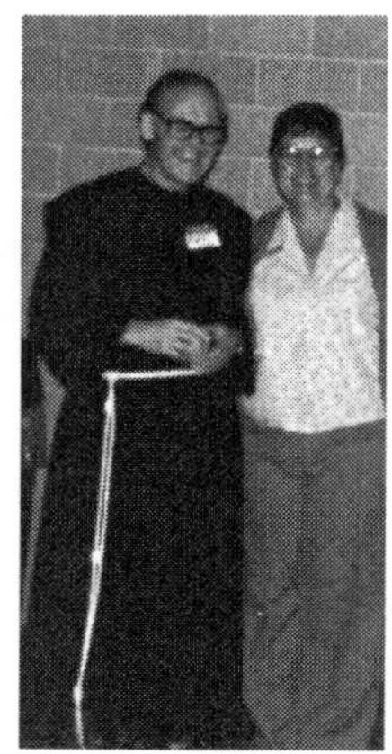

Back to front:Robert (Gooch) Goode, Dee Dobson,Glen-Ann Jicha, Dorothy Nakatsuji.

John Dorman, Missionary Priest of Upper Mazaruni and Upper Cuyuni Region in Guyana

"My Choice For National Heroes"

Keith R. Williams (Guyana Gazette, May 31, 2006)

> *The criteria for heroes set... are virtually unreachable in Guyana.... But never fear, I have two more names for you and, although I am not sure of their mortal status, they will always be heroes in my book.*
>
> *(1) The Reverend John Dorman, MS, an Anglican priest who dedicated his life in Christian service to those who got the least attention from officialdom. He crossed waterfalls, blistering savannahs, and negotiated obstacle-strewn and virtually impassable mountain paths in order to serve the peoples of the Upper Mazaruni and Upper Cuyuni Region. And he did so always with a permanent smile on his face and a jovial: "Well, hello, how are you?" to all he encountered in passing.*

John Dorman was a United Society for the Propagation of the Gospel (USPG) missionary priest in the interior of Guyana for 38 years (1957-95). He was professed in the Third Order while Kale King was Provincial Guardian (November 18, 1980), and Dorman died on July 18, 1998.

The Rev. John F. Twisleton's review of Dorman biography (*Old-Style Missionary* (2003)) is a very good summary of Dorman's heroic work:

> *John Dorman first went to then British Guyana in 1957 and served there*

almost continuously up to his death in 1998. Like many expatriates he redeemed his spare time in correspondence. Canon Dorman's letters have made Fr. Goodrich's task all the easier. They have also been a rich source of encouragement, challenge, and guidance to many over the years. As my own reflection makes clear at the end of the book, I am one who would never have come to visit Guyana had not a letter arrived one day in his familiar, closely woven script. Writing in 1986, John asked me to prayerfully consider joining the Company of Mission Priests team in that land to serve the training of Amerindian priests. I could not find an excuse; such was the spiritual force of John Dorman on occasion!

The need for indigenous priests is demonstrated by one of John's tours of the Rupununi region, before we ran the Alan Knight Training Centre, when he baptised more than 100 children, gave Holy Communion to over 1000 and heard nearly 100 Confessions. It was primarily through John's initiative that the Amerindian communities today have almost 20 priests so that the sacraments are now available to all Guyanese, even those in the remotest parts of the rainforest.

Old-Style Missionary makes riveting reading. It begins with a shipwreck on the Essequibo in which John nearly loses his life on his way to take a Boxing Day Mass. He swims in the dark to safety on Calf Island where he says a Magnificat in thanksgiving. Writing from his hammock in the vestry at Kamarang, he speaks of the "paint on the walls still scarred by the blood the vampire bats have sampled from my great toes." Derek Goodrich describes how John was driven from the Mission one night by a pack of jaguars and on another occasion was arrested by the Venezuelan frontier guards on the pretext of teaching without authority on their soil, a trumped up charge fortunately soon withdrawn.

The missionary priest spends himself in much itinerant ministry: "Towards evening he would reach a Mission for Evensong, Confessions, Confirmation class, then sleep in a hammock, with Mass in the early morning. The work was endlessly varied in pattern and human need. It is concerned with carrying the simple riches of divine love to the simple poor people who need Him," John writes. "Could there be anything more at one with the work of the Gospel than a little boat full of silent and reverent people returning from their Communion; the priest barefoot in alb and stole sitting in the bow and carrying the pyx containing the Blessed Sacrament for some faithful sufferer to whom the Lord travels as on the Sea of Galilee?"

Fr. Goodrich describes John's advocacy for Guyana's Amerindians who are faced with the challenge of integration with Guyanese society as a whole. Mining and logging ventures that damage their livelihood challenge them. The pollution of the rivers by dredging for gold remains a very serious problem. Fr. Dorman writes of how the Amerindians "at every point...live in two worlds, and more and more these two worlds are coming into collision

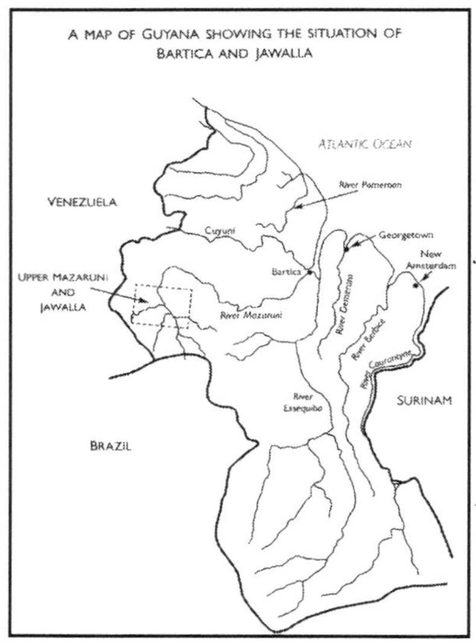

Dorman's Guyana

with their own ancient way taking most of the knocks." When I used to visit him in Kamarang he was always deeply concerned about the heavy drinking and the video shops opened for the mining fraternity and their effect on the indigenous people. The formerly tranquil community had more of the feel of the Wild West with young people being drawn into prostitution.

Between 1975 and 1983 Canon Dorman was involved in a successful international campaign against a major hydroelectric project that would have flooded the Akawaio homelands [cf. Hugo Muller and the Inland Cree, pages 74-80], *including the sacred centre of the Alleluia Church. His refusal to condemn the Alleluia Church, which holds many elements of Christian tradition (but with no Bible or Eucharist) contrasted with the negative attitude of other Christian churches. John succeeded in obtaining associate membership of the Guyana Council of Churches for Alleluia and encouraged his priests and people to hold joint membership. His largest church at Jawalla was built especially to accommodate the traditional Alleluia dance, which would accompany or follow the Eucharist on great feast days.* [See page 200-1]

Fr. Allan Buik's funeral homily is quoted: "True to the best traditions of catholic Anglicanism, both in theory and in practice, he stressed the Creation and the Incarnation as well as the Atonement. His cherishing of God's creation and of the tribes among whom he lived earned him high respect from environmentalists and anthropologists as well as from Christians–Alleluia as well as Anglican.…His devotion to his Amerindians could be paternalistic… (his) foibles were all facets of his love for the people to whom God had sent him, the people for whom he never stopped caring."

The following is a short piece written by Dorman that captures his sense of the presence of God even in the most trying of circumstances: "A View from the Lock-Up" (*El-Dorado*, magazine of the Guyana Diocesan Association, UK, 1972)

> Dear Editor of El-Dorado, you gave me the task of writing about the church and work in our newest parish, Kamarang. It is the setting of an adventure of primary evangelism in what is now our country's loneliest corner. I planned to write a prosaic factual account of the Cuyuni missions.
>
> It would not do. This river is the real road, I think, to El-Dorado: yes, literally and spiritually.

Literally, its rock-strewn torrents pour between untouched gold-bearing hills, fed by sparkling brown-tinged streams where little nuggets and shining dust may still be found in the pools by the fortunate few. When you have travelled by engine-boat at least a week upstream from Bartica, you pass from Guyana into the "Spanish Main," and reach, one day beyond, the Cuyani's largest village, called El-Dorado.

Spiritually too: here they survive, few and almost untouched by the clawing paws of acquisitive "civilization," the calm, wise, gentle Amerindian people, to whom God has given the tropical forest as their teacher. They have learned their lessons there for unnumbered centuries, and theirs is the priceless treasure of a way of life so good that any visitor, not blinded by vanity, would want to walk himself among them to listen and learn its secrets. In tiny villages of Caribe people, poor as the poorest you dreamt of, yet their humanity glittering with the simple secrets that the great world has lost, the real "Golden Man" stands to meet the Church of God, and learn what more God has to give.

We cannot write that story yet. El-Dorado's river welcomed the Church only six years ago, but the doors seem to be closing, closing against the world (which will batter its way in). The area becomes yearly more inaccessible and the little riverside villages are scarcely half as populated as they were when we came. Geography, economics, history are ready to say, "There is no El-Dorado—it was a dream."

Mr. Editor, I arrived here at the river by plane, hoping to write you "the usual article" on the spot. However, the same evening, following a little military mistake (for which most ample regrets have been offered and accepted), I found myself in detention across the frontier, and what follows was written there.

Ambassador in bonds? Scarcely that: just another priest held prisoner on duty, to add to the hundreds or thousands elsewhere tonight in the same position.

Curious how patterns persist from Apostolic times. The circumstances, the pretexts, are often irrelevant to the errand, which is interrupted. But interrupted it is, though, as St Paul found, "the word of God is not bound." It never is.

The soldier with his gun across his knees, who watches us through the open door tonight, while the noise of the barracks on a Saturday night makes sleep impossible, unknowingly speaks to me as plainly as the soldier to whom the Apostle was chained at Rome. His dull green uniform helps him remember he is only one of an army, serving a cause. One soldier in uniform is the army on guard. At the same time, his uniform helps each and all to blend into the forest setting of their service, so well that, with some simple skill, they can almost vanish from the scene.

John Dorman at left along with friends at Kamarang.

I find this an interesting hint to the Church in Guyana, indeed everywhere. The common "uniform" of being disciples, which enables us to recognize each other—isn't it Christ's holy sign of the Cross, carried by us all with gladness as well as tears? This "uniform" is somehow the key to the Church's unnoticed silent power in the world, the hidden yeast at work. Remember Kurutuku down the river, loneliest village I know; I can see Edwin the catechist and Dunstan the school-master asleep in their flimsy homes, among Christ's beloved poor. Five years they've been there, two or three months' mail-time from their own villages; just a hammock, a table, two stools, some books, the roughest meals over a wood fire, a smile for everyone, and duty done as God offers daily opportunity. They're in the uniform of the Christian army, yet invisible to the world, unvisited, unraised, unprompted. This is the miracle of camouflage that the Church is using, to be everywhere, actively fighting evil, as an integrated worldwide force, yet invisible to the dictator who would crush it, or the vested interests who might try to harness it for the enslavement of men born to be free. I pray for the Church in Guyana, uniformed with the Cross.

As I look at this soldier again, just a few feet away, his uniform is somehow concentrated in his belt. Without it he would be an untidy, unprepared, uncouth figure. But belted, he is alert, proud, and ready for anything. The shining buckle is his pride, and the strong webbing gives him a real integration of purpose in his soldiering.

What is our belt? A year ago when I was here in the Cuyuni, I had Winston [Williams] with me, a young Akawaio tribesman who, alone and unaided, persuaded the Guyana Youth Corps to release him from that training, so that he may fulfill the claims of God calling him to train for full-time Christian work. He came with me across the high savannahs and through the streaming forest valleys, northwards to a strange area, to serve as an evangelist on the very same island I was arrested on this afternoon. After that long three days' journey, I had only one night to introduce him to his little flock—"This is my young brother, Winston, who will stay to help you come nearer to God"—and the next day after an early Mass, we waved goodbye, leaving him on the rocky beach with the tall trees behind him, as upright and strong as himself. He is belted with the fact of vocation; the certainty of divine commission; apostleship, if one dare claim that word for each such Christian, as well as for us all. How hopeless it would be if we left that behind.

I look down at the soldier's boots. They must be costly, for the soft pliant leather is laced tightly half-way to the knee, against the hazards of jungle journeys, and yet they are smart enough, with their daily shine-up for the Presidential Guard on parade. St Paul's phrase gives the clue—"Your feet shod with the preparation of the gospel of peace." Two months ago a young man I knew well was travelling by canoe, as his ancestors had done for centuries, from one side of this broad river to the other, from one country across the international water to the other. It was early morning, just dawn.

A rifle shot rang out, and he fell dead into the water, shot through the mouth. Such unexplained violence in a military zone has a terrible power to scatter an innocent population, whose forebears lived indifferently on one side, farmed on the other and fished between. But Peter, the fine old man who with his own hands built the beautiful church of St Faith, at Awatapati (two years' work for the glory of God) would not remove from the scene of the crime. The priest would be coming soon; the people must be here to worship with him. God would take care of them. Those who believe that Christ sends his Easter gifts of peace to the hearts of men must also pay the price to win peace in their homes, to cement peace among the nations.

I smile at the soldier in the lamplight, as I sit writing on the edge of the bed and the tense face relaxes into an answering smile. I bless him with the sign of the Cross, and, after a moment of perplexity, he understands and makes the holy sign himself.

It is night, and, though he is on duty, he has left his cap behind, till he needs it for tomorrow's burning sun. I am glad he has put it aside, for it lets me see him as a man, a brother man, his black lustrous hair somehow placing him not as a soldier, but in that category of which God our Father knows each one by name; just as in some Venezuelan village, perhaps overlooking the shining blue Caribbean as it sweeps west to Panama, his mother would not pick him out easily when the soldier boys come home on leave, marching in battalion pride to the little plaza—until they lift their caps to cheer. Then she can see him at once as her son.

I remember how many hundreds I have been allowed to baptize in this river since 1966: perhaps I could identify the adults by name, but the children, who nestled in my arm and smiled as the cool water flowed over their foreheads, I would soon be stumped for their names if they came in through that open door one by one. But the Church would not, because God could never forget, as a mother may, at times, even wish to forget.

There are many "caps" put on people in Guyana: racial prejudice, social stigma, economic injustice, divisions of inherited culture, home languages not shared, etc. But in the Church you come bareheaded, and each is seen as one to whom God says, "I have called you by your name, you are Mine."

I have still to think about his gun. This is a horror of which I have no expert knowledge. I could not name its parts, nor even explain their uses. Only I know it is made to kill. It is the symbol of fear, of human disunity. Yet one

St. Francis de Sales Church in Kamarang—construction was completed in 14 working days in July 1969 with the assistance of 30 youth volunteers from Guyana, Bermuda, Georgia, and Maine during an International Student Work Tour. John's ashes are buried in the church's graveyard. (Stabroek News, July 30, 2009)

supposes he is proud of it, because it marks him out in the nation, as one who has been trusted with the arbitrament of life and death. In the last resort, life and death are his business.

Perhaps we may say that Satan gives him this ghastly duty, but that God allows him to bear it; just as Our Lord carried the ghastly Cross, the challenge was what to do with it, and He answered by transforming it into a means of life from death.

In a few years—who knows?—the Church in the Cuyuni may be dead. A village is uprooted by remote decree: a sect sweeps in to an illiterate people and with "high-powered preaching" overwhelms with arguments that they cannot read; a new industry is opened and a thousand years of hunting, fishing and farming go by the board. Whatever may come, we live and would die in the cause of Life: in little groups, men, women and children stand up to be counted for Him who is the real Life, along these lovely river banks and in the little islands among the jagged rocks.

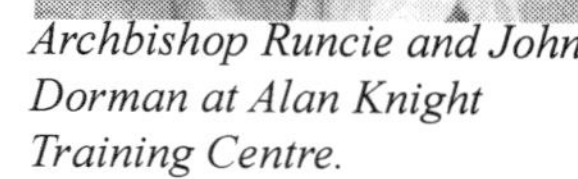

Archbishop Runcie and John Dorman at Alan Knight Training Centre.

What looks like doom is a challenge to jump up and face the darkness, for there is the true light beyond. It is now past midnight and the dawn will come: for you, Dunstan, Edwin, Winston, Peter, old Hannah with the patient smile, little Veronica with the face of the Madonna, all of you.

God bless you through the night till then.

References

Goodrich, Derek. *Old-Style Missionary: The Ministry of John Dorman, Priest in Guyana.* East Harling, Norfolk UK: Taverner Publications 2003.

Moore, Robert J, and Gerald T. Rayner. *Audacious Anglicans: Heroes of the Anglican Communion.* Picton, Ont: Bluejay Pub, 2008, Chapter 15: John Dorman.

Chapter 6: Dee Dobson, Guardian to Minister Provincial 1981-90

John Scott's times as Guardian had plenty of Provincial firsts. However, Kale King's sudden resignation as Provincial Guardian created a huge, new precedent. Since his resignation occured between elections, the Statutes empowered Chapter to choose a new Guardian to complete his term. Dee was unanimously nominated in September, and chosen by acclamation of Chapter to become the new Provincial Guardian.

Dee's Lack of Vision?

In her initial report to the First Order after she had been Guardian for all of three months (from "Guardian's Report to the First Order, February 1982"), Dee made this curious statement: "I realize that our [First Order] Provincial would like perhaps a two or three page outline of a 'vision,' but I really do not feel that such an outline is feasible. We are all seeking the same goal, to be with our Lord in the way of Francis."

Much of the heat in the conflicits of the John Scott era (women's ordination and gay ordination) were dissipated by the time Dee became Guardian. The union of two disparate Third Order Franciscan communities—separated by an ocean, and requiring a new constitution and statues—was finished. Long position papers on big topics or multinational reports from abroad were, for the moment, no longer needed. The central provincial or interprovincial focus of the *Franciscan Times* or *Newsletter* was eroded initially by budget concerns—the single Epiphany-tide issue during Kale King's term cost more than a whole year of issues. As the *Times* temporarily diminished in importance, an inexpensive monthly newsletter, the *Information Sheet*, began. (The complete run of the *Information Sheet* from November 1980 to June 1998 is available, and indexed on the TSSF website.) Moreover, the 1980s also saw the flowering of many local fellowship newsletters. Thus, in the 1980s, the *Franciscan Times* primarily became a pastiche of articles from these local fellowship newsletters rather than articles on big topics or multinational reports.

Parallel to all of this was the demise of the the Provincial Convocations. Chapter realized that "Provincial" Convocations drew few outside the immediate area of where it was held. Moreover, Provincial Convocations were expensive to Chapter because they were underwritten by Chapter funding and controled by Chapter. Dee effectively stopped supporting Provincial Convocations after 1982. (The final Provincial Convocation in Miami during the John Scott era nearly depleted all Provincial funds.)

Dee and John New Orleans Provincial Convocation 1997

These Provincial Convocations were replaced by many Regional Convocations. Dee and Chapter found it easier to focus on regional convocations because they could be created and funded by local groups of tertiaries without Chapter control or funding. Almost from the moment Dee was elected as Guardian, regional convocations began to occur. In 1981, her first year as Guardian, regional convocations were held for the first time in the Northeast, in the Southwest, and five other regions with many scheduled to mark the 800th anniversary of Franciscanism.

Whether Dee Dobson had a stated "vision" or not, the result of Dee's and Chapter's specific, pragmatic decisions effectively decentralized the focus of the Province.

Consider the role of Fellowships in the Province. Originally there was little attention paid to Fellowships. The first mention of a Provincial Officer called the Fellowship Coordinator did not occur until the 1975 Provincial budget; only in the 1981 Chapter was a Fellowship Coordinator described, and it wasn't until 1983—66 years after the Third Order was born—that a draft of the *Fellowship Conveners Handbook* was presented to Chapter for ratification. Is it any wonder then that as late as 1983, only 50% of the members of the Province belonged to fellowships—most were separate pious individuals.

One can also track the relative importance of fellowships by the size of the annual TSSF budget given to the Fellowship Coordinator. Initially the financial commitment to fellowships was relatively small: 7% of that given to the Provincial Chaplain and 50% of that given to the Area Chaplains. However, by the second year of Dee Dobson's first term, 50% of what was given to the Provincial Chaplain and 200% (later 300%) of that given to the Area Chaplains, was budgeted for the needs of the Fellowship Convener.

For fellowships to grow, however, they needed a champion for their interests. This is exactly what Dee Dobson proposed in her first Report to Chapter as Guardian in November 1982:

As you know, Fellowships have been a concern. Some are hale and hearty and emulate Franciscan love, community and commitment. Others could, for the want of a better term, be called mediocre with sporadic showings of commitment. Still others–I can thankfully say, very few–can only be described as disasters. Marie Webner has graciously consented to be our Fellowship Coordinator. It is expected that she will chair

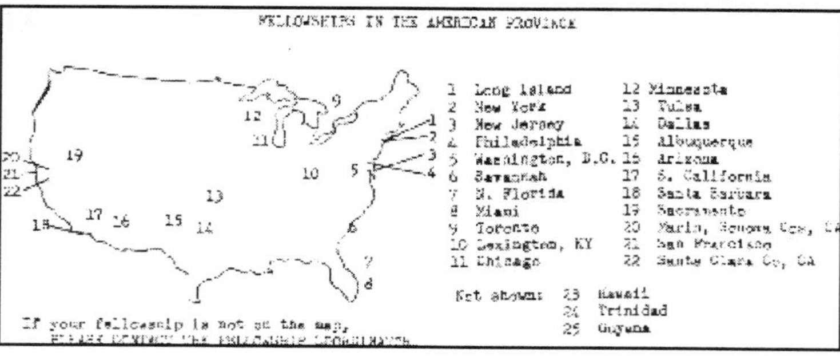

From Franciscan Times, 1990.

a group to draw up flexible guidelines, guidelines that have been distilled from the input of fellowships. In the future when funds become available, we hope to have a training session for conveners. In the interim, Marie and I hope to meet with Conveners at regional convocations.

The Rise of the Fellowship Coordinator and Marie Webner

The position of Fellowship Coordinator, now a member of the Standing Committee of the Province, was absent from the Province's Directory for the first six years of John Scott's tenure (1971-76). In looking for information about the characteristic activities of the fellowships, Provincial Secretary, Helen Webb, had to survey the majority of existing fellowships to discover what their meetings and activities were (*Franciscan Times*, December 1976). That same year, 1976, Marie Webner (26 years in profession) was appointed by Guardian John Scott and confirmed by Chapter to be the "Fellowship Contact Person" (by June 1978 she was using the now familiar title of "Fellowship Coordinator"), and, by the May 1977 issue of the *Franciscan Times*, Marie was writing short articles summarizing fellowship best practices: "Fellowship Partnership" (May 1977) and "A Report Summarizing Fellowship Annual Reports" (June 1978). After one term of three years, in January 1979, John Scott and Chapter named a new Fellowship Coordinator, The Rev. Annjane Tanner of the Long Island Fellowship. For the next three years, "reports" from fellowships became random collections of personal information about who was moving, being noviced, having picnics, etc.

When Dee was elected, Marie Webner was re-appointed as Fellowship Coordinator in 1982 and remained as Coordinator for the next nine years until she was elected as Provincial Chaplain. In 1983 there were 25 Fellowships in the Province, and four regional convocations each year. When Webner stepped down in 1992, there were 38 Fellowships and eight regional convocations. With such a dramatic shift from the John Scott "provincial" settings for convocations to the Dee Dobson/Marie Webner "regional" settings for convocations, Chapter had to redefine the word "convocation" in the Statutes to indicate both "provincial" and "regional" meetings.

In the January 1978 issue of the *Franciscan Times*, "Fellowship newsletters" are first mentioned: *Sursum Corda*, a 16-page newsletter, produced by the Long Island Fellowship, and *The Franciscan Flyer* from the San Francisco area was already up to Vol 2, No. 2. In May 1980, the *Franciscan Times* noted that the Minneapolis Fellowship had produced a bimonthly newsletter; that the *W. I. (West Indies) Franciscan News* was being produced by the Trinidad Fellowship; and a Spanish-language newsletter, *Carta Franciscana*, was being produced in Columbia. In the Epiphanytide 1981 issue of the *Franciscan Times*, the Puget Sound Fellowship announced the birth of their fellowship newsletter, and the San Francisco fellowship announced the publication renewal of their newsletter.

By the time Webner left her position, these six fellowship newsletters had grown to fifteen. Many were rather hastily put together by cutting and pasting typewritten pieces, photocoping the result, and sending it out by post. Many were just one-page, front-and-back affairs including such items as invitations and announcement of upcoming local and regional events; reports of past meetings or events: ordinations, professions, novicings, and the arrival of new postulants; a few poems and short essays; and some reprinting of other fellowship newsletter materials and some forwarding of provincial information.

Two newsletters from the mid-1980s, however, stand out from all the rest: the *Seedlings Tidings* from the Mustard Seed Fellowship in Upstate New York and *Caritas* produced by the Toronto Fellowship in Eastern Canada. Both were substantial pieces of work with typical fellowship newsletter items augmented by the kind of material that formerly appeared in the *Franciscan Times*–extended essays drawn from authors province-wide. In just the first issue of *Seedling Tidings*, Marie Webner and Provincial Chaplain, Robert Goode (Gooch), penned pieces about fellowships specifically for this newsletter (see Gooch's example on the opposite page). In later issues, articles by Bishop Desmond Tutu, Joanne Maynard (editor of the *Times*), Presiding Bishop Edmund Browning, and even Archbishop Runcie were reprinted in this fellowship newsletter.

Franciscan Times and the *Information Sheet* Reflect A New Emphasis on Local and Regional Information, and *Pax et Bonum* Debuts

From 1978 until the 1981 Epiphany-tide issue, Peg Shull edited the *Franciscan Times*. The 1981 Epiphanytide issue was the *Franciscan Times*'s handsomest issue, but it was out of sync with the new emphasis of the Guardian and Chapter on keeping costs down and focusing on the local and regional events. Shull's single Epiphanytide 1981 issue went over the whole year's budget by 30%. As a result, Chapter decided, as of December 1981, to cease publication of the *Franciscan Times*, and to shift publication of all provincial news to the monthly, quick-copy format of the *Information Sheet*. (The *Information Sheet* had only begun publication in November of 1980. The indexed, complete run of the *Information Sheet* is available on the TSSF website.)

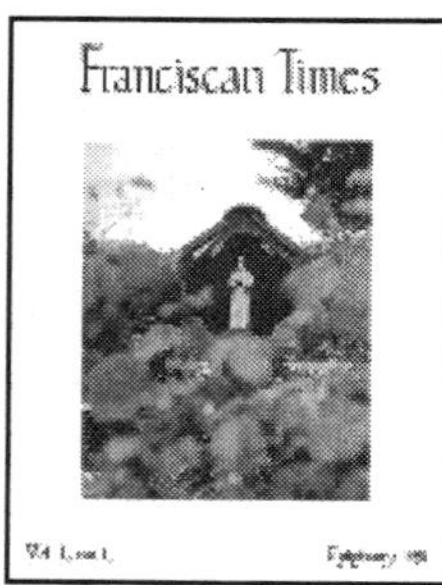

However, the story quickly got complicated because a new editor, Roberta Beisel, was appointed to direct the *Franciscan Times*, and she produced a nicely formatted issue without the use of color, Eastertide 1982. Beisel's version of the *Times*, however, still required a printer to produce it. At the 1982 Chapter, Chapter changed its mind once more and now looked for a parallel production of the *Franciscan Times* and the *Information Sheet*; the *Times* would be a quarterly with feature stories and the *Information Sheet* a bimonthly with more breaking-news information.

Joanne Maynard who had recently written a book, *The Burning Mushroom: And Other Epiphanies*, was appointed as the new editor, and she edited the *Times* for the next eight years until asking to step down in 1990 at the completion of Dee Dobson's terms as Minister Provincial. Maynard's *Franciscan Times* reflected Dee's and Chapter's new emphasis on fellowships and regional convocations and was primarily a pastiche of short pieces gleaned from fellowship newsletters, fellowship annual reports, and regional convocation reports. Like the fellowship newsletters, this pastiche was photocopied, scotch-taped together, and then photocopied. There were few, if any, long, substantial articles, which left a desire in the Order for someplace to publish longer articles, poems, reviews, etc.

To fulfill that desire Terry Rogers and Arthur Wolsoncroft created *Pax et Bonum* getting it endorsed by the 1987 Chapter. *Pax et Bonum* was designed to come out twice a year and be composed of

> *articles by Tertiaries on a variety of issues and from diverse points of view. The overall purpose is to deepen our sense of our Franciscan vocation, stimulate our thinking, and widen our view of the unique gifts and unique lives within our Third Order Community.* (*Information Sheet* December 1987).

Two issues were produced, 1988 and 1990. (Only the 1990 issue has been found and scanned and is included in the *Franciscan Times* collection on the TSSF website.

When Robert Durand succeeded Joanne Maynard as editor of the *Franciscan Times* in 1991, he folded the longer, substantial articles of *Pax et Bonum* into the local and regional focus of the *Times*.

In 1985 Robert Goode (Gooch) Lays Down His Mantle as Provincial Chaplain After 14 Years

For 14 years, Gooch was either the Province's Assistant Chaplain (when that was all the pastoral leadership allowed by the First Order to tertiaries) or Provincial Chaplain during the very formative years of the province in John Scott's era and the first half of Dee Dobson's. He first appeared in the records as a novice in the First Order, but was professed in the Third Order, like the high priest Melchizedek, on an unknown date. Here are two important pieces he wrote, one for a fellowship newsletter, *Seedlings Tidings* and the second in a letter to our Provincial Secretary, Helen Webb.

What a Fellowship is Not

(From *Seedlings Tidings* 1985; reprinted in the *Information Sheet* 1985)

There are several things fellowships are not. They are not an advertising cartel to promote St. Francis. In other words, a fellowship should not be composed of everyone in the surrounding ten counties who likes St. Francis. A fellowship is not primarily a support group. There are, however, many periods in our Franciscan life when the support of a fellowship keeps us going. But a fellowship is not therapy, and a person who is in the formation process particularly should be doing his or her own growing in places other than the fellowship, as well as within the dynamic of the fellowship. It is not always advisable to share your innermost secrets with members of a fellowship. We are not all equally mature. Members come and go; people move. Fellowships, like people, change.

Nor can a fellowship be a substitute for a spiritual director. As Provincial Chaplain, I deal over and over again with situations where the novice counselor, a friend in fellowship, a friendship with a friar, becomes a substitute for a spiritual director. It is too easy for a spiritual director to be just a name on a report form. This is where your trust and confidence should lie. This is where crises and problems should be resolved. All too often, I get requests for release from vows which show that the spiritual director hasn't even been asked for an opinion.

People should bring as much or more to a fellowship as they take from it.

More than anything else, a fellowship is a reinforcement of one overriding fact about us; we are committed to this way of life. Good times, bad times; dry times, full times; we are trying to follow our Lord in the way of St. Francis for the rest of our lives. High Church, Low Church, charismatic, Anglo-Catholic, whatever, our unity lies in the common vow. We live in an age when promises are broken not only frequently but casually, when we are taught to believe we owe everything to ourselves and little to others. It is the vow that separates us from those called to walk in other ways. Yet our vow is only part of our baptismal vow.

Think of the consequences and importance of a vow in terms of the theology of St. John, where THE word becomes a living and effective entity, where THE Godhead itself is described as THE Word. May your word as a Franciscan be an extension of THE Word in the life of the Church.

On The Role of Confession in the Third Order

Provincial Chaplain Robert Goode June 15, 1983 letter to Helen Webb

...As to your queries about confession, the problem is that we all go back so far it is sometimes hard to remember things. Maybe I can jog your memory a bit.

During the tremendous time of change when we abandoned *The Manual* of OSF, you may remember that there were many who were upset at giving up names, habits and the *Credenda*. In a way, it was an enormous change. We began a whole new set of statutes and changed the report form.

During that Chapter and what I believe we called convocation, we agreed on a few things without putting them into elaborate systems of rules in order to avoid the very rigid and legalistic tone of the former manual.You may recall that in a spirit of keeping the basics and partly to conciliate those who were being asked to give up many things, which were precious to them, we agreed that two things were characteristic of the American Province and would be kept. One of them was the recitation of the Daily Office. The other was the fact that confession was a normative practice for us.

I remember this well because I was on the committee that changed the report form, and it was clearly understood that the penitence section would be kept and that it referred to the Sacrament of Penance as well as any devotions, such as examination of conscience that a person saw as part of their Franciscan spirituality. ...So, our policy has always been to talk about the sacrament as being a normative part of our life, rather than to talk of it as "required." Do you understand the difference in tone I am talking about?

We are a voluntary association in the Episcopal Church. No one has to belong to the Third Order. We require spiritual directors, and we require recitation of the Office, none of which are requirements for the ordinary Episcopalian. I believe at least half of the various associates and companions of the other religious Orders not only require the use of the sacrament of penance, but sometimes even attempt to set the frequency. In fact, the Rule of Life of the associates of the Sisters of the Holy Nativity is more rigorous than ours, and, incidentally, you might want to know that they do not allow their associates to become tertiaries.

Anyone who is immersed in Franciscan spirituality knows that the Sacrament of Penance and the penitential life in general is as major a theme as poverty and that our other names are "Little Brothers and Sisters of Penance." That is why the friars, to this day, keep two Lents. Franciscans are the most popular confessors in the world, and there is a whole definitively Franciscan approach to the Sacrament of Penance, as characterized by St. Leonard of Port Maurice. This tradition is very much alive and well today, as evidenced by the fact that while many Roman Catholics have fallen away from the Sacrament, churches run by friars continue to have lines outside the confessional.

With beginners it is natural that there might be questions and some ignorance, but I would suggest you express your puzzlement with someone in this category because a serious objection to the Sacrament of Penance is so incompatible with Franciscan spirituality and tradition as to make someone's grasp of the Franciscan life questionable, if they cannot see this. This is the sort of person who ought to be a candidate for the associates. This is also a time when even Protestant ministers are again hearing confessions, so this kind of reticence on the popular level is very out of touch with what is actually happening.

Now, we do have people in the Episcopal Church who try to make a thoughtful and cogent objection to the Sacrament of Penance. Granted, these are few and far between these days, but the tradition from which they speak is also opposed to vows and blessings and is opposed to the whole idea of the religious life. So, I would find it hard to understand why such a person would want to be a tertiary in the first place. The relationship with a spiritual director is far more intimate and revealing than that with one's confessor, for in it one must lay bare one's besetting sins and the whole pattern and structure of sin in one's spiritual life. So, again, I would be puzzled as to why someone would be willing to have a spiritual director but not a confessor.

I think that what you have done, as a matter of course, is the right way to handle it. Get the person's spiritual director to discuss this with them and show them what a marvelous means of grace it is. I have many times gotten letters from people, perhaps even some you have counseled, who have said that the single greatest blessing of their being a tertiary was that the Order moved them to make use of the Sacrament when they might not otherwise have done so. Occasionally, we do get a newcomer who has not used the Sacrament and who might have been scared off if we had all kinds of material about it in our introductory literature. But the process of being open to all of the things they have to do to become tertiaries makes them especially open to using the Sacrament as just one of many new things that are now coming into their life. Most of the time, however, aspirants are already penitents. So, as I have said above, try to be firm and gentle and talk about the sacrament naturally. People will often grow into things if you give them leadership. We are not trying to whip them into it. Yes, I do expect people to use the Sacrament, but I hope my counselors and formation directors will be tactful, gentle, and firm.

The larger we get, the more diverse we get, and, while we have abandoned many of our practices such as requiring belief in the Immaculate Conception and some of these rightly so, we must be very careful to resist the equally growing pressure to so water down our life so that we end up being a bunch of people of good will who happen to like St. Francis.

I can easily see how it might have happened that something like this slipped past you and for reasons that I have already outlined above, I do not pound on it. I do apologize, however, if there are some counselors who do not understand this. However, because of your experience and the length of time you have been on this journey, I trust you to have a feel for the right touch in dealing with this. Does this help answer your questions?

Provincial Chaplain Robert Goode (Gooch) died Francistide 1998.

Remembrance of Gooch

Masud Ibn Syedullah (Franciscan Times Fall 1998)

Provincial Chaplain Marie Webner Presenting Robert (Gooch) Good With a Commendation.

I remember Gooch as a person who naturally exhibited qualities of humility and joy. He was my immediate predecessor as Provincial Chaplain for the Third Order. One of the things I remember most about him was the way he responded to me being selected to be the next Chaplain. I was greatly moved when, after Chapter ratified the Provincial Minister's nomination that I be Chaplain, he began right away to plan an induction service. It was marvelous! Not only was the rite constructed well, eloquently expressing the duties and responsibilities of the Chaplain, but also Gooch's joy permeated the event. It was as if he were handing over, not only the symbols of office, but a part of himself as well, as a personal gift. He embodied for me, in those arts, the Franciscan ideal of egalitarian relationships. It was from him that I discovered much of what it means to humbly serve and, when the time comes, to joyfully celebrate and support the gifts and ministry of those who follow–to cheer them on.

Election of Masud Ibn Syedullah, TSSF Chaplain 1985-88

Little Chronicle 1985

Masud is the first chief pastor to have developed his vocation as a Franciscan entirely as a member of the Third Order. (Gooch had begun his Formation as a First Order Brother.) Masud's election as chaplain is a significant new move in the life of the Third Order towards autonomy and self-development. For the first sixty years of its existence in the Episcopal Church, the Order was run by a friar-priest. But as research into the early Franciscan roots has shown, the Third Order that St. Francis founded was intended to be an autonomous, self-supporting organization.

Making Chapter More Internationally Representative

In 1986 Ewan Macpherson, editor of *Caritas* (Eastern Canada fellowship newsletter), convener of the Toronto Fellowship, and Area Chaplain, was elected a member of Chapter, but, prior to taking up his duties, received a call from a parish in the UK and thus left the Province. In 1989, in the next round of Chapter elections, Ewan's successor as Convener of the Toronto fellowship, Warren Beal, was elected to Chapter. However, before he took his place on Chapter, he asked to be released from vows. Ruth Duncan of Ontario was then appointed to join the Chapter with voice and vote, and, subsequently when another person resigned from Chapter, Ruth was appointed to fill out that member's term, becoming the first Canadian to be part of the elected Chapter. (Muriel Adey, also a Canadian, was an ex-officio member of Chapter when she was Women's Formation Director at the end of John Scott's terms.)

Presence on Chapter for members from Trinidad and Tobago happened a bit quicker. In 1982, Jackie Richards was invited to attend Chapter, and, in 1985, she became the "Caribbean Representative" and reported to Chapter on events in the Caribbean and South America. In 1989, Jackie became Assistant Formation Director for the Caribbean, and, in 1992, both Jackie and Gloria Waldron were elected to Chapter from the Carribean.

TSSF Formation Moved Franciscanism Beyond The Anglican Communion

(1) Order of Ecumenical Franciscans

From OEF Website, "How It All Began" 2008

In 1980, Dale Trana (name later changed to Dale Carmen) petitioned the Third Order to accept her as a postulant, so that she could learn the spiritual disciplines with guidance. [*Ed. Very much like Father Joseph in 1914 who went to* the *Society of the Divine Compassion (SDC) in England for Formation. He, however, was refused.*] Even though she was a United Church of Christ pastor, she was accepted into the formation program,which became a river of life-giving water to a parched soul. At this same time, God's mysterious planning brought Ron Nuss-Warren, Charles Maxfield, Dale Carmen, and their families together on a farm in North Dakota. It was there that they discovered common ground in the search for spiritual growth. They longed to be nurtured by a Christian community called to serve Christ in the spirit of Saint Francis. Ron, Charles and

Dale were all pastors in the United Church of Christ serving small churches in North Dakota, and they realized the importance Francis gave to accountability in the church. Therefore, they sought obedience and responsibility through proper channels in the United Church of Christ. For the next three years, letters flew between UCC dignitaries, TSSF officers, and an increasingly excited trio of dreamers who sought to form an expression of Franciscan community within the protection and direction of the United Church of Christ.

In August of 1983, Ron Nuss-Warren, Charles Maxfield and Dale Carmen claimed an empty room at Annunciation Priory south of Bismarck, North Dakota, and began to hammer out, sentence by sentence, word by word, a General Rule and Principles for yet another expression of Franciscan community. Their primary building blocks came from Francis' "Rule of 1221" and "Rule of 1223" as expressed in *Source Documents: For the Living Tradition of the Society of St. Francis* (commonly known as the *Book of Roots*) published by the Society of St. Francis.

Over 90% of the words of the "General Rule" and "Principles" of the Order come from these primary documents, and only thosewords were changed that were necessary to have this new Franciscan Order be inclusive of all Christian denominations. After three long days of work and prayer, a fledgling "Rule" and "Principles" were ready for review by the sisters and brothers in established Franciscan communities. Through the grace of God, Br. Robert Hugh, SSF, was nearby in Minneapolis, Minnesota (only 500 miles away!). Dale Carmen hand-delivered the new "Rule" and "Principles" for his scrutiny. Graciously, Brother Robert Hugh offered to stop in North Dakota on his way to California to discuss possible corrections in the document.

On the plains, scattered clouds on the horizon are reason to hope that God may gather them into a thunderhead laden with rain for parched earth. And so it seemed the will of the Lord when, on November 22, 1983, Ron Nuss-Warren, Charles Maxfield and Dale Carmen met a notary at the bank in Parshall, North Dakota, and signed papers of incorporation (by the State of North Dakota) for the Third Order of St. Francis–United Church of Christ. On that same evening, a "Celebrating Birth" service was held at the Parshall United Church of Christ. The main speakers were Rev. George Metcalf, Chaplain of the Minnesota Fellowship of TSSF, and Rev. Marwood Rettig, Conference Minister of the North Dakota Conference of the United Church of Christ. Witnessing to the spirit of ecumenism, the service was blessed by the Lutheran minister, Assembly of God pastor, and Roman Catholic priest–all from Parshall–and the Sisters of the Benedictine Priory at Garrison, North Dakota. Fumiko, a Japanese exchange student, played classical music; the choir offered up "Seek Ye First" and the local priest sang the "Prayer of Saint Francis," accompanied by a Vietnamese-born guitarist.

During the service, the Rev. Metcalf read a framed parchment signed by Provincial officers, blessing us with these words:

We the capitular tertiaries of the American Province of the Third Order of the Society of St. Francis greet you as you begin to provide for a Franciscan expression of the Gospel life in your part of the Lord's vineyard. We pledge to you our fellowship, and our concern and those sharings that occur between brothers and sisters. May your walk in the steps of the Little Poor Man of Assisi be one blessed with peace and perseverance.

The blessing from TSSF was followed by the reading of the Rule and Principles of the new Order. The Rev. Metcalf received the vows of Profession from Dale Carmen, and Dale received the vows of intention to the postulancy from Ron Nuss-Warren and Charles Maxfield. Later, seventy-some worshippers gathered for fellowship in the church basement. A tangible sense of hope and joy permeated the gathering as though they had, indeed, become instruments of God's peace. In some humble way, there was a sense that they had participated in one of God's awesome mysteries.

(2) Secular Franciscans Order (Roman Catholic)

From the OEF Website, "A Little History of OEF Roots," January 2012

[W] hen in 1966 Brother Paul OSF was elected to be the new Minister Provincial, he had a vision for the Third Order that would have it stand free and clear as an Order in its own right, with its own leadership, pastoring and formation, parallel with rather than dependent upon or defined by the life of the Friars and Sisters. When Br. Luke SSF became Minister Provincial in 1970 he supported that vision and over the next eight years, first Br. Robert Hugh and then Br. Mark Francis, had the task of "working themselves out of a job" as Friar Chaplain to the Third Order, visiting fellowships and individual tertiaries to share this vision. So since the late seventies, the Third Order has directed its own life. Peter Funk and Marie Hayes were the first tertiaries to lead Novice Formation, John Scott to lead Administration, and Robert Goode to provide Chaplaincy.

A later Director of Formation was Glen Ann Jicha of Chicago. Glen Ann was working in [*Ed. Chicago's*] Loop and started regularly attending the OFM parish St. Peters. Benet Fonck OFM became Glen Ann's spiritual director, and Benet Fonck was the friar responsible for the Third Order groups in the Province of OFM. He became interested in the structure being developed by the TSSF. Shortly thereafter, Benet was taken to Rome by the American Minister General John Vaughn to become the Friar responsible for the Third Order. Benet took with him the TSSF structure and *Formation Letters,* and, over the next few years in conversation with the OFM Caps and the OFM Conv, SFO was born as the modern expression of the Secular Third Order. The American TSSF structure largely influenced the SFO structure over the 1970s. It is quite amazing the degree of consultation between Anglican and Roman Catholic Franciscans at this time around Third Order structure.

Factoids of the Dee Dobson Era

1981: Fifty people attend Province's first regional convocation in the Northeast.

1982: TSSF joins with the Roman Catholic SFO in the National Franciscan Communication Conference.

- "Convocation" designated to mean not only Chapter-sponsored Provincial meetings but also fellowship-sponsored regional meeting
- International Roman Catholic Congress (CIOF) held in Rome invites Anglican/Episcopal representatives to attend for the first time: John Scott, Dee Dobson, Anita and David Catron from the American Province and Richard Scott from the European Province.

1983: The majority of the professed are not pledging; 1985 finds that less than 300 out of 700 members pledge

- Ken Cox, Men's Formation Director, dies. Alden Whitney becomes the new Men's Formation Director.
- Marie Webner begins drafting the first *Fellowship Convener's Handbook*

1984: Dee Dobson re-elected as Guardian

- Masud Ibn Syedullah elected as first Provincial Chaplain after Robert Goode retires as Chaplain
- MaryAnn Jackman creates the *Dancing Francis* (below) as the American Province's logo

1986: To parallel First Order nomenclature, Chapter votes to rename the "Guardian" as "Minister Provincial"

- TSSF is recognized by the House of Bishops as a Christian Community and enters ECUSA's annual Red Book for the first time

1987: At the end of the Inter-Provincial Third Order Chapter (IPTOC)–the highest level of legislative authority in the world-wide Third Order–TSSF elects Bob Pope of the European Province as its first Minister General of the Third Order

1988: Jack Stapleton elected as Provincial Chaplain resigns within one week; Alden Whitney appointed Interim Chaplain

1989: Chapter studies the possibility of moving the 1991 Chapter meeting to the Caribbean (Chapter 1990 proposed taking a future Chapter meeting to Trinidad in 1993; Chapter 1991 voted down the proposal to take Chapter outside the US)

- Marie Webner is elected as Provincial Chaplain; Anita Catron takes over as Fellowship Coordinator
- Br. Dunstan leaves Trinidad and Tobago ending the First Order presence on these islands
- 50% of professed are not reporting annually; and only one third of Area Chaplains are reporting annually

1990: Ruth Duncan, a Canadian, is invited to Chapter with voice and vote

- 50% of members still not pledging

The Future of the Third Order

Memo by Marie Webner addressed to "My fellow members of Chapter" March 26, 1985.

...Does it occur to you that we are in a singularly unattractive adolescent stage of development? We have simply not decided what we want to be or how to go about it (whatever it is). We wobble....Until we decide what we want to be and how to go about it, we obviously are in no position to take risks. In the long run, however, if we take no risks, we will never reach maturity (that is, our full potential).

I am convinced that a great deal of our identity crisis has its roots in our inability to find a model. We look for one in the First Order, but the model there is not completely appropriate to our large numbers, our scattered members, and the diversity of our members (especially the diversity in understanding). When we turn to the Roman Church for a model, we find that the hierarchical and priest-dominated authoritarianism there is also inappropriate to the Third Order of St. Francis in the Episcopal Church. Another model might be found in professional nonprofit associations, but the goals of these organizations are far removed from our own imperatives. We have already discarded the Third Order model in England because the friars there are sufficiently numerous to continue to provide direction, specifically in the form of a full-time Friar Chaplain.

I believe that our first task as Chapter members is to recognize our uniqueness. Yes, our uniqueness. We can learn from the examples provided by the First Order, the Secular Franciscans, and professional organizations, but we will not find any of these models adequate to our own unique situation.

The first point, then, is that we need to be creative and open-minded in seeking our identity as it unfolds in the patterns of our administrative actions....

How Did Dee Ever Become a Tertiary?

"A Meeting of Franciscans" by Bill Graham, Summer 1998, Franciscan Times

Dee: The Offices were the main reason that I didn't join a lot earlier. I was teaching and just couldn't work them in. We're a lot more flexible now. Tertiaries once wore a garment called a scapular and were to keep their membership rather secret. They were not to wear their profession crosses outside. Now, we encourage them to do so.

Fr. Bill: Dee, who was your counselor when you were a novice?

Dee: I had Peter Funk, and he was excellent. Peter was a freelance writer and still does the monthly "Word Power" section in the *Reader's Digest* magazine. He wrote our first set of Formation Letters.

Fr. Bill: I've met Peter several times, and I've quoted from his letters in sermons, retreat meditations, and Cursillo talks. You couldn't have had anyone better. How did you become interested in the Order?

Dee: I was looking for something to deepen my spiritual life. Brother Dunstan was a particularly strong influence on me.

Fr. Bill: That sounds pretty much the case for me as well. I was influenced by Fr. Scott and Br. Robert Hugh, the First Order Visitor, when I joined. How has the Order changed since you joined?

Dee: I mentioned the reorganization of 1972. Br. Robert deserves much of the credit for that happening. Others helping were Fr. John Scott, Helen Webb, Fr. Warren Tange, Fr. Robert Goode, and myself. We were still under the First Order, but were given a lot more control. We had our own Guardian. John was our first one and served six years in that capacity. I was Guardian for nine years. In 1981, we strengthened our international ties, becoming completely autonomous in 1987.

Denalta (Dee) Dobson died August 15, 2001 in Miami, Florida

Julia Bergstrom, Provincial Chaplain, Franciscan Times

There were expressions of grief at the service, but Dee's family and friends, especially her children, made the open house a joyous occasion. This was the first time I had met her children, and I think they're wonderful. As we know, Dee had many children besides the six biological ones. In fact, several people who were friends of her children in high school flew in because Dee was their mother too. In her honor, her children made her lasagna and key lime pie recipes, enough for 75 at the open house. At the funeral, Br. Robert Hugh celebrated the Eucharist, and Br. Dunstan preached, using the last chapter of Proverbs. We sang "All creatures of our God and King," "Joyful, joyful we adore thee," and "Lord, make us servants of your peace." "The Canticle of the Sun" was printed on the back of the program. Her obituary, written by Bill, Jr., talked about her participation in TSSF. We thank you, God, for Dee's life and witness. There is rejoicing in heaven!

(Left to right) Dee Dobson, Maryann Jackman (creator of the Dancing Francis logo), and Alden Whitney (next Minister Provincial).

References

Maynard, Joanne. *The Burning Mushroom: And Other Epiphanies.* Cincinnati, Ohio: Forward Movement, 1980.

Chapter 7: Alden Whitney, Minister Provincial (1990-1996) and First Minister General from the Province of the Americas (1993-1999)

Expeditious Rise in the Order

Alden's journey through the Order was the most expeditious of any Minister Provincial (and probably any Minister General):

- 1981, in December, Alden was professed.
- 1982, in November, he was recruited to be the Men's Formation Director upon the death of the incumbent, Ken Cox.
- 1983, Alden was ordained as a deacon.
- 1984, Alden was ordained as a priest.
- 1988, when Jack Stapleton resigned as Chaplain after one week, Alden became Acting Chaplain as well as continuing his work as Formation Director for Men.
- 1990, he was elected Minister Provincial.
- 1993, he was re-elected Minister Provincial and, later that same year, Minister General of the Third Order.

The Big Topics Return

The 1980s and the era of Dee Dobson yielded few "big" topics over which TSSF had to wrestle. John Scott's era had women's ordination and gay ordination. Now with the turn of the decade, the "big" topics reappeared with which TSSF had to wrestle. This time it was primarily affirmation and respect for gay rights.

At the 1990 Chapter in which Alden, an openly gay man, was elected Minister Provincial, Chapter passed the following resolution with one abstention:

> *Whereas there has been growing concern about the prejudice and discrimination that have existed in the Episcopal/Anglican Church toward lesbians and gay men,*
>
> *Whereas we, as a religious Order, have pledged to fight against all ignorance, pride and prejudice that breed injustice or partiality,*
>
> *Therefore, be it resolved that we, the Chapter of the Third Order of the Society of St. Francis, American Province, affirm that Christ indwells all persons regardless of sexual orientation; we affirm that we welcome to our services of worship and to all occasions for fellowship all persons; and we affirm*

Anita Catron Miner and Alden Whitney on the steps at Little Portion

that we welcome and encourage full membership in this Order for persons of all sexual orientations.

Further, we encourage those of us who would do so, to educate ourselves and others in the Church about the current pressing issue of lesbians and gay men in a society that is frequently hostile to them; and we commit ourselves to action to end ignorance about, prejudice toward, and discrimination against lesbians and gay men in the Episcopal/Anglican Church and in society at large. (Information Sheet October/November 1990*)*

During the following Chapter (1991), Ken Norian spoke for many in saying that he was troubled by the disunity in the Province and in the Episcopal Church and wanted Chapter to create some bridge between those with traditional beliefs in regards sexuality and those who support same-sex sexuality. Alden as Minister Provincial and Marie Webner as Provincial Chaplain produced the following letter that was then sent out to all members in March 1992:

Dear Sisters & Brothers of the Third Order,

At its annual meeting in October 1991, Chapter was asked by a professed tertiary to affirm a resolution stating that Chapter will surely accommodate differences of opinion concerning moral and theological issues held by various Third Order members in a way that strengthens our fellowship and affirms each member of the Order. All the members of Chapter were in profound agreement with the spirit of the resolution and requested that the Minister Provincial and the Chaplain address the issues in a letter to all tertiaries.

The Rule of the Third Order defines our way of life. It not only supplies the aims of our community, but also provides the ways in which we can serve Christ and the world in the manner of Francis of Assisi. It declares that humility, love and joy are the three notes that mark the lives of tertiaries; without them all efforts are vain. "Where charity and love prevail, there our God is found."

When we are admitted by profession to the Order, each of us pledges to serve Jesus Christ for the rest of our lives, seeking to spread the knowledge and love of Christ, to promote the spirit of love and unity within the family of God, and to live joyfully a life of simplicity and humble service. Therefore, the life of every tertiary must reflect obedience to the principles we have espoused, and the vows that we have made. In these tenets that make up the Franciscan focus, we affirm that the center of our faith is always Jesus Christ, our Lord & Savior. Our preoccupation with Jesus encourages us to live joyfully a life of love leading to sacrifice, and thus, God's purposes are served.

The concerns of Third Order members reflect the concerns of the greater Episcopal Church. We need not rehearse here the details of the issues involving ordination, inclusive language, committed relationships, marriage, and sexuality—to name most of them. In deliberations about the questions, the role of tradition is sometimes measured against the evolution of society (or the dissolution of society, depending on one's point of view). The tried-and-true tripartite approach to solving theological and moral problems by using Scripture, Tradition and Reason seems to have led not to consensus but, instead, to diverse points of view often accompanied by fear and acrimony. In some instances, what one person views as a matter of much needed justice, another sees as a betrayal of moral tradition or of Scriptural theology. Neither "conservatives" nor "liberals" have sole claim to feeling pain, outrage and sadness. There are people of all persuasions who consider leaving the Episcopal Church (and The Society of Saint Francis) in order to maintain integrity of conscience.

How can we respond to divisiveness in our Church and Third Order community? How can we accommodate differences of opinion concerning moral and theological issues? Some say that the Church is in the process of defining the boundaries of the faith. Perhaps the danger in focusing on the boundaries is that of turning attention away from the interior of the faith. Shouldn't we focus much more attention on the essence, the interior center of our faith? The peril of failing to accommodate our differences is of losing the faith altogether.

We are Franciscans who have promised to follow Christ. As the Rule states: "Love is the distinguishing feature of all true disciples of Christ who wish to dedicate themselves to Him as his servants.... Tertiaries seek to love all those to whom they are bound by ties of family or friendship. Their love for them increases, as their love for Christ grows deeper.... Tertiaries have a special love and affection for members of the Third Order, praying for each other individually and seeking to grow in that love." As Christians, we promise to put love first by seeking and serving Christ in all persons, and by respecting the dignity of all persons.

Let each of us commit ourselves again to respecting the views of every brother and sister tertiary. Let each of us love the other so that we are truly "bound into a living whole through [God's] supernatural love.... This unity of those who believe in him will become, as our Lord intended, a special witness to the world of his divine mission."

With this letter you will find a copy of "The Rule of the Third Order of The Society of Saint Francis (For Daily Reading)." It is commended to all tertiaries by all the Ministers Provincial and is being circulated in all five provinces of The Third Order. We pray it will be helpful in your prayer and study, and will promote unity among all tertiaries.

Second Largest Exodus in Provincial History With Resulting Financial Problems.

Within eight months of receipt of this letter from Alden and Marie Webner, 31 people asked for release from their vows or withdrew from Formation, and some found their way to the conservative Anglican Order, Franciscan Order of the Divine Compassion (FODC) (see page 62). The following year, 1993, 43 people asked for release from their vows or withdrew from Formation. Such numbers were double the average (1989 to 1998 Withdrawn/Released/Lapsed as listed in the issues of the *Information Sheet*). This is the second largest exodus from the Order after the 119 withdrew in 1967. The fallout from such an exodus on the parish level is usually severe financial problems. The Order proved no different. At the 1994 Chapter, the Provincial Bursar announced that provincial funds would fall short by $2000 for costs already incurred, and that additional outreach funding for Franciscan Aid and others would have to be postponed. In the soul-searching triggered by this exodus and financial problem, Provincial Chaplain Marie Webner had a theory about what could possibly explain this new exodus. She pointed to the uneven evolution of provincial members moving from an understanding of the Third Order as a "pious guild" of individuals to a community of a religious Order.

Pious Guild to Religious Order: From the Late 1940s and Early 50s to the 1990s

Letter of May 1993 from Chaplain Webner to a tertiary Professed 46 Years

...my very personal experience of it is not unlike your own except that I had the good fortune to have been in the right places at the right times, so that I knew what was going on and was a part of the changes that took place after 1967. I've been on Chapter from the beginning, and so I can certainly share the blame for whatever went wrong and whatever went right. The retreat I conducted after Easter was in Hawaii, where I renewed friendship ties with Gooch (Fr. Robert Goode), who was the first tertiary to serve as chaplain of the Third Order. Prior to that time we had had friars as chaplains. And, of course, I remember the time when the only response to a report (which was a checklist of omissions) was a penance–for women, from the Poor Clares. Anyway—Gooch commented to other tertiaries present that "Marie has been professed in the Third Order since the time it was a pious guild." I thought about that remark and decided Gooch was right. When I was professed in 1953, the Third Order was a pious guild. A guild is, by definition, an association of persons with like interests, and, although members of the Third Order rarely were acquainted with one another, we presumably had a rule of life and an attraction to a Franciscan lifestyle in common. We were required to keep in touch with First or Second Order, but we were not a community. As you well know, all that has changed. When the House of Bishops recognized the Third Order SSF as a "religious community" of the Episcopal Church, it accepted what had been born in the more than 20 years since 1967 (the year of the amalgamation of American and British Franciscan Orders).

So what's good about becoming a community? One of the things I pointed out in my talk in Dallas is that we now have a community network which serves to sound alarms. Part of my experience as a tertiary in 1960 was being in the most extraordinary isolation when my husband was having a breakdown and our marriage was breaking wide open as a result...I knew no other Episcopal clergy, and had no avenue to find support. The bishop who ended up deposing my husband did not strike me as a likely candidate. It is my sincere hope that such a situation will never again occur in the life of a Third Order member. If the Area Chaplain is not a person a member wants to turn to, there are other local members, the Minister Provincial, the Chaplain—or perhaps simply a kindred spirit met and enjoyed at a Third Order convocation. Certainly, I got through my particular hell with a vivid realization of and thanksgiving for the presence of God through it all, but I believe firmly that God normally works through community. Almighty God expects normally to work through members of Christ's Body the Church. I believe we are failing in our vocation as Christians and as Franciscans when we fail to be there for fellow Christians in their need. I believe, in other words, very firmly in the need for community. A pious guild is not a bad thing at all, but to be an organic, dynamic, creative community in touch with the will of God and the need of our brothers and sisters is a far better thing. My particular need was critical and traumatic; I cite it only to make a point. There are other needs, greater and smaller, that a community can and should be offering one another. There are other cases where the parish is not the appropriate community, or the informed community. In our very mobile population, the Third Order is often a point of stability in an otherwise formless chaos.

So what's bad about becoming community? It's the same thing that's bad about the Church in general: we are corrupted by the sins of society, and we fail to become what God intends for us. But it's not only sin and failure. With all the best intentions in the world, we simply make mistakes....In line with your definition of obedience ("to listen earnestly"), I would surmise that we failed in obedience. We did not listen earnestly to you and to the rest of the local fellowship. In all honesty, I have to say that my recollection is that the Formation team (backed up by Chapter) proceeded on the best information available, and I cannot say dogmatically that a mistake was made. But I also feel that members in profession, our brothers and sisters, need to be listened to. They need to feel that we have taken time to listen earnestly. They have every right to be part of the process. Being part of the process may or may not affect the ultimate action, which, after all, cannot be made on the basis of a vote! I do not figure that this is comforting input from me. But, after all, I've been around for donkey's years, and I know we make mistakes. I also know that these decisions are extraordinarily painful and are never lightly made. It's a terrible thing, this business of having to say Yes or No to people who are sure they have a Franciscan vocation. If we say Yes to the wrong people, it will hurt their lives and the community; if we say No to the wrong people, it will do the same. The responsibility is awesome, and decisions are not made without prayer, thought, and consultation.

I hope you will forgive us for making mistakes. Chapter is an elected body, and democratic process confers the right to question. Whoever had the nerve to question in Father Joseph's day? His No was No and his Yes was Yes. If you didn't like his answers, you either shut up or got out. If I had received a message from on high that a friend of mind was "unsuitable for life in the Third Order," I would have considered it a matter of obedience to accept without question.

The Membership Responds Positively—1995 Finances

Perhaps those remaining in the Province after this second exodus remained with a renewed sense of the Third Order as a community that Marie Webner described for within a year the financial crisis was over.

> *1995 has brought an excellent recovery of our financial position. We were able to pay all our debts for 1994, and to enter the 4th quarter of 1995 with a bank balance of over $16,000. The membership of the Order responded to our appeal for help with great generosity—$6,000 plus $1,500 found in Hawaii, project money which had never been spent. Our economic measures regarding travel have helped as well. (from the Minister Provincial Report to Chapter, October 1995)*

Marie Webner, Long-time Servant in the Order

Marie was professed in 1953, and the part of her life prior to the late 60s and the merger of OSF and SSF is told by her in Chapter 2. In 1971, at the time when members of the Third Order took over the leadership of the Order, Marie became involved in most everything from the beginning. As she wrote: "We were privileged to be in on all the "firsts" in terms of statutes, formation program, and fellowship guidelines. Much has changed for the better over the years–but oh! it was exhilarating to lay the first bricks in the Third Order structure."

In 1971 she was appointed Asst. Novice Mistress for Women under Peter Funk's direction. In 1974, she was elected to Chapter, which she served for two terms until 1980. As managing editor of the University of Arizona Press, she used her word-smithing and publishing experience to work on multiple editions of the *Devotional Companion* beginning in 1981. (I joined her efforts for the 3rd edition that came out in 1994.)

Although there were people who worked with Fellowships prior to Marie's appointment as Fellowship Coordinator in 1982, it was really Marie's efforts conjoined with Dee Dobson's focus on the local and regional that changed the face of the Order in the 80s. Directly arising from her work as Fellowship Coordinator, Chaplain Masud Ibn Syedullah appointed her as his Assistant Chaplain to focus on the work of the Area Chaplains.

In 1989, she was elected Provincial Chaplain. As Fellowship Coordinator and Provincial Chaplain Marie wrote more articles for the *Franciscan Times* than any other member of the Order. None were just fluff pieces announcing meetings or reporting on Area Convocations; her's were substantive: "Fellowship as Partnership" (1977); "Gift" A Poem On The Death of My Father (1981); "Community in Fellowship" (1982); "Community Events for Fellowships: Professions and Novice Admissions" (1983); and then her "Chaplain's Journal" that appeared in each issue of the *Franciscan Times* from 1991 to 1994. In 1994 Minister Provincial Alden Whitney proposed her third term re-appointment as Provincial Chaplain, but this re-appointment was not sustained by the vote of Chapter.

Chapter Does Not Sustain Webner's 3rd Term Appointment

From the *Admonitions of St. Francis:* Number 4. Let no one appropriate to himself the role of being over others.

> *"He did not come to be ministered unto, but to minister," says the Lord. Let those, who are set up over others, glory as much on account of that office of superior, as if they were appointed to the duty of washing the feet of the brothers. And, in as much as they are so greatly disturbed on account of the loss of their office of superior than the duty regarding feet, they assemble purses for themselves to the danger of their souls.*

(The footwashing mentioned was not the Holy Thursday ritual, but the duty of cleaning the their fellow friars' barefeet that had trod roads along with horses and other animals. The reference to the "purse" was to the "purse" in the keeping of Judas from which he was suppose to have stolen.)

From an interview with a Chapter member present at the time
Marie Webner had always wanted to be Chaplain. She had been so much a part of the Province for so long that everyone just took for granted that her appointment as Chaplain would be fine and solve a big problem—chaplains are hard to find. Gooch retired after 12 years, and Masud was elected as the next chaplain but served for only one term. The next Chaplain to be appointed was Jack Stapleton, and he had to be replaced within a week by Alden who only agreed to serve on a temporary basis. When Marie was appointed as Chaplain, it worked beautifully for a while, but then there started to be "glitches".

She began making decisions without consulting with others, and changing set programs that others had worked out without first checking with them or anyone else. For example, she wanted to get the *Devotional Companion* printed in a certain way. When it came back from the printer, the page numbers were off from what she wanted. She then spent a huge amount of money to have them completely reprinted; again, without consulting with anyone.

We all arrived at chapter that year in 1994 with the idea that we couldn't vote for her to continue in a third term as Chaplain in the fashion she was demonstrating. None of us had talked to each other about it, it was just a consensus we all arrived at separately from observing her actions. Alden did his level best to help her understand and to prepare her for what he could guess was coming before the vote was taken, but she was not open to it. He tried to get her to withdraw before the vote, but she would have none of that. It was heartbreaking because

she couldn't see it coming, did not understand why people did not want her to continue, and considered the chaplaincy as her right. I remember that, through the entire Chapter vote, flocks of crows were flying around Little Portion, cawing and carrying on.

Webner's Freedom

A 1997 note three years later from Marie Webner
I feel a wonderful freedom to express my opinion these days. I do not want an office or influence. I want to be free to be the person I want to be, pursuing the interests that I have not been free to pursue while working for money or for TSSF....I have sent a finished piece of writing off to a publisher. I think it would be a miracle if I did not get rejections before acceptance, but I feel really good about being embarked on this third career of my lifetime.

Marie Webner died in February 2015.

Factoids of the Alden Whitney Era

1990—With Alden's election, he leaves the Formation Program; Ann Harris is elected as the first person to lead a Formation Program for both Men & Women

1991—Robert Durand and Rik Fitch take over as editors of the *Franciscan Times* and move it beyond physical cut-and-paste into digital desktop publishing with an improved and unified layout

1993—Having just been re-elected for a second term as Minister Provincial, Whitney hosted IPTOC at Little Portion Friary, and was elected Minister General for a term of three years. (Only currently serving Minister Provincials can be candidates for Minister General. Moreover, at this time, one could serve simultaneously as both Minister Provincial and Minister General. However, such simultaneous service is less than optimal, and the Order's Statutues were subsequently re-written so that upon election as a Minister General, one must resign as a Minister Provincial. Thus only Alden Whitney has ever had a three-year coterminous term as both Minister Provincial and Minister General.)

1995—Chapter decides to hold the first Provincial Convocation in over a decade in New Orleans in 1997 and makes Fellowship Coordinator, Anita Catron, leader of this effort. At this point, Nobel Peace Prize winner, Archbishop Desmond Tutu, TSSF agreed to be the keynote speaker.

Ministers General in TSSF

Robert Pope (European Province)	1987-1993
Brian Hamilton (New Zealand Province)	1993-1996
Alden Whitney (American Province)	1996-1999
Keith Slater (Australian Province)	1999-2005
Dorothy Brooker (New Zealand Province)	2005-2011
Ken Norian (Province of the Americas)	2011-2017

Homily delivered by The Rev. Alden Whitney, retiring Minister General on 26 September 1999 in St. Lucia, Queensland, Australia at His Final IPTOC

(See Anita Catron's experience at this IPTOC on page 137)

The text I've chosen for this afternoon is taken from Luke's Gospel, Chapter 24, verse 23: *they came back and told us that they had indeed seen a vision of angels who said that he [Jesus] was alive*."

This service of prayer, renewal of vows, and the installation of Keith Slater to be the fourth Minister General of The Third Order comes at the end of a wonderful week of collaboration and fellowship amongst all the Orders of The Society of Saint Francis. I daresay, our being here together is the actualization of a dream, a vision (if you will) received by many of us quite a long time ago.

Dreams and visions and voices from God have been integral in the Franciscan story. Furthermore, we were reminded earlier this week that all humans possess the divine capacity to dream dreams and to actualize them.

Bonaventure tells us that as "Francis left town to meditate out-of-doors....and as he was passing by the Church of San Damiano which was threatening to collapse with age, he felt urged to go in and pray. There, as he knelt to prayer before the painted image of the Crucified, he felt greatly comforted in spirit and his eyes were full of tears as he gazed at the cross. Then all of a sudden he heard a voice coming from the cross, and telling him three times, 'Francis go and repair my house. You see it is falling down.' Francis (says Bonaventure) was terrified at the sound of the voice, but the power of its message penetrated his heart and he went into ecstasy." We know of course that Francis took the urging literally for some time until Holy Spirit clarified for him the intention of the voice that he had heard.

In a similar vein, Pope Innocent Ill received messages from God and one of them occurred in a dream whilst he was asleep. There is that image of the Pontiff lying in bed asleep with his head propped on his hand—as if he had dropped off into slumber as he was reading—and he dreams that the Church is falling over, so that it lies tilted and useless. And we know that after that, the Pope legitimized the ways and mission of Francis' growing band of Little Brothers. Their Rule and the Principles it embodied were affirmed, and the Order grew and became influential, and effective in its aim to spread the Gospel and, in doing so, to emulate Jesus in lives which embraced poverty.

We all have dreams which may convey pertinent messages for us. There is one dream I recall which I dreamed twenty-five years ago. In it, I was lying in hospital in bed, having had a serious chest operation. The surgeon stood at my bedside and told me: "I regret to tell you, Dr. Whitney, but we opened your chest and examined your lungs. Unfortunately, it was too late, for we saw that your chest is riddled with lung cancer, so we just closed you up.

The dream had a powerful effect upon me. I woke up at once, aghast at the message of the dream, but grateful that it was indeed a dream. I had been a smoker for 24 years, and was still smoking at least 30 cigarettes a day. But somehow that dream had the power to kill the denial that had kept me smoking. And later that day, as I was driving somewhere in the car, I opened the window and threw an almost whole pack of cigarettes out the window. And that (by the grace of God) marked the first day that I began to think of myself as a non-smoker. And my life was changed. I had smoked my last tobacco.

In the Luke's story about "The Walk to Emmaus" there are some women who had told Cleopas and his companion that they had been that morning to the tomb where the body of Jesus had been lain—that the body of Jesus was gone but that they had encountered angels in a vision who delivered to them a message that Jesus was alive. And of course we know how the story goes on from that point.

The Interprovincial Chapter of The Third Order has a story to tell this week. It's a story inspired in part at least by the vision we gleaned from studying a passage from William Countryman's book, *The Good News of Jesus*. This is what it says:

> *"The GOOD NEWS offers only one principle for interaction among human beings. That principle is the equal love of self and neighbor. Every action is good insofar as it conforms to it and bad insofar as it doesn't. It is the principle that must guide both our private, and wherever possible, our public lives if we wish to be people who live out of THE GOOD NEWS .... To move toward a world in which the principle of love is taken seriously will still be a long and difficult process, but it should be possible now in ways that it has not been in the past. We have had ample evidence in this century of the terrible wrongs worked by ethnic and racial hatreds by the contempt of one class for another, or by sexual arrogance. The world will not be safe for any of us until it is safe for us all. However difficult the principle of love, and however demanding and hard at times to define, love is the only moral principle that opens a door to the future. When I truly believe that I am as human as you and you are as human as I, that God loves us indistinguishably, I shall begin building a different kind of world."*

IPTOC has seen a vision of angels who say that Jesus is alive. Tertiaries in all the five provinces have talked about our Third Order as a people knit together in prayer and community, open and ready to include all people. I daresay we have been flexing and stretching this week, as we explored the themes, and formulated concrete proposals which are meant to encourage provinces as a whole, and fellowships and individuals as the parts thereof. We have celebrated our diversity, and asked each tertiary to be risky in embracing and implementing in their lives particularly the 7th, 8th and 9th days of our Principles.

I think its worthwhile to rehearse them again. And some of you may hear some slight but important changes in the wording of them.

Day Seven—The Second Aim To spread the spirit of love and harmony. The Order sets out, in the name of Christ, to break down barriers between people and to seek equality for all. Tertiaries accept as their second aim the spreading of a spirit of love and harmony among all people. They are pledged to fight against the ignorance, pride, and prejudice that breed injustice or partiality because of distinctions of race, gender, sexual orientation, color, class, creed, status, or education.

Day Eight—(The Second Aim cont'd) Tertiaries fight against all such injustice in the name of Christ, in whom there can be neither Jew nor Greek, slave nor free, male nor female; for in him all are one. Their chief object is to reflect that openness to all which was characteristic of Jesus. This can only be achieved in a spirit of chastity which sees others as belonging to God and not as a means of self-fulfillment.

Day Nine—(The Second Aim cont'd) Tertiaries are prepared not only to speak out for social justice and international peace, but to put these principles into practice in their own lives, cheerfully facing any scorn or persecution to which this may lead.

So, we have dreamed dreams this week and seen visions and heard voices dreams and visions, and voices that declare again that Jesus is alive. And in doing so, I think that our vocations have been renewed once again, and that we have been empowered to carry away from this beautiful place the fruits of our work to the more than 30 countries where tertiaries live. Pray with us please, that the renewal we have begun here is in fact just a beginning. AMEN

The Rev. Alden Whitney died May 20, 2000.

Minister General, Provincial Minister of the American Province, Priest, Doctor, Psychotherapist, Sheep Farmer, Friend, A Beloved Child of God

Recollections on Alden Whitney

Muriel Adey

I was not privileged to know Brother Alden as well as many of you: he came onto Chapter after I stepped down in '81, and was only present for half a day at the most recent Chapter where once again I was a member. However, that is not to say that Alden did not greatly influence my life!

In the late 80's and early 90's, I was feeling very ambivalent about continuing to renew my vow and pledge in the American Province of TSSF. Only my Spiritual Director knew how agonized I was. Out of the blue I got a phone call from Alden to say he would be in Vancouver for a conference, and could I hitch a ride on a ferry and meet him for lunch. I did. I was able to freely share my conflicted feelings and feel understood, better yet, we found quiet corner in the nearby Cathedral and Alden accepted my renewal. That was a major turning point!

Moreover, soon after that I read in the *Franciscan Times* that the Community Obedience which is now printed on the inside front cover of the *Principles and Rule* had been accepted by all the provinces of TSSF at IPTOC, including the American Province, as something to do which would help all the provinces feel part of the worldwide TSSF family. As I understand it this was very dear to

Alden's heart and a major contribution bringing all of us on the American continent closer to our European, African, Australasian, and New Zealand brothers and sisters.

For me personally, my heart rejoiced to read once more the very familiar words of the Community Obedience which had nurtured my own formation before I crossed to this side of the Atlantic. As a direct result I felt at home enough, once more, to stand for election to Chapter. Brother Alden saved me from becoming a lapsed tertiary.

MaryAnn Jackman
He was my brother in every sense of the word, and I loved him enormously. If anybody out there has a doubt about how good and wonderful and full of integrity and holiness a gay person can be, here is your gloriously shining example, our former Minister General.

I once told Alden over breakfast in an airport hotel in Chicago if everyone who was gay would come out, things would change enormously for the better. I didn't include myself in that number at the time, though the minute I spoke the words, God revealed to me for a fact that I should have. I confessed that to Alden recently. OK, Alden, I've put my words where my heart is at last. You were out to all the world, in all your hopeful innocence and wonder. Me, too, darling one, after your shining example.

He had great wit and a sense of wonderful fun. We enjoyed each other so much. He said in a note towards the end that he wished he could see me. I was thinking about flying east for a quick visit, and my friend Jo said don't wait too long. I did. (I'm sorry about that, dear Alden.) The last time I saw him was in San Francisco a year or so ago, and we knew when we said a lingering good bye then, I think, that we wouldn't see each other again. We kept up a lively daily email correspondence until he got so ill. I have missed that terribly. I could tell you so many wonderful Alden stories, but I won't. They are mine and I'm going to jealously hold on to them for a while. At least until the pain is less.

References

Countryman, Louis W. *Good News of Jesus: Reintroducing the Gospel.* Cambridge, MA: Cowley Publications, 1993.

Ferrante, Tony, and Paulette Jacobson. *Letters from the Closet.* Sacramento: Tzedakah Publications, 1994.

Chapter 8: Anita Catron, Minister Provincial, 1996-2002

New Orleans Provincial Convocation June 1997

Provincial Convocation 1997, New Orleans

The Provincial Convocation of 1997 in New Orleans was the biggest undertaking of the American Province in over a decade...and probably the biggest undertaking ever. It was put on in an area of the country where there was little or no local support—thus everything has to be done from a distance. The keynote speaker, Archbishop Desmond Tutu, TSSF pulled out of the Convocation towards the last minute. Yet from beginning to end, Anita Catron led the work to make the Convocation happen...and she did it humbly and with aplumb. Moreover it was such a success that henceforth this Province has sought to hold Provincial Convocations every five years. (It could even claim a surplus over expenses of $1330.)

One of our members from Tennessee (John Tolbert) dressed up in whiteface and brown robes as Brother Heriticus and gifted people with hand-forged iron nails. Here's Lucy Blount's reaction to Br. Heriticus (*Franciscan Times* Fall 1997):

> *Precious Sisters and Brothers,*
>
> *My mind drifts back to the first whole day of our New Orleans Convocation. We all were gathering to board the buses to go to our beginning Holy Communion service at the Cathedral. As I walked to the bus, there he stood, the man robed in brown. His back was turned. I just thought to myself, that's a little odd. I don't recognize that shade of brown belonging to any of our brothers and sisters. Then he turned and I saw for the first time his grease-painted face. It was startlingly white. There seemed to be a gladness, a sadness about this clown who called himself Brother Hereticus. As I came closer, I recognized our own John Tolbert from the Southeastern Convocation. I felt a little awkward and a little "distancing" cropping up in me. Was he being serious or sacri-*

legious? I thought of the centuries of brothers and sisters in brown marching by. What would they think? I didn't mind making a fool of myself, why in just a few days I'd be doing so at the talent show [Ed. See related article and photo about Lucy Blount and Lambkins J. Flock], but was this an "approved" activity? I wasn't quite sure. All I knew is that it made me a little uneasy. Chicken that I am, I just stood and watched and didn't get too close, except when one of John's big hugs would catch me off guard.

I remember him silently sitting near the front of the Cathedral on the right-hand side. I remember him silently standing in line at lunch and then sitting silently at one of the dining tables. I remember him sitting silently at one of our later services. I remember him silently standing in the downstairs hallway giving out a gift. I couldn't avoid him. He's my brother and friend. His hand grasped mine and left the present. I looked down. It was a large, primitive iron nail. I looked up and met John's happy/sad eyes and said "Thank You!"

John—alias Brother Hereticus—our Franciscan clown, was willing to be a "Fool for Christ" tangibly, literally. His presence was a profound blessing. He cut very close to the edge. It made my heart cry out "Hey Lucy, how far are you willing to go out on a limb for your Lord, for Francis, for your brothers and sisters in Christ?"

I remember one day gazing into the mirror in our dorm room after brushing my teeth and noticing a big white streak through the side of my hair.

My first reaction was "Oh, dear! I'm aging right before my very eyes." Then I smiled and then I burst out laughing. Hereticus had left his mark on me! Some of his grease paint had rubbed off at the passing of the peace. I carefully wiped it off and went on to the rest of the day's activities.

Later I laughingly mentioned it to John. I once again thanked him for the nail. It was a weighty present, and I asked if he might give me twelve to take home to our Fellowship. It seemed the perfect gift to take back to Alabama's "God's Joyful Fools." He did, and it was. They received them two days ago when we met at the Advent Cathedral in Birmingham for a meeting, lunch, and Holy Communion where I was professed and then there was a reception. Family, friends, Franciscans were gathered. It was a day I'll never forget, never.

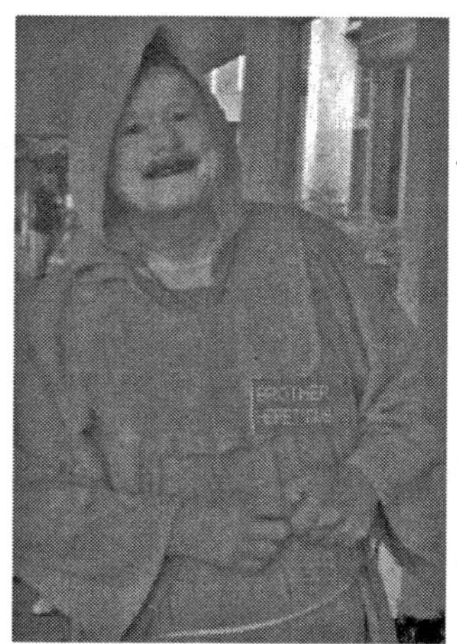
Brother Hereticus

Funny, as I sit writing to you here on the floor in a hotel bathroom so as not to awaken my sister or mother, (we're on a mother-daughters trip to Canada) my mind drifts back and seems to skip from the image of John the Clown to being professed and then back to John the Clown and then to being Professed. The two scenarios seem to be weaving themselves together and becoming one. Maybe it's because it's pre-dawn, and I just need some coffee. All I know is that I can't wait to see the photographs taken while I was making my vows. It wouldn't surprise me a bit if there was an invisible clown present carrying some nails in his hand, ready to distribute them to each person.

Thank you, John. Your happy/sad eyes reminded me of another "Clown of Christ." It is my prayer that I may become as you have become—willing to come close to the edge, to go out on a limb, to do a little hilarious humility dance as our Brother Francis did and all for the love of Jesus.

And now it's time to rise off this cold tile floor and tiptoe back to bed. But first I'm going to take a glance into the mirror, for there might be a little while grease paint still stuck to my hair. If not, I do know it has surely stuck to my soul. I was stuck on by a bear hug and a nail gently placed in my hands.

Lucy Blount and Lambkins

Other events at the 1997 Convocation included Br. Jon Bankert presentation of a play with sacred puppetry in the style of Japanese Noh theater, *An Experience of Saint Francis in India* written by Arthur Little. Sisters Pamela Clare and Jean of the Community of St. Francis gave a presentation on Creation Spirituality based on Matthew Fox's *Original Blessing*. There was also a jazz Eucharist led by Ken and Janet Watts from Florida, and Lucy Blount kept us all captivated with her stories illustrated by a lamb puppet and a whole barnyard of critters hidden away in her hat. (You can see much more of this convocation by viewing the streaming video on the website (*Resources for Tertiaries*).)

1997 Steering Committee (left to right): Dee Dobson, Joan Verret, Carol Tookey, John Brockmann, Gloria Waldron, Julia Bergstrom, Anita Catron, Bob Kramish Secretary, and David Burgdorf

Provincial Convocation 2002, Santa Barbara

Anita and Suzanne Farnham

Just before her second term ended, Anita coordinated another team to design and create another Provincial Convocation with this one in Santa Barbara, California. I had recently read Susan Farnham's books on discernment in community (*Listening Hearts*), and persuaded Chapter to invite Susan as the keynote speaker.

The convocation was surrounded by a eucalyptus grove at the La Casa de Maria retreat center with trails up into the Santa Ynez Mountains rising up behind the retreat center. Some trails led to a lovely pool at the foot of a waterfall where one could relax and cool down from hikes. I was on the planning committee of the Convocation, and the host for the talent show. For most of us the most amazing part of the Convocation was the prayer service and blessing presided over by Masud who was accompanied by Iman Bashar from Baltimore, and Rabbi Carlos Huerta from West Point Military Academy. (You can see much more of this convocation by viewing the streaming video on the website (*Resources for Tertiaries*).)

Responses to the Santa Barbara Convocation 2002

From the British

Five tertiaries **Michael Daws** (the official representative of the European Province), **Margaret** and **Richard Scott**, **Maria** and **John Fox** were privileged to attend the Convocation. Such an event occurs every five years; Maria and John had been to the previous Convocation in New Orleans in 1997, and were so enthused by it that they repeated their participation in 2002. All five tertiaries found the six days in Santa Barbara an unforgettable and moving experience, which is quite difficult to describe because it depended almost entirely on the warmth and capability of the American tertiaries involved. There were around 150 people attending, and everyone who travelled by plane was met personally at the airport by local tertiaries and delivered to the Casa de Maria Retreat Centre! The Centre was set in seven acres of beautiful parkland, complete with a swimming pool, tennis courts, etc and adjoined estates of celebrities such as Oprah Winfrey and Michael Douglas. The theme of the Convocation was "Discernment: Seeking the Mind of God in our Franciscan Life" and the six days were packed full of opportunities to worship, be still, be vigorous, or be entertained. As it is not possible to describe the full scope of the Convocation in any detail we have selected just a few personal impressions of some activities that we felt to be worth mentioning.

- **Worship and prayer** surrounded all that we did. There was Morning and Evening Prayer, a Eucharist and Compline using a specially prepared and bound Worship Booklet. The spirit of the worship and the joyfulness of the singing was almost beyond belief, bringing us to tears on a number of occasions. There was sufficient time for reflection and meditation each day, guided in the Chapel or privately either in a multi-faith Meditation Chapel, through centring prayer, use of a labyrinth, a Peace Garden, or the beautiful grounds.
- **Discerning our Franciscan Life** was the main theme at the Convocation. We were guided by Suzanne Farnham, author of *Listening Hearts*, in how to discern ways forward in difficult situations, both through individual and group approaches. On the individual front we were asked to choose a method of exploring what was in our hearts through arranging a pattern of natural objects on a tray, writing a Letter to God, or developing a short story, hymn or prayer. Small groups were formed to practice a special technique for discerning issues that were lying under the surface within a group. The process was quite revealing, especially the requirement that while listening to others, we were bidden to refrain from interruption but also from formulating our own response. Rather we were asked to allow each other's contribution to be respected, by waiting in silence for the Holy Spirit to inform our responses before speaking; unfortunately there was insufficient time to appreciate the full implications.
- **Peace and Justice Issues** were prominently discussed during the Convocation. There was a special Workshop on the topic, held twice, and a group formed during lunches to continue the dialogue. There was great strength of feeling on these issues, and a special e-mail for 'SSF Peace with Justice' has been set up, to which any tertiary may subscribe.
- **The Interfaith Initiative** was for us all the highlight of the Convocation. The Rev. Masud Ibn Syedullah had arranged for two friends, Imam Moshamad Bashar, John Hopkins University Chaplain from the Baltimore

The essence of shared spirituality at Santa Barbara: Rabbi Carlos Huerta; Jewish Chaplain and Professor of Higher Mathematics; The United States Military Academy, West Point, NY , Anita, Imam Mohamad Bashar Arafat; Founder & Director of Civilizations Exchange and Cooperation Foundation; Baltimore, MD.; Muslim Chaplain, Johns Hopkins University; Rev. Masud, Brother Robert Hugh in foreground, Minister General and Bishop-to-be Keith Slater in back.

Islamic Centre, and Rabbi Carlos Huerta, Jewish Chaplain at the West Point Military Academy, to engage in an interfaith dialogue. This was followed by an incredibly moving service in the chapel, during which the Anglican, Muslim and Jewish clergy intoned their own scriptures. The service commenced with the rabbi sounding the shofar on a ram's horn and the imam intoning the adhan, the Islamic to prayer. At a critical point in the service each of us formed a line to receive the laying-on of hands from the three clergy, in turn. They prayed over us individually, and, finally, we surrounded the three and laid our hands on them. We were charged to be *reconcilers*; it is difficult to imagine a more inspirational experience in this strife-torn world.

- **Finally, the Fun and Warmth** that permeated all that went on was genuinely astonishing. Our universal reaction was "What very nice people these American tertiaries are," and it was like being immersed in a luxuriously warm bath. Michael commented: "A major impact on me was how much I felt in the presence of Francis with a place of much simplicity and celebration of sun, of earth, of water, of people, yet within a world of so much complexity and therefore contradiction. I felt that this was a world that Francis would have recognised and suffered with." There were people present from the Caribbean (three of the seven professed during the week were women from Tobago), Guyana, Canada and all over the United States. There were many First Order Brothers and Sisters, representatives from OFM and SFO; there were tertiaries' friends and relatives interested in TSSF as well. The organisation and administration was superb, the food too extravagant for words, and we all caught our flights home!

We would like to thank Anita Catron, Minister Provincial, and her team for the wonderful time that we spent with them in Santa Barbara. As well as benefiting from our attendance there has been much to learn in terms of organising such an event, and our involvement has stimulated a number of ideas to take home.

From "Good News For The Idaho Guard (July 2002)—Our Father?

Chaplain (COL) Larry Harrelson, STARC Chaplain

The last week of June I attended an international convocation of the Third Order, Society of St. Francis, of which I am a professed member. I was touched beyond expectation by grace. I share some of what happened. It gave me hope for our world, and perhaps it will encourage you as well.

One day we had an interfaith dialogue between a Jewish rabbi, a Muslim imam, and a Christian clergyman. The Christian minister, an Episcopal priest, pastors in New York and works part-time with cadets at West Point. He met the imam (who lives and teaches in the U.S.) at the Taize international prayer community in France. The Jewish rabbi is an active-duty chaplain at West Point.

The most powerful piece for me was the actual interfaith worship service following the dialogue, which was held in the chapel at the Catholic retreat center where we were meeting. The modified Taize worship service was called to worship by the rabbi's shofar (ram's horn) and the Muslim call to prayer by the imam. Sacred readings from the Hebrew Scriptures, the Koran, and the New Testament were done in Hebrew, Arabic, and English respectively. The three faiths were respected, yet nothing was watered down or diminished. Respect for diversity and unity was present.

Our 85th Anniversary of Founding Cake

All who wanted were invited forward to receive the laying-on-of hands—a practice common to Judaism, Christianity, and Islam—and simultaneous prayers by the rabbi, imam, and priest, prayers done in the language and traditions of the three faiths. Most of the 150 convocation participants, including myself, received this spiritual blessing. We were in no hurry, for God's work was being done by us Children of Abraham. Dialogue is important. More important is praying together, with mutual respect.

I am proud to be in the U.S. military and to know that we long have been interfaith in the Chaplain Corps, as we promote the free exercise of religion for all—an expression of our great country. The cards and handbooks we carry as chaplains in the pockets of our BDUs [battle dress uniforms] speak to our calling. At the causality collection points, we prayerfully make our rounds of those not expected to live. If a chaplain of the dying person's faith group is not present, any chaplain uses the appropriate prayers for that person—be the prayers Catholic, Protestant, Jewish, or Muslim.

Novice Mission to Mexico 1999

Anita Catron (from *Franciscan Times* Spring 1999)
For ten days this last March, a group of Franciscans (Brothers Tom, Clark and Guire (SSF novice), Sister Pamela Clare, and I) were invited to do a preaching teaching mission in the Diocese of Mexico. The Rt. Rev. Sergio Carranza, Bishop of the Diocese of Mexico, and Father Vincent Schwahn, Dean of the Seminary of San Andres, organized our nine church engagement. The goal was to share our personal Franciscan journeys, describe the whole Society of St. Francis, give homilies, and learn about Mexican Anglican spirituality—all in Spanish. The churches where we went ranged from small mission churches in outlying areas to large congregations in Mexico City. A few of the Anglican churches were over 100 years old. In general, the Diocese of Mexico is growing.

Perhaps we gained more than we offered. We found the Mexican congregations to be very welcoming, friendly, inquisitive, and open to the idea of "Anglican"

Anita with Graciela Alvarez y Fuentes TSSF in Mexico City

religious Orders. One of the most rewarding experiences took place when we accompanied a priest to the homes of two sick parishioners to pray and visit with them.

The hospitality exhibited by our Mexican brothers and sisters was outstanding; one whole evening was organized around a shared evening meal. One of our group put it quite well: the spirit in the more remote churches was most moving and generally deeper than elsewhere. We even learned about some of the deeply-rooted, pre-Spanish customs woven into the services.

There was even time to tour the pyramids at Teotihuacan, the exquisite Templo Mayor (Tenochtilan), archeological ruins excavated within the last twenty years in the center of Mexico City, the main archeological museum, and to re-master the metro and bus system which is less hectic than I recall from twenty years ago when I was last in Mexico.

I very much enjoyed returning to a country where I once lived for three years and returning to the Spanish-speaking congregation of San Jorge where my own vocation developed. I loved reviving my Spanish language skills, seeing former friends, and being a whole family with my First Order brothers and sister. It was also a real treat to visit two of our four Third Order members who live in Mexico.

Br. Tom, Bishop Carranza, Anita, and Br. Clark

True, we did miss interacting more with the seminary students and learning from them, but, when we return at the Bishop's invitation in Advent 2000, perhaps we can remedy that shortcoming.

TSSF Helps Form the National Association of Episcopal Christian Communities

Franciscan Times, Sping 2000

Four of the Episcopal Church's Christian Communities met with Bishop Rodney Michel of the House of Bishops' Standing Committee on Religious Communities in late February, to report on the formation of NAECC, the National Association of Episcopal Christian Communities. Five of the church's eight canonically recognized Communities have voted to proceed with the formation of this association, which Bishop Michel has hailed as of vital importance for the spiritual growth of the Episcopal Church. As he told the gathering, "You are spokespersons for your community, your parish church, and the Episcopal Church." Religious life is one of the best-kept secrets in the Episcopal Church, and Bishop Michel called on the communities to be more active in the dioceses in which they are resident, taking part in diocesan conventions, and furthering the mission of the church whenever possible. Sparked by input from George Gray (Community of the Paraclete), the association defined its purpose: to "share and commu-

1—Anita Catron and Andrew Wilkes, TSSF
2—Congregation of the Companions of the Holy Spirit
3—Community of the Paraclete
4—Brotherhood of St. Gregory
5—Worker Sisters and Brothers of the Holy Spirit

nicate the fruits of the Gospel, realized in community, with the church and the world." This year's meeting, the third such conference of communities, focused on discernment and formation, and began to explore the Rules of Life followed in each community. Bishop Michel stressed the importance of the discipline of the Daily Office, common to most Rules, as a means to foster a sense of community. As conference convener Tobias Haller (Brotherhood of Saint Gregory) put it, "an invisible wave of prayer washes over the world several times each day as people around the globe open their prayer-books and breviaries, whether alone or in choir." Carol Tookey (TSSF) added that given the international character and the flexible rule of her community, the Office is being prayed in many ways by many voices. The next step for the association is the adoption of by-laws, which will be explored at the next conference.

Reflection by the American Province Representative to IPTOC 1999

Anita Catron, Minister Provincial

The experience of the 1999 Interprovincial Third Order Chapter (IPTOC) in Brisbane, Australia, was one I shall remember fondly; it confirmed that I have been called to follow Christ in the way of St. Francis after almost 20 years since my profession. Indeed I have been called to pray unceasingly. I have been called to love my brothers and my sisters, those whom I know and even those whom I do not know half way around the world. Further, our Third Order aims tell me that I have been called to live simply, to spread the spirit of love and unity within the family of God, and to make our Lord known and loved everywhere.

The IPTOC papers each provincial delegation wrote helped us have an early understanding of one another from province to province but also within our own provinces, where distances are great, and cultures, languages, devotions, and practices are varied. Each Franciscan province truly has its own rich and varied heritage to be cherished and celebrated.

In Brisbane, I had a chance to test once again my various Franciscan callings. I was in a new and different location; new people; new way of expressing the English language; new cultures—both indigenous and Australian; new foods (scones!); new ways of praying the *Daily Office*; new reasons to love my Franciscan family. And yet, it was as though I belonged to this new, far-off setting. During my lifetime I have lived in three other countries and six different American cities, experiencing the diversity of life each offered. To my amazement, my heart recognized the Franciscan charism everywhere I lived or traveled.

One could say, after all, that I've been well grounded in the Third Order Principles for Daily Reading, the intercessory prayers we say for one another around the globe, the Third Order Constitution, our own Provincial Statutes, the new Guide to Love and Harmony: "What first steps can I do today." Suddenly, the community obedience prayer "Both here and in all your churches throughout the whole world..." took on true meaning. Besides the institutional ways of recognizing my callings, there was the mere "being" with one another in study, prayer, work (meetings!), meals, and sightseeing. To me these are all clear callings to witness Jesus in the lives of others wherever I may land or with whomever I may be. They even teach me something about myself, that while I am special according to God's gift of grace, so is everyone else in God's creation. I am called to love others and that love we share really is the glue of our community. Or, as William Countryman said in his book *The Good News of Jesus*, unless I realize that you are as fully human as I am, there is no love (paraphrased).

Interacting with my tertiary brothers and sisters from other countries at IPTOC was part of the heavenly calling I have experienced. We were indeed fortunate to have the advantage of meeting with our First Order brothers and sisters, and one Second Order sister as well, completing the Franciscan family. Both our diversity and our similarities bind us together. Hence, we are called upon to be lovers, paving the way in this needy world of ours toward our ultimate, heavenly calling with God. Our journeys, then, may all be diverse, but the faith we share and celebrate in Christ and Francis, is the same. For that we give thanks.

[*See Alden Whitney's Minister General homily at this IPTOC on page 121*]

L to R, Front to Back: Row 1: Dorothy Brooker (MP, New Zealand); Anita Catron (MP Americas); Joan Verret (Americas); Row 2: Val Tibbey (Australia); Anne Kotze (MP Africa) Marion Nevell (Europe); Back Row: David (Africa); Keith Slater (Incoming Minister General, Australia); Caroline Clapperton (MP Europe); Alden Whitney (Outgoing Minister General); David Burgdorf (Americas); Allen Williams (Europe).

Anita Catron's Final Report as Minister Provincial

As I reflect upon my six years as your Minister Provincial, I am very grateful to each of you here, to all Third Order members and to my family for the faithful support and love during this time of my ministry to the Third Order. The First Order Brothers and Sisters in this Province have also contributed so much to my upbringing, and I consider them family.

Anita Catron Calling Chapter to Order at Little Portion Friary.

I have grown in my own spiritual journey in unimaginable ways, and for that I thank God and the Holy Spirit for leading me. The *Principles* of the Order have undergirded me, and given me an appreciation for the ministry of each Third Order member, and I celebrate the diversity that we share. I could not have designed this path myself; it was entirely God's doing.

There have been challenges—modifying the sacramental confession requirement, reinforcing use of the *Daily Office* in the American Province, helping fellowships grieve in a healthy way, recognizing Community Obedience, being asked to preach sermons at the last minute, and the loss of two former Ministers Provincial. The joys far outnumber the challenges. The joys include seeing the Third Order as a truly global Christian Community, the inclusion of non-Anglicans in the Order, the birth of NAECC (National Association of Christian Communities), the recent Provincial Convocations, the ecumenical relations with the Roman Catholic Secular Franciscans and the Order of Ecumenical Franciscans, the two preaching missions in Mexico, the beginnings of interfaith dialogue, the conversations with the First Order Brothers and Sisters worldwide, the efforts for peace and justice, and much more.

Here are a few highlights of the past year. In November we hosted a celebration of John Scott's ministry, our first Minister Provincial/Guardian, in his Philadelphia home. About 20 members from the NJ and Philadelphia Fellowships attended. We shared our Franciscan journeys, and how we had met John. It was evident from the "stories" that John had touched the spiritual lives of many of us. After all, it was through John that I was introduced to the Third Order.

I had a rewarding experience when I joined Brothers Clark Berge and Tom Carey on the preaching and teaching mission to the Diocese of Mexico. We were well received by Bishop Carranza and the clergy of the dozen churches we visited. The parishioners treated us kindly, always showering us with special meals and stories. One of my best memories was the stay at the "Asilo de Ancianos" (Old Folks Home) in Toluca! Other memories were the penetrating questions people asked us about our Franciscan journeys.

And the Provincial Convocation! A treat in so many ways, and a beautiful California location with time to pray, relax, meet friends, "discern" and hear Rabbi Huerta and Imam Arafat. The blessings from Father Masud, the Rabbi and the Imam were unforgettable.

I urge you as tertiaries to focus on the future vision and hopes of the Third Order, to continue compiling our 85-year-old history in this Province, and to engage the talents and ministries of all Third Order members to further the three aims of the Order.

Thank you for the privilege of being your Minister Provincial.

Br. Robert Hugh SSF Reminiscences

Mary Alice White (Professed 1961) (from *Franciscan Times 2003)*

I do not know the date of Brother Robert Hugh's arrival from England and the merging of our Order and the English Order into the Society of St. Francis. I only know that there came a renaissance within the Order.

Other brothers, of course, came. I believe actually it was 1960 that I first met Brother Robert when he visited Denver. He told a small group of us what the brothers did in England as well as at Little Portion. Now that I think back upon it, I believe that his enthusiasm and knowledge of the brothers' work is what really inspired me to become a full-fledged tertiary in the first place He then and now means so much to the Order and has influenced hundreds of people, I'm sure, to become Third Order people.

Reminiscences by Br. Robert Hugh

(All from memory, so no guarantees as to accuracy in every detail)

I was sixteen years old when I discovered that only ten miles from my high school was the headquarters of a Franciscan Friary organized in the Church of England. I had always supposed that strange characters like monks, nuns, and friars were bound to be Roman Catholic. A weekend visit proved me wrong, and I came under the guidance of Fr. Algy SSF, and his young secretary novice, Br. Michael. When I left school for military draft service in the army just after World War II, Algy suggested I become a Companion (Associate as we would say in this Province), and helped me draw up my first Rule of Life and make my first confession. He was my spiritual director until his death in 1955. After reading theology at Cambridge, and going on to seminary at Oxford, I became a tertiary for the next decade as a parish priest in the Diocese of Durham. First Fr. Francis and then Fr. Reginald were the friars who guided my Third Order journey. I also remember being sent off by bus to be looked at by Dorothy Swayne, a formidable but wonderful tertiary who in the 1930's had worked with Algy in adapting the Principles of the Christa Seva Sangha to become the Principles of the First and the Third Orders SSF. [See page 41.]

In 1964 1 left parish ministry to test my vocation in the First Order SSF, at Alnmouth, Hilfield, and Glasshampton. Only just first professed, I was asked to be one of three friars to visit the OSF Friars in the US as part of an exchange at the time of the amalgamation of OSF and SSF. I was told it was for "a year, or so." At the end of November 2002 I shall have completed thirty five years of "... or so"!

Fr. Algy

For three years I was Novice Guardian at Little Portion, while Br. Luke fulfilled that role in England. In 1970 I made my life profession in New York, and, when Luke returned to the US and succeeded Br. Paul as Minister Provincial, he asked me to become Chaplain to the Third Order, which I did for the next four years.

Br. Paul envisioned the Third Order as free-standing in its own right, with its own administrative, pastoral, and formation leadership, rather than being heavily dependent upon the paternal benevolence and guidance of the friars. Br. Paul had been working to communicate this vision of the Third Order while he was Minister, and I saw it as my trust to further that vision. In accepting Luke's invitation I declared my hope that by the end of my term as Chaplain I should have worked myself out of a job since the role would thenceforward be filled by a tertiary. That did not quite happen since Br. Mark Francis followed me for the next three years, but already much progress was being made. During this time I traveled a great deal to spend time with fellowships and individuals, realizing that it is not really possible to win people to a different understanding of the Third Order by the written word alone. I believe that I managed to visit personally with nearly all the professed during my years as Friar-Chaplain. Many were very responsive to this, but others clearly felt threatened by the SSF/OSF amalgamation. In many cases they had a staunch Anglo-Catholic background, a deep commitment to their profession, and to the friars, especially to Fr. Joseph, which they feared they might lose if the Third Order stood free and equal with the First. Because Paul's initiative coincided with the SSF/OSF amalgamation, quite a number of tertiaries concluded that it was all a scheme that "those dreadful Brits" (who, some of them were convinced, were "Black Protestants!") had hatched. [Ed. *"Black Protestants" means hard-line Protestants who were vehmently anti-Catholic and anti-Anglo-Catholic.*]

I find it hard to believe how different my role as Friar Chaplain to the Third Order was from that of say a Friar Visitor today. If new would-be tertiaries wanted to join, they wrote to me, and I approved their draft rule. If they were ready for profession, my approval as Friar Chaplain was a key part of that. If a newsletter need to go out, I was the one who composed it, and then typed it onto a stencil, put it on the Gestetner duplicator, and lamented as all the 'o's dropped out after the first fifty copies, leaving blobs of ink on the page. Fortunately, numbers were much smaller (my guess is about 150).

Hilfield Friary

Br. Robert Hugh, 1968

Formation was the first area really taken over by the Third Order itself, and I have the happiest memories of visits to Lambertville, NJ, where Peter Funk was composing the first set of Formation letters, as he and Marie Hayes guided those in formation (at first divided according to gender). John Scott became the first administrator of the Third Order (*Guardian* in those days, rather than *Minister*).

In 1979, when Norman Crosbie succeeded Luke as Minister Provincial, he asked me (I was Assistant Minister) to represent him and the Province in the relationships between the friars and the tertiaries. Thus began the "Friar Visitor" role. In 1981, I became Provincial Minister, and, as the CSF Sisters have done, combined both roles. For most of the years since 1987, when my term as Minister ended, I have continued to be Friar Visitor. Participation in Regional arid Provincial Convocations and in the Third Order Chapter have been highlights for my years. Now, as Br. Derek begins his term as Minister, he is combining the roles, ensuring the closest possible links between the First and Third Orders.

Br. Robert Hugh, 2002

References

Countryman, Louis W. *Good News of Jesus: Reintroducing the Gospel.* Cambridge, MA: Cowley Publications, 1993.

Farnham, Suzanne G. *Listening Hearts: Discerning Call in Community.* Harrisburg, PA: Morehouse Pub, 1991.

Little, Arthur, and Leonard C. Holvik. *An Experience of Saint Francis in India.* 1970.

Chapter 9: Problems and Opportunities Spanning Multiple Ministers Provincial & Chapters

Towards the end of Anita Catron's term as Minister Provincial, problems and opportunities presenting themselves to TSSF required the work and efforts of a number of Ministers Provincial and Chapters over an extended length of time. These problems or opportunities were: the selection and election of the first Third Order Bishop Protector; the incorporation of the Brazilian Order of St. Francis (OSF) into the Province of the Americas; and the new "Safe Church" requirements issued from the ECUSA House of Bishops.

The Final Act of Independence from the First Order—Choosing Our Own Bishop Protector

Franciscan Times, Advent 2003

[Ed. "The Bishop Protector in Franciscan terms corresponds roughly to the Visitor in other religious orders, but with us has always had greater significance. He is there roughly to protect the Order from the Church and the Church from the Order. He is a "go-between" in case of crisis and a final court of appeal and advice [within the Order]." (Fisher, p. 140.) As early as 1928 during the move to Mount Sinai, NY, Father Joseph was making reports to a Bishop Protector (Williams, p. 157, footnote 25).]

The first three Bishops Protector of the American Province TSSF functioned as the Bishops Protector **for all SSF Orders in the Americas**: the Brothers, the Sisters, and the Poor Clares. Bishop Paul Moore of New York was Bishop Protector from 1973-89, Bishop George Hunt of Rhode Island from 1990-93, and Bishop Jerry Lamb of Northern California from 1993-2002.

Bishop Moore frequently attended Chapter meetings, and Bishop Hunt led the Chapter's Quiet Day in 1993. Bishop Lamb attended the 1997 Provincial Convocation in New Orleans and was the celebrant at the Jazz Mass. In 2002, Bishop Lamb notified Anita in the final months of her term as Minister Provincial that he desired to retire from his position. After combing the *Statutes* and *Constitution*, Anita could find no reason why the TSSF Bishop Protector should be the same as that of the First and Second Order Brothers or Sisters.

Moreover, at a meeting that year of the Conference of Anglican Religious (CAROA) and National Association of Episcopal Christian Communities (NAECC), Bishop Rodney Michael (Chair of the House of Bishops Committee on the Religious Life) encouraged all Orders and Communities to have Bishops Protector who would have closer oversight and get to know the Communities better. (Probably this was a preamble to the Safe Church Initiative and controversy discussed in "The Red Book, Safe Community and Conflict Resolution, and Going Beyond," p. 160.) Given this situation, Anita Catron as Minister Provincial felt it was time for TSSF, American Province to have its own Bishop Protector.

To begin choosing a Bishop Protector, Anita wrote to Chapter 2002 members soliciting criteria for the selection of a Bishop Protector and names of candidates.*

Methodology for Choosing a Bishop Protector/Visitor 2003

Report to Chapter 2003 by Anita Catron

Task Committee at Chapter 2002 charged with the project to find a successor included:

- Masud Ibn Syedullah (newly-elected Minister Provincial)
- Anita Catron (former Minister Provincial)
- Barbara Baumgarten, Formation Director
- Julia Bergstrom, Provincial Chaplain

How names of bishops to consider were chosen:

- Our current Bishop Protector, Bishop Lamb, gave us names of candidates.
- Anita asked Chapter 2002 members to list qualities of a Bishop Protector.
- Other TSSF members offered names of bishops they thought fit the criteria.
- The Task Committee decided that all 20 bishops named should be considered.

Drafting of letter to bishop candidates:

- Done by Anita; input by Masud and Barbara; final letter designed.
- Letters went out to about 20 ECUSA bishops May 24, 2003.
- Responses from bishops were invited by phone, email or regular mail.

Follow-up calls made to the bishops:

- Masud and Anita made follow-up calls within the month to each bishop.
- Most responded; some were away; all were getting ready for 2003 General Convention.
- Sometimes faxes were required to follow up.
- Sometimes a second call was required.

Thank you letters sent:

As soon as a bishop responded, yeah or nay, Anita responded. If the candidate declined, he or she was thanked for considering the appointment. If the candidate was interested, Anita invited the candidate to meet with Masud, Barbara and Julia at General Convention. Anita explained the process to the candidates, and a timeframe to vote (being Chapter time) was outlined.

Personal Interviews at 2003 General Convention:

- These were set for General Convention with two serious candidates.
- Masud, Barbara and Julia met with the first two bishops.
- Impressions were positive for both.

Voting by Chapter members, 2003:

Each interested bishop candidate was invited to write some paragraphs as a biography. Chapter members would review the bios and candidates per the Statutes and Constitution. The biographies would be published in the *Franciscan Times* in the Fall issue to notify the membership. Voting by Chapter members would take place at Chapter time. The elected bishop would be notified by Masud. The new Bishop Protector's term of 6 years would begin as of Chapter 2003. He would be eligible for another term of 3 years, if it were mutually agreed upon by the bishop and Chapter.

All bishops were gracious and felt honored they had been asked to be considered. Most declined because of restraints on time away from their dioceses or travel conflicts. Most expressed an affinity with Franciscan spirituality and had their own active spiritual lives. Some were already Bishops Protector of other Orders. No women bishops were considered, not because they didn't fit the description, but because none were suggested (a few are already Bishops Protector of other Orders). One positive outcome of the process of choosing a Bishop Protector was wider knowledge of the Third Order in the House of Bishops.

Before being elected by Chapter, Bishop Gordon Scruton of Western Massachusetts wrote regarding his pertinent experiences for becoming Bishop Protector:

For over 30 years I have lived under a Rule of Life both as an Associate of the Society of St. Francis and with the Fellowship of the Way of the Cross, an Order of Episcopal clergy who do not live in community but who share a Rule, gather for yearly silent retreat and for several occasions of prayer and reflection as we seek to live as contemplatives in action in our daily lives. I was Superior of the Fellowship for 10 years.

As Rector of St Francis, Holden, Massachusetts for 15 years, I was led to lots of study and prayer about St. Francis, our patron, and the connections of his life and witness with the life and witness of Christians today. My core mission in life has been as a spiritual guide: talking with individuals; leading small groups, retreats and conferences; helping people discover a deepening relationship with Christ which connects with their daily vocation as representatives of Christ in the world.

Bishop Protector's Address at Chapter— Love Extravagantly

(*Franciscan Times*, Fall 2010)

Seven years after his election as TSSF's first Bishop Protector, Bishop Scruton gave this address at Chapter, and it demonstrates the quality of spiritual leadership Bishop Scruton has offered our Province for many years.

I opened my address by leading Chapter in a Taize song, and then declaring to them that it is a joy to be among them and to talk about us to the House of Bishops. I even requested to be a member of the Bishops' Standing Committee for religious communities to share the Franciscan viewpoint.

This is the first year Ken [Norian, the then-Minister Provincial] *has not needed to call me for some type of crisis. I believe this is a sign of health and growth within the Order. It is a joy to see the Order living and following the Spirit. Even the quality of discussions at Chapter meetings has deepened from when I first was among you.*

One of the tasks of a Bishop Protector is to ask if the Order is being faithful to their charism. In the Franciscan family, this means: how widely are we in love with Jesus? Francis' energy came from his passionate love of God and extravagant love of all his brothers and sisters. I encourage all of you to keep this always in your hearts and minds.

I was at the recent House of Bishops gathering where we prayed at the Mexican border and named some who died trying to cross the border. As a wider church, one current focus should be the status of immigration. In talks with border guards, when asked what can help most, the guards answered: "Get good immigration laws that we can enforce."

As Christians, how are we called to respond? How does God's love fit in this situation? As we look at the Biblical stories, Abraham was an immigrant who sometimes had to lie and steal to survive; the Exodus happened when there were too many immigrant families in Egypt; Jesus himself was a refugee to Egypt; and Paul started Christianity as a religion of immigrants.

We all have immigration stories in our families' history, but we often forget them. If we are to respond in Christ's love, some Christians may need to go to jail in civil disobedience.

As was common in the civil rights days, activists are urged to write the phone number of their attorney on their skin so it's available if needed.

Please pray for all affected and remember our call is to love God, love our neighbors, and love extravagantly.

A Final Blessing from Bishop Scruton

John Brockmann

This is the blessing that I learned from Bishop Scruton, who used it as a leitmotif in his work as Bishop in Western Massachusetts (he in turned learned it from The Most Rev. Stewart Payne, Metropolitan of Canada). Now I use it as a blessing at each service.

May the Lord Jesus, who loves with a wounded heart,
be your love for evermore;
May the Lord Jesus, who serves with wounded hands,
help you serve others;
May the Lord Jesus, who walks on wounded feet, walk with you to the end of the road.
Look for the face of the Lord Jesus, in everyone you meet,
And may everyone you meet, see the face of the Lord Jesus in you.
And may the blessing of God Almighty, Father, Son and Holy Spirit, be with you and remain with you forever. Amen.

Brazil's Order of St. Francis (OSF) and the Province of the Americas—A Tempestuous Courtship

Nearly two decades after this process began, work is still taking place to make this unique relationship a reality. Other Provinces have experienced similar situations: Province of Asia-Pacific has the Papua New Guinea (PNG) Region, and the Province of the Pacific has the Solomon Islands Region. However, Brazil is critically different from either of these other Regions:

(a) the Brazilians had already formed a kind of national organization with local fellowships prior to encountering TSSF, whereas PNG and the Solomon Islands were off-shoots of previously established Provinces; and

(b) Brazil approached the Province of the Americas whereas PNG and the Solomons were already a part of a Province.

The history of the interweaving of OSF and TSSF that follows is derived from the minutes and reports of the Provincial Chapter, from the *Franciscan Times* articles, and from archives of letters and email.

1998

The Order of St. Francis (OSF) began indigenously as an amalgam of First and Third Order members; a community sharing a similar Franciscan spirituality but with different charisms. Thus OSF approached both the Third Order in the American Province and the First Order in the European Province to see where they might fit. The Rev. Cesar Alves contacted the English friars, and spent some time at Hilfield Friary (Dorset, England). Meanwhile, the Rev. Francisco Sales, having just returned from Assisi, started to contact American and English First Order friars asking them how to start a new group of Anglican Franciscans in Brazil. Frei Chico was referred to Cesar Alves, and both were referred to American Province (TSSF) when Anita Catron was Minister Provincial. At the same time, fellowships were begun in Recife and São Paulo (Chapter Report, Brazil, 2003; *Franciscan Times* Easter 2003).

1999

At Francistide, The Primate Bishop of Brazil approved the Rule of Life and Statutes of the Order of Saint Francis (OSF) and canonically authorized OSF as part of the Episcopal Anglican Church of Brazil (Chapter Report, Brazil, 2003).

2002—Fuller Partnership for Latin America in the American Province

David Catron (Franciscan Times Easter 2003)

Few people think about Anglicans, and even less about Anglican Franciscans, when they think of Brazil. Yet a thriving community of Anglican Franciscans is precisely what two members of the American Province found when they traveled there in December 2002. Brother Derek, SSF, Minister Provincial of the First Order, and I, David Catron, a Portuguese-speaking member of the Third Order, spent a week, December 3-10, visiting Franciscans in Recife and São Paulo.

Anglicanism came to Brazil in two stages during the nineteenth century: by way of English immigrants who established themselves in 1810, and through the work of American missionaries who arrived in 1889. At present, the Anglican Church in Brazil (officially called *Igreja Episcopal Anglicana do Brasil*, or IEAB), the Nineteenth Province of the Anglican Communion, has seven dioceses, two missionary districts, and 150,000 members. Their web site in both Portuguese and English is www.ieab.org.br.

Roman Catholic Franciscans have been in Brazil since the early colonial period as in much of Latin America. The origin of Anglican Franciscans is uncertain, but appears to have strong links to the Roman Catholic Secular Franciscan Order, inasmuch as many Brazilian Anglicans are converts from the Roman Church.

At the 1998 Lambeth Conference two Brazilian bishops came into contact with First Order brothers of the European Province and expressed interest in Franciscan religious life. As a result, two Brazilian Franciscans, both priests, visited Hilfield Friary in 1998 and 1999. In the American Province there were several communications from Franciscans in Recife, a major city in northeastern Brazil, asking for closer relations. Eventually Brother Derek was invited to visit at the time of the Diocese of Recife's annual convention, December 5-8, 2002.

Part of the convention's opening Eucharist was devoted to a ceremony in which eight to ten people were admitted as postulants and novices, and others to profession. The Brazilian Franciscans regard themselves as a single Order, the Order of Saint Francis (OSF), embracing both seculars and those who are seeking a community life. They stated a dislike of the ordinal numbers "first" and "third" as suggesting somehow an inferiority of the latter to the former. All members wear brown habits with a white cincture for ceremonial purposes.

Some of the best interchanges and discoveries occurred at lunch and dinner, which was served in the church's ample dining area (part of it outdoors). Br. Derek and I were able to visit with fifteen to twenty men and women, all thirsty for information, as we were about them. Occupations were as diverse as veterinarian, web page designer, teacher, student, retired, and clergy. A number of spouses were present also. Most had come to the Anglican Church from other faith traditions, notably Roman Catholic and Baptist.

On a Saturday, one of the lay brothers took Derek and me to visit the parish church of Água Viva in the nearby town of Olinda. It was an extremely modest facility, not much more than a large metal and concrete storage shed with a sanctuary for worship, a kitchen, and, yes, a dental office. It serves the entire community of Olinda's *lixão*, or landfill, except the land has not been "filled," rather it is just a huge trash and garbage heap. The church ministers to the people who make their living on top of, and whose homes are alongside, the mountain of trash. They scavenge for reusable materials, first with which to make their own homes, and second, to sell to middlemen who come in large trucks to pick up metal, glass, and other recyclables which are then taken to manufacturers.

After visiting the church, Derek and I were taken to the cardboard and metal village where we visited church members and residents, many who live in the midst of incredible poverty, on less than $1 per day.

Later in the day Derek and I were taken to visit the parish church and residence where Dom Helder Câmara, Roman Catholic Archbishop of Recife, served and lived until his death two years ago at the age of 90. Dom Helder, together with the Brazilian (also Roman Catholic) Franciscan Leonardo Boff, was one of the principal architects of Latin American liberation theology in the 1960s and 70s.

On our way home, Derek and I were able to stop for two days in São Paulo, where we met with another ten Franciscans who were also eager for information and closer ties to the Province. And, as in Recife, several in this group were interested in community life. The bishop of São Paulo, who was at the gathering, said that he will shortly donate land about an hour's distance from the city for what can become a friary.

In São Paulo we got our first serious look at, and discussion of, the founding documents of the Brazilian Franciscans. While their *Principles* are the same as the rest of the American Province, their *Rule of Life* does not match any of our source documents. Like the Roman Catholic Secular Franciscan Order, on which many of their forms are based, the Brazilians accept a single *Rule* for all.

Out of nowhere, it seems, has come a highly organized, nationwide group of Anglican Franciscans in Brazil, numbering 30-50 people, who are keenly interested in establishing a relationship with our Province.

Geographically, of course, they are already in it, but they know little of our processes, our constitution, our statutes, and our way of life. This is a stunning opportunity, and the American Province is already taking advantage of it. On April 27, Formation Director Barbara Baumgarten and I will travel back to Recife and São Paulo for a week of discussions on formation and on to create a Rule of Life. In late May the General Secretary of the Brazilian OSF will travel to New York to take part in the First Order Brothers' Chapter.

Latin America, so long a neglected part of the American Province, may be on its way to a fuller partnership.

2003

In **April and May**, David Catron and Barbara Baumgarten traveled to meetings in Recife and São Paulo to explain the formation process and to invite the Brazilian Franciscans to join TSSF (Chapter Report, Brazil, 2003). Br. John George also went to a Synod meeting in Brazil (Chapter Report, Brazil, 2003). Barbara Baumgarten wrote a follow-up letter on the formation process to both groups in Recife and São Paulo proposing that the Formation program of the Province of the Americas largely be duplicated in Brazil with the language translated from English to Portuguese.

In **May** the General Secretary of the Brazilian OSF traveled to Little Portion on Long Island, New York to take part in the First Order Brothers' Chapter, and it became apparent that one of the difficulties for OSF was their reticence to distinguish between First Order Brothers and Third Order Brothers and Sisters (Chapter Report, Brazil, 2003).

Masud Ibn Syedullah, Minister Provincial, receiving Dom Celso Franco de Oliveira, Bishop of Rio de Janeiro, as a Postulant.

Also in **May**, the newly elected Minister Provincial Masud Ibn Syedullah sent out invitations to the Brazilians to establish a covenant relationship (Chapter Report, 2003). Copies of this letter were sent onto the Brazilian bishops for their review. Both Frei Chico (Diocese of Recife) and Cesar Alves (Diocese of Sao Paulo) were invited and accepted the invitation to join Chapter 2003 at Little Portion.

While Frei Chico and Cesar Alves were present at Chapter in **October**, Chapter debated drafting a Concordat inviting the Order of Saint Francis (OSF) of Brazil to join the Third Order, Province of the Americas (Pentecost 2004 *Franciscan Times*). When this topic came up for discussion and vote, a number of Chapter members urged a go-slow approach by prototyping this relationship before committing to it in a Concordat. Other Chapter members called upon others to "trust in the Spirit," and to approve the Concordat. In the end, the motion to draft a Concordat and offer it to OSF passed.

2004

From April 19 to May 3 Masud Ibn Syedullah, Minister Provincial and a number of other key leaders journeyed to Brazil with the Concordat to meet with the Primate of Brazil, Dom Orlando Santos de Oliveira. Dom Orlando signed the Concordat and offered ongoing support. Dom Orlando noted that the TSSF's presence was not a U.S. idea, but a response to Brazil's invitation. The following is the article that appeared in the *Franciscan Times*.

The Araçatuba fellowship: (left to right, front) First Order Br. Severino, Elisabet Pessoa, Rosana Pacheco w/daughter Laura, Alvaro Antunes, (2nd row) Barbara Baumgarten, Rev. Sérgio Pacheco (guardian), David Catron, (in back) Bro. Laurindo.

TSSF and OSF (Brazil) Sign Concordat!

Barbara Baumgarten Franciscan Times
Pentecost 2004

Last October at Little Portion, Chapter drafted a Concordat inviting the Order of Saint Francis (OSF) of Brazil to join the Third Order, Province of the Americas. To follow up on that decision, four delegates—Masud Ibn Syedullah, Minister Provincial; David Catron, translator; Anita Catron, Los Latinos Coordinator and myself, Barbara Baumgarten, Formation Director—went to Brazil from April 19 to May 3, to meet with the various OSF fraternities (a.k.a. fellowships) throughout Brazil.

Masud Ibn Syedullah, Anita Catron, and Cesar Alves, with Franciscan brothers at The City of God, Rio de Janeiro.

We began with a visit in São Paulo to the Regional Guardian, The Rev. Cézar Alves, Brazil's equivalent to a Minister Provincial. After a day in São Paulo, David and I traveled overnight by bus to Araçatuba in the state of São Paulo, to meet with the Rev. Sérgio Pacheco and their local fraternity. The Diocese of São Paulo has recently purchased a farm for the Franciscan community to operate as a drug rehab residential program for teens. This program trains them in farming, community living and academics. Currently, the farm includes a house for twelve, and another for two Franciscan brothers. However, in the near future, three more buildings will be constructed: one for housing forty teens, one for offices and community activities, and another for a retreat/conference center.

While David and I were in Araçatuba, Masud and Anita traveled to Rio de Janerio where they met with Rio Diocesan Bishop Dom Celso de Oliviera and The Rev. Stephen Taylor (an English-Portuguese speaker) at the Cathedral. At a fraternity meeting of OSF members, Masud and Anita had a chance to talk about TSSF both in the Americas as well as its worldwide community. Later at the Eucharist, Masud received Bishop Celso as a postulant. It was a joyous occasion; a Roman Catholic friar friend of the Bishop delivered the sermon, making it a truly ecumenical event.

Masud Ibn Syedullah and Cesar Alves with Dom Orlando Santos de Oliveira, Primate of the Episcopal Anglican Church of Brazil, as he signs the Concordat, pledging his support.

After the service, 75 people gathered for a reception honoring both the Bishop and the TSSF visitors. The next day, Masud and Anita took a bus past the famous *Christ the Redeemer* figure on Corcovado Mountain, the well-known beaches, and finally to the "City of God" (Cidade de Deus) in the outskirts of Rio. (The "City of God" was featured in a recent motion picture of the same name.) The government moved a large population from the beaches to this new location. Nearby is the Episcopal Church, a center for Franciscan social ministries where some literacy is taught to both adults and children.

Two issues of a community newspaper have been published, and the intention of the paper is to involve the whole "City of God" community. Everything is done on a shoestring but well and with heart. For Masud and Anita it was unforgettable; the level of commitment and courage of the Franciscans engaged in this ministry is reminiscent of the early days of Francis and the Franciscan movement. Next on their itinerary, Masud, David, Anita, and I traveled to Caruaru, in the state of Pernambuco in Brazil's Northwest. There we met in a regional Chapter meeting with representatives from most of Brazil's fraternities (Recife, Caruaru, Natal, São Paulo, and Paraíba).

After a morning of prayer and Franciscan reflection and study, the Concordat was read, discussed and unanimously ratified! The Regional Chapter meeting closed with a Eucharist and some sharing. The Franciscans were the first guests at a newly opened retreat center, which was transformed from a couple's villa home. The couple proved to be gracious hosts who joined in many of the TSSF/OSF activities.

From Caruaru, the TSSF delegation flew via the Recife airport to the southern city of Porto Alegre in the state of Rio Grande do Sul. We were met by Christina Winnischofer, the General Secretary of the Igreja Episcopal Anglicana do Brasil (IEAB), the Anglican Province of Brazil. Christina did much for the delegation; she arranged all of our in-country travel, hosted us in Porto Alegre, and introduced us to the Primate of Brazil, Dom Orlando Santos de Oliveira who then explained that the initiation of a Franciscan Order in Brazil was his long held dream. After hearing the details about TSSF he signed the Concordat and offered ongoing support. Dom Orlando noted that the TSSF's presence was not an U.S. American idea, but a response to Brazil's invitation.

Masud, David, Anita and I then boarded a bus and headed six hours west to Santa Maria where Bishop Jubal Neves had been trying for ten years to create a Franciscan presence in his diocese. We met with a dozen people who were anxious to explore TSSF, especially the *Principles* and the structure of the Order (the Community Rule and the personal rule). Bishop Jubal showed us the diocesan food project where bread is baked, and produce and medicinal herbs grown. This food project is a cooperative effort with the community of Santa Maria to help feed the poor and fund the diocese.

David and I rode six hours by car to Concórdia, in the state of Santa Catarina, to stay in the home of Luiz and Lúcia Sirtoli. Luiz had been a Roman Catholic Franciscan friar for 16 years before marrying Lúcia. Thus Luiz has a profound understanding of the religious life, in general, and the Franciscan charism in particular. Luiz and Lúcia share in daily devotions that include song, scripture and meditation.

David and I concluded our time in Brazil by attending the Diocese of Santa Maria's convention at the invitation of Bishop Jubal. There were repeated allusions to the Franciscan life throughout the convention, and a warm embrace for us. At the closing Eucharist, 12 new members were welcomed into the Franciscan Order. It was a moment of profound joy and humility; indeed it was a tangible moment of being "bound into a living whole through the love we share in Christ" (*Principles*, Day 27).

At the following **October 2004** Chapter, Minister Provincial Masud Ibn Syedullah pointed out:

> *Since the Third Order is part of a world-wide Order in the Anglican Communion, it is necessary for the Interprovincial Third Order Chapter (IPTOC), composed of representatives from the five TSSF provinces, to approve entry of OSF, Brazil into TSSF. IPTOC was scheduled to meet in late August/early September of 2005 at the International Franciscan Study Center at Canterbury, England. Between now and then, it was our task to clarify the particulars of our relationship with OSF towards making a proposal for its inclusion, which will be reviewed by IPTOC next year* (MP Report to Chapter 2004, *Franciscan Times*, Advent 2004).

Masud later wrote about this additional work in preparation for IPTOC.

> *Following the signing of the Concordat, there was subsequent work done by Anita, David, Barbara, and me to clarify the roles and responsibilities of regional officers and their responsibility (as regional officers) to the provincial officers and Chapter. It was that document that was presented to IPTOC—the final document (superseding the Concordat) which was accepted by Brazil, our Chapter, and IPTOC, which paved the way for Brazil to be a region of the Province of the Americas—subject to the Chapter of the Province of the Americas. IPTOC received OSF into TSSF as part of the Province of the Americas, with the understanding that authority rests in the Provincial Chapter. All of this is spelled out in the documents presented to IPTOC upon which they made their vote of acceptance.*

Just after Chapter in October, David and Anita Catron retired from their U.S. jobs and moved to Brazil to help facilitate the Concordat.

The Catrons in Brazil

Franciscan Times, Advent 2004

David and Anita Catron began their long-awaited retirement on October 20, 2004, as they departed Atlanta in the company of Fr. Sérgio Pacheco for Araçatuba, Brazil. Araçatuba is a city in the state of São Paulo, about 500 km to the west of the city of the same name, with a population of about 250,000. The Catrons chose Araçatuba for its central location (easy access by bus or air to most of the Third Order fellowships in Brazil), its temperate climate, and because Sérgio offered them the use of his parish office for Third Order business.

Within days of their arrival, David and Anita found convenient housing, a one-room efficiency apartment within walking distance to the church, and they ordered the installation of high-speed internet at the church office. During their second week, they received a visit from Fr. Cesar Alves, who is the founder of the Brazilian Order of St Francis (OSF) which seeks integration into TSSF, and who was at Chapter last year with his colleague, Fr. Francisco Sales of Recife.

Sérgio, Cézar and the Catrons drew up an outline for a proposed TSSF structure in Brazil. Cesar that there is only one professed TSF in Brazil to date, Fr. Luiz Sirtoli, in the Diocese of Santa Maria, formation was deemed the most important project. At the invitation of both Cézar and Sérgio, David will serve as Formation Director for Brazil, and will name AFDs in three regions, the Northwest (Recife and neighboring states), Southwest (São Paulo and neighboring states) and South (Porto Alegre and neighboring). A Treasurer will also be named and will begin collecting pledges and pledge monies with a view to helping the Brazilian TSF become financially independent, or nearly so, by the time of IPTOC next summer or Chapter in the fall.

On the weekend of November 5-7, the Bishop of São Paulo, Dom Hiroshi Ito, conducted his annual visit to Araçatuba, and the Catrons got to spend a fair amount of time with him. He, like most of the rest of the bishops of Brazil, is extremely supportive of OSF/TSSF in Brazil. Accompanying Bishop Ito was our own First Order Brother Tom Carey, who until April, 2004 was living with those OSF brothers in São Paulo city who hope to integrate themselves into SSF. Tom has an ambitious travel schedule planned to visit most of the fellowships in Brazil, and David and Anita hope to accompany him on some of them.

David and Anita will travel to visit Luiz in the week of November 8-13 to share with him the outline they prepared with Cesar and Sérgio, and to discuss the shape of the formation classes they will conduct throughout Brazil during the coming year. Generally, they will attempt to meet with each fellowship twice, once to discuss the Principles and Community Obedience, and a second time to conduct a rule writing workshop.

In December the Catrons hope to travel south again to visit the Brazilian Primate, Dom Orlando Santos de Oliveira, and the Provincial Secretary, Christina Winnischofer, both of whom have been supportive of Third Order work to date and whose continuing support will be important going forward as OSF integrates itself into TSSF. Other Bishops they hope to visit will be the bishops of Pelotas, Santa Maria, Curitiba, Brasília, Rio de Janeiro. The bishops of Rio and Santa Maria were received as TSF postulant and novice, respectively, last April. Some readers may know that the Bishop of Recife, Dom Robinson Cavalcanti, has been inhibited by the Brazilian House of Bishops due to his schismatic behavior arising out of opposition to the ordination of the Rt. Rev. Gene Robinson. This would be problematic for the Catrons' work in that diocese, where the majority of Brazilian OSF are to be found, except that the Suffragan, Dom Filadelfo Oliveira, is supportive of OSF/TSSF and is functioning, for all practical purposes, as Diocesan. Brazil is an immense and diverse country, equal in size to the United States, and the Catrons look forward to discovering as much of it as possible in the coming years.

....

After five months, October 2004 to February 2005, Anita returned to the U.S. while David stayed on working in Brazil.

2005 The Third Order Chapter

Franciscan Times, Summer 2005

In **May** Barbara Baumgarten stepped down as Formation Director of the Province, and relocated to Brazil as a consultant to Brazil.

The Interprovincial Third Order Chapter (IPTOC) met in **August** at the International Franciscan Study Center at Canterbury, England and unanimously agreed that the Order of St. Francis (OSF) in Brazil be recognized as part of the Third Order of the Society of St. Francis (TSSF) and be joined with the Province of the Americas.

At **October's** Chapter meeting, Masud Ibn Syedullah finished his term as Minister Provincial, and Ken Norian was elected as the new Minister Provincial.

In **December** (2005), the Brazilian-professed members selected three candidates for Regional Minister, and The Rev. Francisco Sales of Recife was elected as Regional Minister. They then began a process of electing other leaders (Chaplain, Formation Leader, Treasurer and Fellowship Coordinator) residing on the regional level and coordinating with their provincial counterparts. (Report on the Latinoamericano Ministry for Standing Committee–January 17, 2006 *(*Anita Catron *Franciscan Times,* Summer 2006)

2006—The Honeymoon and the Tempest

Everything was proceeding so well that the Minister General of TSSF, Dorothy Booker, traveled to Brazil with Anita Catron, to deliver profession crosses and officially welcome the Brazilian fellowships into the worldwide structure of TSSF. Her story is as follows:

TSSF Minister General Travels to Brazil

The Rev. Dorothy Brooker, TSSF Minister General Franciscan Times, Summer 2006

Pilgrims are people who journey in faith into the unknown. How true this was for me. Leaving the security of the plane at São Paulo (the largest city in Brazil of more than 11 and a half million people), I was met by Brother Cesar, SSF, a First Order Brother, and Anita Catron, TSSF, who is the Consultant for the Third Order Franciscans in Brazil, and our journey began. Little did I know that although we had some sense of itinerary we would find ourselves planning the next day or days on the spot, responding to the fellowship requests to visit and finding the cheapest, easiest and safest way to get there.

Little did I know that in a short three weeks, Anita and I would have traveled 16,000kms (10,000 miles) by plane, bus or private car, visiting São Paulo, São Gabriel, Porto Alegre, Erechim, Belo Horizonte, Brasilia, Recife, Caruaru, Salvador, and Rio de Janeiro. As we met with fellowships and spent time with those who were officers in Brazil, time was spent in helping to equip and to enable them to understand the structure of our Order more fully.

It was good to catch up and spend time with The Rev. Francisco Sales ("Chico"), who was present at IPTOC, and who has been elected as the Regional Minister.

Back: Christina Winnischofer, Dom Orlando (Primate IEAB), Juliano Cavedon, Ana Lúcia Machado, Dessordi Leite. Front: Anita Catron, Andrea Machado, Minister General Dorothy Booker, Paul Bassoto, Porto Alegre Fellowship.

It was also apparent that some felt isolated, since they were far away from the fellowship meetings, and it was a wonderful opportunity to show them a way to feel "community." The Brazilian and American websites are a good example of community.

Brazil is part of a large continent with eight Dioceses and two Missionary Dioceses, most with a growing Franciscan Third Order, all finding that the Franciscan way of meeting Christ anew in those they meet to be humbling, exciting and challenging. The Church in Brazil (Igreja Episcopal Anglicana do Brasil) lives like all our Provinces in seeking ways to discern and to dialogue with those in our Anglican Communion who walk a vastly different path.

We both received encouragement and support from seven out of the eight Bishops we met and, in turn, encouraged three of them in TSSF formation.

At that moment the elections were taking place for Chaplain, Formation Director, Secretary, Treasurer and Fellowship Coordinator on the regional level. Once this has been completed, they will be able to help the many novices and postulants to discern their call to a religious life. The worldwide TSSF community needs to support and uphold them in our prayers; many of them are working in areas with the marginalized and the very poor.

The reason for our visit was to formally receive each Fellowship and to present each Professed with the Profession Cross. This was done during a Eucharist, or other services, as well as informal gatherings. It was good to have the Diocesan Bishops present at each place. The Primate (our deputy Bishop Protector there) was also in attendance at one such gathering.

As we received each fellowship we used the following words, with Anita translating into Portuguese:

> *At the Interprovincial Third Order Chapter, August 2005, held in Canterbury, England, it was unanimously agreed that the Order of St. Francis in Brazil be recognized as part of the Third Order of the Society of St. Francis and be joined with the Province of the Americas. As Minister General, it is with great joy that I am here to receive you and to recognize you as Professed and Novices and to encourage those who are beginning their journey as Postulants. To those who are Professed we now present you with your Profession Cross. Wear it as a member of our Order. Wear it proudly and may the Lord accept your offering and give you grace to persevere. To those who are*

Novices and Postulants, may the Lord continue to bless you on your journey towards Profession.

This short ceremony was concluded with the Blessing St. Francis gave to Brother Leo. There are two First Order brothers, Cesar and Evanildo, who were to be received at some point by Brother Jude and Brother Tom from the Province of the Americas, arriving as we left.

It has been a great privilege to represent you all as Minister General with the newest members of our family, and I thank you all for enabling this to happen through our Central Fund. It has been a wonderful privilege to travel with the Brazilian Consultant Anita, who was my voice in Brazil each day.

The Tempest—Fallout from Chapter October 2006

Ken Norian, elected as the new Minister Provincial at 2005 Chapter, chaired his first chapter meeting in October. (For Chapters 2003–06, Provincial Chapter paid the way of two Brazilians to come to each Chapter.) However, immediately following this Chapter meeting a number of parallel actions took place resulting in approximately half of the tertiaries in Brazil withdrawing from formation or asking for release from vows. The leaders other than the Regional Minister withdrew, and the Regional Minister resigned. ("Minister Provincial Report, Chapter 2007," *Franciscan Times,* Christmas 2007).

Four internal actions in TSSF that triggered these events included:

- In 2005, Barbara Baumgarten resigned as Formation Director of the Province, and relocated to Brazil to act on her own as a consultant to the Brazilian tertiaries.
- A norm was passed at Chapter 2006 that the Region of Brazil send an English speaker to participate in Provincial Chapters since translation efforts at Chapter were proving onerous and causing misunderstandings.
- This norm that was intended to be applied only to the Brazilian Chapter representative was miscommunicated by the Brazilian regional leadership as to be applicable to all members. Predictably, the reaction by the Brazilian members was that such actions were "authoritative" and "imperialistic."
- In 2006, some high profile personal relationships polarized the Brazilian-region.

To these four internal TSSF/OSF problems, came the external problems of havoc in the the Episcopal Church in Brazil (*Igreja Episcopal Anglicana do Brasil*). As early as Chapter 2003, troubles in the Church in Brazil were being reported by Brazilian visitors to Chapter, such as:

> We also ask the brothers and sisters of SSF and TSSF to pray for us, since we now have troubles being Franciscans. In North Brazil, the conservative and fundamentalist church branches are in the majority, and we are having some problems. Some of our priests are being persecuted for having a pastoral outreach for gay people; they also do not like our liturgy and our

manner of dress (our habits); the way we pray for the saints; and things like that. It got worse after the ECUSA Convention decisions [to permit same sex unions and allow gay bishops]. The conservatives started to tell us not to establish any contact with the United States or with any other First World countries. They (even the Diocesan Bishop of Recife) called ECUSA "liberal," "revisionist," "non-creedal," and "almost non-faithful." They said we must only officially link up with Africa and Australia (they mean Sydney). We have been non-officially threatened (since they cannot officially interfere inside the religious Orders), and some of our members have lost their jobs in the Church (dismissed).

Finally although not directly affecting the situation, those members of OSF who had opted for a First Order expression of their Franciscanism encountered trouble in their own coordination with the Provincial Chapter of SSF, and several went on a leave of absence.

In December, Ken Norian received approval from Chapter to issue this letter:

Dear Franciscan Brothers and Sisters in Brazil:

In 2003, several members of the Order of Saint Francis (OSF) in Brazil approached the Society of Saint Francis to determine the possibility of a relationship that might exist between the two Orders. There were those in Brazil who felt called to a First Order vocation of celibates living in an intentional community, and those who felt called to a secular or "Third Order Vocation."

The Third Order, Province of the Americas, Society of Saint Francis and OSF through conversation and dialogue agreed on a Concordat of understanding in October 2003. This Concordat presupposed that the Region of Brazil would likely seek to form a separate province at some future date in the Third Order, Society of Saint Francis. The exact nature of this relationship was not clearly defined. Reference was made to a "Companion Region," something not recognized in either the Statutes of TSSF or The Society of St. Francis. In recognition of this goal, a regional leadership would be elected that would mirror the structure of TSSF in the Americas and other Provinces worldwide, but not as a separately governed leadership at this time. (This would be accomplished in the context of OSF professed members in Brazil being professed in the Third Order, Society of Saint Francis, and those in formation eventually professed in TSSF).

Much progress was made in translating formation materials and other documents from English to Portuguese. Last year an election was held to select those individuals who would hold regional positions such as Minister, Chaplain, Formation Director, etc.—all on the regional level. Earlier this year, individuals were received into TSSF from OSF.

Since our Provincial Chapter meeting in October 2006, there has been an unfortunate series of events that has led to serious contention and division in Brazil. Several entire fellowships have expressed that they have withdrawn from TSSF. Other individuals have as well. Many of the previously elected officers are included in those who have withdrawn. The TSSF Chapter expresses its regrets for any unintentional role it may have had in contributing to the feelings leading to these decisions.

It is clear that the situation that has evolved in Brazil is one that holds no prospects in the near future for establishment of a separate province in the worldwide Third Order, Society of Saint Francis–which was the driving force behind establishment of a regional organization of officers that paralleled the Provincial organization. It is appropriate at this time to abandon the regional structure in Brazil and implement a structure typical of the rest of the Province.

TSSF in the Americas is comprised of sisters and brothers from the United States, Canada, Colombia, The Dominican Republic, Ecuador, Guyana, Jamaica, Mexico, Nevis, Trinidad and Tobago. Tertiaries in these countries are equal partners in the work of the Province. Tertiaries from all countries are able to serve on Chapter–and many do. Depending on the number of tertiaries in each country, Area Chaplains, Area Formation Directors, and Area Bursars may serve the people in their respective countries. In non-English speaking countries, Chapter relies on bilingual tertiaries to facilitate communication within the Province. This arrangement has worked successfully for many years–both serving the needs of tertiaries in many countries while benefiting from the diversity represented by all in the Province.

The situation in Brazil should not be any different, and should have the same opportunities for success. Franciscan tertiaries in Brazil may choose to seek release from their vows in TSSF and associate themselves with whatever community nourishes their Franciscan vocation. We would look forward to maintaining the same fraternal relationship with other Franciscans in Brazil as we do with Franciscan communities both within the Anglican Communion and in other denominations. Franciscan tertiaries in Brazil who choose to remain in TSSF should be assured that their Franciscan vocation will be respected and will continue to be encouraged and nurtured in the same way that tertiaries throughout all countries in the Americas are.

I am sure many of you may have questions. Not all the answers have been fully developed, and not all questions have easy answers. Anita Catron has been designated as the Consultant to Brazil, and you should feel free to work through her for the immediate future for either general questions, or specific questions that you have for me or for Chapter.

Amidst the disappointment and frustration many of us are experiencing at this time, we should not fail to remember the Franciscan charisms of peace, love, charity, humility and joy. I am confident that those who seek to live in the spirit of these charisms will continue to walk together as brothers and sisters in Christ and Francis.

To enact this letter, Chapter adopted unanimously the following resolution:

> We encourage and support ongoing and future direct communication in English and cooperation between regional and provincial officers in Brazil. Moreover, we empower the Regional Minister of Brazil to *appoint* assistants to serve in positions, which may be made vacant. The 2005 Addendum to the Norms concerning the *election* process for officers in Brazil is no longer needed and is to be removed.

The dramatic change in the relationship of OSF and TSSF in the year 2006 shook the very foundations of all the work that had been accomplished, and silence descended.

2007—Brazilians Live a Franciscan Life on Local Levels with No Regional Structure, and No One to Officially Coordinate with the Provincial Chapter

At Chapter 2007, Dessórdi Peres Leite was present representing Brazil. Since it was of utmost importance to institute a formation program and a way to care for the professed, Sérgio Pacheco was approved as AFD, and Anita Catron as Area Chaplain. In order to best serve the fellowships of the two major regions, Dessórdi Leite was approved as Assistant Fellowship Coordinator, and he was to be assisted by Christina Winnischofer.

Bishop Naudal, Anita M., Bill B, Carmen Gomes (Curitiba).

2008

In March Anita Catron Miner and Formation Director Bill Breedlove made a 10-day trip to ensure that Assistant Fellowship Coordinator, Christina Winnischofer, had all the materials and help to perform her job (*Franciscan Times*, Summer 2008). Anita Catron Miner and Bill Breedlove's trip included visits to five cities. Despite the absence of Regional leadership, local and fellowship TSSF life continued. In Campinas (State of São Paulo) there was a growing fellowship. Sérgio Pacheco, the AFD for Brazil, was not only performing his AFD task but also growing his fellowship. Anita and Bill professed two members and two others renewed their novice vows. The fellowship in Rio met once a month, and was getting ready for the profession, novicings, and reception of a postulant.

During the summer of 2008, on the hillside above downtown Rio de Janeiro, in the barrio of Santa Teresa, Bishop Celso Franco de Oliveira with the help of the Third Order Franciscan community established Casa Franciscana (*Franciscan Times,* Summer 2009).

At October's Chapter, Brazil's regional representative, Christina Winnischofer, shared news from Brazil. She has been working on bringing together all the fellowships in Brazil and has contacted them all, finding: there are 28 professed, 25 in Formation, and three-and-a-half fellowships are sound and will hopefully offer a solid basis upon which to grow. (Christina observed that she thought that the OSF/TSSF in Brazil had been growing too fast with many joining without fully understanding what profession meant.)

Dom Celso's Street Eucharistic ministry. Here is a YouTube of the 10th anniversary of this ministry. https://youtu.be/WYPBkXTpn3Q

2009

At October's Chapter, Dom Jubal Pereira Neves was the representative from Brazil. There was a great deal of discussion about creating committees to clarify a process for formation and accountability that fits Brazilian culture beyond just translation of materials. Currently there are only a few identified leaders, and they are overextended. The vast size of Brazil (almost as large as the USA) is a factor. Representation is needed from the north, central and south.

2010

At October's Chapter, Dessórdi Peres Leite was the representative from Brazil. He reported that in Formation there are four Inquirers; eight Postulants; and five Novices. Dessórdi explained that given the size of Brazil, no one can speak for the whole country, only their own fellowship. The dioceses of Brazil do not work together, making it difficult to unify Brazilian tertiaries. They have 400 years of Roman Catholic example and theological and cultural differences. In their Church of Brazil, there is no Sacrament of Reconcilation, almost no spiritual direction, and words like "Rule" and "obedience" are understood negatively.

2011

At October's Chapter, Ken Norian, outgoing Minister Provincial, summarized his experiences of Brazil over his two terms; that the relationship had been an ongoing challenge:

> The sense of community between the north and south of Brazil is an issue, and there is less connection to TSSF Province of the Americas. No local leaders have arisen. There are active local fraternities/fellowships who clearly display a Franciscan charism with much zeal. Our visibility, however, into their Formation is nil as is communication with those who have been professed there. We've made several visits there, and have always invited a representative to Chapter. There has been nearly no contact in the past year. I confess to some level of burnout on this matter, as it has consumed a tre-

> mendous amount of time and energy over the past six years. Clearly, the current situation is not sustainable—and has been languishing for nine years.
>
> With a North American-based liaison, it seems that the current situation would continue with limited effectiveness especially in regard to Formation and care of the professed. It is believed that there needs to be a local committee in-country to discern God's call for that vital Franciscan spirit that does exist (Minister Provincial Report, Chapter 2011).

A letter was composed that went out to all the brothers and sisters in Brazil assuring them of the Province's prayers, love and support, and belief that local discernment is vital to respond to the Spirit of God that is calling them into the way of St. Francis. Barbara Baumgarten was contacted to serve as an initial animator since was living in Brazil and was familiar with formation.

2012

At the October Chapter with the newly-elected Minister Provincial John Brockmann there was a request from Barbara Baumgarten for some funds to underwrite "retreats/gatherings" around Brazil since she told Chapter that this was the most natural way for Brazilians to come together. (They had also just created their own Facebook page, which Provincial Chapter helped to fund.)

2013—The Resurrection of the Courtship

As October Chapter was approaching, Chapter asked for some kind of report from Barbara and Brazil regarding the previous year, and how the funds that had been sent had been spent. Disappointingly, Chapter was informed that at least two "retreats/gatherings" had been planned, but were canceled for lack of interest. One last "retreat/gathering" was scheduled right at the time of our Provincial Chapter October 2013. So we waited, and voted more support money at that Chapter with the proviso that a report would be forthcoming.

In late October and early November 2013, the report of a miracle occurred. Not only did this last scheduled "retreat/gathering" take place, but at the "retreat/gathering":

- a regional chapter was constituted;
- a Regional Minister elected (Barbara Baumgarten),
- a Secretary (The Rev. Francisco Sales, the former Regional Minister), and Bursar were also elected; and
- a sizeable amount of money was collected to support the ongoing efforts of the Region.

In one stroke, this "retreat/gathering" of the Brazilian members of TSSF returned to the pre-Chapter 2006 understanding of a Region within the Province with locally elected officers.

2014

Beginning in January 2014, Provincial Chapter moved to a quarterly conference call to consider professions, releases, etc. The Brazilian Regional Chapter elected a person to profession in late 2013, and Chapter approved a process whereby the Brazilian Regional Chapter would do the work of formation and discernment, present the Provincial Chapter with the relevant materials and then the Provincial Chapter would ratify or not ratify their elections. Finally after eleven years, a practical, working organizational relationship was established between the Region and the Province, but the Province would have the final confirmation of all elections to profession as required under the *Provincial Statutes*.

In May 2014, based upon the success and work in January, Provincial Chapter established a parallel procedure for releases of Brazilian members from vows and two were released; and Provincial Chapter also moved to link the regional and provincial Fellowship Convener and Bursars. As Chapter in October 2014 approached, all seemed to be working according to plan until the reality of the Brazilian election to profession schema was revealed in discussions. Because all elections to profession are done at one time during an annual retreat prior to the meeting of Chapter, all Provincial confirmations proved to be superfluous to the Brazilian regional decisions. At this Chapter, Tom Johnson was elected Minister Provincial and the process of resolving the Regional/Provincial relationships continued.

Annual Christmas Mass Held in the Street in Downtown Rio de Janeiro, 2014.

(1) Nicholas Wheeler, British missionary priest, giving Eucharist to street community. (2) Serving the food line. (3) Street child opening a gift from Toys for Tots sponsored by American Consulate. (For more information see Franciscan Times, Sum. 2010, "Street Mass Ministry–Rio de Janeiro," p. 1.)

The whole process, thus far, has taken 18 years and work from five different Minister Provincials and six different Chapters. There was an initial burst of enthusiasm and promise followed by a time of treading water. The personal and the organizational became thoroughly confused, leading to an organizational collapse of the Third Order Region in Brazil. In 2014, there are signs of a rebirth, but so much still needs to be resolved. This episode in our history is still looking for a finale.

The Rev. Steve Best .

The Red Book, Safe Community and Conflict Resolution, and Going Beyond

Like the work with Brazil's regional organization and status, wrestling with Safe Community and Conflict Resolution took the work of two Ministers Provincial and two different Chapters.

Background

In 1986, TSSF was recognized by the ECUSA's House of Bishops Committee on Religious Orders and Other Christian Communities as a Christian Community and entered ECUSA's annual "Red Book" (*The Episcopal Church Annual* the official directory for ECUSA) for the first time. Appearing in the "Red Book" gave creditability to TSSF as an authorized organization. (The effort to be included and recognized by the House of Bishops Committee on Religious Orders and Christian Communities was led by TSSF Chaplain Fr. Robert "Gooch" Goode and Fr. George Metcalf of Minnesota.) This recognition allowed TSSF to participate in Conferences on Religious Life sponsored by ECUSA.

However, the cost of such public recognition and authorization eventually became apparent. As the scandals of sexual abuse and improprieties in all the churches became known in the 1990s, and, specifically, as questionable sexual improprieties by members of the SSF First Order hit the newspapers…and as the Church Insurance Company was hit by claims from a former SSF novice, the House of Bishops (HOB) Standing Committee on Religious Orders and Christian Communities (SCORC) inititiated new requirements in 2005. The SCORC began putting pressure on Religious Orders (e.g., our First Order brothers and sisters who live in community) and Christian Communities (those Orders not living in community like TSSF) to be more accountable to the House of Bishops and be subject to increased monitoring. The process by which this would be accomplished was that the Bishop Protector would meet with every professed person over a period of years, and that everyone in a Christian Community would have to undergo a background check.

However, such a procrustean solution failed to recognize that TSSF, the largest Christian Community in ECUSA, was unlike any enclosed communities because members of TSSF are a quite widely dispersed community. Thus, quite practically, how could a Bishop Protector interview every member? How could every aspirant afford a background check? Moreover, TSSF in the Province of the Americas crossed national and provincial jurisdictions, so how could ECUSA impose its rules on non-ECUSA bishops and provinces of the Anglican Communion?

At Chapter 2005, Minister Provincial Masud Ibn Sydeullah worked with Chapter to create the "Safe Community and Conflict Resolution" committee to look at the health of the whole person (body, mind, and spirit) in relationship with the TSSF community including racism, baptismal values, and the worth of the individual. The Committee included the Chaplain, Formation Director, Minister Provincial, and other members representing differences races, ethnic backgrounds, genders, and sexual orientations.

At Chapter 2006, newly-elected Minister Provincial Ken Norian and Chapter agreed to adopt a new "Safe Community and Conflict Resolution Policy" for trial use for two years with an annual review by Chapter. Another document worked on by the same committee addressed the requirements imposed on the Order by the Standing Committee on Religious Communities (SCORC) of the HOB if we were to continue being recognized as a Christian Community and to be listed as such in the *Episcopal Church Annual*. The Rev. Steve Best, who had worked on these issues within his own diocese, was a key animator of this whole process.

Two documents were produced.* The first requested that the Order's official recognition by ECUSA be withdrawn because of the impossibility of properly fulfilling the requirements of the House of Bishop's Standing Committee on Religious Communities. At the same time, this document points to the official recognition afforded the Province of the Americas, TSSF by its constitutional position as one of the four component parts of the worldwide Society of Saint Francis recognized by the See of Canterbury.

Once the problem of official authorization was disentangled from the actual work that was needed to ensure Safe Church policies in TSSF, a second document was created which spelled out exactly how Safe Church policies were to be implemented in TSSF. This document was published in the *Franciscan Times* in toto, and, ever after, all officers and all new postulants are required to sign an acknowledgement of receipt form and send it to the Chaplain.

2007 Chapter held a mid-review of the Safe Community and Conflict Transformation Policy, with a workshop at the Provincial Convocation serving as a way to illustrate how this process of conflict resolution can work. Steve Best stressed the necessity of not ramroding the process through the membership but of letting it be one of formation. Regional representatives will serve to put the policy into context through relationships, adding another dimension to their work.

2008 Chapter created a system to record basic and required information on leaders (report, renew and contribute) plus safe community information on a database for all of the professed. The "Safe Community" document was approved with a change in emphasis on transformation from conflict to growth. The language also became more theological for example, using biblical examples along with reflective questions.

At **2009 Chapter**, Minister Provincial Ken Norian reported attending the NAECC (National Association of Episcopal Christian Communities), which is a gathering of representatives from many of the Christian communities in North America. He reported that TSSF was fully embraced regardless of our "official status with the House of Bishops." (Moreover, TSSF is still listed in the "Red Book".) The other Christian communities were very interested in our journey with the Safe Community Covenant and considered us in the forefront on this issue.

All the concern disappears with Chapter 2009 not to reappear until **Chapter 2013** when a review of records and reaffirmation of the Safe Community process occurred.

References

Fisher, Michael. *For the Time Being: A Memoir*. Leominster: Gracewing, 1993.

The Episcopal Church Annual. Wilton, Conn. [etc.: Morehouse-Barlow [etc., continuing]

Williams, Barrie. *The Franciscan Revival in the Anglican Communion.*London: Darton, Longman & Todd Ltd; 1982.

Chapter 10: The Evolution of Justice, Peace, and the Integrity of Creation (JPIC): 1998-2013

To accurately use a sundial you need a graph of the Equation of Time. The Equation of Time represents the facts that, although both celestial solar time and human watch time can symbolize the passage of time, both are independent in the passage of time they reveal. Only occasionally during a year and only then at irregular intervals during the year, do the two coincide. Moreover, the relationship between the two sometimes shows the sundial to be revealing time at a slower pace than watch time, and, at other times, faster than watch time.

The Equation of Time in all its complexity can also visually represent the relationship between the timing and personalities of Chapter and the elected officers in the Order, and the timing, personalities, and highlights of the efforts of those who make up the volunteer leaders of the Justice Peace and the Integrity of Creation (JPIC) (formerly the Justice and Peace group JP)) in the Province of the Americas. Sometimes Chapter and JPIC coincide with individuals who are members of both and who can coordinate the united efforts of both—but that is unusual and unpredictable. Most of the time Chapter and JPIC operate independently in their activities, in the individuals involved, and in their efforts at coordinating themselves.

Just as the long-term problems and solutions of the last chapter escaped the neat metronome of Chapter and Minister Provincial election cycles, so too the story of JPIC escapes such predictable cycles. Justice, peace, and concern for God's creation have been Franciscan concerns from Francis' earliest work. Many individual members of the Third Order have labored in these areas for years and continue to do so on an individual basis. These Franciscan core concerns produced in turn: a Chapter focus group, commissions, a number of Province-sponsored events, and finally the theme for an entire Provincial Convocation in 2013. Moreover, JP and JPIC actions led the Province of the Americas to become included in Franciscan endeavors beyond the Anglican Communion: **Franciscans International** (FI, a primarily Roman Catholic-based, non-governmental organization (NGO) at the United Nations serving as a Franciscan ethical/moral presence) and later **Franciscan Action Network** (a Washington, DC lobbying group acting as a a Franciscan ethical/moral presence in domestic US politics).

Like many aspects of the Province of the Americas, leadership in the area of Justice & Peace (JP), later Justice, Peace & the Integrity of Creation (JPIC), rested on the resourcefulness, perseverance, and organizational skills of a few very key volunteer leaders. The first generation of leaders included Carol Tookey, Terry Rogers, and Emmett Jarrett, who were succeeded by the second generation of leaders, including Joyce Wilding, Francesca Wigle, Verleah Kosloske, and Dianne Aid.

Justice and Peace (JP), A Chapter Focus Group 1998-2001

In **1998**, Masud Ibn Syedullah reported to Chapter that a committee had been formed from members of the First and Third Orders (Minister Provincial Anita

Catron, and former Ministers Provincial John Scott and Dee Dobson, and soon-to-be Minister Provincial Masud) to listen to concerns of the Orders and to provide guidance in matters of justice and peace (JP). Individual tertiaries were urged to join Franciscans International (FI), and the *Franciscan Times* that Fall published this description of FI:

Franciscans International, a Non-Governmental Organization (NGO) at the United Nations has General Consultative Status with the United Nations Economic and Social Council. (The Anglican Communion also has a representative to the UN whose office has the same NGO status.)

Franciscans International is a network of the Franciscan Family (trans-denominational) collaborating on world issues; a forum for the poor to have a voice at the United Nations; a place where the Franciscan Family and the 185 UN representatives of the member states, the UN civil servants and other NGOs can share the heritage of Saints Francis and Clare for peace; and a clearinghouse of UN information on global concerns vital to the Franciscan Family in its global mission in the world. Through collaboration, education, and action, the mission of Franciscans International is: care of creation, peacemaking, and concern for the poor.

As an Order, Chapter 1998 voted to contribute $300 dollars to Franciscans International. It winds up, however, that it is more advantageous for FI in UN-NGO reckoning if individuals rather than groups contribute and join, and thus all Chapter members voted to join Franciscans International as members.

In **1999**, Carol Tookey, John Tolbert, Joan Verret, and Fr. Charles Roland from Guyana met as the Justice and Peace group at Chapter. The Peace and Justice Group sponsored Fr. Roland's trip to the US to be part of a 12-member delegation to the World Bank IMF annual meeting to present the necessity of Third World debt forgiveness. (Fr. Roland is an Amerindian from a community on the Guyanese/Venezuelan/Brazilian border. His people are very isolated; no phone, no mail, no roads, yet there are about 20 tertiaries living in this region. For more on this community, see Chapter 13.) Charles wrote this letter to describe his visit:

The reason for my coming here was to attend the Jubilee 2000 on the topic of cancellation of Third World debt of which Guyana is one of the countries mostly affected. To be honest with you I did not really know about the situation which this heavy burden of debt was causing in my country. Then I too did not realize that so many Christian bodies, such as Franciscans International, the Peace and Justice Group and many others were in solidarity with these effects on Third World countries which face such hardship. Guyana is for one in a state of poverty, especially in the interior, where our native people feel the squeeze more. We do not have proper medical facilities, no drugs to treat the people who are sick. The education system is on the point of collapse, where there is no finance to pay the teachers. All these were reported, and I know for a fact that careful attention was taken by those who were listening. I'm now aware, and realize that many people in the US were not conscious of the real situation in Guyana, and I am happy that I was able to come and relate the true story of what is really taking place in our country by this. I will say that my visit was worthwhile and I have a new vision and understanding and which gives me new hope that brothers and sisters in the US are concerned and will voice our problems to higher authorities.

In **2001**, Carol Tookey was joined by Terry Rogers, Brenda Cummings of Trinidad, and Emmett Jarrett, who together constituted the JP committee at Chapter. The committee urged a renewed concern and commitment for peace and international and national justice. Thus, by 2001, the three key players in JP (soon to be JPIC) were creating events in these areas. All three brought with them JP experiences outside of TSSF to their work. Carol was trained as a nurse and hospice worker, then deacon, eventually priest, and has spent much time as a missioner in Navajoland following in the work started by H. Baxter Liebler (see Chapter 2). Terry Rogers was also trained as a nurse and worked as a companion of the Catholic Worker House founded in NYC by Dorothy Day. Terry has used her nursing skills during trips to the West Bank of Palestine. Emmett Jarrett, prior to his work with JPIC, was a parish priest, published poet, the president of the Episcopal Urban Caucus, a leader in the Episcopal Peace Fellowship, and, with his wife, had just begun a type of Catholic Worker house in New London, Connecticut. (For much more on Emmett, see Chapter 14.)

First Province-sponsored JPIC Action-2002: Telegrams to President Bush

At the 2002 Chapter, JP became JPIC—Justice, Peace, and the Integrity of Creation, and a motion was made to create an annual JPIC Commission be appointed by the Minister Provincial. The Commission's job was to bring before Chapter and the Third Order the ministries for justice, peace, and the integrity of creation as expressions of the Second and Third Aims of the Order in the *Principles* of the Third Order; to seek out and celebrate, through publication, the living examples of such witness and ministry in members of the Third Order; and to bring before Chapter such policies and programs of the ministries of justice, peace, and the integrity of creation as may be appropriate for adoption by Chapter, or as a commendation to the membership of the Order, or otherwise recognized or celebrated.

However, such organizational concerns took the backseat when on the Friday of the 2002 Chapter meeting, Congress voted to grant George W. Bush the the use of military force in Iraq (an outgrowth of the war in Afghanistan). Two actions were initiated that day in JPIC's recommendations to Chapter:

1. That the Third Order Chapter send to President George W. Bush a telegram stating "We beg you not to go to war with Iraq but to work through the United Nations for a peaceful resolution of this crisis."
2. That a JPIC letter be sent out to all TSSF members by post and email as follows:

Brothers and Sisters,

As followers of the Prince of Peace we are called to be instruments of God's peace. We commend to you these words of Thomas Merton:

Instead of hating the people you think are war-makers, hate the appetites and disorder in your own soul, which are the causes of war. If you love peace, then hate injustice, hate tyranny, hate greed–but hate these things in yourself, not in another.

As a way to work actively for Peace, the Third Order commends to each member of the Order these three activities:

i. daily prayer

ii. weekly fasting

iii. regular acts of generosity and self-denial

We also suggest the daily use of the World Prayer for Peace found in the Devotional Companion:

O God, lead us from death to life, from falsehood to truth. Lead us from despair to hope, from fear to trust. Lead us from hate to love, from war to peace. Let peace fill our hearts, our world, our universe. Amen

JPIC Prayer and Witness Actions: 2004 to 2008

JPIC's Prayer and Witness actions began in 2004 as a response to the War in Iraq. Two years later JPIC action focused on the anticipated controversy and dissension at General Convention of ECUSA held on June 2006 in Columbus, Ohio. Two years after that, JPIC action became a worldwide response by all the TSSF provinces to the anticipated controversy and dissension at the Lambeth Conference of Bishops in Canterbury in 2008.

First JPIC Prayer and Witness Action, 2004: Union Square Witness

Growing out of the earlier action, at the 2002 Chapter, Carol Tookey and JPIC Commission members decided to sponsor a Witness for Peace in Union Square in the heart of New York City on September 11-17, 2004—the third anniversary of the attacks on the World Trade Center. Emmett Jarrett, a newly elected member of Chapter, quickly took a guiding hand by pointing out that the Dominicans had set up a tent there for a month and dedicated themselves to fasting, prayer, and interaction with the community to preach Christ and peace in the "marketplace."

Here's how Carol Tookey wrote up a report on this action for the *Franciscan Times*:

A Jesuit priest who teaches Buddhism and preached the Gospel in limericks; a young college student recently transported from the Midwest to New York City; a Buddhist woman preparing for a peace action; filmmakers in desperate search of a tent; a Jewish man who thought our work was important but who was startled when we said we weren't collecting money; a street person whom we named "the angry Brit" who thought **we** *were*

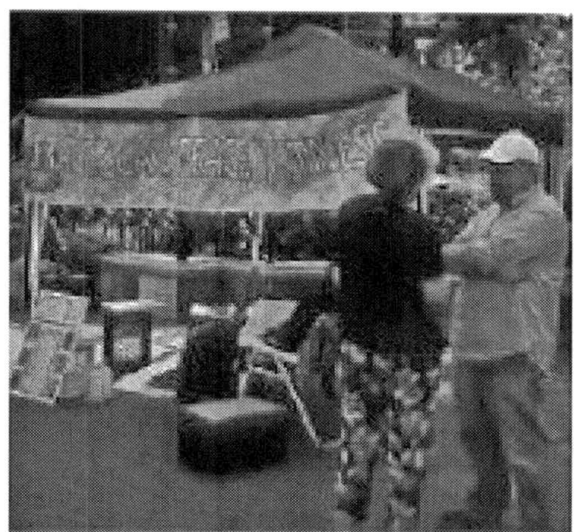

Terry Rogers and Charles McCarron in front of tent.

crazy—these were just a few of the visitors to our Franciscan Peace Witness, held September 11-17 in Union Square, New York City. JPIC members gathered Friday evening for prayers and preparation. Saturday morning we began a ritual cab ride from 1st Avenue and 1st Street to 14th and Union Square with all our props: lawn chairs, tent, posters, and a Franciscan "altar" created from a Rubbermaid tote, a piece of cloth and a San Damiano cross. Our booth was assembled with the homemade and donated, and held together with twine and duct tape.

Having no park permit for the weekend, we sat under the shadow of Abraham Lincoln (the tent not being permitted on those days) and were available to passers-by to look at our display, pick up a brochure or peace prayer card, or engage us in conversation. By Monday we were allowed to take our regular place and set up our tent in the "Gandhi Triangle"—an area of Union Square adorned with pampas grass and a statue of the famous exemplar of non-violence, Mohandas K. Gandhi.

Every morning before moving out to the park, we prayed the Morning Office in community. Most days we were able to engage the Word of God in Gospel Based Discipleship, a format of African Bible Study developed by the Episcopal Church's Native Ministry Office. Franciscans came and went through the week: Charles McCarron to teach us the finer points of setting up the tent and bring us the fine banner produced by his partner; Ken Norian, stepping in for his lunch break from his job in Manhattan; our Minister Provincial, Masud; Lyndon Hutchinson-Hounsell, Lynn Herne, Pam Moffitt, and Evelynn Mackie who helped staff the booth throughout the week; Ellen Rutherford who came for our closing event; Antonio, one of our brothers from Brazil; and Friars Derek and Graham who lent dignity and humor to our gathering.

And through all of this week there were the visitors—people from all walks of life—curious about what we were doing, giving us words of support, asking questions, sometimes challenging us–but always engaging. At the end of each conversation we would ask the visitor if there was something we could pray about for them. It was amazing to see what the offer of ministry meant to people. Some intercessions were general— "world peace"—but others were very personal—"for my mother who's having brain surgery tomorrow," "healing for my relationship with my daughter." So at the end

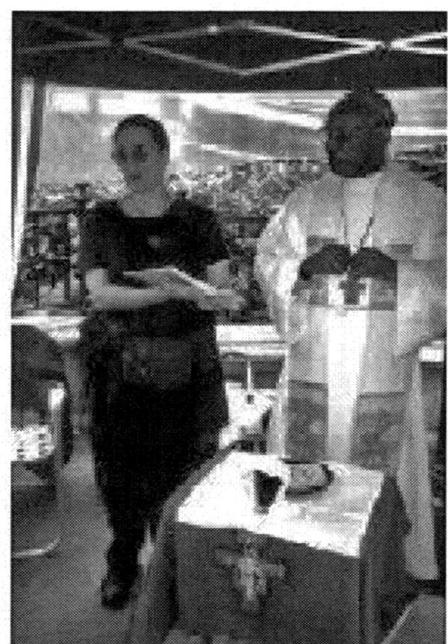

Carol Tookey and The Rt. Rev. E. Don Taylor, Assistant Bishop of New York.

of each day, before we packed up, we gathered around our little altar and offered these concerns up into the heart of God.

We finished off our week on the Feast of the Stigmata with a Eucharist under the tent. The Rt. Rev. E. Don Taylor, Assistant Bishop of New York, presided and offered an inspiring homily on how we are all called to bear the signs of Christ into the world. As the dismissal was given, we began to disburse, catching cabs and trains for home.

The JPIC Committee is so grateful for all who lent their support in so many ways—money to help pay for our meals and cab fares, donated items, prayerful solidarity from across the Province, for all who visited. Most especially I'd like to thank Terry Rogers for all her "diaconal" ministry in planning, organizing, setting up, getting permits and generally putting it all together—and to Fr. Emmett Jarrett for his spiritual and theological leadership, and for being a wonderful teacher.

Here's how Lyndon Hutchison-Hounsell wrote up his impressions on this action for the *Franciscan Times* in "A Canadian in Union Square:"

It's a warm sunny day in September, and here I am on a plane to Newark again. I'm headed for another meeting of JPIC (Justice, Peace and the Integrity of Creation Commission of the SSF). Except this time I'm also going to participate in the Franciscan Peace Witness in Union Square in the middle of Manhattan.…I find the warm smiles and hugs of Terry Rogers and John George Robertson waiting at the Peace Witness booth. Later, Emmett Jarrett and Carol Tookey return from a little walk...and then a little later Lynn Herne arrives...and a little after that Ken Norian arrives on a break from work.

I have no idea what to expect when I get there. Am I going to be walking around with placards saying MAKE PEACE, NOT WAR!? Am I going to be handing out pamphlets to everybody who walks by to get them to change their attitudes and become non-violent activists? Am I going to dress up as a victim of war and show everyone first hand the horrors of armed conflict?

Well, there were pamphlets, and we were indeed a witness. We were a presence in Union Square for a whole week, and I had the privilege of being a part of this for about one day. We didn't force people to change their minds. We didn't scream out "Repent or you will bring the end of the world!" No, we were witnessing. We were there to show the people who walked by that there were people in our world who thought there was a better way to address conflict in our world. We were there to be pastors to those who came up and needed to share their painful stories of war and personal conflict. We were there to offer prayers at the end of each day. And so I had the privilege of joining some of my Franciscan brothers and sisters in caring for the world and in sharing our hope for a better non-violent way of living together and solving our differences.

Our storyboards with the Franciscan Peace Pledge and Martin Luther King Jr.'s Principles of Non-Violence were very attractive to people. These are pastoral documents that expressed our longing for reconciliation. These were documents that attracted people because I think they are welcoming statements and inviting statements that asked people to think differently for just a moment. This Franciscan Peace Witness provided a place of hope for some of the people we met. I believe our presence there courageously showed people that there are people who think differently about how to live in our global family, and it allowed some people to discover that they were not alone in thinking differently just like us. It was in the spirit of Gandhi's saying, "You must be the change you want to see in the world," that I spent my time there, and the humble statue of Gandhi lurking over our shoulders was a helpful reminder.

As a Canadian immersing myself into the American milieu just a couple of months before a presidential election, I felt a little out of place, and I didn't want to go around pulling splinters out of others' eyes by saying things like, "Well, we didn't go to Iraq!" After all, our government isn't perfect. We may have protested the war in Iraq, but we did so with some apathy. My government certainly didn't condemn others for going into Iraq. Canadians pride ourselves on being "Peacekeepers," but it would be even better if we were "Peacemakers." It would be better if we were a little more proactive about finding peaceful solutions before the conflicts escalate into war and genocide. It's not easy being a witness to peace but, as Franciscans, we have an example to follow. Francis went in with the love of God and the spirit of Jesus to convert the sultan. Francis was trying to find a better way to share the land. I believe we are all called to find a better way as we work at spreading harmony and love, and as we work at becoming people of humility, love and joy in everything we do. Sometimes the task seems so daunting, yet so simple.

Second JPIC Prayer and Fasting Action, 2006: General Convention, Columbus Ohio

At Chapter 2005, Emmett Jarrett presented the idea of our Order offering a Franciscan prayer and fasting action at the General Convention of ECUSA being held June 2006 in Columbus, Ohio. (Emmett and others anticipated that widespread controversy and dissension would occur at the Convention. In 2004, the Archbishop of Canterbury and a consultative group had created the Windsor

Report, which called for a moratorium by all provinces in the Anglican Communion on the use of rites blessing same-sex unions. Since it was unlikely that General Convention would vote to adhere to this call, there were widespread fears that some schism in the province would occur.) This General Convention action followed on the heels of an IPTOC 2005 letter to the Archbishop of Canterbury and signed by the Ministers General of the First and Third Orders and the Abbess of the Poor Clares with the following message:

> *We offer to the Primates and to the members of the Anglican Communion a model of moving forward as Church: walking in the way of Saint Francis of Assisi whose embrace of the leper and the way of non-violent love knit together a universal family of Christians, rooted in the Gospel, growing in joy and simplicity and extending a Reign of God marked by justice and peace.*

A resolution was drawn up and adopted unanimously: *RESOLVED, that the Chapter of the Third Order, Province of the Americas, Society of St. Francis, approves and authorizes a Franciscan Witness of Prayer and Fasting during the General Convention of the Episcopal Church in the USA, June 13-21, 2006.*

When the Witness of Prayer and Fasting was carried out the following summer, here's how Terry Rogers described the experience (*Franciscan Times* Summer 2006):

> *The body of Christ, the ark of salvation, the vine and the branches, the sheepfold, treasure in earthen vessels...*
>
> Praying for several hours a day in the Meditation Chapel at General Convention was a time to anchor myself in the church, "that wonderful and sacred mystery." I started making a list of scriptural and traditional images for the church, so those images could fill my imagination both in the chapel and as I went out and talked to people. There was a powerful contrast between the timeless church and the church very much in time–yet they're one–like the unity of Christ in the Incarnation.
>
> *The new Jerusalem, a royal priesthood, stewards of the secrets of God, salt of the earth, the bride of Christ....*
>
> Gazing at the San Damiano cross we had brought, of course, made me think of the Franciscan call to rebuild the church. Each day we discovered more Franciscans: exhibitors, volunteers, deputies, bishops, convention secretaries, etc. Each were focused on the given task, so there was not nearly enough time to really visit with anyone, yet we were able to count on our mutual affection and helpfulness, and many of us shared Evening Prayer each night.
>
> *Living stones, the temple, a light to the nations, Christ's ambassadors, the kingdom of God.....*
>
> There were two very large icons in the chapel, one of Jesus and the other of Mary holding the Christ child. Praying in the presence of these images–human bodies and faces–began to get through to me: was every human being, made in God's image, in whom Christ dwells, created to shine in glory like

> the golden radiance of these icons? I am so blind to this reality, so quick to dismiss and to judge.
>
> When I see the icon, the body of Christ, I am looking right at the church, beautiful and richly alive.

Emmett Jarrett also described his experience at General Convention in this way in the *Franciscan Times*:

> Susan Pitchford, in her book ***Following Francis: The Franciscan Way for Everyone***, refers to Franciscans as "the lunatic wing of the Church" and a number of us were at the Convention as part of a ***Franciscan Witness of Prayer and Fasting*** for our Episcopal Church. I counted at least 20 tertiaries, four First Order brothers, and two sisters from the Community of St. Francis, as well as two or more tertiaries from other Franciscan religious communities. We may not have been lunatics, but we were different! We weren't official delegates; we weren't advocating any positions; and we weren't selling anything. We were Franciscans who came to fast and pray.
>
> The Third Order has never before had a formal presence at Convention, although the First Order sisters and brothers have. Terry Rogers observed that this was the first time in her years as a tertiary that "the Order has sent me to do something." Indeed, we were sent by Chapter, which endorsed our prayer and fasting witness at its meeting in October. The idea came from the August 2005 meeting of IPTOC in Canterbury, England, where the assembled leaders of all three Orders sent a letter of support to Archbishop Rowan Williams and all the Anglican Communion primates for their efforts for unity in the Communion in a time of division and conflict. At Convention, we passed out a prayer card with the "instruments of your peace" prayer on one side, and an explanation of our witness on the other. This said in part:
>
> *We believe our Church is afflicted by the "deaf and dumb demon" that the disciples were unable to cast out (Mark 9:14-29), of which Jesus said, "This kind cannot be driven out by anything but prayer and fasting." In company with Anglican Franciscans around the world, we are here to offer a model of moving forward as Church: walking in the way of Saint Francis of Assisi whose embrace of the leper and the way of nonviolent love knit together a universal family of Christians, rooted in the Gospel, growing in joy and simplicity, and extending a Reign of God marked by justice and peace.*

Prayer and Fasting at General Convention.

People present at the Convention, no matter what their positions on the various issues that divide the Church, expressed gratitude for our prayers and our openness to the Spirit's guidance and willingness to pray for everyone. Our presence seemed to lighten the solemn tone of the first few days of Convention, which was indeed serious about the issues confronting the Church, and we shared in the general excitement over the election of the Rt. Rev. Katharine Jefferts Schori of Nevada as the presiding bishop of the Episcopal Church.

The brothers and sisters in their brown habits fit in with fellow religious at the Consortium of Anglican Religious Orders in the Americas (CAROA), but tertiaries were present in the Meditation Chapel and throughout the Convention area talking with bishops, deputies, exhibitors, and visitors about the Church and asking them how we could pray for them. Every day at 6 p.m. we prayed the Evening Office in the Chapel for the intentions people had expressed. Some were for the Spirit's guidance for Church leaders, others for healing and various personal intentions. We prayed for all.

We came from all over. I came from New London, Connecticut picking up Terry Rogers in New York City and driving to Columbus. Carol Tookey drove from New Mexico and arrived the same day. The three of us "anchored" the Franciscan Witness, along with Amy Nicolson and her husband Gil from North Carolina. Ruth and Bob Manson from Pennsylvania were active, as well as Betty Wood from Wyoming, Dianne Aid from Seattle, and Charlie McCarron from Long Island.

Our Bishop Protector, Gordon Scruton of Western Massachusetts, was there, along with TSSF Bishops Jim Kelsey of Northern Michigan, Mark Sisk of New York, Mark MacDonald of Alaska, and Nedi Rivera (an Associate) from Seattle. Dom Celso Oliveira of Rio de Janeiro was also present and was introduced to us by Anita Catron. Brothers Jude, Clark, Eric and Wade from SSF, and Sisters Jean and Maggie from CSF were also present and active.

Franciscans at the General Convention met together on Friday, June 16, to share with one another what the Lord is doing in our various Orders. It's not possible to say what the "effect" of our prayer and fasting was on the life of the Church gathered in convention, but we didn't do it for effect. We see our witness as part of our Franciscan charism of poverty and joy to be shared with the wider Church. We believe God will use our work to God's own purposes, still a mystery to us.

Since not everyone could afford the time and money to travel to General Convention in Columbus, Yvonne Koyzis Hook created a 24-hour prayer vigil over the TSSF-Yahoo group to accompany those who were physically present at the Convention. Here is her description of her "accompanying" experience from the *Franciscan Times*:

> Ten days before the start of General Convention, the question came up on the TSSF-Yahoo group forum as to what we as Tertiaries could do to support the efforts at General Convention, and of the Episcopal Church in general.

It was suggested that we organize a 24-hour prayer vigil to run continuously for the entire duration of Convention, and I was asked to organize it. I emailed all the Franciscans in the U.S. and by the first couple of days of Convention, all our slots were filled! Most of us signed up to pray for a slot one hour a day; some signed up for different slots depending on their changing schedules. Some signed up for two slots, and some who were not able to make the one hour commitment agreed to do their *Daily Office* with special intentions, or to hold Convention in their prayers during their travels that week.

All in all, I heard from about 30 tertiaries, which is an amazing level of participation for something that sprang up spontaneously over the internet! We were able to keep a continuous chain of prayer for General Convention operating the entire time it was in session. I especially want to thank those who signed up to pray in the wee hours of the night—bless you for your commitment!

For myself, I found this vigil to be both deeply rewarding and very frustrating! As a very high energy person who usually dashes off Morning Prayer in 15 minutes, the commitment to pray for two hours a day (I signed up for two slots) represented a great challenge. The overwhelming lesson I learned from my praying is that I now feel called to begin praying for spiritual renewal—both for myself and the Episcopal Church. After a lifetime of being a Christian, and 12 years as a professed tertiary, I would like to fall back in love with God again! I think this is God's call to all of us.

Third JPIC Prayer and Witness Action, 2008: Lambeth Conference in Canterbury

Following up the IPTOC 2005 letter to the Archbishop of Canterbury signed by the Ministers General of the First and Third Orders and the Abbess of the Poor Clares, as well as the American Province's Witness of Prayer and Fasting carried out at the General Convention in 2006, all the provinces of the Third Order decided to sponsor a Franciscan praying presence during the Lambeth Conference in Canterbury in 2008. Again, the leaders of JPIC and of all TSSF anticipated controversy and dissention.

In recent history, the Lambeth Conference met once a decade as a consultative body of more than 880 bishops from around the world. Attendance at the Lambeth Conferences is by invitation of the Archbishop of Canterbury. Notably absent from the list of those invited in 2008 were Gene Robinson and Martyn Minns. (Robinson was the first Anglican bishop to exercise the office while in an acknowledged same-sex relationship. Minns was the head of the Convocation of Anglicans in North America, a splinter group of American Anglicans; the Church of Nigeria considered him a missionary bishop to the United States, despite protests from Canterbury and the U.S. Episcopal Church). At least 250 Anglican bishops, mainly from Africa, were planning to meet at a rival conference in Jerusalem.

Here is Terry Rogers's description of her experience at this Franciscan Praying Presence during the Lambeth Conference in Canterbury in 2008 (*Franciscan Times,* Summer 2008).

> In the city of Canterbury, a five minutes' walk from the cathedral, is an enclosed green space known as Greyfriars. A small river runs through it, and it contains gardens full of blossoms and a small meadow of wildflowers. Next to the meadow is a small building, all that's left of the medieval Franciscan friary. Upstairs is a little chapel in the custody of SSF, and three SSF brothers live on the grounds of the enclosure. Down along the river, over a footbridge, and past more gardens is a large white house, and on the lawn was a shining white tent with tables, chairs, vases of flowers, and Franciscan pictures, which was used for hospitality. This was the setting for the TSSF Praying Presence during the Lambeth Conference from July 16th to August 3rd.
>
> Our TSSF Minister General, Dorothy Brooker (from New Zealand), and the TSSF European Province Minister Provincial, Richard Bird, were there for all this time, joined by Ann Savage-Lewis, a tertiary from Wales. Our own Sr. Joyce CSF and Brs. Eric and Max SSF came from California to join the Praying Presence for many days, and a number of tertiaries from the UK came for an hour, a day, or several days. I came for the last nine days and stayed with Ann in the large house, which was being renovated to be the new home for the SSF brothers.
>
> Our days had this schedule: 9 am Morning Prayer, 10-11 am Bible Study of St. John's Gospel, 12 noon Eucharist, 2-3 pm Contemplative Prayer, and 5:30 pm Evening Prayer. At every time of prayer these words were used: "We pray for those taking part in the Lambeth Conference, for those who declined the invitation, and for those who were not invited."
>
> During the day, both for times of prayer and for hospitality, we welcomed visitors from the Lambeth Conference—bishops, their spouses, other lay and clergy participants and volunteers working at the exhibition hall. On the first Sunday afternoon that I was there we welcomed many of the Franciscan Bishops Protector as well as tertiary bishops, their spouses, and the Franciscans working on the chaplaincy team for the conference. All relaxed in this place of quiet beauty and enjoyed tea, scones, and fresh strawberries and cream. It was a treat to see Gordon Scruton, our own Bishop Protector, there, as well as to meet tertiary bishops from all over the world.

Getting ready for Stations of the Cross: Dick Bird (holding the cross) Minister Provincial, European Province; Dorothy Booker, Minister General; Bishop Keith Slater (dark shirt), former Minister General.

My time there was a wonderful blend: lots of quiet focused prayer in community, as well as Franciscan mirth and story-telling. Each day we served morning coffee and tea and a simple sandwich lunch to visitors and those joining us in the prayers.

The TSSF Bishop Protector in Southern Africa, Merwyn Castle, came to celebrate the Eucharist for us one day and over lunch talked about his diocese and its work with AIDS patients and AIDS orphans. Br. Reginald, SSF, celebrated for us on the 55th anniversary of his profession and told us stories about Br. Algy, one of SSF's founders [see pages 136 and 137]. Bishop Mark Dyer, the retired bishop of Bethlehem, Pennsylvania (where CSF once had a house), shared our Bible study one morning, and told us about his month with the Missionaries of Charity in Calcutta, working with the sisters on the streets, and being asked by a disfigured and homeless man with leprosy to lay hands on him, which, with great trepidation, he did. "I have never in my life," he said, "except for the Eucharist, felt so close to Christ as at that moment."

And we Franciscans all felt time melt away, and the reality of Francis's own conversion was present to us.

I was there for one Friday and participated in the Stations of the Cross, and was so moved that our previous Minister General, Bishop Keith Slater from Australia, came down from the conference that day just to join us in the Stations. We made a small procession all around the wildflower meadow, stopping at intervals for each station, with Richard Bird carrying a hand-made wooden cross. I became very aware of the thickly planted meadow, filled with purple, white and gold flowers, all about knee high. I began to see it as an image of the church, the purple flowers on the same level with all the rest, but adding their own vivid color, the whole meadow completely dependent on God for its life, for water, for sunshine, for fertility—vibrant with health and beauty.

On the last day of the Conference there was a 6 pm closing Eucharist in the cathedral, only for Lambeth participants. Ann and I went down and stood on the sidewalk near the cathedral gate, where the bishops and their spouses would walk down from where their buses dropped them off. It took about an hour for busload after busload to make their way on foot through the street lined with volunteers with golden sashes. This was our first and only chance to really see all the people for whom we had been praying. Only in actually seeing them would I have ever truly realized how many of them are not of European descent—at least half. There they came, dressed in all shades of purple as well as some other colors, tall and short, dark and light, bishops and spouses. We began waving at them and calling out, "God bless you, bishops! God bless you, brothers and sisters! Travel safely! Go in peace!" for the hour's time that it took for all of them to reach the gate. Nearly all of them returned smiles and waves, and those we knew beamed and rushed over to hug us and thank us and all Franciscans who were praying for them.

And those thanks include all of you in the Province of the Americas, whose prayers were added to ours.

The Advent of the Franciscan Action Network—2007

Emmett Jarrett

More than 130 members of the Franciscan Family, leaders and Justice, Peace and Integrity of Creation representatives from 69 provinces, congregations, Secular Franciscan regions and ecumenical partners from throughout the United States, met March 7-9, 2007 in Baltimore, MD to discuss and discern ways to bring a more visible and effective Franciscan presence to the effort of repairing relationships to establish justice in the world. In this meeting, Franciscan friars, sisters, seculars and ecumenicals called for themselves and the larger U.S. Franciscan Family to "speak with one Franciscan Voice in order to effect the transformation of national social policy." The gathering represented the largest U.S. Franciscan group ever assembled in the U.S. solely to discuss ways to be better advocates with persons who are poor, marginalized or victims of injustice.

Emmett Jarrett

Participating from the Order of Ecumenical Franciscans (OEF) was Br. Craig Robert Miller; Carol Tookey and Emmett Jarrett represented TSSF. Emmett Jarrett was elected to serve as the joint representative (OEF/TSSF) on the newly appointed Steering Committee.

Building from the first day's input, the participants in the historic meeting moved from why we should have an organized Franciscan Voice for Advocacy to how we should establish it. The group collectively wrote a Vision Statement (see below) calling the Franciscan Family to work together for social transformation. From the Vision Statement, the participants then committed themselves to having further dialogue and finding the resources to establish a broad-based Franciscan Family Commission for Justice, Peace and Integrity of Creation, as well as a Center for Action based in Washington, DC.

The meeting ended with the newly appointed steering committee anointing the assembly. With this action, participants sealed in prayer the commitment they verbally made to one another to work together to establish structures that can bring the voice and spirit of St. Francis and St. Clare to a world that is crying out for transformation.

Following is the Vision Statement that guides the work of the steering committee, the commission, and the Center as together they work to advocate with one Franciscan Voice for Justice, Peace and Integrity of Creation:

Vision Statement of the Franciscan Family

We Franciscan brothers and sisters, Religious and Secular, from throughout the United States, gathered together in Baltimore, MD to discern the possibility of a unified Franciscan Voice for justice. With great concern for dehumanizing issues in our society, we recognized trends contrary to our calling as followers of Christ. We see that we have the power to effectively advocate for the redistribution of resources, the responsible care for creation, and the healing of relationships within the Franciscan Family, the Church and society. To these ends, we commit ourselves and call all members of the Family to speak with one Franciscan Voice to effect the transformation of national social policy. By walking with our brothers and sisters who are poor and marginalized, we intend to advocate for peace and to reaffirm the dignity of all creation.

From the beginning, TSSF has been an integral part of the Franciscan Action Network (FAN) as the Franciscan Family Commission for Justice, Peace and Integrity of Creation was renamed. At present, two of the second generation JPIC leaders are FAN Action Commissioners, and former Minister Provincial Masud Ibn Syedullah was appointed to FAN's Board of Directors.

Canticle of Creation Pilgrimage, Province-sponsored JPIC Action-October 2008

One of the last actions of this first generation of leaders was a pilgrimage of thirteen TSSF members led by Carol Tookey around the Four Corners area of New Mexico, Arizona, Utah, and Colorado. Their goals were to:

- celebrate the beauty of creation in this unique landscape and multi-cultural area,
- observe the impacts of our lifestyle on this fragile ecosystem, and
- look at alternative lifestyles that are more sustainable and harmonious with God's Creation, all in the context of a shared spiritual journey.

Here's how six participants in the pilgrimage described the Canticle of Creation Pilgrimage (*Franciscan Times*, Winter 2009).

Wes Patterson

Monday we traveled to Farmington, New Mexico and stopped and prayed near the Four Corners Power Plant fueled by rather dirty local coal. When we stopped to view the plant and its plumes of polluting smoke and carbon-dioxide, we spontaneously began picking up the litter along our road. If only the pollution from the plant were so easily removed from our atmosphere! We celebrated a moving Eucharist at the side of Shiprock, an imposing mountain holy to the Navajo and visible from afar in every direction. Monday afternoon we traveled to Window Rock, Arizona.

Pilgrims enjoy a Canyon de Chelly overlook on our "Brother Wind" day. (l to r) Carol Tookey, Pat Millren, Terry Rogers, Caroline Benjamin, Ashley Steinhart, Amy Nicholson.

Tuesday we visited Canyon de Chelly in Arizona, where we learned about a people that were forced in the 13th century to leave their homes because they had developed a population

Front Row Kneeling (l to r): Pat Millren, Judi Thomas, Ashley Steinhart, Terry Rogers, Wes Patterson. Back Row Standing (l to r): Caroline Benjamin, Carol Tookey, Janet Wakefield, Becky Thomson, Butch Trainor, Judy Trainor, Gil Nicholson, Amy Nicholson.

and lifestyle that could not be sustained through a drought. Tuesday afternoon we traveled to Bluff, Utah.

Wednesday in Bluff we walked through the Stations of Creation–a 12-station walking meditation based on Francis's *Canticle of the Creatures*. Ashley had found a dozen powerful photos on the web to mark the stations that emphasized the Bible readings and reflections in the text written by Colin Wilfred SSF. Following the stations, we were able to walk to the bank of the San Juan River and spend some quiet time in meditation about how each of us can help to preserve our world.

Thursday we traveled to Cortez, Colorado, where we had a lunch of locally grown ingredients at Let It Grow, accompanied by some insights from the owner about the importance of gardens and of local ingredients that don't require more energy calories for transportation than we realize in consumption. We then visited Turtle Lake Refuge, where Katrina introduced us to some non-typical foods (weeds?) that are readily available locally. At sundown, we visited the Ft Lewis College Hesperus Observatory. Many of us had our first opportunity to see the extent of creation, from the moons of Jupiter to an emerging galaxy well beyond our Milky Way.

Friday we visited Carol's solar-powered home in Aztec, New Mexico–an example of a lifestyle with minimal carbon footprint. On our return to Albuquerque, we visited Chaco Canyon, a national park that includes extensive stone structures built 850-1250 AD, and abandoned when a drought caused food production to drop below levels needed to support the population.

Saturday, 4 October we celebrated Eucharist and returned home, with wonderful spiritual development growth, and an enormously important appreciation for the need for all of us to change our lifestyles to protect God's Creation.

Terry Rogers

Franciscans can lead the way in protecting God's Creation on earth! Here are some of my memories from the Pilgrimage:

- We had a Eucharist out in the desert, using a rock slab for a table in the wilderness.
- We visited St. Christopher's Mission in Bluff, Utah, founded by H. Baxter Liebler (see Chapter 2); we found his grave in the churchyard. I also spent

time praying in the mission's small, humble cemetery in a nearby field.

- A wildlife expert met with us in a picnic area on the bank of the San Juan River and told us about the effect of dams and non-native species on the plants and animals in and near the river.We each were asked to bring a small vial of water from our own watersheds, which were poured into a common bowl. We then renewed our baptismal vows and were blessed with the water.
- We walked along a path on the rim of Canyon de Chelly and sat gazing at the rose-red-orange canyon walls, glowing in the afternoon sun. On the canyon floor we saw a ribbon of rich green foliage and we rested there in wordless contemplation and wonder.

Janet Wakefield

Of the many beautiful and a few disturbing sites we passed or visited, one image particularly remains in my mind - the FCPP - the Four Corners Power Plant near Farmington where we stopped and prayed. The FCPP and its sister plant, the San Juan Generating Station, are among the largest power plants in the U.S. These plants are emblematic of environmental controversies and concerns all over our country. They are the main contributors to the 6th worst air pollution in the U.S. (Farmington, NM area), causing respiratory problems (asthma), high carbon dioxide emissions, and mercury pollution to the water. (Don't dare eat the fish!) Since these plants and a controversial plant about to be built are on the Navajo Reservation, EPA regulations do not apply. They do, however, supply needed jobs to a very poor people.

As we drove along, we were encouraged to think about and explore alternatives. In the Southwest solar power is an obvious solution and some people are pioneering the way. We visited Carol Tookey's new solar-powered home and saw the panels and their infrastructure. Some people are even able to sell their excess power back to the grid. New housing developments could be required or given incentives to be solar/alternate-energy powered.

We need to consider our own regions/localities and explore what kind of alternative energy makes sense in them. I live in northern New York, so solar power alone wouldn't be a good choice, but wind power is very feasible and, in fact, it is growing here. I mean to learn more about this.

Decentralizing power production has advantages—local control is more apt to create local interest and awareness and ownership (both literal and figurative). Local power production is also less vulnerable to natural and man-made disasters. And the same could be said for local food production. As we go more local for both energy and food production, we become more personally involved and we build relationships and connection with others.

Bill McKibben, author of *Deep Economy*, says connection is the basis of happiness! Funny how it all fits together: Creation/joining the Mystery/deep ecology/awareness/moving toward the One. My commitment is to be/stay connected, to support local green food and energy production, to share the joy and beauty of the natural world.

Becky Thomson

The prints of the photographs I took during our pilgrimage arrived this week. I stopped today and spent time reviewing the remarkable event we experienced in the Four Corners area. I find I am unable to describe what happened then.

Oh, there was the intellectual aspect of the Retreat. I really felt challenged by the presentation on the Franciscan Theology of Creation, by the extensive bibliography, and the very thoughtful discussions at each site. I will be chewing on the information for a very long time. I feel challenged to do something for my community. I am researching community gardens in New Orleans, where I will be moving. There is quite an active association there.

I went on the pilgrimage seeking some peaceful time with God. I needed to get away from all the "white noise" of my too busy, too complicated, too empty life. I looked forward to having time to just be. I did receive what I sought and so much more. I had the absolute joy of gentle quiet and loving conversations with God and brother and sister Franciscans.

Perhaps the photograph that I found myself returning to look at the most was one that spoke of quiet love. It is a shot of Carol Tookey driving the van. She and Ashley Steinhart did an amazing job handling those large vans on very challenging roads! It is when I look at that photograph of my dear friend that I am reminded of a non-tangible, perhaps unanticipated aspect of the week. There was so much quiet love, acceptance, and community with fellow Franciscans. Carol and Ashley worked so hard to plan a truly remarkable pilgrimage. They gave us the chance to see, hear, taste, and experience the theme of the week in an atmosphere of friendship and cooperation. We are an odd lot, we Franciscans. Yet, I had the opportunity to have a great retreat in an atmosphere of such friendship. Carol, hunched over the steering wheel with the vista out the window behind her, reminds me of all the loving effort she and Ashley put into this pilgrimage.

Pat Millren

Perhaps the most moving experience for me was walking into the Church of the Good Shepherd, an Episcopal mission on the Navajo reservation, early one morning for shared silence and later, Morning Prayer. What caught my eye most was not the enormous empty cross with large silver embellishments hanging in the center. It was the small and delicate Stations of the Cross along the walls on each side of the sanctuary. All the figures were Native American. They brought tears I could not fully understand that kept erupting during our service. I've thought a lot about this experience. Perhaps it was the realization in a different way that Native Americans have helped Christ bear so many burdens of our (non-Native-American) lives and culture. Perhaps, extending that idea, it was the realization that the Earth itself and all (non-human) inhabitants help Christ bear the burdens of our continuing excesses. As I wrote to my niece yesterday, I realized that usually I see the Stations of the Cross in the context of men and women of Christ's day relating to/helping Christ. These stations in the Church of the Good Shepherd brought the story forward for me, into the last century, and into today, through the agony of the Earth. I suspect this experience will be with me a long time.

Caroline Benjamin

Carol Tookey and Ashley Steinhart couldn't have planned this pilgrimage any better and every aspect of it obviously had the imprint of their loving touches. There was so much beauty to see and experience that it far outweighed the ugliness of some things (like the power plant on the Navajo reservation spewing pollutants into the air and the San Juan River). I came out of the whole experience with hope that, if we all do what we can to make the environment better, we'll save Mother Earth and her resources.

The Green Committee at my church, St. Christopher's in Bandera, Texas, asked me to make a presentation about this trip yesterday to the adult Sunday school, which I did, and they seemed spellbound and enthused about making positive changes in their lives. Someone asked whether I came back hopeful or discouraged, and I assured her that I was hopeful because I knew that we could spread the message like yeast in bread. Our priest asked me to start getting the word out to our congregation about things we could do on a personal level by having a short entry in each monthly newsletter. I told him it would be easy to have a box on a page with something each person could add to their lives easily. I gave them the environmental action handout we were given, on "avoiding, seeking, and advocating." I told them I was doing advocating by talking with them and they could pass the message on to their circles of friends. So, THANK YOU, dear sisters!!

Caroline Benjamin and Terry Rogers explore Pueblo Bonito in Chaco Canyon on "Sister Death" Day.

Second Generation JPIC Action-Provincial Convocation of June 25-30, 2013

A Franciscan Search for Action and Healing: First Peoples and Sacred Lands—Insignificant in the Eyes of Many, Precious in the Eyes of God.

It was a long five years between the Canticle of Creation Pilgrimage in 2008 and the next Province-sponsored JPIC action. There were plenty of individual members doing JPIC-type actions in the Province ranging from medical missions to Liberia [See page 252] and peace visits to the West Bank. However, between 2008 and 2013 a change in the key players of JPIC occurred, moving JPIC to a new generation of leaders. Emmett Jarrett died of cancer in October 2010, yet in the year prior to his death he made a six-week, 800-mile peace pilgrimage around southern New England. Carol Tookey, after so many years on Chapter as Formation Director and being a voice for JPIC on Chapter, reached her term limits and had to step down from Chapter. She and her tertiary husband moved to New Mexico where she continues to carry on her JPIC work on the local parish level in Navajoland. Finally, Terry Rogers began to shift her efforts to focus more on the Formation Program.

Now a second generation of JPIC key players (Joyce Wilding, Francesca Wigle, Verleah Kosloske, and Dianne Aid) emerged, and, just as Generation 1 leaders brought their prior experience and interests, so too did Generation 2. Some of their experiences were with Generation 1 leaders in other organizations. Joyce Wilding came from the area of corporate organizational consulting, moved into program development for the seminary at the University of Sewanee, and specialized in environmental justice. Francesca Wigle came from long experience in the peace movement in the U.S., prison ministry, and as an Action Commissioner with the Franciscan Action Network (FAN). Dianne Aid has been very active in the immigration movement and is president of the Episcopal Network for Economic Justice. Verleah Kosloske brought her experience with the Episcopal Public Policy Network and Episcopal Peace Fellowship.

Joyce Wilding.

Francesca Wigle.

In 2010, at the Western Convocation, Dianne Aid experienced a program called "Holy Poverty, Lessons from First Nations People." When she was asked by Marilynn Mincey, Provincial Convocation 2013 leader, to develop the program for the convocation, Dianne went back to her rich earlier convocation experience. This is how Dianne explained her program:

Dianne Aid.

Verleah Kosloske.

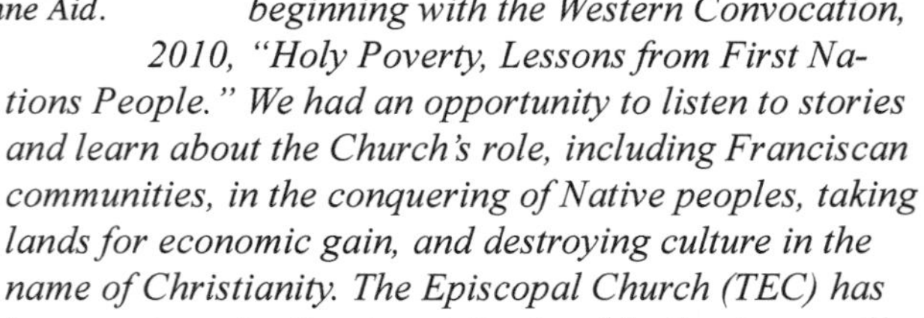

A significant part of our TSSF Province of the Americas Convocation, 2013, will be dedicated to exploring the impact of the Doctrine of Discovery with Native brothers and sisters in our Church. We were inspired to explore this doctrine beginning with the Western Convocation, 2010, "Holy Poverty, Lessons from First Nations People." We had an opportunity to listen to stories and learn about the Church's role, including Franciscan communities, in the conquering of Native peoples, taking lands for economic gain, and destroying culture in the name of Christianity. The Episcopal Church (TEC) has been paying attention to spiritual and justice issues affecting Native communities for the last several General Conventions. In 2009, the Episcopal Church became the first Christian denomination to officially repudiate the Doctrine of Discovery, soon to be followed by The World Council of Churches, and since, other denominations have joined this growing act of repudiation.

In her pastoral letter of May 16th, 2012, The Episcopal Church Presiding Bishop Katharine Jefferts Schori, wrote, "We seek to address the need for healing in all parts of society, and we stand in solidarity with indigenous people globally to acknowledge and address the legacy of colonial occupation and policies of domination." The Church has begun to take time to hear the stories and to profoundly grieve at long-lasting pain inflicted on native communities throughout the Americas. This profound call for healing and reconciliation seems to be a fundamental call of Franciscans to heal divisions by calling communities of people into dialogue and lasting, loving relationships.

The keynote speakers that Dianne recruited were many of the same ones who spoke at the 2010 Western Convocation, including Elsie Dennis (Co-Chair, First Nations Committee, Diocese of Olympia) and Kathryn A. Rickert, a member of the School of Theology and Ministry at Seattle University. Luckily, Dianne and others were also able to recruit Bishop Mark MacDonald, one of our five TSSF professed bishops. Bishop MacDonald, who grew up among the Ojibway people, was recruited by the Canadian Anglican Church to be the National Indigenous People's Bishop. They were also able to recruit the Rev. Canon Robert Two Bulls, the missioner of the Department of Indian Work and Multicultural Ministries for the Episcopal Church in Minnesota and vicar of All Saints Indian Mission in Minneapolis. Robert is also an Oglala Lakota Oyate. Our own Jeffrey Golliher, environmental representative for the worldwide Anglican Communion at the United Nations, completed the lineup of keynote speakers.

Bishop Mark MacDonald.

One of the key aspects of the whole Convocation was the communal participation in a "Lament Over the Doctrine of Discovery" created by Kathryn A. Rickert. She had presented it a year earlier at General Convention in Indianapolis, Indiana. Here is the description of this Lament that she gave to the *Franciscan Times*, Fall 2013:

Somewhere along our tradition this powerful prayer form has gotten lost. For the most part we think of our relations with God and each other in terms of petition, praise and thanksgiving. If we look more closely at both the Old and New Testaments we find that lament is absolutely necessary for our prayer—practice one without which Christianity (and Judaism) don't work very well.

Jeffrey Golliher.

It's not that we don't need those other prayer forms; we do. But they are incomplete without both individual and communal prayers of lament. In a way, lament is the beginning of all deep prayer—that unguarded, honest crying out to God in trust, hope, and sometimes desperation. Lament declares the situation in which we petition, give thanks, and praise God.

If all that is wrong with the world were only "all about us," then perhaps the prayers of repentance would do. It's not!

The pattern of laments as we find them in the poetry and narratives of Scripture include the poetry of the psalms, the prophets such as Jeremiah, Lamentations, the narratives of lament – Israel crying out to God from slavery in Egypt; Abraham checking in with God four times as to the arrival of the long-promised son; Moses crying out to God, "get me help or kill me...you have given me more children than I can manage."

Those emotions include (but not only) fear, anger, rage, grief, longing, and doubt. This speech comes from the depths of our lives—the uncovered, real places of intimate real-life experience. It isn't always nice, but it is powerful and faithful.

When we find ourselves praying in this way, it leads to an intimate, faithful, risky, authentic human-divine relationship. Authentic lament does not come out with tones of arrogance, disrespect, or privilege, but, rather a voice of vulnerability and openness to the most difficult and most beautiful parts of life.

Laments are a temporary tool that is absolutely necessary for our relationship with God, the Creation and with each other. Lament is NOT a lifestyle, nor a personality type. Lament in the biblical tradition begins and ends not because our grief is necessarily ever finished, but because God is both within and beyond our grief. If I am honest I must tell you that I don't know with precision just how it is that laments work. I can see what they do, and I have some understanding as to how. But so very much of this continues to be far beyond us.

Centerpiece of the Lament Laden With Symbolic Objects.

If anything can begin to respond to the horror, rage, and grief generated by the genocide, racism, and white privilege that is at the core of so much of our very painful American history, it is the cross of Jesus. So far, it is as much as I am able to do to bring these wounds to that cross together with you so that we might begin to open ourselves and the structures of our world to this very expansive compassionate love that we find in Jesus the Christ.

Praying together in this way with laments makes it embody our strong emotions, bringing those "loaded guns" out of hiding into the Light where healing may enter in sharing this together with God and with each other, not alone or private anymore.

There is much, much more from Kathryn and from all the speakers in the *Franciscan Times* edition of Fall 2013. There were many published reactions to this Convocation, but one of the most heartfelt is the following.

Sonya Riggins-Furlow (*Franciscan Times*, Fall 2013)

This program was an important one, it affected me in a way that I am still having a difficult time explaining to others as I talk about the Convocation. I felt my internal systems overloading beginning with the moving Four Directions Prayer. Reconciliation with Peoples of the First Nations as a theme was poignant and needed, to say the least.

This Convocation was my goal, I was looking forward to it, since being diagnosed with Stage 2 Thyroid Cancer, through tests, biopsies, surgery and radioactive iodine treatments; I was going to Minneapolis!

All the material was prepared with excellent forethought, all the speakers were well versed and moving and perhaps a little history may explain how the week truly affected me.

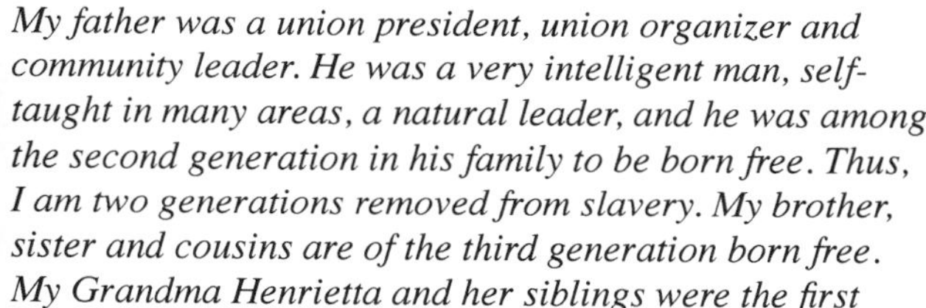

My father was a union president, union organizer and community leader. He was a very intelligent man, self-taught in many areas, a natural leader, and he was among the second generation in his family to be born free. Thus, I am two generations removed from slavery. My brother, sister and cousins are of the third generation born free. My Grandma Henrietta and her siblings were the first generation of the Hall family born free to their mother, who was born a slave and freed by President Lincoln. In the corner of North Carolina where they were all slaves and later freemen, they had an intimate relationship with the Waccamaw Siouan and Lumbee Tribal Nations, to which we have a familial connection.

Being a descendant of slaves, a descendant of Native Peoples in America, a descendant of Reconstruction, Jim Crow, segregation and the civil rights movement, in this year of our Lord, two thousand and thirteen, I am continually exposed to racism and prejudices by others in various settings and venues.

I wondered very early in the week what I was to do with this program information. I have a phrase that I use, if it does not apply, let it fly. But, could I let it fly? Could I close my ears and run away into a corner of my imagination and forget the entire program, of course not.

The night of the Lament made it certain to me that all this information was relevant to me somehow in this place, at this time. When I learned of the Native American boarding schools and the total attempt of cultural assimilation and destruction of history, tribal beliefs and ways plus the other stories being told with great care, I wept.

And, I wondered why everyone else in the room was not prostrate on the floor before God weeping and wailing for this horrific history of our nation.

I realized that I was in a very high emotional state and if I did not get a hold of myself I would be heading for an emergency room. I was so affected. At the peace, I left the Lament and making the long trek back to my room, I prayed and prayed, then suddenly I curled into bed, still weeping I drifted asleep.

Miraculously, in the morning I felt alright. It was amazing. Joy certainly comes in the morning. It was upsetting to hear stories of the Doctrine of Discovery. They were as disturbing as slavery, lynching, Jim Crow, the segregated South, and everything else man can do to his fellow man.

I knew for me that I would continue on my path of treating people with dignity, decency and Christian respect. I also know in my heart that my fellow Franciscans will do the same.

The Second Aim of our Order sets out, in the name of Christ, to break down barriers between people and to seek equality for all. We accept as our second aim the spreading of a spirit of love and harmony among all people. We are pledged to fight against the ignorance, pride, and prejudice that breed injustice or partiality of any kind. So be it! So be it! Amen and Amen

References

McKibben, Bill. *Deep Economy: The Wealth of Communities and the Durable Future.* New York: Times Books, 2007.

Pitchford, Susan. *Following Francis: The Franciscan Way for Everyone*. Harrisburg, Pa: Morehouse Pub, 2006.

Chapter 11: The Canadian Story in Our Province

The Story Thus Far

In Chapter 1's large-scale overview of the Province, we saw that by 1955 the number of tertiaries gathering in three different provinces (British Columbia, Alberta, and Ontario) had sufficient numbers to begin creating Canadian Fellowships. By 1995, British Columbia and Ontario were among the top 5% concentrations of tertiaries in the whole Province.

In Chapter 4 on John Scott's era, there was the heroic story of Hugo Muller's work with the Inland Cree of Northern Quebec in their fight against the James Bay Hydroelectric Project, and the books of poems and essays that he wrote. Chapter 4 also observed that in 1975, the first Provincial Convocation was held in Racine, Wisconsin, and it focused on a discussion of three position papers by E. Will Drake, Judith Robinson, and Michael Hollingshead. E. Will Drake has been professed for 45 years, and is the longest professed member in Canada. His paper in 1975 may, in fact, be the first presentation by a Canadian at any TSSF meeting. When Drake wrote his paper, he was working as a social worker for the Canadian Government in the Northwest Territories.

Moreover, in the last chapter on the evolution of JPIC, we read of tertiary Bishop Mark MacDonald's appointment by the Anglican Church in Canada to be the bishop to all indigenous peoples of the country, and his participation in the 2013 Provincial Convocation.

Canadian House of Bishops invited all Canadian Christian Communities to come together for the first time—TSSF was well represented by Diane and Frank Jones of Vancouver (first row center).

In March of 2014, the Canadian House of Bishops called the first meeting of all monastic communities in Canada. Diane Jones, a member of Chapter, and Frank Jones, Vocations Coordinator for the Province, were invited to attend along with 11 other monastic communities, including:

• The Worker Sisters of the Holy Spirit • Community of the Sisters of the Church
• The Jeremiah Community • The Sisterhood of St. John the Divine
• The Order of the Holy Cross • Oratory of the Good Shepherd
• The Emmaus Community • Contemplative Fire • Holy Cross Priory.
• Threshold Ministries • The Society of Our Lady Saint Mary

Thus by 2014, TSSF in Canada was recognized as one of the 12 monastic communities of Canada by their House of Bishops.

Canadians on Chapter

In 1986, Ewan Macpherson, editor of *Caritas* (newsletter for Franciscans in Eastern Canada), a member of the Toronto Fellowship, and Area Chaplain, was elected as the first Canadian member of Chapter, but took a call from a parish in the UK and left the Province before he could serve.

In 1989, the next round of Chapter elections, Ewan's successor as Convener of the Toronto Fellowship, Warren Beal, was elected to Chapter. However, before he took his place on Chapter, he asked to be released from vows.

Diana Finch.

In 1990, Ruth Duncan of Ontario was appointed to join Chapter with voice and vote, and, subsequently, when another elected Chapter member resigned, Ruth was appointed to fill that member's term, becoming the first Canadian to be part of the elected Chapter. Previously, Muriel Adey, also a Canadian, was an ex-officio member of Chapter when she was Women's Formation Director at the end of John Scott's era and was later elected to Chapter in 1998.

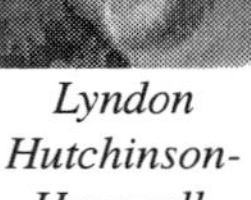

Lyndon Hutchinson-Hounsell.

In 2001 Diana Finch, Fellowship Convener of the Little Sparrow Fellowship (Eastern Canada), was elected to Chapter to be succeeded by Lyndon Hutchison-Hounsell in 2004 and Marilynn Mincey (British Columbia) in 2010. (Duncan, Finch and Hutchison-Hounsell were all from Ontario Province). In 2010, Marilynn Mincey was appointed to one of the most difficult and time-consuming roles in the Order as the Chair of the 2013 Convocation Committee. (The previous Chapter described the success of this endeavor.)

Marilynn Mincey.

Canadian Identity as Tertiaries in the Province

There had always been nationalities other than those of the USA in the Province: Guyanese, Jamiacians, Trinidadians, English, etc. However, none had ever attempted to create a national identity as a group of members in the Province. Newsletters from London to Trinidad and Jamaica had always focused on the life and consciousness of the fellowships, and never on a separate national identity.

However, in the Spring of 2000, Lyndon Hutchison-Hounsell initiated the *Franciscans Canada (FC)* newsletter whose function he explained in the first issue:

> *Over the past couple of years, as I have been in the formation process for the Third Order, I have noticed that there are few scattered Franciscans in Canada. I was thinking that it would be helpful for us to know a little more about each other; that which nurtures our spirit, our ministries, and our dreams and passions. As I have used the Anglican Franciscans Email List I have also noticed that our numerous American sisters and brothers are often discussing national political issues and action that can be taken. For*

all these reasons, and with the encouragement of two of our sisters, Muriel Adey and Diana Finch, I thought it would be useful to start this newsletter.

Hutchison-Hounsell envisioned a four-fold focus for the newsletter:

First, "People of Francis!" will list key contact people in Canada.... Second, "People with Spirit!" will include particularly inspirational prayers or poems or stories that may help to nurture our spirit. ... Thirdly, "People with Work" would include a short article about the work one of us is doing as ministers of Christ following in the footsteps of Francis and Clare. Finally, "People for Justice" would include a short article and information regarding justice issues here in Canada and how we can act and make a difference in our country and in the world.

His newsletter was only published from 2000-06, but it proved so important to the Canadian tertiaries of the Province that Harold MacDonald continued it as a monthly online-only newsletter, *THAW!*, from 2006 to 2008. (Both sets of newsletters have been posted and are downloadable on the TSSF Historical Documents webpage.)

Here are some of the stories collected in *Franciscans Canada*. First, an emigree from the European Province, Muriel Adey. Notice how she experienced the differences between our Province and the European Province:

My "formation" took place in England where we then lived, and where I'd been a Companion for over ten years. It was possible, there, to go to specifically Franciscan retreats, led by one or other of the friars. And for many, it was also possible to visit, or stay, at one or other of the Friaries and take part in the worship there.

"Here and in all your churches throughout the whole world we adore You O Christ, and we bless you, Because by your Cross and Passion You have redeemed the whole world."

These words got ingrained in my being as they were heard in the holy awe of the Friary, and the heightened spiritual awareness of being on retreat. I mourned, on coming to Canada and meeting with North American tertiaries because these words were absent from regular meetings here, even though they are printed on page 59 of our Devotional Companion. I guess because the meetings, or at least the worship part of the meetings, didn't take place in a church.

"May our blessed Lady pray for us, May St. Francis pray for us, May St. Clare pray for us.... (and so on).

Muriel Adey and Br. Geoffrey, Minister General (see Chapter 4).

These words ended the Third Order Office, which also included the prayer above, wherever it was said, and especially when Professions, Renewals and Admissions were part of the Office. Here in North American this prayer is part of the Profession, Renewal and Admission ceremony, so I didn't lose touch with that, except that being an isolated tertiary there weren't many opportunities to be present except for my own Renewal. In those days Holy Communion was mostly in the early morning, even in the friaries and on retreats, and the previous evening's Compline always ended with the words "Come in the dawning of the day and make thyself known in the breaking of the bread." Wonderful words to end one's day with—looking forward to the next morning's meeting with our Lord! I still say them even though the meeting is no longer at dawn.

When the edition of the Principles which we all now use in North America first came out, I was joyful beyond measure to see Community Obedience there at the front, and to hear that at the International Provincial Third Order Convocation (IPTOC) in 1996 there had been an agreement to use it in all provinces to help bind us all together. This was the first time that I really began to feel at home in the TSSF on this continent! And with the suggested reading from the Principles, Intercessions from the Directory, other prayers from the Devotional Companion, it makes a very satisfactory Office in itself in those parts of the Third Order family which aren't obligated to do an Office according to the Prayer Book. Just as the inclusion of the Community Obedience helped me to really feel at home in this branch of the TSSF after being in Canada for 29 years of profession and serving on Chapter and as Formation Director for part of that time, I hope that others who emigrate here will find it being used, for that would help them also to feel at home. (FC, August 2000)

Later Muriel wrote about her experience as an elected member on Chapter:

For the past three years it has been my privilege to be an elected member of the Third Order Chapter–the only elected member from west of the Great Lakes as someone commented, and also the only Canadian to have ever been on Chapter. (I was Formation Director for women from 1974-81, then elected in 1998 for three years.) I was invited to be Celebrant at one of the Eucharists during Chapter–a humbling experience, an awe-ful one, in the chapel at Little Portion. Since Chapter had been talking about the variety of people God calls to explore the Third Order way, and how that very variety causes our structures to adapt and change, and since one subject comes up year after year in this regard, that of trying to discern whether a person is cut out to become a professed member of the Third Order SSF, or whether a person would thrive better in another context, I drew on the Theme of the Roses as I had experienced it myself, this time applying it to membership in TSSF, and in a Fellowship.

Supposing a person seems not to fit in with the members of the Fellowship, or with the Principles of the Order—what can the Fellowship, or the Counselor do? The gardener in the meditation first rejected the rose, but when she or he discovered the rose growing better than before, though in another place, cultivated that place and gradually extended the garden to include it, thereby improving the garden greatly. Using one's imagination, I'm sure there are other scenarios, which one can picture. As I continued to reflect, I thought of transplanting the rose back into the formal garden and building a trellis for it, thus increasing the variety there. However, I have to admit that this alternative doesn't appeal to me as much as the one of extending the garden to include it! Of course, we always have to appeal to the examples of Francis and Jesus when the need for discernment arises.

Finally, any professed member can stand for election to Chapter with other professed members proposing and seconding them. The nominating committee does its best to ensure that all areas are represented. For example, though I was the only one elected west of the Great Lakes, there were ex-officio people from the Western US. I feel sure that if another Canadian stood for election that person would have a good chance of being elected! (FC, Christmas, 2000)

Ruth Duncan, on the other hand, experienced little spiritual differences between Canadian and American novices:

As a Novice Counselor for TSSF I deal mostly with Franciscans in the United States of America. It wasn't until TSSF Chapter ordered me to become Area Chaplain for Eastern Canada that I got to know more of us here in Canada. There really isn't much difference. They and we have exactly the same problems drawing up and keeping our Rule of Life. I am just like the rest of you with the same problems and no better answers. However, as I struggle to help TSSF novices sort out ways to keep their rule, I am forced to struggle with my own. (FC, October 2000)

In June 2006, Harold MacDonald began *THAW!*, a follow-up to Lyndon Hutchison-Hounsell's *Franciscans Canada*. In *FC*, MacDonald wrote of his Franciscan awakening:

The beginning of my discovery of Francis happened when I was 16. Br. Douglas came from England in 1944 to stay at our school, hoping to find a base for a Franciscan community on Vancouver Island. His simplicity and refinement touched my being. I have never been far away from Francis since then. In 1975 Frances and I went to Assisi and saw the very places where much of Francis's life happened! We now live on the shore of Lake Winnipeg, overlooking 22 kilometres of water to the other side. Our yard is a sanctuary for birds and flowers in the summer. In the winter, there are birds, which tumble over our feeders, companions in the cold. Our winterized cottage is adorned with a sumptuous view of the lake through large windows, which enhances the simplicity of our home with an elegance not found in the richest residence in Winnipeg. (FC, August 2001)

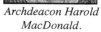

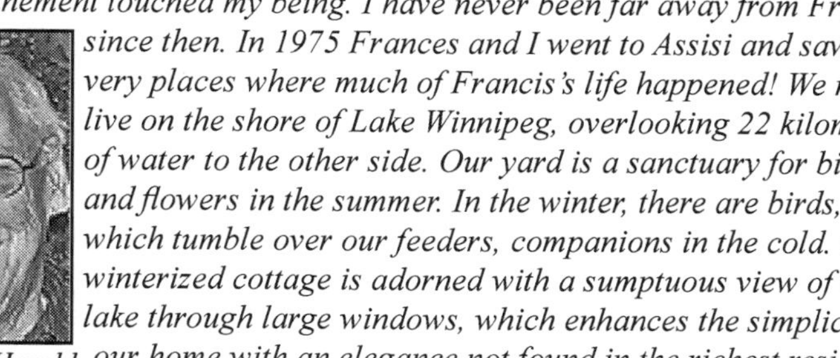

Archdeacon Harold MacDonald.

In *THAW!*, here's how MacDonald described his goals in the first issue:

> *Who we are. "Canadian" means that we will seek symbols, metaphors, for the Franciscan life that come from our experience in this great, northern land. The word "Thaw" is an example. It suggests the physical reality of our Canadian experience. It also suggests the effect of Franciscan life on the soul; or I should say, of the Risen Christ on the Franciscan soul ready and willing to accept Him. "Anglican" means that we will concern ourselves with experience in the Anglican Church of Canada. And "Franciscan" means, well... you know that already. I take "Living with the Principles of the Third Order" as a good basis* (*Thaw!*, June 2006).

In his second issue MacDonald wrote about the isolation of Canadian tertiaries:

> *Isolation is a fact of life for Canadian Franciscans, too. In only two regions are we numerous enough to have fellowships. The rest of us are scattered singly over hundreds of miles.*
>
> *What do we mean by "isolation"? What does it feel like? What causes it? How does one cope with isolation? These are both Franciscan and Canadian questions. Your thoughts would be welcome.*
>
> *It may help to know that "isolation" and "solace" come from the same Latin root. Simply put, isolation is lack of solace, lack of consolation, lack of the normal kinds of kindship and friendship which bring comfort regularly. Even for inner-directed people, solace needs an actual presence, a flesh-and-blood reality. Yet people have endured the lack of normal relationships in the north and came to value and find solace in the very loneliness of the life. Among those who to value and find solace in the very loneliness of the life in the north were the wives of clergy, Hudson's Bay Company employees and Northwest Mounted Policemen, the northern "Trinity" prior to WWII. They are studied by Barbara Kelcy in her book* ***Alone in Silence: European Women in the Canadian North before World War II****. We will not be surprised to read that faith carried the women through the trials of northern isolation. Kelcey writes:*
>
> *"Along with transiency, religious faith was the most constant theme throughout the sources, for all these women, not just the missionaries. It is their Christian faith that stands out above all else. It was their faith that made the experience tolerable, even exciting. Those with a strong faith saw the good in the situation, no matter how difficult it all seemed. Those whose lives are controlled by more secular forces might find such faith incomprehensible, even alarming, and difficult to appreciate that like Inukshuk, this faith was solid and tangible and symbolic of optimism. For them, their God's presence was almost palpable in the northern emptiness.*
>
> *In* ***North to the Rime-Ringed Sun****, Isobel Hutchison echoed other Arctic writers when she declared:*
>
> *We are alone in silence here*
> *Here ample footsteps throng*

The Peace of God breathes all around,

And fills this place with song.

I think these women were sustained also by their intellectual interests. They wrote journals and letters. Their minds were inhabited by descriptions, observations, and local knowledge. They kept busy, too, with the daily round. It took a lot of energy to keep up the standard of English social manners. In all their years of northern separation they never changed their recipes!

Those days have long gone. Isolation and the search for solace has taken on new and destructive power in modern times, when the emptiness of the north has been filled with images of consumer overabundance on the TV. One sees and learns to desire conveniences and distractions available in the south. One needs solace. One seeks comfort in commodities easily shipped by air cargo. One loses the ear to hear the peace of God in the land or in the chill night air, or in the shimmering northern lights. "Alone in silence" is a forgotten resource. Then where will we find solace? (Thaw!, July 2006)

Perhaps being a Canadian tertiary is railing about the U.S. president and his stupidities:

GEO-POLITICAL SICKNESS

I have discovered that a prime reason for not feeling well, for feeling a general nausea, is that I am reading the newspapers.

In particular, I have been reading about the President of the United States declaring unequivocally that he wants to initiate World War III.

He is going to bring this about by attacking Iran. My complexion is green.

Nobody else wants this to happen, except Israel. As to the Middle East, there is some doubt whether Israel is supporting the USA in further destruction of the Arab nations or the USA is supporting Israel. It is a moot point who is calling the shots in Washington as everybody knows.

Certainly God does not want this to happen: the bombing of Iran, that is. St. Francis doesn't want this to happen.

Let's take Francis first. Francis was into little things: things of today, things you could reach out and touch, things that were immediate. Like Jesus, Francis was not interested in things several removes away, such as "taking thought for the morrow, what ye shall eat and and what ye shall drink and what ye shall put on." George W. Bush, however, and his neo-cons, disdain the present (which they can know) in favour of the future (which they cannot know). And so we read of great plans to destroy 134 (plus or minus) sites of nuclear production in Iran in the days to come; we do not read about conversations today between world leaders and the leaders of the next target of USA military power. That is what is so terribly un-Franciscan about geo-politics right now. It's "Shoot now, talk later."

It is as if the devil is not the once-great archangel, but a little boy, intent on mischief and wanting to do something memorable in the short time still available to him. Even if it's a thing of astonishing stupidity.

Francis would walk across the sand and start a conversation. Francis would speak peace. Unfortunately, George stays in the White House and speaks war. That's what turns my stomach. It is the lack of common sense and decency in these affairs. One comes to recognize imbecility in one's enemies; it is sickening to find it among one's friends.

As for God, our nausea is nothing compared to God's rage. The Bible knows quite a bit about "wrath" when God is thwarted. Is that what we can expect: God's anger against the USA and Israel? Once the torch bearer for God, but now turned in disobedience? Could we expect God, therefore, to destroy the USA over the horrors which have been perpetrated or contemplated publicly?

One might say, "Yes." We see that God is already undoing the USA. Think of the truths that were revealed by Katrina. Think of the debt of the world's richest nation. Think of the scorn expressed throughout the world towards a nation that could have been the herald of peace. Think of the persistent hypocrisy over the oft-promised justice for Palestine and the formation of a Palestinian state. Think of 9/11. Think of the fear which awakens many Americans, think of porous borders and elements of lawlessness in the population. Think of the love of violence displayed from the President down.

But God is not predictable. God changes the divine mind. Nineveh is to be destroyed in the morning but by the evening it has repented and God is merciful. God consults widely. God listens to everyone: people and rulers, victims and criminals. For this reason God is slow to act as decisively as we think advisable, more slowly than, say, George W. Bush. George is a lot faster than God at deciding to drop bombs. When God decides for war, it is because the time for consultation is over and because the injustice of a given situation is unbearable in heaven, and because the toppling of a human warmonger is the only way towards peace and justice. So it was in 1939.

So God is slow to declare war on Iran (or Iraq) and slow to declare war on the USA. God gives both a multitude of signs and those who have eyes may see them and repent.

God cannot be taken for granted. There is no telling what God can and will do. God is sovereign. Therefore be careful, be prayerful; be slow to judge and quick to praise. And to make friends with one's enemies. (Thaw!, November 2007)

(However, if Harold had looked at the website and book, *Sorry, Everybody: An Apology to the World for the Re-Election of George W. Bush*, he might find that the sentiment of many Americans was not too far different than that of the Canadians.)

Canadian Poets

Hugo Muller wrote poems written in response to the plight of the Inland Cree (Chapter 4). Harold MacDonald is probably the Canadian with the most poems appearing in the *Franciscan Times*. He retired to the family cottage on the shores of Lake Winnipeg, which he loved, and there his creativity burgeoned through writing, song and poetry. Harold's community continued to grow by way of the internet and included many correspondents, including Bishop Desmond Tutu.

MacDonald's dozens of essays, hymns, sermons and poems can still be found on the *Highland Shepherd* website (http://www.msgr.ca/msgr-7/harold_macdonalds%20muse.htm).

He died in 2009.

Here are three of his poems that most directly focus on Francis.

Simple Francis

Simplicity's a soul undistracted;
all things it knows straight on, a well-coming.
It feels the roughness of the leaf, the humming
bee it hears; opens up if interacted

knows the smoothness of the water's flowing
the touch of wolf: the fur, the ears and eyes;
the call of birds, their lovely songs and cries.
Smell, sight and taste, alert the act of knowing.

Through the senses Francis life encountered,
received with joy that which the senses found
and poverty removed what would confound.
Intense his knowledge, no instant squandered.

With less, the Poverello learned the more
And nature sprang into the human mind
as it is. Itself! After it's own kind!
Discovered in the form that God out-poured.

Look at the creatures of the earth today
their beauty lost to a demonic creed;
no priest to cherish them as God decreed
their mystery, marvel, friendship in decay!

Francis come again! Recover what first you found
Free us from the bonds with which the earth is bound.

With the Leper's Kiss

With the leper's kiss Saint Francis left the world
it was the wall's small gate to open field
where sun and breeze see blossoms meekly yield
and joy waves in the wind, a flag unfurled,
and in the air the bleat of Christ the Lamb.
Where death is spring, and all again begun
the inmost life is bright with morning's Sun,
where sound the living words, I am, I am!
Not of the world yet one with all that is
(more so, than those who wish to leave it not
content with that which they themselves begot)
possessing all yet knowing naught is his.
It is God's goodness fills before and after
the Poverello heard the sound of laughter.

A Monk at Heart

Watchful, I see the opportunities
for praise and giving thanks more clearly now;
to God obeisance, less to neighbours bow;
more occupied with God's simplicities.
The Godly vision at the core of me -
long avoided or ignored - a monk's heart
beats inside, flooding every other part.
(Do not clean hearts produce morality?)
But nothing's sure except for this small thing;
the time is almost up, the life is past;
few throws remain, the dice are almost cast
no resplendent gift now to the party bring.
I will enjoy the thought of God these final days
and use what few remain in poetry of praise.

References

Hutchison, Isobel W. *North to the Rime-Ringed Sun: Being the Record of an Alaska-Canadian Journey Made in 1933-34.* London: Blackie, 1934.

Kelcey, Barbara E. *Alone in Silence: European Women in the Canadian North Before World War II.* Montréal: McGill-Queen's University Press, 2014.

Zetlen, James, and Ted Rall. *Sorry Everybody: An Apology to the World for the Re-Election of George W. Bush*. Irvington, N.Y: Hylas Pub, 2005.

Chapter 12: Masud Ibn Syedullah, Minister Provincial 2002-2005

(From material provided to Chapter members by Masud as its members were considering his election as Minister Provincial in 2001)

Background

My life among Third Order Franciscans began in 1976 in Chicago, while in seminary. I was noviced in 1979 and professed in 1983. I have served the Order in several capacities: founder and convener of the Oklahoma Fellowship; organized and established the South Central Regional Convocation; served as member of Chapter; served as an Area Chaplain; and served as the Provincial Chaplain. Currently, I serve as an Assistant Chaplain, Co-Convener of the New York City Fellowship, and I represent the Third Order on the Ecumenical Committee of the Roman Catholic Secular Franciscans. My wife Janice and I have just celebrated our thirty-first wedding anniversary and have two adult daughters. I pastor the Church of the Atonement, Bronx; and am Director of *Roots & Branches: Programs for Spiritual Growth.* I also serve on the Ecumenical and Interfaith Commission, the Episcopal-Muslim Relations Committee, the Liturgical Commission, and the Standing Committee of the Diocese of New York.

Masud's Vision for the Third Order

I entered the Third Order in response to an intense attraction to the life, lifestyle, and ministry of St. Francis; becoming close friends with some wonderful people who were tertiaries; and a desire to deepen my commitment to God and to the work of God. Through the years, these three categories have remained attractive to me and continue to inform and form my life. I believe the Third Order has something to offer the Church (and the world) and want to offer my skills to further its mission. We live in a challenging, yet exciting period of history, for both the Church and the world. Never before has it been more vital that people of various cultures, races, and religions learn to live together and even to appreciate and to affirm each other. It is increasingly evident that many people, disillusioned with the superficiality of much of religion, are seeking deeper spiritual life. It is further increasingly evident that many of the struggles and conflicts both within the Church and in the world have their roots in injustice, greed, and disrespect. In the midst of terror and mistrust, much of the joy and spontaneity of life is missing. These are but some of the challenges and opportunities facing Franciscans today. Our spiritual tradition, a combination of contemplation and action, is a rich resource to help guide us through the challenges of our time—not only for ourselves, but also for the sake of our parishes and the various communities we serve. What we face today is not much different in substance from that faced by Jesus, Francis, and Clare in their times. Our task is to be focused, spiritually centered, and courageous to act under inspiration of the Holy Spirit. The background that I have in the areas of spiritual formation, pastoral care, and multicultural and interfaith experiences are available to the Order as we seek to engage and to respond to the challenges of our time. I am willing to offer leadership to our Order as we seek to provide ways for our membership to be inspired and spiritually fortified, as well as to encourage and establish ways that we can be faithful witnesses to peace and justice in the Church and in the world. Were I to serve as Minister Provincial, the three aforementioned factors would remain central to the themes of my work: attraction to the life, charism, and ministry of St. Francis; commitment to close friendship among us as a community; and a commitment to engage God and the work God gives us to do.

Hallmark of Masud's Term

One can generalize on the effects of Anita Catron's term, Masud's immediate predecessor, and observe that she was able to achieve a balance of a local fellowship and regional life with whole-province endeavors in the Provincial Convocations. Given such a healthy balance in the Province, the hallmark of Masud's tenure was reaching out beyond the customary boundaries of the Order:

--reaching out geographically in pushing forward the Concordat with Brazil (Chapter 10) and supporting the medical mission to Guyana;

--reaching out ecumenically to the Order of Ecumenical Franciscans and to the Secular Franciscan Order (Roman Catholic) in creating the Joint Committee on Franciscan Unity;

--reaching out within ECUSA in leading a revival of National Association of Episcopal Christian Communities (NAECC) composed of religious communities canonically recognized by the House of Bishops; and

–reaching out politically by taking a public stand on national policies concerning the initiation of the Second Iraq War.

At the first Chapter he chaired as Minister Provincial in 2003, a motion was made and accepted to change the name of the province from the *American Province* to the *Province of the Americas*.

Reaching out Geographically: Medical Mission to Guyana, 2004

Part 1. The Reconnaissance Trip To Guyana 2003

Barbara Baumgarten (Bennett) (Provincial Formation Director) (Franciscan Times)

On February 2, 2003, Julia Bergstrom and I (Barbara Bennett) flew into Georgetown, Guyana along with Guyanese tertiary Eunice Edwards, who had earlier attended the Trinidad and Tobago Convocation with us. The trip began with a visit to Bishop Randall George, who offered a warm welcome along with a word of warning about the instability and violence in Guyana. We were not to leave Eunice's side at any time, for any reason, while in the Georgetown area.

The afternoon was spent obtaining permission to travel to the interior of Guyana to visit tertiaries Charles and Celian Roland. Normally, such permission must be obtained weeks in advance, but by God's grace, the Minister of Amerindian Affairs agreed to grant our travel into Imbaimadai on Thursday, February 6. No small miracle was this!

In the meantime, Bishop George arranged an appointment for us to meet with the Chief Medical Officer of Guyana the following morning. Dr. Rudolph Cummings gave us complete instructions on how to arrange a medical mission into the interior if a team of Third Order members desired to undertake such a ministry. The Amerindians rarely receive medical care by trained physicians and nurses; many suffer from malaria, TB, gastro-intestinal disorders, and malnutrition.

After leaving Dr. Cummings, we traveled up to West Coast Berbice to spend time in Eunice's home. Eunice took us to the end of the road where a ferry must be caught if one wishes to continue on to New Amsterdam. Along the way, she showed us the seven churches served by her local priest. Eunice's home is next door to one of the churches where she serves as a lay minister. The priest depends upon the lay ministers to do nearly everything except absolve, bless, consecrate, and perform weddings. The cemetery is situated between her home and the church, where a number of her ancestors lay and keep watch over her. The day ended with the singing of hymns and saying Evening Prayer with Eunice's extended family of nine.

Laren Gordon and Marjorie White, both postulants since 1997, appeared at Eunice's home midday Wednesday. Their dedication to TSSF was apparent and then was celebrated with their novicing at Evening Prayer and with feasting. En route back to Georgetown, we stopped off at the President's College, the only residential college in Georgetown. Eunice's granddaughter was delighted to see her grandmother and to be treated with some spending cash.

At 6:45 a.m. Thursday morning, the Bishop's driver, Patrick, came to drive us (Julia and Barbara) out to Ogle Airport to catch our flight to Imbaimadai. After going through customs and waiting for the weather to settle, we climbed aboard a small bush plane to make a one-hour flight into the jungle of Guyana. One other passenger and cargo accompanied us on the bumpy and loud flight (ear plugs were a must). Upon arrival at the Imbaimadai airstrip, we were relieved to see Fr. Charles Roland waiting for us, and we were surprised and delighted to see that Fr. Winston Williams was there as well. Fr. Williams explained that we were going to get into a boat and go up the Mazaruni River to Jawalla—a four-hour ride in a motorized open canoe.

Barbara Baumgarten (Bennett) and Fr. Charles Roland en route from Jawalla to Imbaimadai on the Mazaruni River of Guyana. Hidden is Fr. Winston Williams who is steering.

The brown river was low and much care was taken to avoid rocks and other objects. Along the way, the green jungle was thick and quiet. Occasionally, we saw miners or Amerindians going about their daily tasks. Due to the mining, most of the wildlife has moved deeper into the jungle, but we spotted a red snake and a baboon.

Jawalla sits high on a rise above the river. The settlement is spread over a great area and is connected by the river and trails. The Rolands, Julia, and I stayed at a comfortable diocesan guesthouse as did another couple who were in residence to help with the Bible translation program. The diocesan house had chairs with backs, a "kitchen," a common area (where we spent many hours "gaffing" or talking), and three bedrooms. Absent were running water, electricity, bathroom, window screens and other amenities taken for granted in the States. An outhouse was situated nearby and the river was used for bathing. Celian, a trained cook, and Dorina Williams were happy to have a "kitchen" area and cooked many wonderful meals for us. The staples included rice, cassava bread and some type of stew or fish—all cooked over a small kerosene stove.

Celian Roland, Barbara Baumgarten (Bennett) Fr. Charles Roland and Julia Bergstrom during sermon at church in Jawalla. Seated figure on right is lay reader and local midwife, Rita.

Each day began with the beckoning of the conch shell to Morning Prayer and Eucharist at the Anglican church. On Friday, we were invited to eat lunch with Dee and Ray, the American couple in residence at Jawalla to translate the Bible into Akawaio (ek-a-whyoh), the local language. Ray and Dee have been in residence for five years. They spent their first four years learning the language and giving it written form since Akawaio is an oral dialect. Now they are translating the Bible with a team of Amerindians brought in from throughout the region. At lunch, the whole team joins under the thatched roofed, open eating area (like a covered picnic area) for a common meal. We were warmly welcomed by all and enjoyed the stories of many while eating "one pot," a hearty fried rice. The days ended with the loud "whistle" of beetles that announce the setting of the sun, and sometimes the call of the baboons could be heard which resembled the sound of wind blowing through trees.

On Saturday, we joined the only other Christian church in the area for their weekly service. The Amokokopai Alleluia Church meets in a large, open thatched-roof building with backless benches circling the perimeter of the space. A simple table sat in the middle of the room with a basket on it for donations. We were invited to speak, and Winston translated what Julia said. The three-hour service, held in Akawaio (Fr. Williams translated periodically), consisted of preaching and witnessing until the final hour when we joined arms for a meditative chant-dance. The words and steps were repetitive, making it easy for us to fully participate, even if we did not understand what we were singing. The dance concluded by moving everyone outside to another communal eating area where cassava bread, dried fish and cassak (a popular wine made from cassava) were served. While this was the "social hour after church," it felt more like Eucharist, or even the feeding of the 5,000. We were richly blessed indeed to be welcomed into the community.

Across the river and down the trail a bit, sits Jawalla's one store, which sells a limited variety of packaged foods and supplies. Outside the store is a benched area with a television and VCR. A generator is used to power the unit. Arrangements were made for us to show our videos from the Santa Barbara Provincial Convocation and to share stories about the Third Order. Many Amerindians came to hear and see the white visitors. Again, we experienced a warm welcome and strong interest in who we were and what we were about.

The Anglican church sits in the middle of the area where we stayed. It was surrounded by the Williams's rectory, the diocesan guesthouse, the local school and the Bible translation center. Services out of the *West Indies Book of Common Prayer* are held on Wednesday, Friday and Sunday with Morning Prayer preceding the Eucharist. On Sunday, Julia and I preached about TSSF. Fr. Roland recorded the sermon, and Celian translated from English into Akawaio even though most of the congregation understands English. After Sunday services, we lunched, then headed to the boat for our journey back to Imbaimadai.

Imbaimadai is a mining settlement, which lacks the tranquility and cleanliness of Jawalla. The miners have a huge generator that runs loudly during the night in order for them to have light; when they have a successful day finding gold or diamonds, celebrations run at full volume through the night. Their disregard for the environment is evident by the trash strewn about and the damage done to the river.

Part 2. The Medical Mission Trip To Guyana 2004

Brenda M. Stewart (from the *Franciscan Times*)

With God all things are possible. Mission Accomplished. After months of preparation, including lots of frustrations, the Medical Mission to Region 7 became a reality. The Medical Team, which consisted of Dr. Milan Schmidt, Dr. Tupper Morehead and Nurse Sheila Morehead was scheduled to arrive in Georgetown on Saturday, September 4, 2004, and leave for Region 7 on Sunday, September 5, but Hurricane Frances had other plans.

Dr. Schmidt arrived as scheduled on Saturday, September 4, but Dr. and Nurse Morehead had to postpone their flight for September 4 because the Miami Airport was closed due to Hurricane Frances. Tupper and Sheila displayed their

Christian commitment to this mission because of the efforts they made to get to Guyana on Sunday, September 5. They flew to New Jersey, took a cab to JFK, where they made connections to Georgetown. Persons with less interest and faith would have aborted the trip and could not have been faulted for this.

The team went into Region 7 on Monday morning, September 6, accompanied by Mrs. Celian Roland and her son. Mrs. Roland, who resides in Georgetown, volunteered to go in with the team to prepare meals, and to assist her husband Fr. Charles Roland in matters relating to the mission. All food and water was bought in Georgetown and sent in with the team. It was interesting to see the passengers and cargo being weighed to determine that no more than 1500 lbs. were taken on board. Thankfully it was a fair morning, and the takeoff was smooth.

Imbaimadai health worker and Drs. Schmidt & Morehead.

They were met by Fr. Roland and members of the community who were there from the previous day because, although I tried to speak with Fr. Roland to inform him of the delay, the reception was so poor that he could not hear what I was saying, but he had all confidence that his Franciscan Brothers and Sisters of the team would arrive. After treating people at Fr. Roland's community, Imbaimadai, the team went by hired boat to Fr. William's community, Jawalla, where they treated the members of his community. Over 500 people were treated by the team, which returned to Georgetown on Thursday evening, September 9, and got a well needed rest Thursday night and Friday.

We all left Georgetown on Saturday, September 11. Fr. Roland reported that the members of the Good Shepherd Church asked him to say how grateful they were for the visit of the Medical Team, and for the needed treatments that they received. He said that the people were elated that their Church and the Franciscans cared for them, and that this was the first time that they had ever gotten this kind of attention. He said that the Medical Mission was a great success. Fr. Williams reported that the people in his area appreciated the visit, and sent their thanks to Chapter, and all who made this mission a reality.

Dr. Schmidt reported that he treated 151 persons with medical problems, including cardiovascular disease, cancer, diabetes, worms, gynecological problems, pains, headaches, asthma, etc. Almost every person displayed some degree of malnutrition, and would benefit from vitamins. Almost everyone complained of having had malaria, but it was difficult to document this since he had no means of making a diagnosis. There is further need for diagnostic testing for heart disease, cancer screening, etc.

Each community had two health workers, one of whom is retired. They had three months of formal training and felt qualified to give injections, interpret malaria slides, give First Aid, etc. They had some knowledge of antibiotics, but supplies are very limited without refrigeration or electricity. There is nothing to make blood smears. The microscope available has a "cloudy lens" and uses only natural light. The health workers are willing to improve their skills.

There is a need for examination skills and health education, e.g., videos or CDs could help. There is a local store that could assist. Topics should include hygiene, family planning, AIDS prevention, and the proper use of medication. Health workers would like to provide better stabilization, e.g., fluids etc., and transportation for serious cases.

Most employment seems to be related to mining, and there is concern that this may be reaching its end. Farming is done, but hunting is minimal. Fishing yields are low, reportedly due to pollution from the mines. Mercury poisoning directly from fish and water should be a concern, but the local citizens have no knowledge of it. Sanitation is very problematic, and toilet facilities are poor. Most persons, especially children, are barefoot. Soap, toothpaste, and places to wash are needed.

The Church is well supplied and is dedicated to spiritual leadership but lacks material resources. The priest does not have a cross and is in need of stoles and vestments. A VCR and church education materials would be welcomed. A personal Study Bible, typing paper and envelopes would be appreciated. Packages should be sent to Fr. Roland's wife, who lives in Georgetown. The outside of the box should be marked "DONATION TO THE CHURCH," and a letter inside should state this.

Conclusion

During the preparatory stages of this mission, Dr. Rudolph Cummings, Chief Medical Officer, was very helpful and was our contact person in Georgetown for all matters relating to this visit to Region 7. On my initial visit to Georgetown, the Jamaican Consulate in Guyana made the initial appointments for me to see Dr. Cummings and the Minister of Amerindian Affairs, and provided transportation.

Dr. Cummings met and held discussions with the Medical Team before they left for Region 7. He visited the hotel on Friday to see the team after their return, but it was late, and they were resting since they had to leave for the airport before 5 am. I spoke with him, and he was grateful for the assistance given to the people in Region 7, and has promised his support for future missions.

Medical mission at Fr. Roland's house with members of his congregation.

Mrs. Sheila George (the Bishop's wife) was very helpful. She arranged accommodation for my initial visit, also transportation from the airport. She assisted in any way that she could during the preparations for the mission, and met with the team after they returned from Region 7. The hotel staff and drivers were helpful and polite, and this made our stay easier. The written reports from Drs. Milan Schmidt and Tupper Morehead are available. Nurse Sheila Morehead did a tremendous job.

I thank Chapter for giving me the opportunity to coordinate this mission, which was an education on the lives of our brothers and sisters who are in need of the simple things of life. They live a life of poverty, simplicity, and humility, but the love and joy that they exhibit supersede their lack of material possessions.

Observations by Tupper Morehead *(Franciscan Times)*

Thank you, brothers and sisters of the Third Order, for enabling myself, my wife, Sheila, and Milan Schmidt, M.D., to visit the villages of Imbaimadai and Jawalla in Region 7 of Guyana. As you know, Imbaimadai is home to Charles and Celian Roland, and Jawalla is home to Winston and Dorina Williams. Brenda Mae Stewart of Kingston, Jamaica, worked tirelessly over the period of a year to make arrangements with TSSF, the Guyanese government, The Church of the Province of the West Indies (The Most Rev. Drexel Wellington Gomez, Primate), and the Diocese of Guyana (The Rt. Rev. Randolph Oswald George, Bishop) so that a short-term medical mission trip might become a reality. Brenda met us at the airport and attended to every detail of the mission. She also arranged for us to meet another tertiary, Eunice Edwards, of Guyana. Brenda enabled us to have a discussion with the Chief Medical Officer of Guyana, and invited Bishop George's wife to have tea with us.

As I reflect upon our time in Guyana, I am moved by the presence of the Holy Spirit in community. I live in Norris, a small town in the Appalachian region of Tennessee, yet I have brothers and sisters in Guyana, Jamaica, and throughout North and South America; these brothers and sisters love me, pray for me, and welcome me into their homes as part of their family. This family of tertiaries extends around our fragile planet Earth, and this family holds me in its arms of steadfast love every day of my life. As I pray daily using the Third Order, Province of the Americas Directory, I am aware that the spiritual presence of our community is as vital a part of me as my own breathing.

Love in community allows a white, privileged physician raised in affluence in the U.S. to let go of fear and become completely dependent upon his Amerindian brothers and sisters living in the interior of Guyana, the poorest country in South America. Although to visit a faraway place without central air-conditioning and heating, roads, automobiles, television, electricity, plumbing, potable water, or anti-terrorism squads might make some Americans uncomfortable, I felt no fear. Rather, I felt the love of God in community with Franciscan tertiaries in Imbaimadai and Jawalla, and I was continually cognizant of the ongoing prayers of my brother and sister tertiaries back home in the States. In spite of the obstacles of hurricanes, rearrangements in travel, sleeping in airports, getting medications through airline security agents, it was love in community that fortified me with endurance, faith, humor, and persistence.

That same love in community causes me to reflect upon the reasons why our brothers and sisters in Guyana and throughout most of the world must live without clean water, housing, food, education, and access to healthcare. Simple things, like immunizations, mosquito nets, vitamins, toothbrushes, soap, clean water for washing and drinking, flooring, shoes, antibiotics, antifungals, alcohol, anti-parasitics, contraceptives, condoms, and tuberculin skin tests are not available to these, our brothers and sisters.

Is it just our money that is required of us who live in America, where 80% of the world's resources are controlled by 6% of the world's population? I have been enlightened by our brothers and sisters in Guyana, and I have realized that what is required is both our presence and our money. I don't know why it took me fifty years to realize this. Although our visit was short, the places and faces, the smiles and the laughter, the praying and the singing, the simplicity of realizing that each day is a gift–those things will last forever for both those tertiaries in Guyana and for we tertiaries from the States. I understand the sacrifices that American tertiaries had to make to enable Sheila, Milan, and me to visit Roland, Celian, Winston, and Dorina. Some may have fasted, some may have begged, some may have dipped into savings and retirement accounts, some may have passed up buying a needed item, in order to make this outreach possible. We thank all of you. And we particularly thank you for your prayers, which took away our fears and eliminated all of the obstacles. We are a community without boundaries, and indeed our love and joy destroys all barriers between people. The Good News of Jesus of Nazareth and the Good News of Father Francis is "There is another way to live." In a culture where "Leadership" workshops, trainings, and classes abound, let us remember that Jesus and Francis call us to follow rather than to lead. Thank you all and thank you, community, for being countercultural, and providing the fellowship meetings, the retreats, the convocations, and the *Principles* which have given me the freedom to follow Jesus and Francis, rather than to lead Jesus and Francis.

Sheila Morehead *(Franciscan Times)*

I can't remember ever being so excited about meeting new friends and being an instrument for God's mission. We have been on several medical missions before, but, maybe because this one was in the planning stage for so long, I was really anxious to get there. That is, until Mother Nature's interference resulted in one major hurricane after another to cause our plans to be so sidetracked. But as "GOD'S WILL" will be done, we went a day late from Tennessee to Georgia, to New Jersey, to New York, to bypass Florida to get to Trinidad and finally to Guyana 36 hours later than planned! I was so saddened to hear that many people traveled long distances by foot and canoe to set up a welcome party for us on Monday in

Sheila, Tupper, and colleagues.

Imbaimadai. But because we couldn't get there until Tuesday, they ate the party food and made the long journey back to their remote villages.

We arrived in Georgetown, Guyana, very late on Sunday night and were met by our warm Franciscan welcome committee, Brenda and Leonard Stewart. After two nights of no sleep, our room was perfect, if only it weren't located on top of an all night jazz club!

The next morning, Tupper and I met our Franciscan mission-mate, Dr. Milan Schmidt. There was a bond at first sight! After breakfast and more detailed instructions we packed up supplies and headed for our small plane that would carry us into the interior of Guyana to visit the indigenous people of Imbaimadai and Jawalla. We left the coastline and after over an hour of travel looking at rainforest and rivers we suddenly saw before us steep mountains. The view was awesome! We landed on a dirt-covered field and were suddenly surrounded by smiling faces and warm welcomes from the village people who wanted to carry everything for us. We were probably the only white faces most of these people had ever seen, but even the children were not afraid and ran up to us for hugs. Of course, we went straight to the village Church of the Good Shepherd and were formally welcomed.

On the steps of Fr. Roland's Church of the Good Shepherd in Imbaimadai.

My dream for this mission was to be a presence to let these people know that they were cared about and also to listen to their stories. I wanted to know about their needs, their concerns, their struggles and what brought them joy. I just wanted to hear their stories, and if we were able to do some health education and healing while we were there that would be good too. But most of all I wanted to live among them and share the Holy Spirit.

We were truly in another world far from the comforts of home, but the true blessings were the ones we received from these beautiful people.

Over the next three-and-a-half days we set up six (four-hour) clinics and saw 450 patients between Tupper, Milan, and myself. Most of the time we saw patients with upper respiratory colds, skin infections, diabetes, abdominal pain, back pain, and fatigue. But I'm sure we were also seeing a lot of malnutrition, TB, worm infestation, and malaria. Our ability to do testing for diagnosis was very limited. We had to rely on the history we were told (mostly through interpreters) and our five senses, along with our clinical experience. There was also a huge amount of the Holy Spirit flying around for support to us and the patients.

Some of our accomplishments were only short-term fixes and, when the vitamins, worm meds, and malaria medicine ran out, they were back to where they had started. The long-term effects of our visit will be more clear as time passes.

Immediate reflections tell me that these Amerindians have basic needs for human growth and development. Clean, safe water and proper nutrition is what they need first. They need carpentry assistance getting their housing up off the bare dirt ground. They should have basic toothbrushes and toothpaste. A visit by a dental team would be very productive. Education on healthy ways to dispose of garbage and human waste would improve their conditions. Birth control was the number one request by the women. The children complained of abdominal pain, fatigue, and fever.

The Spirit Shop owner does have a satellite, a TV and a VCR. Some of the villagers asked for health education material to be sent in the forms of tape and written handouts. The Spirit Shop man agreed to play the educational tapes for the community. Would I go back to those primitive villages where there was no electricity, no running water and hot temperatures? YOU BET I WOULD!!! I left a piece of my heart and soul with the Amerindians of Guyana.

Reaching out Ecumenically: Establishing the Joint Committee on Franciscan Unity, 2004

From Minister Provincial Report to Chapter 2004

God has also been calling us to deepen our ecumenical relationships, particularly with non-Anglican Franciscans. In February, the Joint Committee on Franciscan Unity was launched with the convening of representatives from its three founding Orders: The Third Order, Society of Saint Francis, The Order of Ecumenical Franciscans, and the Secular Franciscan Order (Roman Catholic). Its mission statement declares that:

> *For the sake of all Creation, we are called to bear witness to the essential unity of the Church, the Body of Christ, by working towards Franciscan unity at all levels of fraternal life. We will achieve this through dialogue and collaboration among the Orders which follow Christ in the tradition of Francis and Clare.*

Furthermore, its organizing principles state that:

> *Acknowledging that they share a common Franciscan charism and are committed to bear witness to its dedication to the work of Franciscan unity, members of the Joint Committee work together in ways that demonstrate mutual respect, honor, and affirmation of the several gifts each brings to the work of the committee... Central to its vision of Franciscan unity is its call to engage efforts toward reconciliation among its sponsoring Franciscan Orders and the ecclesial bodies they represent.*

Diana Finch was elected to be Chair of the Joint Committee. This work is also exploring uncharted waters. Pray that God will grant it wisdom as it engages its work of reconciliation.

Inviting Brother Christopher, a monk of the New Skete Orthodox Monastery, to lead Chapter's Quiet Day also represents a step towards further ecumenical relationships. Already the Monks of New Skete have asked that we serve as a resource to their community as they seek to create a way to organize and provide spiritual formation for lay and clergy who seek to be in relationship with their community. The process of hearing the voice of the Holy Spirit and responding continues.

(Masud also invited Brs. Bill Short and Wayne Hellmann, OFM, the editors of the new "Omnibus" entitled *Francis: Saint, Founder, Prophet* to be the keynote speakers at the Provincial Convocation in Endicott, Massachusetts in 2007.)

Reaching out Within ECUSA in Leading a Revival of the National Association of Episcopal Christian Communities (NAECC)

Summer 2005, *Franciscan Times*

Representatives of eight Christian Communities met in New York City in May 2005 to map out the future of their national association. Chaired by the Rev. Masud Ibn Syedullah, the meeting revived the National Association of Episcopal Christian Communities (NAECC), which is made up of religious communities canonically recognized by the House of Bishops.

In the year to come, NAECC plans a campaign to increase the visibility of its members, including a brochure and a website. The association also began to explore revision of the Church canons to clarify that members of churches in full communion with the Episcopal Church, such as the Evangelical Lutheran Church in America, are eligible for membership.

The Rev. Br. Tobias Stanislas Haller, Brotherhood of Saint Gregory, was elected as Chair, with three other officers: Vice-chair, Cathy Cox, Rivendell Community; Treasurer, Bill Farra, Community of Celebration; and Recorder, Br. Carle Griffin, Community of the Paraclete.

Br. Tobias Stanislas said, "We spent our first evening together telling about our communities and the many ministries of our brothers and sisters. I expect future meetings to be hosted by members in every region of the U.S. We also committed ourselves to offer support to fledgling communities and to active participation with the House of Bishops Standing Committee on Religious Communities." Br. Tobias Stanislas, as Chair, will serve as the NAECC representative to this body.

Reaching out Politically: Taking a Public Stand on National Policies

Easter 2003, *Franciscan Times*

Easter greetings to you all!

This past Holy Week and Easter Day celebrations were, by far, at once the most buoyant, yet the strangest that I think I have ever experienced. Who can explain all the reasons why worship experiences may affect us in one way or other at a particular time? Yet, for me in my parish here in the Bronx, there was a profound sense of drama throughout the week—from the exuberant cheers and gripping foreshadowing of the Passion on Palm Sunday, through the intimacy of footwashing and Eucharist on Maundy Thursday, the meditations of sacrificial love on Good Friday, and culminating with the joyous shouts of "Alleluia.

Christ is risen!" at The Great Vigil of Easter on Holy Saturday and Easter Sunday morning.

What drama! Such a progression: from joyful expectation, to brutal execution, to the new life of resurrection. Such is the central week of the Christian year and such is the story of our lives. Such is the ongoing story of our journey of faith in Christ.

That week was strange in that it was also a time in the history of our world when the war in Iraq was still being waged with indications that it would soon come to an end. What a turbulent time in the life of the world! What a strange moment as the Church was living out, through its liturgy, the drama of the cosmic conflict of good and evil.

What an "out of joint" kind of time. What a time for Christians to be proclaiming the victory of God over death, sin, evil, and corruption. What a challenging juxtaposition of events. It was really too much to take in. It will surely take time to digest, if we will.

As the season has progressed and we have been given the word that the combat portion of the war is over, we are left with an awareness that some significant changes have happened, yet the contrasts persist. An old regime is gone, a country lies in disarray; people are free from a tyrannical government, people are left without homes, family members, body parts. People have new freedom. People have new hope. People are unsure about the future. It is somewhat reminiscent of the opening lines of *A Tale of Two Cites*, "It was the best of times. It was the worst of times..." It is in such times that we need to know the reality of the resurrection. It is in such times that every fiber of our being yearns for the reality of new birth, the restoration of true goodness.

As we of Christian faith continue through this season to proclaim the reality of the Risen Lord, may we also continue our prayers and actions for peace and reconciliation in the world that it may be restored. As our shouts of "Alleluia" ring, may also our shouts for justice persist. May the joy and experience of Easter life not be only for some, but for all. May we be vigilant in our efforts to make it known that the Lord is risen indeed over all corruption, sin, death, and destruction.

Towards Maturity in Christ and Franciscan Spirituality

Final Report to Chapter as Minister Provincial (Franciscan Times Winter 2005*)*

In my report to Chapter last year, I said that during the past few years, "It is as if the Holy Spirit is calling us to move to another level of maturity, being thankful for what we have been and done, yet calling us onward to what we can be and do." That perception continues to ring true to me as I reflect on the events of the past year, particularly within the context of the last three or four years in the life of the Order.

There are at least three characteristics of maturity that I can identify:

1. Openness to listening to and responding, with care, to others;

2. Openness to changing the way we do things when it is for our good and/ or that of those with whom we are in relationship; and

3. Openness to taking risks that enable peace, reconciliation, wholeness, and health.

During the past three years, our Order has been challenged, time and again in each of these areas, to expand our minds, hearts, and spirits in order to respond to the mission God calls us to embrace. The Way of Christ and Francis is such that it receives us as and where we are at the beginning of our journey, then calls us onward to higher heights and to deeper depths of faith, love, and trust as we continue on the path. Such a journey is not always easy, nor predictable, and it is certainly not one that we control if Christ is indeed the Lord of our life, but one that we learn to walk with increased awareness of the faithfulness of God as we continue on the Way.

During the past few years, the Lord has brought before our Order several areas of mission and ministry that were new to us. While most of our energy during at least the past twenty years has been focused on the internal life of the Order, with matters of structure and formation, during the past few years there has been an enormous increase of missionary energy directed to work beyond the Order as well. The internal work of the past was necessary for the health and growth of the Order at that time. We are now in a new place where we must be attentive, not only to the internal life of our community, but also to ways that we reach out beyond ourselves. We began to turn the corner about four years ago.

After years of many activists among us often feeling that they were on the fringe of our community—that their concerns were not central to the focus of the Order—an increased number of our members, as well as the Chapter, began to endorse and participate in more public actions for justice and peacemaking. Our membership in Franciscans International, the Peace and Justice listserv, peace and justice oriented devotional and resource materials, Chapter's letter to President Bush urging non-military efforts for peace in Iraq prior to the invasion, our presence at the Franciscan Witness for Peace in Union Square, New York City, as well as the medical mission to the interior of Guyana—all of these and more represent a new era in the life and work of the Third Order in this province. It was clear at IPTOC that the Province of the Americas has become one of the leaders in expressing our interior spirituality in more exterior ways. It is an inspiration and encouragement to our brothers and sisters in the other provinces.

Also in the past year, we entered intensified relationship with Franciscans beyond the Anglican Communion, namely in participating in the creation and support of the Joint Committee on Franciscan Unity, an historic effort towards mutual regard and collaboration among Franciscans of all Christian traditions –Roman Catholics, Anglicans, and Protestants. One of the results of this collaborative action is that the Minister General of the Roman Catholic Secular Franciscans (SFO) has invited the Minister General of The Third Order to attend and participate in the Secular Franciscans' international Chapter in Assisi in November of this year—a first in the history of Roman Catholic and Anglican Franciscan relations. Furthermore, there is scheduled for February of 2006, a Conference on Franciscan Unity to be held here at Little Portion Friary, bringing together leaders from the Roman Catholic Secular Franciscan Order, The Order of Ecumenical Franciscans, and The Third Order. This is also a major step beyond any that we have ever taken before.

As your Minister, I, along with representatives of two other Christian Communities of the Episcopal Church/USA (The Brotherhood of Saint Gregory and the Community of the Paraclete), was responsible for calling together representatives of the other canonically recognized Christian Communities in the Episcopal Church to re-establish the National Association of Episcopal Christian Communities. Its purpose is to enhance communication among the eleven communities, to share resources for mission and outreach, to give support to newly forming communities, and to be a collective voice for the religious communities of our classification to the Church at large and to the ECUSA House of Bishops, in particular.

Each of the areas of new exploration that we have engaged during the past few years has challenged us towards greater maturity in Christ and Franciscan spirituality. Each one challenges us to be more open—more open to listen to and to respond with care to each other—more open to do things differently than we have done them in the past—more open to risk for the sake of justice and true peace —ultimately, more open to the Holy Spirit of God.

As we move forward, there are at least four more areas that demand our maturity in Christ and Franciscan spirituality:

1. We are currently in the midst of seeking ways to better assure ourselves and the Church that we are committed to being a safe place. Committed to hold each other in esteem as gifts of God, we further commit and discipline ourselves to attitudes and behavior that in no way demean, endanger, or exploit others in any way. Along with other religious communities of the Episcopal Church/USA, we are working along with the Standing Commission on Religious Communities of the House of Bishops of the Episcopal Church/USA to set in place standards of spiritual formation, sexual boundary training, and other means to educate and discipline ourselves in ways that provide a spiritually and emotionally safe environment among us in our Order. As a community dedicated to reflect the nature and glory of Christ, such an expectation is consistent with our Principles and Rule. The challenge for us is in the detail of how we, being such a large and dispersed community, can meet such an expectation effectively.

2. As a community living under vows, it is necessary for us to honor those vows. Each professed member of the community has the responsibility to:

A) Renew our vow annually,

B) Report annually to the Area Chaplain, and

C) Make a financial pledge and contribution to the Order annually.

These three are the core responsibilities to be regarded and maintained by each member of the Order. Each one is an expression and indication of our commitment to be in community with each other, to support our common life as well as our mission.

3. The next generations need to know what is life-giving and exciting about living a Franciscan Christian life. Participants of IPTOC were enthusiastic about identifying ways to share life with the younger generations. They are already the Church of today and need to be aware of what an extraordinary resource the Society of Saint Francis can be to giving definition and direction to the life in Christ. A part of the responsibility of mature adults (elders, if you will) is to offer leadership and guidance to those who come after. What a tremendous resource we can be to those who are seeking alternative ways of thinking and living in today's world.

4. The Anglican Communion is in a time of stress, seeking how it may move forward as a body in ways that will authentically represent Christ in the present world, amidst the various cultures where it exists. There are great disagreements as to what voice it should have in the world. As Franciscans, we intuitively understand that our foundational call is to be radically and passionately committed to love God and each other at all cost. Francis lived a life that demonstrated his determination to express such radical love to all—even to those the Church wished to exclude or even to eliminate. I was encouraged that the Interprovincial Chapters of The Society drafted and sent a letter to the Archbishop of Canterbury and to all of the Primates of the Anglican Communion commending them to be radically committed to each other as family who, although not in agreement about some things, are in agreement that they are related to each other and are committed to honor each other's differences of opinion. We in this province will surely have the opportunity to invite our brother and sister Anglicans to a more mature understanding of what it means to be family.

None of this can be accomplished in our own strength. As Day Thirty of the *Principles* reminds us, "Humility, love, and joy, which mark the lives of tertiaries are all God-given graces. They can never be obtained by human effort. They are gifts of the Holy Spirit." May God grant us his Holy Spirit, more and more, to grow into the maturity that we need to accomplish the good work committed to our charge.

References

Armstrong, Regis J, J A. W. Hellmann, William J. Short, and Francis. *Francis of Assisi: Early Documents. Vol. 1-Saint, Vol. 2- Founder, Vol. 3-Prophet.* New York: New City Press, 1999-2001.

Chapter 13: Ken Norian, Minister Provincial 2005-11; Minister General 2011-

An Unlikely Background for a Minister Provincial?

Over a number of articles in the *Franciscan Times*, Ken Norian shared his unique background for a Minister Provincial.

Masud Ibn Syedullah, right, passing on the role of Minister Provincial to Ken Norian in 2005. In background, Sister Jean CSF and Julia Bergstrom.

> *My undergraduate degree is in finance and I have an MBA. For 20 years I worked in nearly every aspect of radio broadcasting, including off-air and on-air work. I have five kids, including two biological, one adopted and two stepchildren – after seeing them all go through adolescence not much can get me too stressed.* (*Franciscan Times,* Fall 2011)

> *In 1984 I was drawn to a spirituality that was charismatic, contemplative, ecumenical, evangelical, and sacramental – all at the same time. I've found, in the Third Order, a way of life that supports who I am and what I do. With respect to what I do... I've earned my living for most of my life as a manager. Most recently, working in the financial community on Wall Street in New York City for Reuters. There are very real challenges working in an industry that personifies all that Francis was not about while attempting to espouse a Franciscan spirituality. (Franciscan Times,* Summer 2005*)*

> *I was professed in the Province of the Americas in 1989. In 1996 then Minister Provincial Alden Whitney wrote a little note in the Franciscan Times announcing that Carole Watson would not be standing for another term as Bursar, and I wrote to Alden expressing an interest and was elected Bursar. For three terms (nine years) I served in that position.* (*Franciscan Times,* Fall 2011)

Two years later (1998) something momentous happened:

> *...then Minister General, Alden Whitney, and I were talking about the emerging World Wide Web and how we might be able to use it as a vehicle to promote TSSF and provide resources for tertiaries. I had no experience in HTML/Web design. However, I did have an account with an Internet provider, and I registered the tssf.org domain in 1998. I woke up one rainy Saturday morning* [December 12, 1998]. *My day was pretty open. So I made myself a cup of coffee and picked up a book on HTML web page design and started reading. I played around for a few hours, eventually got dressed after my second or third cup.*

Sometime in the early afternoon I switched from coffee to beer and began to design and code [the website]. *After more than I am comfortable owning up to, around dinnertime, I was able to post the first rudimentary TSSF web page. For several years, this hand-coded web page was the foundation for continuing minor improvements* [1998-2005]. *Back in the day, TSSF in the Americas was one of the first Episcopal Christian communities to have a web presence, and was certainly the first in the Third Order province globally* (From a personal email June 24, 2014). [See Apendix to this Chapter]

Ken worked with two Ministers Provincial very closely as Bursar (Anita and Masud), and more briefly with a third during transition (Alden transitioning from Bursar Carole Watson who was a very pre-computer bursar). In his statement for his Minister Provincial nomination, Ken pointed out how he had "had the opportunity to participate with many individuals in our Order's leadership on Chapter and on Standing Committee....I've served the Order as Area Chaplain, Formation Counselor, Formation Class Leader, Fellowship Convener and Webmaster." (*Franciscan Times*, Summer 2005)

In 2002, Ken stood for election as Minister Provincial along with Masud, Jacqui Belcher, and Caroline Benjamin (Provincial Secretary). Masud was elected, and Ken worked as his bursar. In 2005, Ken, along with Terry Rogers and Anita Catron stood for election as Minister Provincial, and this time Ken was elected.

Most Ministers Provincial have been elected to this position from roles that have had a "pastoral" background (Chaplain, Formation Director, Fellowship Coordinator). So as a person with an MBA literally working on Wall Street, I was both humbled and more than a bit frightened by the prospect of serving as Minister Provincial. An important lesson I learned is that God's grace is a powerful and amazing gift. We all have strengths and weaknesses, and, if we are open to the working of the Spirit, God will bless us and work through us. (*Franciscan Times*, Fall 2011)

Following Up Masud's Outreach Initiatives

The explosive outreach initiatives begun during the three short years of Masud Ibn Syedullah's tenure as Minister Provincial basically took the two terms of Ken Norian's Minister Provincial tenure to work out in detail incorporating (or attempting to incorporate) them into the internal life and structures of the Province. Much of such overlapping and long-term experiences of the Province were captured in Chapter 10: the ongoing tumultuous work managing a "proto-province" in Brazil; and the ongoing work with the House of Bishops in ECUSA around the policies of "Safe Community." With the former, the evolution of the relationship with Brazil continued after Ken's two terms concluded; with the latter, Ken proved to be a skillful canon lawyer capable of crafting a solution that pleased all parties, clarified the Province's position in ECUSA, and even left our standing as a "listed" Christian Community in ECUSA's Red Book [See Chapter 10]. Ken continued to work with, support, fund, and attend meetings begun during Masud's tenure in the Joint Committee for Franciscan Unity and the Franciscan Action Network.

In his Minister Provincial report to Chapter in 2008 (at which he was unanimously elected to a second term), Ken, himself, described his work "as a manager – reinforcing our existing ethos." Since Ken had to use most of his two terms as Minister Provincial to support and incorporate the outreach efforts of Masud, he was left little time and space for his own new Provincial initiatives. Moreover, during his tenure as Minister Provincial, he had to respond to the death of the one of the Province's heroes, Emmett Jarrett.

Emmett Jarrett (JPIC Mover and Shaker) Dies, 2010

Emmett's death in 2010 hit Ken hard. Ken always explained how it was his ongoing debate and dialogue with Emmett that allowed him to grow beyond his MBA training and his Wall Street work assumptions. At the funeral Ken was joined by (left to right) Joyce Dupont, Gary Mongillo, Janet Moore, Masud Ibn Syedullah, Danni Bellows, Bill Breedlove, Paul Jakoboski, Rick Bellows, and Jocelyn Linneken.

From the New London Day (newspaper)

[Emmettt] continued to live a life of love and service to the community exemplified by his work with the Homeless Hospitality Center, the Voluntown Peace Trust, and his participation in the ongoing life of St. Francis House.

He worked his way through Columbia University discovering his vocation as a poet. He taught English in Crete from 1966 to 67, wrote a study guide to Shakespeare's *Hamlet*, and continued writing poetry. On his return to the United States in 1967, he helped found Hanging Loose Press, and published several books of poetry. After "meeting Jesus on the Taconic State Parkway," he attended the General Theological Seminary in New York City and was ordained in 1976.

He and his wife of 27 years, Anne Scheibner, met as staff to the Brooklyn Urban Hearings on "The Role of the Church in the City" in 1980. Fr. Emmett served as national president of the Episcopal Urban Caucus from 1992 to 1995. He edited two EUC publications: *For The Living of These Days: Reflections on the Rule of Life of the EUC* and *To Heal the Sin-Sick Soul: Toward a Spirituality of Anti-Racist Ministry*. After he became a member of the Third Order of the Society of Saint Francis (TSSF), he and Anne returned with their children, then ages 14 and 10, to Anne's home region of southeastern Connecticut in 1999. Their intention was to try an experiment in "intentional Christian community," which became St. Francis House at 30 Broad Street in New London: "a place of prayer, a house of hospitality, and a center for peace and justice ministry."

In 2005 a new collection of Fr. Emmett's poetry, *Wild Geese Flying South,* was published by St. Francis House's Jubilee Publications. *Broad Street Blues: A Reader in Radical Discipleship* chronicled the development of the ministry at St. Francis House. Modeled in part on Dorothy Day, Peter Maurin, and the Catholic Worker movement and starting with the idea of listening to and engaging with neighbors, the work of St. Francis House took shape with different members of the House engaging in various endeavors.

With the Rev. Eric Swanfeldt of Uncasville and other walkers, Fr. Emmett participated in three of the now annual Peace Pilgrimages starting in 2006 and walking between 270 and 800 miles each year. In 2008 he gave the closing statement at his trial as one of 34 defendants arrested for their Guantanamo witness at the Supreme Court in Washington, D.C.

New London Day

Kathleen Edgecomb, October 12, 2010

Emmett Jarrett, an Episcopal priest known for his love and kindness to all, died Saturday the way he lived—at peace, in a home filled with books, religious icons and a community of family and friends. "We were all there with him. He shared his life and his love of life, and he shared his death with us all. It was a privilege and an honor," said his friend, Paul Jakoboski, vice president of Gemma E. Moran United Way/Labor Food Center. Jakoboski has lived for the past 18 months at St. Francis House, the home at 30 Broad St. that Jarrett and his family opened to any and all.

Jarrett, 71, helped organize the New London Homeless Hospitality Center Inc. and was a popular figure in the antiwar movement. For years he was a regular at peace vigils at the base of the Soldiers and Sailors Monument, participated in three Peace Pilgrimages across Connecticut and was arrested several times while protesting the war in Iraq.

But he is most remembered as the man who opened St. Francis House on Broad Street ten years ago. It was an experiment by Jarrett and his wife, Anne Scheibner, to create an "intentional Christian community." It was a place to pray, a center for peace and justice ministry, and a home that welcomed the homeless, those in transition and those looking for a more spiritual life. "To me, he was the closest thing to Jesus Christ," said Judy Mann, a member of Temple Emanuel in Waterford, who met Jarrett ten years ago and helped him start the homeless shelter. "He emulated goodness in everything he did. He had an angelic aura all around him. He was the most peaceful man I ever met," said Mann, director of volunteer services for the New London Community Meal Center Inc.

Jarrett, who was known as "Father Emmett" to most of those who knew him, had a background in English, wrote poetry, served in the Army from 1959 to 1962 and became an ordained Episcopal priest after meeting Jesus on the Taconic State Parkway.

His wife said he had some kind of spiritual experience on the highway in upstate New York and decided to devote his life to living in what he called a "beloved community," where people are committed to paying attention to what's happening to the poor and the marginalized around them.

"He wanted to bring peace to a world that has lost its way," his wife said.

Dick Marks of Silver Springs, who arrived last week to be with his friend during his final days, said Jarrett had an uncompromising view of Christianity that was not just "something you do turning out every Sunday morning."

"He changed my spiritual outlook," said Marks, who has known Jarrett since 1987. "He made me much more concerned about our neighbors and all people around us."

Nora Curioso's first encounter with Jarrett was in 2006 when Jarrett and others were carrying coffin-shaped boxes through Norwich to protest the Iraq war.

"He felt people should see the coffins of soldiers that the government was not letting us see," said Curioso, who works at St. Francis House. "I think his legacy will live on not only in New London. ... Homeless people around the county were touched by him, even if they never met him."

Cathy Zall, executive director of the Homeless Hospitality Center, said she met Jarrett in 1999 when she read a letter he wrote in an Atlanta, Ga., magazine about "intentional Christian communities."

Zall, who lived in Old Lyme at the time, called him. "I was instantly sucked into the vortex of him," she said.

Jarrett challenged people to live with more concern for others than for themselves, Zall said. "He could have been a high-paid rector in a big Episcopal church, but wanted to live according to the Gospel among people who needed him," she said.

Jarrett, who allowed homeless people to live on his porch and offered his home to anyone in need, was diagnosed with cancer in December 2008. Up until a few days before his death he was active and attending community events, including the Homeless Dance fundraiser last month at Ocean Beach Park.

Interview with Emmett Jarrett During One of His Peace Walks

Tracy J. Sukraw, Diocese of Massachusetts Newsletter (Winter 2008-2009)
What are you learning from your walk?

> Humility and courage. I'm a Third Order Franciscan. The only saint quoted in the Rule is Bernard of Clairvaux, and he says that any spiritual community must be founded on humility if it's going to have any chance of success. What do we understand about a nation being humble? I don't begin to justify terrorist actions, but what if our country after 9/11 had chosen not to lash out with power and enormous strength, but instead to humbly say, what can we do to find out what caused this? What I'm learning is to connect the personal virtue of humility, which I work at like all of us, with the idea that there is something for the community to be humble about as well.

In terms of courage, it doesn't take a lot of courage to walk. You just have to stay off the main roads! Part of it is to be willing to have only a handful of people—or even nobody—show up. And that's O.K. There it is.

Why the no-show, do you think? I don't hear the church talking about peace much.

No, you don't. The churches largely are not involved in the peace movement. What if the Episcopal Church said: We don't buy the war. It's not a just war, we can't participate, let's not pay war taxes. And some of us, this is our commitment; we earn sufficiently little money not to pay taxes. And yet live very full lives. You don't need a lot of money to be happy.

Rev. Swanfeldt of Uncasville & Fr. Emmett walking a peace pilgrimage.

Why are the churches not involved?

Partly we're so concerned with institutional survival and maintenance that we don't take courageous stances. I mean, many people do in many situations. The work that people do, for the homeless, for social justice, all those things are great. But when it comes to conflict with the main society, we're very, very hesitant about that.

What are you hearing from people along the way?

A real concern for what our children's lives are going to be like. It's clear that our children's lives are not going to be like ours. In part that may be a good thing. We might get closer to some realities. I mean, I'm not hoping for a depression, but with the economic turndown, we may have to stop being as consumerist as we are. I hope we do stop being as consumerist as we are.

It sounds like this is as much about storytelling as it is about walking.

Absolutely. That's the thing. We show up—we're stupid enough to walk 800 miles in six weeks, and that attracts people to come and say, who are these nuts?—and then we have a chance to ask them to tell us their stories, tell us what they yearn for. And as often as not, what you yearn for is connected to a story somehow.

How is the act of walking biblical?

Well, if you think about it, Jesus walked up and down Palestine. People go on pilgrimages to Canterbury, to Rome and to other holy places. A pilgrimage is a walking to some place for a purpose, and the purpose is always a spiritual one, always to get in touch with the center of one's self, which is somehow the center of God's heart. Life is a journey, and it's on a road.

What can people do in their day-to-day lives to work for peace?

What's wrong with our society and our world won't change on Jan. 20 [Inauguration Day]. People can make a public witness. It's important to say these things we believe in public. Associate with people in your churches, in your synagogues. Get involved with interfaith concerns. There are secular people who are yearning for peace. All those kids out on Boston Common yesterday, very few of them seemed to represent faith communities, but they're working for peace. We can learn from them. They can learn from us. Frankly, in environmental terms, the culture is going to have to live more simply. It's possible for some of us to begin to do that now. One of the best meals I ever had—and I love good food, rich food— was with Phil Berrigan [peace activist and Ploughshares Movement cofounder] at Jonah House in Baltimore. We had some lettuce and tomatoes grown in their garden, some bread they had baked themselves, some peanut butter and some jellies they had made and water. It was nourishing, it was healthy and it provided a table around which conversation could happen. And of course, that's the Eucharist, isn't it. You know, we gather for the wedding banquet, as in today's Gospel reading [Matthew 22:1-14], we eat and drink and are nourished in both body and spirit, and that's where the kingdom begins to be.

What People Expect of Franciscans: God's Mission for Us in Today's World

A Sermon preached Emmett Jarrett at the Holy Eucharist at the Provincial Convocation of the Province of the Americas, Endicott College, June 27, 2007

As I was preparing to come to this Convocation last week, friends asked me where I was going. To a gathering of Third Order Franciscans, I explained. Their eyes crossed. What could be better, I asked, than spending six days with 129 Franciscans? Answer: Spending six days with 130 Franciscans!

Our Minister Provincial, my friend Ken Norian, mentioned yesterday that in the early days of the Order, "Chapter" was not a leadership group making decisions for others, but a gathering of hundreds – even thousands! – to pray together, renew their commitment to Christ and one another, study the Scriptures, and discern God's call to them for the future…rather like this Provincial Convocation!

Let us remember the difference between an institution and a movement. In an institution, a few people at the "top" make decisions for the many "below." In a movement, the people who do the work make the decisions!

So – I am privileged to be with all of you today to speak of a growing "movement" within the Franciscan family, and indeed in the Church as a whole. Not just Anglican Franciscans, and not just the Episcopal Church.

That movement is, I believe, a movement of the Spirit. That movement is people responding to the leading of the Holy Spirit. It is a movement of disciples who want to respond to Jesus' command to "love one another" as He loves us. It is this kind of love that will, I believe, help us to put the internal conflicts in our Church in perspective, and work together as disciples on the mission of Jesus Christ: to proclaim the Kingdom of God as it comes near to us in Christ's love, and to heal those who are broken by the savage power of the American Empire.

This movement of the Spirit in our time is founded on our growing awareness that the mission of Christ is to proclaim and practice ***God's justice*** in a cruel and destructive world, ***God's peace*** in a world at war, and to ***care for God's creation*** in ways that reflect our understanding that it is not ours to own or exploit or destroy but to care for tenderly as a mother for her child – or, perhaps better – as a mature person cares for an aging mother.

The mission, therefore, of the Church, and of the Franciscan family, is the mission of God's justice, peace, and the integrity of creation.

We are not naïve about this mission. It's not a matter of birdbaths and soup kitchens, important as those are, but about the ***revolutionary transformation of society*** – starting with our society in the United States of America. We must stop the wars in Iraq, Afghanistan, Palestine, Darfur, and elsewhere, and start a revolution of values to break the cycle of endless war that we are running on like lab rats on a treadmill.

How can we do this – we who are sinners ourselves, no better than our ancestors? It is not easy, and the task will not be done in a few days or even years.

But remember the context of Jesus' new commandment to love one another as he has loved us that we heard in today's Gospel [John 13:31-35]. Judas, the disciple who betrayed him, has just shared intimately with Jesus a morsel of bread, which the Lord had dipped into the stew at the Last Supper and given to his friend, perhaps even placing it in his mouth! Judas has now left the table and gone out to betray Jesus to the religious and imperial authorities, who will torture him and murder him on the cruel cross. When Judas leaves, Jesus says, "Now is the Son of man glorified" (John 13:31), and then he gives his disciples the "new commandment" of love. It is not to warrior heroes or plaster saints that Jesus commits his mission, but to us. The test, for us as for the first disciples, is love. People will know that we are his disciples if we love one another.

* * *

In March of this year, Carol Tookey and Craig Miller (Order of Ecumenical Franciscans), and I attended a conference of 137 members of the Franciscan Family in Baltimore as your representatives. The 134 others were Roman Catholic Franciscans, and they organized the conference, but we were made welcome by everyone, beginning with the Friars of the Society of the Atonement from Graymoor (see Chapter 2).

We gathered to pray and talk together to discern if God is calling the Franciscan Family to speak with one voice in the center of world power about justice, peace, and the integrity of creation. One of the speakers, Joe Rozansky, OFM, a Midwesterner who works in the OFM JPIC office in Rome, posed the issue as a question: "What do people expect of Franciscans?" This was his answer: "People expect three things of us: commitment to the poor, peace-building and nonviolence, and care for the Creation."

That question, and those answers, make sense to me. I invite you to think about them as you go through our time together at Provincial Convocation, and reflect on how we are meeting these expectations, and what more we can do together, ecumenically, to meet the Lord Jesus' test of love for us as disciples and Franciscans.

First, commitment to the poor. Christians are committed to the poor because Jesus was committed to the poor. Not only did He teach that the poor are "blessed" (Matthew 5:3), but the Son of God "became poor although He was rich, so that by His poverty you might become rich" (II Corinthians 8:9). St. Francis in his time embraced poverty because Jesus Christ was poor, and to follow Christ meant to be poor with him.

The Churches in our time have nearly forgotten the poor Christ. Our "affluenza" has led to what Gibson Winter once called "the suburban captivity of the Church." We must return to the Lord, in whose footsteps we follow, by embracing the poor.

Leonardo Boff, a Brazilian Franciscan, in *Francis of Assisi: A Model for Human Liberation*, reminds us that the Church has gone through three stages in its relation to the poor. Originally it was a Church "of the poor" because its members, even though not all were slaves or impoverished, were powerless, an enemy of the state, a threat to the Roman Empire by their very existence, subject to criminal penalties as an illegal religion.

This changed when the Emperor Constantine embraced Christianity in 325 AD and made it the state religion, an "Established Church." The Church became rich in worldly terms, and a lot of Christians went to the desert to found monastic communities that sought to live in the poverty of Jesus. The rest of us enjoyed the spoils, built big churches, and exercised power. But the Church never completely forgot the poor. (How could we?) We became a Church "for the poor," establishing schools and hospitals, benevolent societies and sanctuaries for the needy. A powerful Church, identified with the powers, took care of the poor in a paternalistic way, as a matter of charity. Everyone had his or her place in this world: the rich, to obtain salvation by doing good works, gave alms to the poor. The poor learned patience under their afflictions, and provided occasion for the rich to give alms.

Something new is happening in our time. First in Latin America, and then around the world, Christians have begun to awaken to the injustice of poverty. We have begun to realize that the wealth some of us enjoy is related in profound ways to the destitution others experience. In Latin America this awakening was called a "preferential option for the poor," and so the Church has begun to be a Church "with the poor."

Thinking about the poor in these terms leads to a new understanding of what it means to be disciples. Those of us who are privileged – and wealth is not the only form of privilege – some of us are privileged by being white, or male, or "educated" – may give away money, but we cannot escape the privilege of race or gender. But we can begin to be committed to the poor, to stand with them. We can begin to see the world through the eyes of the destitute.

In my own life, that is where ministry with the homeless in New London CT has brought me. To see the world as the poor see the world is to understand the role of wealth and power, and the ways in which I share in it. To stand with the poor is to opt for a different way of living. It may have something to do with discipleship, with love as not a warm fuzzy feeling but a decision to follow Jesus.

Second, peace-building and nonviolence. The Bishop of Assisi once said to Francis, “I think your life is too hard, too rough. You don’t possess anything in the world.” Francis replied, “My Lord, if we had possessions, we would need weapons to defend them.”

Christians, of all people, should know that there is an intimate connection between possessions and violence, both personally and socially. When I think in terms of my money, my house, my wife and children, my profession, my country…, I am not far from being willing to use force to keep you from obtaining what is mine. Peace is not the absence of war in the Bible. Peace, eirene, pax, shalom, is abundance, community, family, safety, a covenant relationship with God and God’s people. But when we equate our good with our possessions, we are willing to kill to protect them.

Last year, I went with a group of friends, led by a 75-year-old United Methodist minister, on a two-week, 270-mile walk around the State of Connecticut. We called it a “pilgrimage for peace,” and said we were “praying with our feet.” One of those pilgrimage days was September 11, five years to the day after the terrorist attacks on the World Trade Center and the Pentagon, the icons of U.S. economic and military power. But it was also the 100th anniversary of Mahatma Gandhi’s first satyagraha, in South Africa in 1906.

The history of the 20th century – the bloodiest century in human history – world wars and the Holocaust, the Cold War and now the “war on terror” – is a history of millions slaughtered in wars that did not bring peace or democracy. But the same century, looked at from the perspective of the poor, is the century of nonviolent revolution. Nonviolent actions have brought freedom to India, South Africa, and our own Civil Rights Movement, the fall of the Berlin wall and the collapse of the Soviet Empire. No military force was used in these struggles, but the peaceful resistance of ordinary people brought an end to tyranny.

The connection between peace and the poor is not merely economic, but it is at least that. The U. S. spends $2 billion a week on war in Iraq, but doesn’t have money to provide good schools for our children or health care for 47 million uninsured, of whom a third are children. I’ve learned from my experience what the great American nonviolent advocate, A. J. Muste, taught: “There is no way to peace. Peace is the way.” Francis likewise taught us to greet friend and “enemy” alike with the salutation: “May the Lord give you peace!”

Third, care for the Creation. Christians, Jews, and Muslims declare that “we believe in one God, the Father Almighty, creator of heaven and earth.” We did not create the earth on which and from which we live, God did. As Biblical people, we are not the “owners” of Creation. God is “the only landlord.” Our faith invites us to imitate God by resting on the Sabbath. We are also taught about "Sabbath economics" in the story of the manna from heaven. God commanded the people in the desert to "so gather it that everyone has enough to eat. . . ." They did, and when they had gathered, "he who gathered a large amount did not have too much, and he who had gathered a small amount did not have too little" (Exodus 16:16,19). Each one had "enough," and "enough" is the biblical standard.

Because God knows our acquisitiveness, our possessiveness, God provided the Jubilee for the redistribution of land – the "capital" of early societies – every fifty years. Leviticus 25 teaches us that we cannot sell or own the land in perpetuity, because it is not ours; "the land belongs to the Lord." Likewise we may not own slaves, exploit workers, or charge interest on loans. Bankers, beware!

This sense of the creation as God's gift to be shared, rather than our possession to be owned, hoarded, exploited, points to the solution to the environmental crisis. There is, after all, enough for everyone to eat – even with six billion people on the planet. There is enough for all our need, but not for anyone's greed. So the care of Creation – the third expectation that people have of Franciscans – is related both to peace and the poor.

In Genesis, human beings are created to cooperate with God by tilling the earth and caring for it (Gen. 2:15-17). In Jesus' teaching this vision of creaturely solidarity and of the earth as home is revived. "Notice the ravens; they do not sow or reap, . . . yet God feeds them. . . . Do not seek what you are to eat and what you are to drink, and do not be anxious. All the nations seek these things, and your Father knows that you need them. Instead, seek God's kingdom, and all these things will be given you besides" (Luke 12:24-31). Our vocation is to share, not only our wealth with each other, but the earth itself with the other creatures, to the praise of the God who created all of us.

Francis picks up this theme in the "Canticle of the Creatures," composed at the end of his life. This is not the sentimentalized birdbath Francis, but the realistic man of his times who knows his place among the other creatures ***because he has learned his place among the poor.***

* * *

So there you have it. I believe people "will know we are Christians by our love." We will be known as Jesus' disciples, not by our liturgical correctness or our theological orthodoxy, or even by our Franciscan habits, but by our orthopraxis. We will be known by our fruits.

If we are what the Franciscan Family is calling us to be – committed to the poor so that we have poor members in our congregations, and our Church is truly standing with the poor, we will be disciples. If we are willing to make the changes in our lives that surrender possessions and embrace love of enemies, if we become peace builders and actually practice nonviolence, we will be disciples. If we treat the earth, our mother, whom we share with all other people and creatures, with respect, and acknowledge God's sovereignty, we will be disciples – and Franciscans.

All this is practical stuff. We live it or we lose it. Dorothy Day, founder of the *Catholic Worker*, who was Franciscan in spirit summed it up:

> *What we would like to do is change the world – make it a little simpler for people to feed, clothe, and shelter themselves as God intended them to do. And, by fighting for better conditions, by crying out unceasingly for the rights of the workers, of the poor, of the destitute – the rights of the worthy and the unworthy poor in other words – we can, to a certain extent, change the world; we can work for the oasis, the little cell of joy and peace in a harried world. We can throw our pebbles in the pond and be confident that its ever widening circle will reach around the world. We can give away an onion. We repeat, there is nothing that we can do but love, and, dear God, please enlarge our hearts to love each other, to love our neighbor, to love our enemy as well as our friend.*

Then Jesus will truly be able to say to us, "You are my disciples." Then Francis will say to us, as he said on his deathbed to his first companions, "I have done my part. May Christ teach you to do yours."

Provincial Convocation 2007, Endicott College

From June 26th to the 30th, 2007, the Province of the Americas held its Provincial Convocation at Endicott College on the shores of Massachusetts Bay 20 miles north of Boston.

Reflections on the Convocation from Dianne Aid

First of all, to even be able to get to Provincial Convocation was a challenge, and I had lots of support from brothers and sisters. To them, I am humbled and honored.

Your faces, my brothers and sisters, are precious to me. I remember sharing meals with Brenda and Leonard Stewart, Winston Williams, Brenda Cummings. Knowing our Franciscan Community brings about peace and community–it is hope for the Anglican Communion and for anywhere in the world where there is strife. It also highlighted for me the responsibility we have as a U.S.-dominated membership to listen and learn from the gifts that come from other places.

They came from around the world: Trinidad, Africa, England, and New Zealand.

The programs were excellent. I think many of us who have visited Assisi would have loved to have had the knowledge imparted to us by our presenters, especially the *Virtual Basilica*. The highlight for me, however, was the JPIC panel and hearing the stories of our Third Order brothers and sisters and what they do in their day-to-day lives as vocational Third Order Franciscans. Carol Tookey shared from her life story and her daily efforts (along with her husband) to live as a committed steward of the environment. Seemingly simple things are really challenges for us in our high-tech, fast-running world to adopt; i.e., buying locally and foods in season, how far we drive, how easy it is to jump on planes, using more and more damaging fuels. I have really taken this to heart and am looking at ways I can follow Carol's example.

Beverly Hosea was present with her mother, Peggy, and Bill Berge with his son, Brother Clarke, SSF. It was wonderful to see and be present with extended family members.

Ken's Notion of a Tertiary

Ken Norian's entry in Anglican Religious Life 2008-9, p. 173 (edited by Petå Dunstan)

In the new edition of the *Anglican Religious Life 2008-9,* TSSF is listed in addition to SSF, along with details on each Province. Ken wrote an essay on what it means to be a tertiary, and it gives us insight into what the Third Order means to him:

> *This is a question often asked since it is a term not in the vocabulary of most people. Tertiary has a Latin derivation indicating "third." Members of a Third Order are then called tertiaries.*
>
> *So, what is a Third Order and, more specifically, The Third Order of the Society of Saint Francis? Why are people called to this Order? What do tertiaries value about being Third Order Franciscans? The answer to these questions begins with Francis of Assisi, who was called by God to rebuild the Church.*
>
> *Francesco Bernadone was the son of a wealthy merchant who was born late in the 12th century in Italy. Through a powerful conversion experience Francis came to mirror the love of Christ and the living Gospel so closely that nearly everyone who met him wanted to follow his way of life. He realized that not everyone could or should take up a celibate life of poverty and homelessness, yet he recognized that people unable to do this were still drawn to serve God with deeply committed hearts and lives. Long before Francis was born, groups of men and women in ordinary secular walks of life were living under rules and vows as members of "Third Orders." Francis saw this as appropriate answer for many of his followers and so, over eight hundred years ago, the "Brothers and Sisters of Penance," later known as "Third Order" or "Secular Franciscans," came to be.*
>
> *The Anglican Franciscan movement began in the United States, England, and India early in the twentieth century and merged into the Society of Saint Francis. The Third Order of the Society of Saint Francis is a fully independent Order with its own provincial and worldwide Constitution, Rule, Principles and Statutes.*
>
> *Tertiaries are no less committed than Friars or Sisters who live in community. Our vocation is lived out in a different and, some would say, more challenging way. We are not "wanna be" nuns or friars, a "pious guild" nor a devotional society. We are lay and clergy, single or in committed rela-*

tionships, serving God as we are called, in the ordinary occupations of life. Because we are an Order, the shape of our lives is formed in the context of the Order's Principles and Rule.

There are three Aims of the Third Order that summarize our mission. First we seek to make our Lord known and loved everywhere. By word and example, Tertiaries witness to Christ in their daily lives. By prayer and sacrifice, we help forward God's work wherever He has called us.

We seek to spread the spirit of fellowship, love and harmony within the family of God. By working happily with people of different race, color, creed, education and opportunity, tertiaries seek to break down the divisions in the world. We try to live in the spirit of the prayer written in the spirit of St. Francis: "Lord, make me an instrument of your peace."

We strive to live simply. Acknowledging that everything belongs to God, we seek to use His gifts wisely and to be good stewards of this fragile earth, never destroying or wasting what God has made. We provide the things necessary for ourselves and our families without demanding luxuries. We seek never to forget the needs of others.

Tertiaries seek to serve God through prayer, study and active work for the Kingdom. Tertiaries are called to prayerful lives—of openness to God and to others. The Eucharist is the heart of our prayer. While Tertiaries give first place to the study of the Scriptures, we also seek to widen our understanding of the Church's mission, of our Franciscan vocation, and of God's world. Tertiaries seek to discover what God wants us to do. In our daily work and lives, we try to serve God and work for the good of others. The best service we can offer is to reflect the love of Christ, and to show his joy and peace to others by example.

Tertiaries seek to live their lives in a spirit of humility, love and joy. While most Tertiaries do not physically live together, we are truly a community that is knit together in community and prayer. We are called daily to share in an offering of prayer for each other. We rejoice in all of the marks of a Christian community - a rule, shared prayer, well wrought liturgies, a formation process of several years, shared stories, spiritual friendships and heroic pioneers like Francis and Clare. The mutual support we offer each other in all aspects of life, especially in ministry and prayer, is most appreciated by members of the Third Order community. This support stems from the unconditional love and acceptance from others with similar commitments to seeking and serving Christ in all people. Tertiaries make a lifetime commitment to live a Rule of Life in company with the sisters and brothers in their Order.

If you are striving to be a peacemaker, feel called to action and contemplation, are yearning for a deeper relationship with God, passionate about social justice, concerned about ecology, the poor, and the marginalized then the Third Order may be a place where you can find a spiritual home.

There are several thousand Anglican tertiaries around the world in many countries organized around five Provinces, including the European, African, Australian, New Zealand, and the Americas.

As St. Francis said at the time of his death: "God has shown me what was mine to do; may God show you what is yours to do."

Last Musings of a Minister Provincial

Time it was, and what a time it was.
It was; A time of innocence, a time of confidences;
Long ago it must be, I have a photograph;
Preserve your memories, they're all that's left you.
(Paul Simon, "Bookends")

Hopefully there will be more than memories after 15 years on Chapter, the past six of them as Minister Provincial. Hoping that, by the grace of God, I've been able to contribute significantly to the Third Order, Society of Saint Francis in the Province of the Americas. Those who know me well know that I'm a VERY nostalgic person. My family tells me that I spend too much time in the past. Truth is, I believe that all that we've done in the past is a part of who we are now and what we are becoming.

A little over 15 years ago then Minister Provincial Alden Whitney wrote a little note in the *Franciscan Times* announcing that Carole Watson would not be standing for another term as Bursar, and I wrote to Alden expressing an interest and was elected Bursar. For three terms (nine years) I served in that position.

Most Ministers Provincial have been elected to that position from roles that have a "pastoral" background (Chaplain, Formation Director, Fellowship Coordinator). So as a person with an MBA literally working on Wall Street, I was both humbled and more than a bit frightened by the prospect of serving as Minister Provincial. An important lesson I learned is that God's grace is a powerful and amazing gift. We all have strengths and weaknesses, and, if we are open to the working of the Spirit, God will bless us and work through us.

It's hard to imagine, but 15 years ago, the internet was in its infancy. I built TSSF's first webpage with simple coding on a rainy Saturday that began at 8 a.m. with coffee and ended 12 hours later with a pint... or two. We've come a long way since then, electronic communications becoming a part of our lives and greatly enhancing our ability to share more immediately. Our Statutes have changed. Dozens of members of Chapter have contributed to the life of our Order. The "norms" have been added to and modified. The Anglican Communion has gone through changes and growth, not entirely without pain on the part of some. Some of our sisters and brothers have died, while others have moved through our community and moved elsewhere. Many have persevered with joy and continue to be a witness to Franciscan spirituality in our faith community and others.

In writing my last "Minister's Musings" I'm tempted to tick off accomplishments. Isn't that what folks do when leaving a ministry or career? True, but that's not what we are about as Franciscan Christians. Every one of us in TSSF is a lesser brother and sister individually; collectively we are a powerful witness to making Christ known and loved, spreading the spirit of love and harmony and living simply after the example of Brother Francis. We are all channels of grace through whom God's mighty work is done.

For the first time since the founding of our Order in the Americas there are four living former or current Ministers Provincial or Guardians (Kale King, Anita Catron, Masud Ibn Syedullah, and me). Very soon there will be five. I commend to your thoughts and prayers the election of a new MP, trusting that the Spirit will move to select the person of God's choosing.

After my term is over in October, my prayer will remain the same, that "we may glorify God's holy name after the example of Saint Francis and win others to God's love." May God's peace and joy be with us all—always.

Election as Minister General 2011

Ken was elected to be Minister General of the worldwide Third Order in August 2011. This was only the second time that a Minister Provincial of the Province of the Americas was elected to this position (previously Alden Whitney served one term 1996-99):

> *Every six years three representatives from the five provinces of the Third Order, Society of Saint Francis gather for an Interprovincial Third Order Ch apter. The 2011 IPTOC was held at Holy Cross Monastery in West Park, NY, USA. We gathered together with the Interprovincial First Order Chapters of the First Order Sisters and Friars. We gathered together in our respective communities and together – celebrating our identity as sisters and brothers united in the Society of Saint Francis.*
>
> *The Third Order was represented by Nolan Tobias (MP), Stewart Lane, and Cynthia O'Ehley from the African Province; Ken Norian (MP), Barbara Leonard and John Brockmann from the Province of the Americas; Salley Buckley (Assistant MP), Helen Granowski and Harold Joinoba from the Province of Australia, Papua New Guinea and East Asia; John Hebenton (MP) and Bobbi Wilson from the Province of Aotearoa, New Zealand and Polynesia with Melanesia; Joanna Coney (MP), Tom Keighley and Jackie Alexander from the European Province. Dorothy Brooker, our Minister General, led and facilitated the gathering.*
>
> *In the course of our time together one of the points of business was to elect a new Minister General [a majority of all representatives present, but only standing Ministers Provincial are eligible to be*

Ken's instillation by Bishop Protector General, The Most Reverend Roger Herft AM (Archbishop of Perth and Metropolitan of the Province of Western Australia).

elected]. I am humbled and excited to serve our community in this role. The role of the Minister General is principally to ensure that the constitution of the Third Order is observed, to coordinate the interprovincial life of the Order and to encourage a sense of worldwide community. [Franciscan Times, Fall 2011]

In 2015, Ken was elected to an unprecedented distinction for the Province of the Americas, the first person from this Province to be re-elected to a second term as Minister General.

References

Anglican Religious Life: A Year Book of Religious Orders and Communities in the Anglican Communion, and Tertiaries, Oblates, Associates and Companions, 2008-2009. Norwich: Canterbury Press, 2007. (edited by Petå Dunstan)

Boff, Leonardo. *Francis of Assisi: A Model for Human Liberation.* Maryknoll, N.Y: Orbis Books, 2006.

For The Living of These Days: Reflections on the Rule of Life of the Episcopal Urban Caucus edited by the Rev. Emmett Jarrett, 1986.

Jarrett, Emmett, and Sarah Jarrett. *Broad Street Blues: A Reader in Radical Discipleship: Reflections and Articles from St. Francis House Troubadour 1999-2010.*, Jubilee Pubications/ St. Francis House, 2010.

Jarrett, Emmett. *To Heal the Sin-Sick Soul: A Spirituality for the Struggle against Racism.* Boston, MA: Episcopal Urban Caucus, 1996.

Jarrett, Emmett. *Wild Geese Flying South: New Poems.* New London, CT: Jubilee Publications, 2005.

Appendix: The Evolution of the Province of the Americas Website: 1998-2016

The story of Ken Norian's first creation of the Province's website was told in his chapter. The website changed little for seven years, but in May 2005 Ken came up with a new design.

In 2006 Ken passed on the webmaster duties to Clint Hagen in Texas, who was a novice at the time and an expert at web design. Clint moved through two more iterations: 2006 and November 2013. It is interesting to compare and contrast these websites to observe the changing nature of the Province over its fifteen-year evolution.

One of the biggest changes involves the presence of the Roman Catholic SFOs on the website. In 1998 they were not present at all on the website. In 2005 they were relegated to "Non-Anglicans/Non-Episcopalian"—somewhat of a negative definition. Finally, in 2013 they were just listed as part of the "Franciscan Family." What is shown by website design is the hard work over many years of the Joint Committee on Franciscan Unity.

The other biggest change only comes in 2013 when resources for Spanish and Portuguese members, which were formerly hidden away in deeper levels of the website, are now presented front and center on the homepage, thus indicating the growing awareness and role of non-English speaking members.

Original color screen captures of these websites can be found by searching for tssf.org at the Internet Archive Wayback Machine (https://archive.org/web/).

Ken Norian's 1998 original design was little changed up to May 2005.

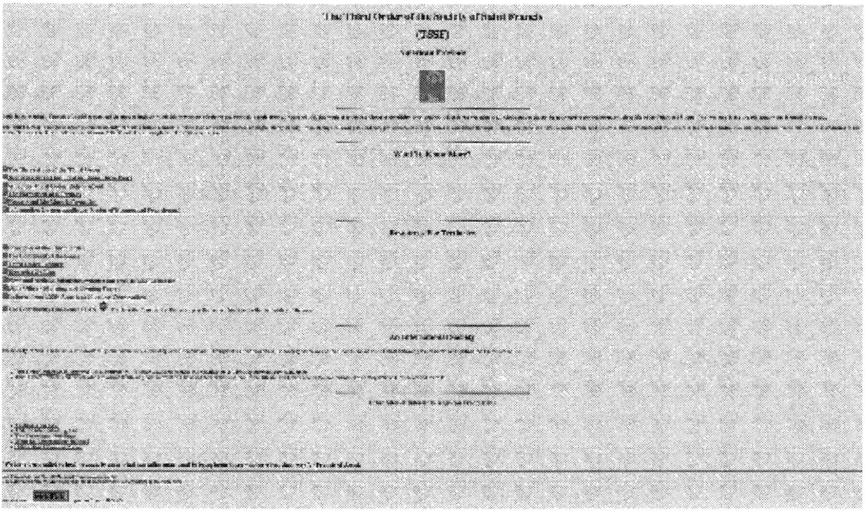

22 Links

Each link takes the reader into another page and then back to the main page.

26 Links
Each link takes the reader into another page and then back to the main page.
New items in this version include a specific link to the Roman Catholic SFOs and links to all other Provinces in the Order.
To make room for these new links, the six "Other Sites of Interest" were pulled.

The right-hand large illustration of Francis came from a public relations triptych display for dioscean conventions designed by Jacqui Belcher, then Provincial Secretary.

Ken Norian's May 2005 design.

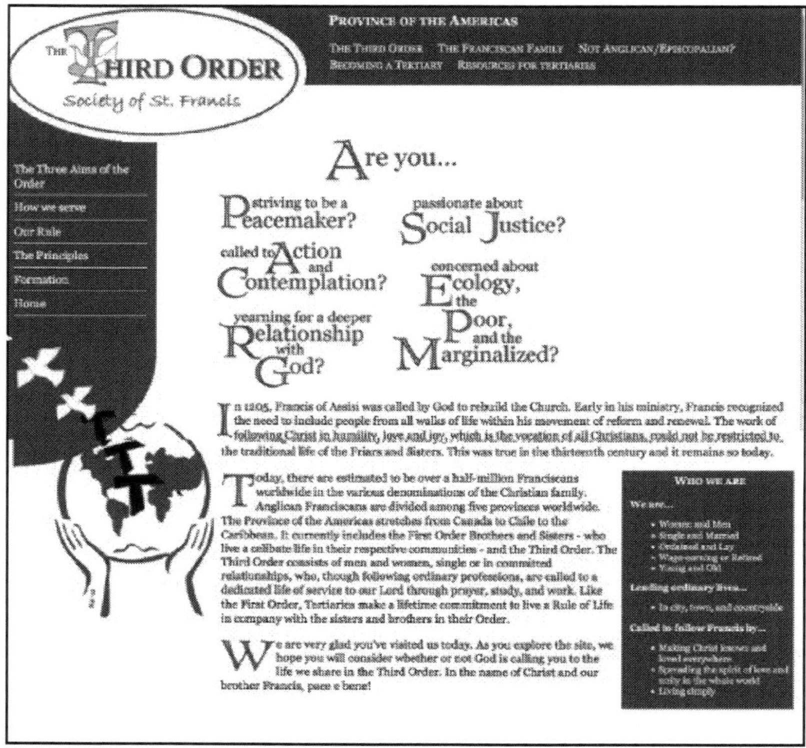
PROVINCE OF THE AMERICAS
THE THIRD ORDER
THE FRANCISCAN FAMILY
NOT ANGLICAN/EPISCOPALIAN?
BECOMING A TERTIARY
RESOURCES FOR TERTIARIES
THE THIRD ORDER
Society of St. Francis
The Three Aims of the Order
How we serve
Our Rule
The Principles
Formation
Home
Are you...
striving to be a Peacemaker?
passionate about Social Justice?
called to Action and Contemplation?
concerned about Ecology, the Poor, and the Marginalized?
yearning for a deeper Relationship with God?
In 1205, Francis of Assisi was called by God to rebuild the Church. Early in his ministry, Francis recognized the need to include people from all walks of life within his movement of reform and renewal. The work of following Christ in humility, love and joy, which is the vocation of all Christians, could not be restricted to the traditional life of the Friars and Sisters. This was true in the thirteenth century and it remains so today.
Today, there are estimated to be over a half-million Franciscans worldwide in the various denominations of the Christian family. Anglican Franciscans are divided among five provinces worldwide. The Province of the Americas stretches from Canada to Chile to the Caribbean. It currently includes the First Order Brothers and Sisters - who live a celibate life in their respective communities - and the Third Order. The Third Order consists of men and women, single or in commited relationships, who, though following ordinary professions, are called to a dedicated life of service to our Lord through prayer, study, and work. Like the First Order, Tertiaries make a lifetime commitment to live a Rule of Life in company with the sisters and brothers in their Order.
We are very glad you've visited us today. As you explore the site, we hope you will consider whether or not God is calling you to the life we share in the Third Order. In the name of Christ and our brother Francis, pace e bene!
WHO WE ARE
We are...
Leading ordinary lives...
Called to follow Francis by...
Living simply

Clint Hagen's May 2006 design.

There were only ten links from the homepage, however, each one takes the reader into another page and deeper into more information or offsite to other websites. Thus the homepage is greatly simplified while keeping all previous information available at deeper levels.

Now the specific link to the Roman Catholic SFOs not only comes up by clicking "Not Anglican or Episcopal" but also by clicking on "The Franciscan Family."

Not visible from the homepage is a password-protected Secure Area in which documents of the Order are kept in a way that web bots cannot access.

There are also many more resources available for downloading and use, i.e., brochures and posters that can be printed as needed rather than stockpiled and mailed.

Again, the illustrations come from the public relations triptych display for dioscean conventions designed by Jacqui Belcher.

You can also observe the great visual simplification of the homepage with only two colors.

The Third Order

Society of St. Francis
Province of the Americas

About The Third Order | Joining Our Order | The Franciscan Family | Resources & Links | Español & Português | Contact Us

Are you...

concerned about
Ecology?

Clint Hagen's 2013 design.

Now there are only six links from the home-page, down from 26 in 2005.

However, all previous information is available at deeper levels, from popdown menus offering as many as ten links to another group of pages.

Now resources for Spanish or Portuguese members are right on the homepage.

Also Clint has decided to use photographs as often as possible to transmit the message formerly only given in text.

The photographs are dynamic in that they change in the homepage display, and entire videos from the Provincial Convocations are stored and available.

Also the website has the digitized archives of the Province, ensuring their safety and security over prior physical methods.

The Contact Us area is also dynamic in that the need to post and update actual email addresses moves behind the scenes with just generic email addresses offered.

Finally, the design of this website allows smartphone users to create bookmarks that show up as "apps"--so that, for example, the daily and monthly items of the Community Obedience change day by day when clicked on a smartphone.

2016 homepage (top).

TSSF Website New Look (2016)

Lucinda Dyer (Franciscan Times, Fall 2016*)*

While the new site has a very different look, the majority of the original content was retained, and the way the site's navigation bar is organized will be familiar to members. There are two new design elements. The first is "blocks" (with text and a graphic) on the homepage that link to sections entitled *About the Third Order, Joining Our Order, The Franciscan Family, Programs, and Resources*. The second is links to a live Facebook feed, the *Franciscan Times*, the *Daily Office* and Obedience, and contact information for Spanish and Portuguese speakers appear at the top and bottom of each page.

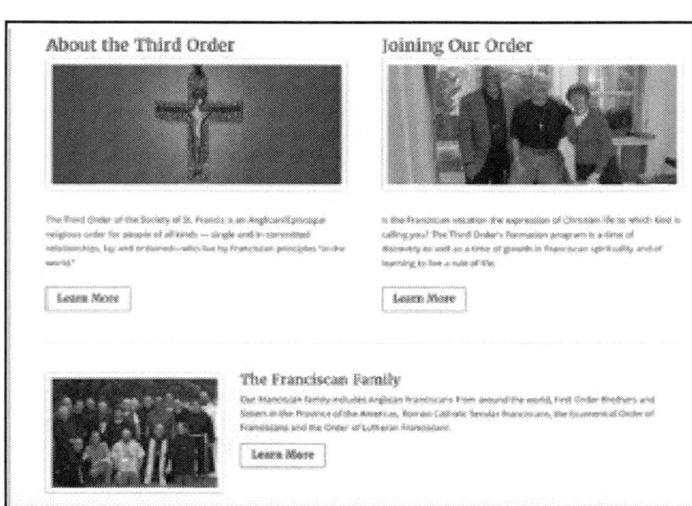

2016 design blocks, which appear on the lower half of the homepage.

Chapter 14: John Brockmann, Minister Provincial 2011-4

How I Grew in the Order

This history of the Province of the Americas has moved from a macrocosm view of statistical large-scale generalities in Chapter 1 through the individual histories of the Ministers Provincial and the stories of what happened during their time in office. In this chapter the history of the Province moves from the macrocosm to the microcosm with the most specific memories of a particular Minister Provincial, me, and my 25-some years in the Province. Looking back on it all, my experiences in the Province almost seem *Forrest Gump*-like in the opportunities I have had to work with many interesting figures of the Province and experience so many important events of the Province .

My Beginnings in the Order

As an English professor at the University of Delaware, I spent many of my summers teaching short writing courses on four continents—a kind of busman's holiday since teaching writing was what I did during the regular semesters. On those long, dark, over-ocean flights the question "What profiteth a man to gain the whole world and yet lose his soul" would often haunt the moments before I closed my eyes. Finally, at the end of one such a trip, I marched into the office of the rector of our campus parish, Bob Duncan (who later became first archbishop of the Anglican Church in North America), and I asked if he could help me find some stability in a life of prayer lived as a lay person.

He gave me Martin Thornton's *Christian Proficiency* (1959), which I devoured, and, using it, I created a Rule of Life and began living it. Duncan then suggested that I talk with his vicar, Rev. Jack Stapleton, who had been elected Chaplain of our Province and then resigned in 1988 (See Chapter 4), and later asked for release from his vows in 1995. Jack suggested that I could more deeply live my Rule of Life in the company of others who were also trying to live a Rule of Life as lay people if I joined the Third Order of the Society of St. Francis. Thus, I applied to be a postulant so that I could more easily live my Rule of Life. I was officially received as a postulant on 5/20/1990; noviced on 5/09/91 and professed in 1993 at Graymoor.

Thus when I began Formation, I was not *consciously* drawn into the Order by a knowledge of Francis and Clare, by an attraction to the Franciscan charism, or by romantic notions supplied by films like Zeffirelli's *Brother Sun, Sister Moon*. However, *unconsciously*, in the deep ways that God woos us, it was entirely fitting that I applied for postulancy in the Franciscan Third Order.

Growing up Roman Catholic, when it came time for Confirmation, all confirmands were encouraged to choose a new "spiritual" middle name. I was very excited about adopting a "macho" spiritual name like *George* from St. George who slew dragons or *Lawrence* after St. Lawrence the Deacon who withstood his tortures and even made light of them. However, my mother would not let her eldest son take on such ego-boosting spiritual names. Her retort to my choices was: "John, you need to take the name *Francis* from St. Francis of Assisi so that you can learn some humility." Perhaps, then, it was the grace of Confirmation bestowed in that new middle name that marked my future spiritual path as revealed to me at just the right time and in just the right way—God's kairos time and place.

Graymoor—The Northeast Convocation (NERC)

Drawing TSSF members from Virginia to Maine, the annual August meetings of NERC always had the reputation of being the largest of all the regional annual convocations as well as being the convocation home for many of past, present, and future TSSF leaders mentioned in these pages. This was the regional convocation home for John Scott, Alden Whitney, Masud Ibn Syedullah, Ken Norian, Terry Rogers, Emmett Jarrett, Jane Ellen Traugott, Lynn Herne, Rick and Danni Bellows, etc.

For years NERC met at Graymoor Friary in Garrison, New York, the site of the first Franciscan foundation in the Episcopal Church, the Franciscan Friars of the Society of the Atonement. However, the monks and nuns of this Order left the Episcopal Church in 1908 to join the Roman Catholic Church (See Chapter 1).

On first arriving at the top of the long driveway zigzagging to the top of the mountain, the front of Graymoor always appeared to be a huge Stalinist edifice—all square and strictly utilitarian in design. Yet, once one arrived at the back of the building, there was a beautiful and unusual compound. A cliff outcrop by the crypt of Father Paul (founder of the Franciscan Friars of the Atonement) looked out over the surrounding Taconic hills and mountains and down the Hudson River to distant New York City (see the very beginnings of the *Day in the Life of Convocations* streaming video on the TSSF website under *Resources for Tertiaries)*. In this back compound was also the small St. Francis Chapel with a life-size statue of Francis, its face supposedly composed from his death mask, and the marble used for the altar came from Mt. Alverna in Italy, the site where Francis received the Stigmata.

I met John Scott, the first Third Order Guardian, many times here at Graymoor. Ken Norian would mysteriously invite a select few to the meditation room where incense abounded. Jane Ellen Traugott usually brought her tambourine, and in one memorable year Masud taught us about Taizé, its chants and prayers. Alden Whitney always came to the Northeast Convocation where I found him to be the "Very Model of a Modern Minister Provincial"--smart, insightful, with a certain weight of spiritual authority casually expressed. Alden received my profession here at Graymoor on August 28, 1993.

Graymoor was so important to me that when I married a wonderful woman named Sarah, we spent the tail-end of our honeymoon in 1994 attending NERC. A year later, Sarah and I presented the three-day program at Graymoor using multimedia and small group discussions formulated after Steve Allen's old show *Meeting of the Minds*. Our program asked participants to explore how many of the actions of Franciscan saints contrasted or even contradicted the traditional principles ascribed to Francis (e.g., Francis was a peacemaker, but St. Joan of Arc was a French war leader; Francis embraced poverty, but Sts. Kings Louis and Ferdinand had riches; Francis ordered his monks' books to be destroyed in Bologna while later St. Thomas More wrote them and was one of the most learned men in Europe). (Portions of our presentation are captured on the *A Day in the Life of Convocations* made in 1995 and available for streaming from the TSSF website under *Resources for Tertiaries*.)

At NERC, time was always set aside for Chapter members to acquaint participants with what was going on in the Province at large. From one of these meetings led by Alden, I learned that the *Devotional Companion* was in the midst of being revised. I was only a novice, but one of the Franciscan books I found that opened my eyes to the wide world of Franciscan saints through the centuries was *The Poverello's Round Table* (1959). From it I was keen, as a married man, to have included in our new *Devotional Calendar* the married Franciscan couple Luchesio and Buonadonna (April 28). I also discovered a wide number of TSSF heroes or saints from other Third Order Provinces, e.g., Yona Kanamuyezi of Rwanda-Burundi, Jan. 23, and John Bradburne of Mutemwa, Sept. 5. Thus I was very interested in expanding the *Devotional Calendar* to include all these Third Order saints and heroes. (Twenty years later, in 2014, Carol Tookey again revised the *Devotional Companion* that includes the *Devotional Calendar*. I worked with her to include new Franciscan heroes from our Province: H. Baxter Liebler, Nov. 21, Desmond Lionel Morse-Boycott, Aug. 9, and Hugo Muller, Nov. 3.)

Helping with the *Franciscan Times*

Once, in fulfilling our Rule's call for a yearly retreat, I was making a silent weekend Advent retreat in Burlington, Vermont. My bottom-bunk-mate was an older man who was pretty good at staying silent. Over the course of the retreat, I saw that he was also an adept at choosing the driest logs and lighting the fire in the cabin's hearth, rubbing the backs of people he evidently knew from years past, and generally being the guru of lovely, warm places to meditate. It was only in the last three minutes of this retreat when words were finally allowed to pass that I found out I had bunked with just about the only Third Order Franciscan in Vermont; his name was Robert Durand.

From that weekend of silent communion onward, Robert was a gracious mentor to me in the Order. We both were technical writers, and we both were adept at using computers for desktop publishing. He always had a kind word of encouragement for me as well as lots of red pencil marks for the articles and poems I submitted to him when he was editor of the *Franciscan Times* (Summer 1991 issue to the Lent 1996 issue).

At one point Bob Durand took me to my first fellowship meeting, The New England Fellowship (Br. Juniper Fellowship) on the outskirts of Boston which was presided over by Judith Gillette, who was for many years an Assistant Formation

Director. Mona Hull was also at the meeting. Mona had been the first treasurer of the TSF Corporation (see Chapter 3). She had worked with Paul Sabatier's research materials that he had gathered for his 1893 biography of St. Francis. These materials were then donated to the Boston Public Library. (Her 1962 dissertation was titled *The Usefulness of the Original Legend of Saint Francis of Assisi in Religious Education.*) In these research materials she told us of seeing an actual document signed by the Poverello as well as a wood-bound breviary of an early monk. (Paul Sabatier, a French Protestant, wrote the first modern historical biography of St. Francis in 1893. It was put on the Index of Forbidden Books for Catholics in 1906.) There were many others at the fellowship meeting who were TSSF, SFO, Ecumenical Franciscans, and just good fellow travelers. Judith's husband David is one such fellow traveller, and he has a talent for woodworking; he fashioned a wooden Tau cross on a leather strap which I wear each Sunday when I celebrate the Eucharist.

All too soon, Robert Durand moved to Hawaii where he found that his ministries and his consultant work made it too difficult for him to continue as editor of *The Franciscan Times* (FT). Thus, with the Fall 1996 issue, I followed in his footsteps as editor and designer. (The same October 1996 Chapter that voted for me to become editor also voted for Ken Norian to become bursar. I was also nominated during that Chapter to run as Minister Provincial along with Julia Bergstrom (Asststistant Chaplain) and Anita Catron (three term Fellowship Coordinator) was elected.) However, as editor of the FT, I was required to meet with Chapter each year, and, for many years, I was accorded voice and vote.

Becoming a Priest Forever in the Order of Melchizedek

In 1995, my Bishop in Delaware, Bishop Cabell Tennis, knew that to express my TSSF Rule of Life, I was teaching Education for Ministry (EFM) and my university core course on Biblical and Classical Literature as a full professor (Study); had voluntarily done three units of hospital chaplain internship (CPE as my Work/Service); had gone through our multi-year formation process; and had just finished a program in spiritual direction at Shalem Institute. Moreover, Bishop Tennis, like many bishops, had the perennial problem of small parishes that could not afford full-time clergy salaries and benefits. So the Bishop approached me and a few others to create a novel path to ordination, a variation on Canon 9. (Canon 9 had originally been designed by the National Church for places such as isolated rural villages. Bishop Tennis, who had been a canon lawyer, reasoned that the whole of the small Diocese of Delaware could be seen as such a "village.") He required that if I and my compatriots promise only to serve as priests in the Diocese of Delaware, to be bi-vocational, and to serve only in small, financially strapped parishes, then he would agree that we would not have to go to seminary but would complete a program of local tutoring in order to pass the General Ordination Examination. God graced me in rural Delaware to have within five miles in one direction a retired dean of a British seminary, and, in the other, a retired leader of interprovincial policies from the National Church. So I and ten others entered this program.

However, by the end of the program, I was the only one ordained as deacon (May 1997) and then priest (December 1997); all the others had dropped out or been asked to leave. Then within a month of my December ordination, Bishop Tennis retired, and the incoming bishop ended this special ordination program; no one ever again would be ordained in this fashion. And then, within a short time, General Convention abolished the Canon 9 priesthood, and "regularized" all Canon 9 priests so that there would not be a two-tier system of priesthood within the Church. Thus I was ordained in a completely unique fashion only by the grace and timing of God—I very much feel to be a priest in the Order of Melchizedek. (Masud Ibn Syedullah was the preacher at my ordination.)

Provincial Convocations

Provincial Convocation 1997

The next year I was part of Anita Catron's team putting on the Provincial Convocation of June 1997 in New Orleans. Among other duties, I would jog along the streetcar tracks each morning to a French bakery, *The Staff of Life*, to buy the bread for the Convocation's daily Eucharist.

Provincial Convocation 2002

Just before her final term ended, Anita pulled together another team to design and create a second Provincial Convocation in Santa Barbara, California. I had recently read Suzanne Farnham's books on discernment in community (*Listening Hearts*), and persuaded Chapter to invite her as the keynote speaker.

The convocation was ensconced in a eucalyptus grove at the The House of Maria retreat center with trails up into the Santa Ynez Mountains rising up behind the retreat center. Some trails led to a lovely pool at the foot of a waterfall where one could relax and cool down from hikes. I was on the planning committee of the Convocation, and the host for the talent show. For so many of us the most amazing part of the Convocation was the prayer service and blessing presided over by Masud who was accompanied by Iman Bashar from Baltimore, and Rabbi Carlos Huerta from West Point Military Academy. (You can see much more of this convocation by viewing the streaming video on the website under *Resources for Tertiaries*, and by reviewing Chapter 8 on Anita Catron Miner's time as Minister Provincial.)

The Delmarva Fellowship, Br. Juniper's Seesaw

Though Provincial and Regional Convocations were important experiences for me, it was life in the local Br. Juniper's Seesaw Fellowship in Delaware that kept the Spirit alive for me month in and month out. When I was teaching at the University of Delaware, I would attend the newly formed Br. Juniper's Seesaw Fellowship that had branched out from the Philadelphia Fellowship with John Scott. (To understand our moniker, re-read Chapter 9 of the *Little Flowers of St. Francis*.)

At one time, the Philadelphia Fellowship with John Scott was the epicenter of the Province of the Americas. However, by the time I was professed, the number of people meeting in center city Philadelphia was dwindling while at the same time more were meeting in the Princeton, New Jersey area to the north where Peter and Mary Funk lived (see Chapter 3) and in the Wilmington, Delaware area where I lived and where Frances Baum lived. She was the first and only professed member of the Third Order in Delaware for many years, having had her profession received by Br. Robert Hugh in Assisi while she was on a pilgrimage with him in 1990. She was known by her first name Joan for some years of her life, but, upon profession, she resolved that all would call her by her middle name, Frances. And, so we all did.

In addition to Frances in our Fellowship, there were a number of Delaware people I met while attending NERC at Graymoor: Bonnie Barnidge who transferred from the Roman Catholic SFOs and Angie Rummel, our long-time visitor. A number of participants in my EFM classes that I mentored or my directees joined the Order. Some persevered like Nancy Woodward and Russ Bohner, while some followed alternative spiritual paths like Paul Garland who left Formation and became an archbishop in the Orthodox Church of Canada in the U.S.A. Together with Alice Banks from Norfolk Virginia, the Fellowship expanded and contracted as members from Virginia, Pennsylvania, and New Jersey came and went.

One of the most memorable events of our Br. Juniper's Seesaw Fellowship for me was a Blessing of the Animals in Lewes, Delaware. During that Blessing, I gave a presentation along with a storyteller/holy person of the Nanticoke Tribe (local native people of Delaware) during which he and I explored for the audience the places of coincidence of Franciscan spirituality and understanding of nature with the Nanticoke spirituality and understanding of nature.

Life at Chapter 1985

MaryAnn Jackman (Information Sheet October 1985)
Those of you who have participated in Fellowship retreats and area convocations, when we are able to share a bit of live-in community, will know how very special those times are. There is a certain bonding that takes place in such a family setting, working and praying together, sharing ideas, laughing together, sharing a meal, working through a hard problem, discovering more of who we are in relationship with each other and in our Franciscan vocations. Many things stand out as high points, and I'd like to share a bit of the joy I felt with you all.

First, I found that Kale King, who has always been special to me, was coming in on the same flight from our transfer point in Chicago. Greeting Kale at O'Hare as we boarded was the beginning of it. When we arrived at Islip, Dorothy Nakatsuji [See page 92] was there. Although we'd never met before, I knew her, it was as if we just picked up a life-long conversation we'd left off a few minutes ago.

The depth of sharing, loving, and openness among us all was amazing throughout the whole week. It felt as if the Kingdom had arrived. (We certainly felt your prayers!) Masud's installation as Chaplain has to rank among the highest of the high points. The. Rev. Robert Goode ("Gooch") adapted the "Celebration of a new Ministry" from the BCP to our needs, and Masud was presented in turn with

- a Bible ("be among us as one who proclaims the Word"),
- the Formation Handbook ("help us form new brothers and sisters in the Franciscan life"),
- a stole ("be among us as a priest"),
- a cope ("help us celebrate the joys of the Franciscan life"),
- a cross ("remember the past for this is part of who we are"),
- oil stock ("be among us as a healer and reconciler"), and
- the Statutes ("obey these statutes and do not forget that our ministries flow from the bishops of the Church).

Gooch's sermon was eloquent and moving. The whole process was one of numinous joy, and is something I will never forget.

The activity of the Holy Spirit was so apparent, and not just in the work we did—at one point I was talking to Alden Whitney about one of the novices in the men's program whose address we had not known since his seminary graduation last June—he's a really special one, and just as I said to Alden "I wish I knew where he was," the phone rang for me—the lost novice calling to say hello and tell me where he was! Zap! The Lord was obviously "at it again" all through the week.

Another high point was the wild and wonderful game of Trivial Pursuit (won by Br. Kirk SSF & Jackie Richards!) that went on until midnight. The deck was obviously stacked—at one close point near the end, it was The Rev. Alden Whitney's turn to answer and the fate of the game practically hung on that answer—what question did he draw? "Name the authors of the four Gospels." But the all time favorite question was "which leg of a chicken is most tender?" This led to a continuing joke, and David Nard and Alden quoted freely from "The 1938 USDA Study," giving number of trials per chicken, etc. We all laughed so much that we were sore from it.

There were quiet times, thoughtful times, serious times, too. Much work was accomplished. The day before Chapter officially opened, Br. John George SSF facilitated an all-day discussion of our assets and liabilities, and where we would like to go from here. Long-range goals were discussed, and during the course of the week, many of these began to fall into place, proceeding organically from our growth and development.

The strongest points seemed to be that we need to share the leadership workload, possibly on a regional basis. This is developing beautifully with the increased responsibilities of Area Chaplains and the AFD programs now operating in both men's and women's formation, and through the leadership arising out of area convocations); that we need more post-profession support and involvement (this also proceeds from the newly expanded Area Chaplains' roles); and some upgrading of the formation program (already being planned and implemented). We all saw exciting new possibilities.

We have come from being more an adjunct to the First Order than anything else to being an Order in our own right, independent but related to the First and Second Orders, and fully self-determining. Our Guardian now has equal status with and shared responsibility for all three Orders in the province with the Ministers Provincial of the First Order and the Mother of the Second Order. It was clear from the results of the meeting that we know who we are and have some idea of where we're going, and that we remain open to where the Lord wants to lead us is most important.

My Life at Chapter 1995 to 2010

During the 15 years I attended Chapter at Little Portion Friary each October I did so most often as the editor of the *Franciscan Times*. During this time I was also an elected member of Chapter for two terms and then, after three years, another term. The choices and initiatives of the Ministers Provincial who guided Chapter during the years I attended, Alden Whitney, Anita Catron, Masud Ibn Syedullah, and Ken Norian, are reported in each of their respective chapters, so I will only tell you about the general experience of attending Chapter.

On one hand, attending Chapter was like experiencing a mini-Provincial Convocation every year. Where else would you get the opportunity to work on projects and have discussions with tertiaries from all points of the Province: Canada, East and West Coast US, the Caribbean, Guyana and Brazil? Where else would you hear reports of what's going on in the Third Order in Africa or New Guinea? Where else could you pray along with First Order brothers and sisters as well as Second Order Poor Clares?

On the other hand, Chapter could be very much like a three-day meeting of a parish vestry with endless voting, discussions, and subcommittee work. However, unlike most vestry meetings I have attended, Chapter is always wonderfully leavened by the communal recitation of the Offices and a daily Eucharist. During each eucharist officiated by a Third Order priest, we honored the various Eucharistic settings of the Province: Canadian, West Indies, USA.

Eucharists at Chapter, as at a Convocation, include annual renewals, and the installation of various officers and prayers of thanksgiving for officers stepping down. The most solemn of the Chapter eucharists, for me, is always the one in which we pray the necrology for the year. Name by name those who had died that year are read aloud, and one or more Chapter members who knew the person voice a short remembrance. At one Chapter when I was Minister Provincial, the ashes of one of our professed were interred in the very simple graveyard of the friary. We processed out holding the Friary's new statues of Elizabeth and Louis (our Third Order patron saints), I dug the small hole, and we said the prayers, and interred the ashes.

Day 28 of our *Principles* observes that tertiaries "delight in fun and laughter, rejoicing in God's world, its beauty and its living creatures, calling nothing common or unclean." Thus there always seemed to be time after all the work of the day for a late evening run to *McNulty's Ice Cream Parlo*r, a celebration of Ken Norian's wedding engagement, a taste of a Caribbean carnival including a limbo stick, or sing-alongs of praise and folk music from the 1960s, 70s, and 80s with a local Third Order musician.

Surrounded each year by so many people, who with God's grace, work long and hard to make the Province of the Americas alive, I am often reminded of those of the past who worked just as hard but have, for one reason or another, asked for release from their vows and have left the Order:

- Warren Tanghe who worked hard to create the Province's original Statutes and organizational structure and C. David Burt wrote one of the three position papers to carry to England to begin the process of consolidation with TSF and TSSF;
- MaryAnn Jackman who created the logo of the *Dancing Francis* (1985), and who wrote about Chapter just above, edited the *Information Sheet*, was Provincial Secretary and served in many roles;
- Jacqui Belcher, who edited the *Information Sheet* for so many years and created the triptych and its illustrations we still use at diocesan conventions;
- John Tolbert, who was Br. Heriticus at the 1997 Provincial Convocation (see pp. 130-1) ; and
- Marie Webner and Jack Stapleton, who were both Provincial Chaplains.

For all of these men and women who worked so diligently in this Province, God, thank you for the time we had together.

Minister Provincial 2011

Our Provincial Guardians and Ministers Provincial have come from many different areas in the Province:

- John Scott and Masud Ibn Syedullah had been Provincial Chaplains,
- Anita Catron Miner had been Fellowship Coordinator,
- Ken Norian had been Bursar,
- Kale King and Dee Dobson had been general members of Chapter, and
- I was the first to come from Communications and Publications.

Four Ministers Provincial at the Minneapolis Provincial Convocation 2013: Ken Norian, Masud Ibn Syedullah, John Brockmann, and Anita Catron Miner

When Ken Norian resigned after two terms as Minister Provincial to take up his duties as TSSF Minister General, I was elected without opposition.

Attending to Infrastructure of the Province

I had always been deeply embarrassed when informed of the overwhelming percentage of professed in other Provinces who financially contributed to the needs of the Order. The Province of the Americas' percentage of professed contributing usually came in last among all the Provinces. This had been a problem since the time of John Scott:

- Only 43% of the professed contributed in 1982, and the Order moved into deficit spending;
- There were special mailings in the *Information Sheet* related to stewardship during Dee Dobson's tenure (1985);
- We went into debt in 1994 when Alden Whitney was Minister Provincial, and
- Failure to contribute financially was a focus of Chapter in 1998 and, in 1999, a task force to investigate was established.

This problem keeps reoccurring despite the fact that the threefold marks of profession–Report, Renew, and Contribute–have been repeatedly publicized.

Thus the Provincial Bursar, Tom Johnson, and I decided to take a look at the list of the professed to see who had failed to contribute financially for a span of at least three years—the most easily observed mark of profession. We discovered 80 professed people in a province of 500—nearly 16%—had not contributed for at least three years. We then worked with the Chaplain to discover how many of these had also not reported and renewed. Sadly, we found nearly all had not.

Then, to my great discouragement, we observed that, among such folks who did not "Report, Renew or Contribute," there were Area Chaplains and Fellowship Conveners—the face and first responders of the Province—who were not achieving the minimum threefold marks of profession. Sadly, this was nothing new. Five years earlier in 2006, the Provincial Fellowship Coordinator discovered that a number of Fellowship Conveners were not reporting, renewing, or contributing as was expected of all professed members. Chapter at that time passed a Norm that any person holding a leadership position in the Province must meet all three marks. Five years later, a number of those holding a leadership position in the Province were still not meeting the three marks of profession.

To rectify the situation, Tom Johnson and I composed a series of personal snail-mail letters and were able to whittle down the nearly 80 professed people in the Province who had not renewed, reported and contributed to 12 (or from 16% to 2%). Most of those we contacted were pleased to be recalled to their vows and intentions…a few objected strenuously, and a few asked for release from their vows. However, by 2013, the local leadership of the Province and nearly all of the professed in the Province were meeting the threefold marks of profession: Report, Renew, and Contribute.

Over Extended Travels of Ministers Provincial

Ken Norian's Minister Provincial Report of 2006 mentions another aspect of our Province's infrastructure that was problematic:

> *One of the areas that presents a challenge to a Minister Provincial is the amount of travel away from home that is requested. I would like to extend my appreciation to Ann Harris, Lyndon Hutchison-Hounsell, Anita Catron and Masud Ibn Syedullah, who represented TSSF at the CSF Chapter, the OEF Chapter, Brazilian gatherings and the NAECC. This year I was privileged to attend the gathering of the Joint Committee on Franciscan Unity, a regional gathering of the OEF, two Standing Committee meetings, the First Order brothers Chapter, the Northeast and Southeast Convocations, two gatherings of Franciscans International, and the European General Chapter at York, UK.* (Minister Provincial Report to Chapter, 2006)

No MP prior to Ken was expected to attend so many functions outside the Province or the Order. Moreover, the funding for attending so many functions was quite confusing; most funds for participating in such meetings came from the MP's "discretionary fund." meaning that advanced planning and budgeting for such expenses were largely missing. Thus I created the position of Coordinator of External Relations and offered it to former Minister Provincial Masud Ibn Syedullah, who is expert in this area of external relations. He agreed to coordinate and propose budgets for all who would attend the myriad meetings outside the Province or the Order. Thus, henceforth there would be budgets and constraints in fulfilling travel and meeting commitments outside the Order or beyond the Province.

Chapter Becomes Peripatetic

No one wanted to disrupt the traditional practice of Chapter's annual meetings at Little Portion Friary (LPF) that had been taking place since the late 1970s. Little Portion Friary was familiar; Little Portion Friary brought our leadership into close contact and worship with the other Orders in the Province; and it was a beautiful location on the north shore of Long Island. (See "A Pilgrimage to a Modern La Verna" p. 21, or Peter's Funks's description of his visit in 1961, pp. 48-9) However, at the 2013 Chapter, our First Order representative apprised us of the possibility that LPF would not being available to TSSF for meetings within the very near future because LPF would be sold. (See Appendix below.) Suddenly we found we needed to reclaim our nearly forgotten Franciscan charism of being peripatetic—of being like Jesus:"Foxes have dens and birds have nests, but the Son of Man has no place to lay his head." Francis had embraced this peripatetic aspect as a foundation to the Order, and so too had the Province when it met all over the continent during the days of John Scott. A very positive aspect to becoming peripatetic was that it would give Chapter opportunities to learn more from local fellowships and members and to make Chapter more transparent and available to the general membership.

As Anita Catron Miner, Bill Graham and I traveled home from Chapter 2013 by taking the hour-and-a-half ferry across Long Island Sound, we all pulled out our laptops and began to imagine locations where Chapter could meet for the next three years by looking at the addresses of Chapter participants to minimize airfare costs while meeting in convenient locations. Thus for 2014, we chose to meet in Boston, hold our meetings free of charge in my parish, and stay at an OEF-recommended location, the Walker Center in Auburndale. For 2015, we chose Chicago and the Cenacle Retreat & Conference Center, and for 2016, we chose the San Damiano Retreat Center in Danville, CA. In addition to minimizing airfare costs based upon Chapter participant's home addresses, all three are near mass-transportation so the usual costs required for taxis and shuttles to Little Portion Friary on Long Island could be dramatically reduced.

Continuing Care for the Professed

The Province is pioneering this work for the whole Third Order by creating a "Celebration of an Anniversary of a Profession," the idea of sabbatical pilgrimages, and the incorporation of wisdom from our elders into the life of the Province and the Order.

Election of a Minister Provincial at the First Peripatetic Chapter

Chapter 2014 was the first peripatetic Chapter convened away from Little Portion, and I hosted it in my parish in the outskirts of Boston, Massachusetts. The first order of Chapter business was the election of a Minister Provincial. I stood for re-election to a second term, and Tom Johnson was also nominated. In this election process, our Bishop Protector called for a never tried before election process to be accomplished by silent discernment rather than open discussion. After the majority of Chapter approved this new process, Tom Johnson was elected. (The closest parallel in our Provincial history to this occasion was the vote not to re-elect Marie Webner as Provincial Chaplain in 1994.)

Mere Thanks Are Not Enough

After I had finished writing, designing, and editing the Fall issue of the *Franciscan Times*, I sent it to our newly elected Minister Provincial, Tom Johnson, for his review and approval prior to being posted on our Provincial website. Unbeknowst to me, an introductory paragraph was added, reproduced below:

Mere Thanks Are Not Enough

As the Fall issue of the Franciscan Times goes to press, it is appropriate that we celebrate the service and ministry of John Brockmann as Minister Provincial for the last three years (2011-2014). This term of service followed years serving on Chapter, as editor of the Franciscan Times, as archivist and historian, and as a leader in the Northeast Regional Convocation.

John's term as Minister Provincial was a creative season reflecting a long and dedicated ministry to the Province of the Americas. Those years of service provided both history and wisdom as he endeavored to take the helm and to lead us forward.

Under John's leadership and guidance, significant steps were taken to move the Order forward in visionary ways. He led Chapter in "going peripatetic" after many years of meeting at Little Portion Friary, SSF, on Long Island, New York. He brought Chapter to Boston, Massachusetts, for its first meeting away from the "womb," hosting our meetings at his parish – Grace Episcopal Church, Norwood, MA, and coordinating – even cooking – our meals in the parish hall. He guided us as we elected Dominic George as Provincial Chaplain, Anita Catron Miner as Provincial Secretary and Liz Peacock who will begin service as Formation Director in December 2014. He envisioned a new, more efficient way to relate to outside organizations and steered Chapter to elect Masud Ibn Syedullah as Director of External Relations. He encouraged a new emphasis on Justice, Peace and the Integrity of Creation (JPIC), and led us to elect Joyce Wilding as JPIC Animator.

John's leadership produced very real advances in the integration of the Regional Chapter of Brazil into our Provincial Chapter, in the areas of formation, election to profession, finance and local fellowship coordination. He helped streamline procedures of the Province for electing persons to profession, as we moved to quarterly phone conferences so that candidates did not have to wait months and months for Chapter's decision to profess.

All this, while keeping the Order moving forward and... continuing to edit the Franciscan Times, writing the history book, and in all the other ways, big and small, of ministering to benefit the Third Order, Province of the Americas.

John, we celebrate you, we thank you, and we wish you God's peace and rich blessings in the months and years ahead.

Appendix: Our Motherhouse, Little Portion, to be Sold; A Reflection

Ken Norian, Minister General (from Franciscan Times, Fall 2014)

Some of you have had the opportunity to spend time at the "motherhouse" of SSF in the Americas, Little Portion Friary in Mt Sinai, Long Island, New York. It is where the brothers of the First Order and the sisters of the Second Order have made their home since the 1930s. What follows is a communication from Br. Jude the Provincial of the First Order in the Americas. Not articulated is that 80 percent of the members of the community are aged or infirm.

In my conversations with Br. Jude, I suggested that even a once-roaring fire that has been reduced to embers can still be brought to life, but, if a bucket of water is thrown on it, it will surely be extinguished. Jude and a few others are looking for a way to keep the First Order alive in the Americas. The tertiaries on Long Island are a fraction of all the members of TSSF in the Americas. Personally, though, this is hard, since Little Portion Friary was the place I "found Francis," and it was a source of stability for me for many years.The chapel of my profession 25 years ago this month has already become a garage with parked cars. I suppose there is a lesson there that Francis kept reminding his early followers: it's not a place, it's an ethos and the Spirit.

Keep the First Order brothers in the Americas in your prayers as well as the First Order in all their other provinces. Over the last few days I've reflected on how vitally important the Third Order is to the preservation and vitality of the Franciscan charism in the Anglican Communion.

Letter from Br. Jude, Minister Provincial of the First Order Brothers, SSF

Dear Brothers and Sisters of the Third Order,

As most of you know, the First Order Brothers have been meeting in a special Chapter this week in Los Angeles with Bishop Jon Bruno, our Protector, with outside advisers and Fr. David Burgdorf TSSF, [former Provincial Chaplain] *helping to facilitate our meeting. It was a difficult meeting as we faced some of the issues ahead of us. It became clear that with our shrinking numbers and the number of elderly and infirm, we could no longer continue to maintain the present number of houses we have; that together with the fact that new people looking to join us are excited about our urban ministries and working with the poor; and the cost to repair and bring Little Portion up to code (three and a half million dollars), not to mention the fact that it requires six active brothers to run the plant, brought us sadly to the conclusion that we had no alternative but to leave Long Island. This was not an easy decision to make since Little Portion has been our home since the 30s.*

We plan to fence off and maintain the cemetery as a place of burial for members of the First and Third Orders, build a Memorial Garden with access from the road, and secure funds from the sale of the remainder of the land to set up a trust to care for the plot. We hope other members of the Third Order in the area will help us see that the place is well–maintained. As you can imagine, all of this is going to take some time, and it will be a slow process to achieve it all, probably 18 months to 2 years. Please pray for the brothers as they undertake this major shift in their lives and as they seek to renew and revitalize their ministry and the call to "Rebuild the Church' in what could be a new and exciting way.

With our love and prayers,
Jude ssf

References

Farnham, Suzanne G. *Listening Hearts: Discerning Call in Community*. Harrisburg, PA: Morehouse Pub, 1991.

Habig, Marion A. *The Franciscan Book of Saints: First Published As the Poverello's Round Table*. Chicago: Franciscan Herald Press, 1959.

Hull, Mona C. *The Usefulness of the Original Legend of Saint Francis of Assisi in Religious Education*. Boston University Graduate School PhD Disserta tion University Microfilms Inc., Ann Arbor, MI, 1962.

Sabatier, Paul. *Vie De S. François D'assise*. Paris: Fischbacher, 1894.

Thornton, Martin. *Christian Proficiency*. New York: Morehouse-Gorham, 1959.

Zeffirelli, Franco, Graham Faulkner, Judi Bowker, and Alec Guinness. *Brother Sun, Sister Moon*. Hollywood: Paramount Pictures, 1988.

Chapter 15: Tom Johnson, Minister Provincial 2014-

As the son of missionaries, Tom spent much of his early life overseas, first in China and then in Bolivia. In his late teens and early twenties Tom was employed by the American Bible Society in Venezuela for two years, and later in Colombia where, at age twenty, he was placed in charge of the entire Colombian enterprise with two local offices and over 20 Colombian employees. After two years in Colombia, he identified and trained the first Colombian national executive.

Tom graduated from UCLA and Fuller Theological Seminary and was ordained a minister in the United Presbyterian Church. He served for another 11 years with the American Bible Society, first in Chicago and then at New York headquarters where he became a senior executive in charge of the "Ways and Means" Division, including direct mail fundraising, church relations, public relations, and deferred giving. In 1997, Tom was ordained a priest in the Episcopal Diocese of San Diego, and served for five years as Vicar of St. Hugh of Lincoln, Idyllwild, CA, followed by four years as Rector of St. John's, Indio, CA and, concurrently, Vicar of Santa Rosa del Mar, Desert Shores, CA. While Vicar of Santa Rosa del Mar (a Spanish-speaking congregation) he arranged the purchase of property and supervised the installation of a church building. He retired at the end of 2006.

Tom was professed in the Third Order in 2002 and served as retreat leader for a Southern California Convocation and, briefly, as convener of the St. Bernardine Fellowship. He and his wife Susan (also a professed member of TSSF) moved to Northern California in November 2008, where they are active in the Living Waters Fellowship. Tom had been TSSF Bursar since December 2009, (replaced by David Lawson-Beck in 2014). He is currently a Priest Associate at Trinity Episcopal Church in their hometown of Folsom. Tom speaks Spanish fluently, Portuguese passably.

Letter to Fellowship Conveners, March 2014

"I cannot easily find an example of a church that since the end of the Roman Empire has found renewal without there being flourishing religious communities." "...we need a wild burst of fresh and Spirit-fuelled imagination about Religion (religious communities) in the 21st Century."

Archbishop Justin Welby

March 28, 2014
Dear Sisters and Brothers in Christ and Francis,

At our Chapter meeting in Boston, Bishop Scruton, our Bishop Protector, spoke about the rapid and enormous changes that are taking place in the world around us, including in the Church. We are living in a 21st century that has quickly left the 20th Century behind and is thrusting us ever deeper into dizzying change. In our Franciscan world, we see the struggle with change that our First Order is confronting as is the Community of St. Francis.

In this context of a changing world, and as we approach our 100th anniversary, I believe we in the Third Order Society of St. Francis Province of the Americas must take time to re-evaluate who we are. I am asking that we place a high priority on ***re-envisioning*** what "…rebuild my Church" means for us in the 21st Century. That we place a high priority on ***re-envisioning***, to paraphrase Francis, "what is ours to do" as we move into our next 100 years of service to the Church.

I have arranged for Jeff Golliher to lead Chapter – at its next meeting – in an in-depth time of reflection, discussion and discernment centered on the kind of ***re-envisioning*** I'm calling for. This will be the beginning of a longer discussion as we move toward our Centennial Provincial Convocation.

I am writing to you, because I want every tertiary to be a part of this discussion in one way or another. Thus, I am asking you as a Fellowship Convener to plan for your Fellowship to have some serious discussion about this in one or more of your meetings and to share your opinions and insights with me so that you will have input to our discussions next October.

As a religious community within the Anglican Communion, we can – and should – be a channel of God's Spirit to bring renewal to the Church (i.e., rebuild) as we, like Francis, experience renewal ourselves. I pray, that through the commitment of each and every tertiary, we can experience what Archbishop Welby called "a wild burst of fresh and Spirit-fueled imagination" that will define a truly Franciscan walk that is a powerful witness in the 21st century world.

Notable Initiatives

Tom Johnson

Several tertiaries helped to develop a study guide to assist in the "re-envisioning" exercise. Fellowships, Convocations and many individual tertiaries responded to the call with a plethora of thoughts, ideas and suggestions that formed the basis for Chapter in 2015 to continue the discussion, pointing toward our Centennial Convocation in 2017.

Continuing to focus on "re-envisioning," my most recent pastoral letter asked us all to shift our focus from TSSF as an "organization" to TSSF as an "organism" in which each member, as part of the body, has an essential role in expressing her/his unique gift and function that together become the "leaven" that can transform the Church and the world.

Responding to a growing interest in the Third Order in Spanish-speaking countries in Central America and the Caribbean, I asked Jim Hagen to take over responsibility for promoting TSSF in those countries. Jim travelled to Guatemala, El Salvador, Dominican Republic and Puerto Rico, discovering a vibrant interest among Spanish-speaking Anglicans. In order to properly address unique cultural and geographic situations, Chapter agreed to appoint a

Special Formation Director for Latin America to work with Jim Hagen and **local individuals** to create appropriate formation programs in each country. This is a three-year program with the Special Formation Director for Latin America reporting annually to Chapter.

With Rick Simpson as our new Provincial Chaplain, we have been working to invigorate the Area Chaplains, particularly to encourage a more pastoral ministry rather than just receiving reports. Newly elected Fellowship Coordinator, Peter Stube, has articulated an ambitious vision for helping TSSF Fellowships to become active mission centers. Liz Peacock and her Assistant Formation Directors have been working to infuse into our Formation program a strong sense of "shepherding" by the Formation Counselors. Through these Pastoral Officers we are endeavoring to open our lives and our Province to " *a wild burst of fresh and Spirit-fueled imagination"* as called for by Archbishop Justin Welby.

Minister's musings...

Tom Johnson

While reading Professor Pazzelli's book, *St. Francis and the Third Order*, I recently found myself disturbed–at least initially–by his use of the term *evangelical* to characterize the Franciscan movement. However, I soon realized that I was reacting to what the term *evangelical* had come to mean in the current Christian context, which had evolved into something quite different from what Professor Pazzelli was describing.

The Reformation brought to life the term *evangelical* to describe the Protestant Churches who based their teaching on the "Gospel." It also came to contrast the Reformed Churches from the Calvinists. Gradually, the term came to describe various movements in the Church that hung onto conservative theological stances. And in our own time, the term *evangelical* frequently describes those churches often called fundamentalist and which are politically aligned with the "right wing;" thus my initial dismay at Pazzelli's use of the term with reference to Francis.

However, as I looked a little more closely, I came to realize that he was using the term to describe the Franciscan "way of life" that was patterned according to the "Gospel" in imitation of Jesus. He was translating "vita apostolica" as "evangelical life." So, once again I was drawn back into the basic Franciscan charism–living as Jesus showed us and told us to.

This reminded me of another word from the early days of the Third Order that has come to mean something quite different in our own time. The early members of the Third Order were called the "Brothers and Sisters of Penance." In the early church, penitents were those who had been excluded from receiving communion through the sacrament of Penance. Over time, the administration of Penance became less burdensome, but nevertheless continued as a way to atone for one's sins.

In the 12th and 13th centuries, however, there developed a number of penitential movements – including the Franciscan Third Order – that described those who "repented" and "turned to follow Christ" (metanoia) as Brothers and Sisters of Penance–or often as Penitents. This somewhat different use of the word, once again, points to the Franciscan emphasis on living the Gospel.

I recently read an interview of Pope Francis published in *America*. In it he was asked about the specific place of religious men and women in the church of today. He said, "Religious men and women…are those who have chosen a following of Jesus that imitates his life in obedience to the Father…. In the church, the religious are called to be prophets in particular by demonstrating how Jesus lived on this earth."

This brings me to what I feel is a very important statement in a document from our Formation Team – Formation Guidelines: Reporting, Part 1: "The old view was, counselees were expected to write six postulant reports and 24 novice reports, then would be considered eligible for profession. The reports could be done at their own pace. If they didn't report monthly, the process would simply take longer."

That approach had some serious drawbacks, and we're doing things a bit differently now. It isn't the report count that qualifies a novice for profession. **The focus now is on whether or not the applicant is living the Franciscan life, and growing in humility, love and joy.** The reports are merely a tool for reflection and personal growth, to allow the counselor to provide support and guidance, and as a way to gauge whether or not the candidate is suitable for making life vows in TSSF.

As we all think and discuss and pray about how we can best be Third Order Franciscans in the 21st century, let us not forget that it's all about **living** the Gospel life as exemplified by our little brother Francis.

Kathryn Challoner, TSSF– Medical Missions to Africa

For years, Kathryn Challoner (Professed 2005) has traveled to Liberia on medical missions to Liberia on vacation from her medical work in the Department of Emergency Medicine at the Keck School of Medicine of University of Southern California. She has created a scholarship fund, Challoner Medical Mission Fund, and Tom Johnson both as bursar and then as Minister Provincial has been a big supporter of her work as well as financial intermediary. You can read about her Medical Missions in 2003 and 2011 (Summer 2003 issue and Winter 2012 issue of the *Franciscan Times)*, a report of how she received a grant from Franciscan Aid to fight Ebola in Liberia (Epiphany 2015 issue of the *Franciscan Times*), pictures of medical graduates who have benefitted from her scholarship fund (Fall 2015 issue of the *Franciscan Times*). Kathryn was awarded the 2015 Humanitarian Award by the California Chapter of the American College of Emergency Physicians.

Ground Zero Liberia—Ebola

Kathryn Challoner (from Franciscan Times Summer 2015)

That is what the Liberians call the northern part of Lofa County. This is where the Ebola virus killed two-thirds of the villagers leaving hundreds of orphans. This is where Benedict and I travelled this week. We crossed the St. Paul River and drove to Bolahun where Benedict was born.

There at Ground Zero, Benedict and his group (Baffa) are building a huge new school, and a dormitory (orphanage) for the Ebola orphans. The school is close to completion. Classrooms have blackboards but no desks or seats yet. We have a computer room almost assembled. We have just installed a generator so adults can attend night classes. We have a new library and we are installing shelving. All school supplies are free and the minimal tuition for all Ebola orphans has now been paid (thanks to several donations from members of my parish, Bishop Breidenthal of Southern Ohio and the generous work and gifts of the Third Order). I wish you could see it!

We already have 320 students enrolled. Benedict and I attended the opening day Eucharist with the students in the old packed St. Mary's church (once used by the Anglican Order of the Holy Cross). And suddenly the children began to sing and to dance in their places. A girl would lead off then the whole congregation would join in. The percussion drums played by one of the boys would begin to beat, and one of the girls would chime in with the *shekere* (a percussion hand drum from Africa, consisting of a dried gourd with beads woven into a net). All I could think of was "Dear Lord, with all these children have been through and they can still sing like this."

Benedict, of course, had to make a speech as the President of Baffa, and he stated I was his American mom. The priest then–not to be outdone–stated that since Benedict was everyone's Father, it followed that I was everyone's Grandmother. I had been hoping for grandchildren and suddenly I had 320 of them.

We also travelled to the Anglican Leper Colony–the oldest in Liberia. The WHO provides the boxes of medicines but there are shortages of food and dressings. Benedict and I made hasty arrangements for immediate deliveries-along the way scooping up "Uncle," a frail emaciated old man, to drive him to the nearest hospital for a chest x-ray. His chest x-ray cost $20 US dollars, which of course, is prohibitive for the average Liberian and so was covered by the medical mission fund of the Third Order.

In the leper village, babies clung to Benedict's and my clothing whimpering to be picked up. I was trying to follow the no contact Ebola rules, but I sure felt sympathetic when Benedict suddenly scooped up several in his arms.

Then an even more gut-wrenching point of the day–we travelled to the Ebola villages.

Benedict's truck was loaded with rice, schoolbooks, hand sanitizer, crayons, pencils and pens. As we made the deliveries, we faced the devastation this virus had caused. One village had an Ebola memorial—27 names out of one small village were painted on a simple stone. The children in the village wandered with hurt lost eyes and clenched fists–signs, Benedict told me, of severe depression. We told them that we loved them, that these gifts were from others who loved them and a new school had just opened where they were welcomed and which was free to them.

The village leaders—Christian and Muslim—encouraged the little ones to try and go. One day they would have a story to tell of what had been lost in their villages–a story to be remembered when there was no one left to tell–of this horror that had destroyed their families and lives. I met the wife of the first nurse who died of Ebola while trying to care for his patients. She had five children and was destitute. Benedict spoke to her promising, rice, food, a free schooling for her children, and that we would always be there for her. How right this place was for this new community. "Ketobaye" is the Liberian word for Hope.

TSSF in Cuba

The TSSF presence in Cuba is growing very quickly. In March 2016, Raciel Prat was received as a novice by his priest, the Rev. Armando Delgado, who is also his Spiritual Director. In February 2017, the Rev. Haydee Lugo (Rector of Saint Michael's and All Angels in Ceballos) and Yulién Yuslán were welcomed as postulants during a break in the meetings of the 108th Annual Synod of the Episcopal Church of Cuba. The ceremony was presided over by their diocesan bishop, the Rt. Rev. Bishop Griselda Delgado del Carpio, Bishop of Cuba. Also on that day, Raciel and others were given the opportunity to convey a message on behalf of the Third Order to the synod assembly, and Bishop Delgado del Carpio expressed words of praise and offered a brief explanation of the Order. (Jim Hagen as Hispanic Ministry Coordinator has been their liaison and helped create a Hispanic Facebook page (*La Tercera Orden Ministerio Hispano Sociedad de San Francisco*).

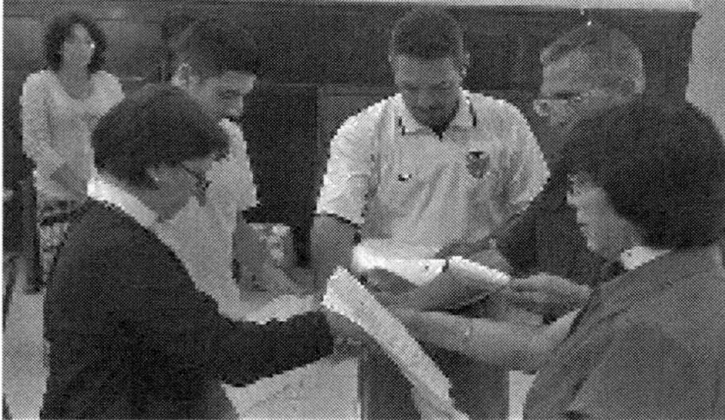

(From left to right): the Rev. Haydee Lugo; Yulién Yuslán, Raciel Prat, the Rev. Armando Delgado, and the Rt. Rev. Bishop Griselda Delgado del Carpio.

References

Pazzelli, Raffaele. *St. Francis and the Third Order: The Franciscan and Pre-Franciscan Penitential Movement.* Chicago, Il: Franciscan Herald Press, 1989.

Chapter 16: Eight Authors of the Province of the Americas

We have already read of six authors who have been members of the Province of the Americas: Desmond Lionel Morse-Boycott (Chapter 1), H. Baxter Liebler (Chapter 1), Peter Funk (Chapter 3), Hugo Muller (Chapter 4), Harold MacDonald (Chapter 12), and Emmett Jarrett (Chapter 14). Here are eight others with reviews or excerpts drawn from the *Franciscan Times*.

William Haynes, Professed 1989

A Physician's Witness to the Power of Shared Prayer (1990); *Minding the Whole Person: Cultivating a Healthy Lifestyle from Youth Through the Senior Years* (1994); *Is There a God in Health Care?: Toward a New Spirituality of Medicine* (2006.)

Is There a God in Health Care? Toward a New Spirituality of Medicine
Review by Jonathan Steinhart, MD TSSF (Franciscan Times, Summer 2008)

Is there a God in health care? This is a good question for providers and patients, which is all of us, and particularly for those of us who are Christian and Third Order. The question implies a familiar dichotomy: science vs. religion, faith healing vs. technology. As a child, I watched on television, along with my parents, Oral Roberts "heal" people with a hand on their forehead and an incantation. This looked like all faith and miracle, and no science. In many years of medical training, I laboriously studied the sciences, which underlie medicine and the technology, which makes it possible, and there was no mention of God or the role that religious faith may have in healing. Both these events and the divisions they implied are decades ago.

Fortunately, times have changed. There is now an ongoing dialogue between scientists and theologians, and medicine acknowledges that there is more to healing than drugs and surgery. Still, it is easy to compartmentalize our lives into the secular and spiritual. However, we, who are in the Third Order are challenged by our Rule to dissolve this barrier. Drs. Haynes and Kelly address issues of spirituality and medicine in their new book. Dr. Haynes is a retired cardiologist and Third Order Franciscan and Dr. Kelly is an associate of the De La Salle Christian Brothers, university professor, and Bonhoeffer scholar. Their exploration of these issues is comprehensive.

They examine familiar issues such as prayer and healing. Should doctors pray with and for their patients? Dr. Haynes became a strong believer in this practice over the years and, when appropriate, prayed with and for his patients. He says, "Indeed by praying with their patients, doctors can help God become a consoling presence for them in their suffering."

They look at the role of health care in terminal illness. It is in this sphere that theology and medicine can enhance each other's effort. Healthcare providers can now do much to relieve physical suffering, but only by addressing the emotional issues and the spiritual concerns which may underlie them can they fully treat the needs of many of their patients. The issues of forgiveness and reconciliation are often critical to a patient and his or her family at this time, and caregivers such as chaplains, social workers, and therapists can assist medical personnel in addressing these concerns.

Using Jesus as the model healer, they have an excellent chapter on "Listening from the Heart in Health Care." They believe that some of the charm and maybe therapeutic power of Jesus is that he took the time and effort to listen to people who often were not heard in their society. The key to being a good listener is avoiding judgments based on preconceived attitudes and stereotypes. The joy that comes through medicine is the trust that develops between the caregiver and the person who has come for help. This only comes through active and unhurried listening, something that is important for us in the healthcare professions to realize as the increased workload, paperwork, and abundance of technology decrease our face-to-face time with patients.

In a chapter entitled, "Healing Services: Miracles, Cures, and Hope," they look at the role of contemporary healing ministry. Sometimes a well-known religious healer such as Father DiOrio, with whom Dr. Kelly had a personal experience, fills this role. His daughter had a brain tumor and her condition remarkably improved and stabilized after an encounter with Father DiOrio at a communion service. They point out that Father DiOrio always makes it clear that he is not the healer but a conduit for the healing love of Jesus, the Divine Physician, [Ed. See parallels with Emily Gardener Neal later in this chapter] and that Father DiOrio always counsels those who come to him to continue their medical treatments. Though less dramatic, both authors are strong supporters of the healing ministries in the church and its outreach ministries.

The authors briefly address contemporary social factors that affect health care: lack of universal health coverage in this country, a predilection for advanced weaponry and violence to solve problems, an environment with a diminishing water supply and replete with toxins. These problems go far beyond the reach of individual health care providers and the institutions with which they work. They believe we must foster in our lives and our churches a spirituality that respects the environment, advocates for the poor, and seeks justice and mercy first to address global problems. Is not this what we are all about as Third Order Franciscans?

So where is God in healthcare? Drs. Kelly and Haynes lead us to believe that He is to be encountered on many fronts: in a physician's office, in a healing service, in intercessory prayer for the sick, in advocating for greater healthcare access, in the laboratory and the operating room. They do not suggest that "faith, prayer, and a spiritual relationship with God" are to be substituted for capable healthcare providers using modern medicine. They believe that God acts in health care through the spiritual life of healthcare providers, through the healing ministries in and out of the church, and through God-given advances in modern medicine and technological breakthroughs.

Over the years my parents become supporters of Oral Roberts and lived their final years in University Village, a retirement center in the shadow of the tall towers that once housed his medical school. They also inspired and help put a son through medical school. The frontiers of medicine and theology are continually expanding and merging, and I recommend this book to readers who are interested in new insights in this emerging dialogue.

Lucy Blount McCain, Professed 1997

Letters from a candidate's wife: it looks like a rough ride, but there's a rainbow in sight. (1994), *"Lamkins J. Flock, get off that heap!": an adult fable.* (1997), *Letters to the Precious Group.* (1990), *The Story of Lucy What's-Her-Name!: And Your Name Too!* (1990), *Lenten Love Letters.* (1998), (and with Mary Barwick) *I Love You Greater Than Space!* (2013).

Lenten Love Letters an excerpt (*Franciscan Times*, Winter 1998)

From "A Foreword" by The Rt. Rev. Henry N. Parsley, Jr., Bishop Coadjutor of Alabama

Lent is sometimes called the ***ver sacrum****, the sacred spring of the church. These letters have a spring-like quality which can help renew our sense of God's grace in all of life and find the inner rebirth to which this holy season invites us. May they cheer you and kindle your faith as they have kindled mine.*

Precious Sisters, Good Friday

My name is Mary, the Handmaiden. I am Jesus's mother. He is the Messiah, the Lord and Savior of the world. He is the Messiah, the Lord and Savior of the world! I know. At the Annunciation I was told by our Father God Almighty's messenger. At His birth, shepherds and wise men recognized and worshipped Him. At His nine-day-old presentation to the temple, holy Simeon and Anna proclaimed Him. John the Baptist knew. His disciples knew, first the twelve and then hundreds, even thousands who followed Him knew. The miracles. The fulfilled prophecies. My Son Jesus is the Messiah, the Lord and Savior of the world!

But where is everybody now? I don't understand. I kneel on the ground looking up. My eyes are fixed on His. I'm trying to give Him strength with my gaze. There is an excruciating pain in my heart. My head is throbbing. My breath has become labored like His. Am I also dying? Once again I don't understand. I don't understand what's going on. But, that's all right. I've learned that I don't have to understand, but rather I have to trust and in trusting comes acceptance and I can, I must, I will proclaim my eternal continual response to our Lord God. "Yes."

My precious, precious sisters. I am in agony. If I could, I would climb up on that cross and die in my Son's place. You know I would, all mothers would. Right now I have to stay here as if glued to this spot.

"God is Love. My Son is the Messiah. God is Love. My Son is the Messiah." This thin line of words has become my Hymn, my chant, my lifeline. "God, give me the strength to see this moment through and once more say 'yes'."

Sisters, do you still want to be a handmaiden, a servant too? Today I am clothed not only in humility, but the garment of love has also been added. God's ways are not our ways. I know beyond a shadow of a doubt that our Father God's love is about to crash through this darkness and that my Son's Messiahship is about to be eternally proclaimed.

My arms are outstretched. I seem to be dying too, dying to self as I look upon Him. At the same time, this exquisite sense of love seems to be blossoming.

Look. Look! Do you see? Do you feel? Do you sense the same? Stretch your arms out. Look up into His eyes. All else seems to be dropping, drifting, departing away. This Light—This Love—In this darkness. Ah! "Yes, Lord, Yes."

I Love You Greater Than Space

Review by Janet C. Nail (Franciscan Times, Summer 2013)

Remember finding *The Song of Solomon* in the Bible when you were in junior high school? This was a book that your parents and teachers definitely did NOT want you to read! In fact, they seemed to be embarrassed that it was included in the Bible. Maybe they tried to etherealize it by describing it as an analogy of God's love and pursuit of the church.

Anything but the love of a man and woman! I feel that Lucy Dunn Blount may have been influenced by the Song of Solomon in writing *I Love You Greater Than Space*, a paean to the love she shared with Duncan MacLeod.

Lucy and Duncan met at Monteagle Sunday School Assembly. Both are wounded and healing; he is a widower, she a divorcee. Their mutual attraction may have come to nothing had not Duncan's daughter learned that Lucy made an annual retreat to St. Mary's, an Anglican Convent in Freeland, England, a convenient mile-and-a-half from the MacLeod home in Long Hanborough.

Two months passed before their first date; in another two months they were married, and their love was so strong it was obvious to everyone they encountered. Again, they were in Monteagle, as the season was coming to an end. After a grand day of activities, they retired to their room. In the middle of the night, Duncan awoke in obvious pain. Sitting up in bed, he took a deep breath and made motions with his arms as though swimming; then he was still, dead of a massive heart attack.

They had been married a glorious 623 days.

Their love story, told in poetry by Lucy, is not a delicate, unearthly tale. It is as much part of the world as Lucy and Duncan are, concrete, hearty, and solid. This is a love of flesh, of conversation, of silence, of walks and meals and drinks in the evening. It is walking hand in hand, admitting that she is smitten by his very blue eyes. It is rejoicing in embraces and caresses. It is the love for which God created man and woman.

Stylistically, the book includes three parts. "Soaring Songs" is the story of the courtship and marriage. Each stanza of a poem is written as a haiku, an interesting conceit that differs from the usual notion that a haiku stands alone, complete. This gives flow to the poetry and saves it from the facile rhythm of most love poetry (who has not suffered from the "See Saw, Margery Daw" scansion of those magazine poems?).

The progress of love is so real that one occasionally feels like a voyeur reading it, but it is not embarrassing. It feels somewhat like sitting with old friends whose marriage is so grounded in love and in God that you bask in the warmth! You feel your own relationships enriched.

The second part, "Duncan Doodle-Dog," is the achingly beautiful effort to explain Duncan's death to their grandchildren, to ease their grief. In so doing, she embraces her own and moves to releasing him to God. I found myself choked up reading this section (and if you can read the story of the stuffed dog without tearing up, you have lost something!)

The third part, "Ta, Gorgeous," is the sad journey of learning to accept the change from wife to widow. Everything ordinary is now strange; a journey to Birmingham, being home alone for the first time, introducing herself at a retreat—all is changed, changed; a terrible beauty can be born only through the bedrock of her faith, of his faith. She sees them as separated yet together, looking forward to the day they will be together again.

Faith in God is the continuing golden thread in these poems. Loving God made it possible for Lucy and Duncan to love one another, loving God made it possible to continue life with a shout of "Grateful, grateful!"

Read *I Love You Greater Than Space* to reassure yourself that love is of God, and all your love is part of God.

Jeff Golliher, Professed 2004

A Deeper Faith: A Journey into Spirituality (2008),

Moving Through Fear: Cultivating the 7 Spiritual Instincts for a Fearless Life (2011)

A Deeper Faith: A Journey into Spirituality.

Review by Masud Ibn Sydullah (Franciscan Times, Winter 2008)

A Deeper Faith is an extraordinary book of spiritual guidance. Written in a style reminiscent of C.S. Lewis' *Screwtape Letters,* Jeff offers spiritual direction in the form of letters, responding to letters sent to him from a spiritual directee. Such an approach helps to create a sense of intimacy and personal care as Jeff engages the questions, concerns, and life situations of the directee.

A Deeper Faith is written for a broad spectrum of people on a spiritual journey. While being absolutely appropriate and helpful for dedicated Christians, it is quite accessible to the seeker–those who are not quite sure what path they may want to take, but are committed to responding to the call of Spirit in their lives.

The book is honest, addressing nearly all aspects of human experience and the life of faith. Jeff courageously shares his own experiences and challenges of faith and faithfulness. Remarkably, he strikes a balance–telling enough of his own story to be self-revealing without being self-indulgent. The style convincingly conveys the relationship of a faithful spiritual director/soul friend sharing with another on a spiritual journey. Organized in chapters relating to the Liturgical Year of the Church, one is able to relate the concerns of the letters to the themes of the Church Year, as well as have empathy with both the director and directee as the author guides us through what one of the collects of *The Book of Common Prayer* calls "the chances and changes of life."

I highly recommend *A Deeper Faith*, and since we are just about to enter Advent, it would be a perfect time to begin. However, wisely, Jeff has written this book so that it really does not matter when, or with what chapter, one begins to read. In any case, one is invited (and guided) into *A Deeper Faith.*

Moving Through Fear.

Review by Mary Teresa Rogers (Franciscan Times, Summer 2011)

Jeff Golliher is a great storyteller. Because I know him, I can hear his North Carolina accent behind the stories he tells in *Moving Through Fear*. Many of these stories are from his childhood in the rural south; some from his adult life as a priest. All the stories illustrate a very particular encounter with fear and the chance to move through and past it.

Early in the book he tells the story of St. Francis and the wolf of Gubbio. Later on he talks about his first meeting with a terrifying three-foot-long snake when he was five years old, and his subsequent teenage and adult fascination with snakes. All of which led up to a seemingly simple event on St. Francis Day at the Cathedral of St. John the Divine in NYC, when he and other clergy sat in the cathedral garden to bless hundreds of pets:

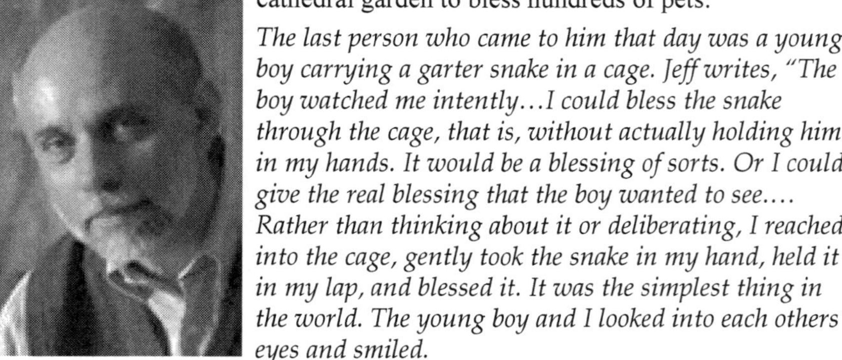

The last person who came to him that day was a young boy carrying a garter snake in a cage. Jeff writes, "The boy watched me intently…I could bless the snake through the cage, that is, without actually holding him in my hands. It would be a blessing of sorts. Or I could give the real blessing that the boy wanted to see…. Rather than thinking about it or deliberating, I reached into the cage, gently took the snake in my hand, held it in my lap, and blessed it. It was the simplest thing in the world. The young boy and I looked into each others' eyes and smiled.

The simplest thing in the world—that is what many of Jeff's stories add up to. Although he is clear that fear is sometimes just what we need to respond to a real danger, so much of our fear needlessly complicates our lives.

The spiritual practices he suggests—those that nurture and cultivate the seven spiritual instincts—are simple as well. That's part of why this feels like such a Franciscan book. It's also earthy: rejoicing in the details of a swarm of bees, of the sacredness of a family meal, of the spiritual struggles of children who are bullied and who fight back, of the last and intimate visit with a dying friend.

It is characteristically Franciscan that Jeff ends with an epilogue called "In Defense of Joy." "The defense of joy is the best of all possible defenses," he writes. When he took up the practice of searching for joyful people, the ones he found helped him open his eyes to see even more. "Joyful people insist on creating and living the kind of life that they believe we are all meant to share." Looking for joyful people–a practice that is deeply incarnational.

Susan Pitchford, Professed 2004

Following Francis: The Franciscan Way for Everyone. (2006),

God in the Dark: Suffering and Desire in the Spiritual Life. (2011),

The Sacred Gaze. (2014)

Following Francis: The Franciscan Way for Everyone.

Review by Ted Witham, Former Minister Provincial of Australia

Susan Pitchford's new book is written with love and insight. I liked it for two main reasons:

1. It reminded me of my own journey as a novice in the Third Order of the Society of Saint Francis 25 years ago towards a fuller realisation of my vocation as a Franciscan.

2. Pitchford's struggles with aspects of our life like simplicity and chastity inspired me to go deeper into those areas in my life to make it conform a little more to what a Franciscan might be.

Novices will appreciate the way some of the jargon of the Third Order has been demystified by showing how words like "Rule," "Joy" and "Obedience" are concepts that can reinvigorate Christian living.

The chapter on prayer as desire and fulfilment shows a second great influence on Susan Pitchford's life, Teresa of Avila. In his 2006 encyclical *Deus Caritas Est,* Pope Benedict XVI approves the idea that eros is a characteristic of God.

God's desire for us–as Pitchford shows by reference to Teresa as well as Francis –is the basis of the life of prayer. Thomas Keating's phrase "exuberant mysticism" describes Franciscan prayer well.

Following Francis is funny. It frequently made me chuckle out loud. Wry and humorous observations, say of birds from a window, are exemplars of how following Francis is fun.

Susan Pitchford knows the cost of being a Franciscan, having, for example, foregone tenure as a professor.

Such decisions are painful and difficult, not the least because colleagues either can't understand or are threatened by these decisions.

These personal examples give the book its strength. For many of us in the U.S. and Australia, the challenge of being a tertiary is complicated by our middle class lives. In our wealthy countries, it can be counter-productive to give away all our money and possessions. We are held by so many safety nets–most of which we middle-class folk make good use of–that trying to stand aside from our wealth might simply make us dependent not on God, but inappropriately on other people.

I struggle with these issues, and I was very encouraged by Pitchford's struggles with them.

And I enjoyed going on "Franciscan road trips" to Ghana and Cambridge in England. Pitchford shows imaginative ways in which we can bridge the great divide between us and the poverty in this world.

With its easy-to-read style and helpful exercises at the end of each chapter, this book is clearly aimed at Third Order members starting out, but would be equally helpful to anyone considering how Franciscan spirituality could refresh their Christian life.

Tertiaries and others who have been on the Franciscan journey for some more years can continue to gain from insights into retreats as *yichud*, into the power of the Profession vows and their renewal each year, and so on.

I read many good books about the life of Francis, some excellent books about the ideal of Franciscan spirituality and the story of the Franciscan family. But this book is about being a Franciscan, in particular about being a Third Order Franciscan. It's an insider's book, and as such will be helpful for many.

God in the Dark: Suffering and Desire in the Spiritual Life.

Review by John Brockmann (Franciscan Times, Summer 2011)

We have all profited from Susan's 2006 book, *Following Francis: The Franciscan Way for Everyone*, in how she ruminated on our formation material in *Forming the Soul of a Franciscan.* Susan's new book is introduced on her website:

> *"Eros is one of God's names." The late Dorothee Soelle wrote these words in* The Silent Cry: Mysticism and Resistance, *and Christian writers are increasingly meeting God under this strange and ancient name. A growing number of books address either our longing for God or our grief when suffering comes and God seems far away. What is lacking is work that shows the relationship between our longing and our grief.* God in the Dark *portrays suffering and desire as the two faces of passion, and passion itself as the essential energizing force of the spiritual life.*
>
> *Western Christianity in the twenty-first century urgently needs to know both sides of passion. The religious routines, partisan squabbling and mundane daily upkeep of the institutional church often obscure the passionate love at*

the heart of the Gospel. Overburdened by the demands of our lives, we settle for an hour of peace each week over intimacy with the living God, and what began as a love affair cools into a banal religious complacency. God in the Dark *invites readers to reconsider the God whom the Bible describes as both "love" (I John 4:8) and a "consuming fire" (Hebrews 12:29).*

There is also an acute need among spiritual seekers for a better understanding of suffering, especially spiritual suffering. Many people were shocked to learn through her letters that Mother Teresa had spent much of her life in a state of spiritual darkness. The struggle to reconcile this with her reputation for holiness reveals that the role of darkness and suffering in the spiritual life is not widely understood. God in the Dark *invites readers to reinterpret the dark nights of their lives, to learn that darkness is not necessarily a place of failure and abandonment, but can be a place of intimacy and growth. When we learn that God does some of his best work in the dark, we will be drawn there by our desire, and when the night closes in around us, we will welcome its embrace.*

Alan Jones, Dean emeritus of Grace Cathedral, San Francisco, wrote the Foreword of the book and this is what he had to say about it:

'There be in God, some say, a deep but dazzling darkness.' The 17th century poet Henry Vaughan expresses a vital truth, which is explored with intelligence, passion and humor by Susan Pitchford. In spite of her disclaimers to be a theologian, her book is a discerning work of the moral and theological imagination. It is an exploration well suited for our times, marked as they are, by both shallowness and fierceness in religion. The God of God in the Dark *is passionate and intractably mysterious. And because we are all made in that divine image, so we too are driven by passion to embrace the unknown. Spirituality isn't a 'product.' It can neither be bought nor sold and Susan Pitchford skewers this misunderstanding with down-to-earth accessible writing, marked with humor and honesty. The book is refreshing and yet stands in a long mystical tradition. It is a great gift for a floundering, atomized culture—water in the desert.*

John Michael Talbot had this to say about the book:

Susan R. Pitchford has penned (or at least word processed!) a new book with a master's touch in God in the Dark. *Coming from a Franciscan orientation, she has tapped into a broad spectrum of the ancient mystical heritage of Christianity in a way that speaks to the average person in a fast-paced, modern world. Readers will find it a fine addition to their modern mystical books, or a great introduction to the mystical tradition for new seekers and first-time readers.*

Stuart Schlegel, Professed 2000

Wisdom from a Rainforest: The Spiritual Journey of an Anthropologist. (1998) (This book was later made into a New York play in 2005 entitled *Kegedewan*, which means *The Gift*.) In the play, Stuart informed me: "At one point, my which means *The Gift*.) In the play, Stuart informed me: "At one point, my bishop (in the play, a much more self-righteous and pious guy than was actually the case!) says to me on an occasion when I come out of the forest for a break: "Father, did you teach them the gospel?" and I reply, "Bishop, they taught ME the gospel."

A reviewer of the play wrote: "*Kegedawan* is that rare example of theater that is potentially both cathartic and eternally memorable. Its exploration of individuality, gender identity, freedom of will, and grace under pressure is breathtakingly remarkable."

The book was a finalist for National Book Award in the Philippines. Stuart received lots of email in response to the book, but he told me he prizes this one most: "I received an email from a British soldier in Basra, Iraq, which was their area of responsibility, and he said that he had been given a copy of *Wisdom* by his padre (their term for chaplain, as you know — who knows how he got ahold of it!), and he was deeply moved to read about such a nonviolent, loving people amidst the terrible carnage all around him.)

This was the excerpt and dialogue that appeared in the *Franciscan Times*, Summer 1998.

Prologue

This book is a love story.

In the middle of a dark night in July 1967, deep in a Philippine rainforest, I realized that my son Len, sleeping beside me on the bamboo slat floor of my tiny house, was sick. The heat of his feverish body had awakened me. Rain, which had begun the day before, pounded loudly against the grass roof, but I could still hear him moaning. Len was only six years old, and his mother—who knew much more than I did about sick children—was far away. But I knew that he was too hot. I woke him up and gave him an aspirin with a little water I kept by the sleeping mat. As the night went on he became hotter and hotter. I lit a kerosene lamp, climbed out of the mosquito net we were sharing, and poured more cool water. I sponged off his arms and legs, hoping that by cooling them I might bring down the fever. Perhaps it helped; I couldn't tell. Len kept moaning and I waited impatiently for morning, my mind filled with dark apprehension.

We were in a place called Figel, a small Teduray settlement alongside the Dakel Teran River on the island of Mindanao. Len and I had walked in the day before, wading across the wide river numerous times. It was a long, hard, full day's trek into the heart of the forest.

Morning finally came and—at last—I heard the playing of gongs which greeted each sunrise in Figel. I saw several Teduray friends up and stretching in the morning mist, their sleeping sarongs cowled over their heads against the damp coolness of the new day, and I called for them to come over and look at my son. By then he seemed to me to be much worse. He had lost control of his bowels and bladder, and he was obviously seriously ill.

Several women and men discussed the situation among themselves. They saw my fear and concern, and some of the men said that they would leave immediately and carry Len out to the coastal town of Lebak, where there was a large plywood factory that had "my kind of doctor." Normally the trail to Lebak involved fording the winding river about a dozen times as it snaked its way to the sea. But that would be impossible now: the night's hard rain had swollen the river, removing any hope of crossing it. It was strong and swift and twice its usual arm pit depth. People never tried to go to town under such conditions. But my Teduray companions saw that I desperately wanted my son to see the coastal doctor, and knowing this touched a deep chord in them, in their understanding of how life should be lived. The Teduray I knew in Figel never ever took someone's wants or needs lightly. They were willing to risk their lives to take him there.

They would attempt this unimaginably dangerous trip even though they were certain that Len's illness was due to his having unintentionally angered a spirit. The Figel people had no concept whatsoever of germs, or even any awareness of what my kind of doctor did, and although no one said anything, I knew they had informed one of the Figel shamans, who would litigate with the offended spirit as soon as possible to effect a cure.

One of the men quickly cut down two six-foot lengths of bamboo from a nearby grove and hung a sarong between them. We then put Len, who seemed to me barely conscious, in this makeshift stretcher. The trek would be agonizingly slow with the river so treacherous; no one would ever attempt it unless forced to by an emergency. But within twenty minutes of the gongs' announcement of the dawn, we were off. Our little group— six Teduray men, Len and me—made its way, deliberately and torturously, along the full length of the the flooded, furious river, clinging to its banks. Fear for myself and my friends' safety now joined my anxiety about Len's condition. In many places the men carrying Len had no firm footing and, their muscles taut and glistening with sweat, were forced to grasp exposed tree roots or shrubs as the river crashed by just below them. The going was slow. Although we stopped for very few breaks, the day passed all too quickly and we were still far from the coast.

After sundown darkness filled the forest, but our little band struggled on. There was a half-moon for part of the night, but not much of its light penetrated the canopy of high trees to reach us on the forest floor. When the night became too dim and the darkness too dangerous we paused and made torches of tree resin applied to the end of short sticks. As we continued along the river banks, we held the torches high with our free hands so that we could see where to put our feet and grasp for firm handholds.

I stumbled alongside my sick and frightened son trying to comfort him, awkwardly keeping up as best I could with these men who had spent their whole lives on this river and in this forest. I put cool cloths on his forehead and spoke to him whenever we stopped for a break or to switch litter bearers.

The trip was a twenty-hour nightmare of physical exertion and danger. We crawled along the river through most of the night, resting only occasionally for a few short moments—which seemed to refresh the Teduray but which did little for my fear and heartache. I knew the breaks in the pace were necessary—it was incredible that these men didn't need more of them—but Len seemed to be getting hotter and weaker, and the horrible possibility that he might not make it weighed on me.

Just as morning was about to dawn, we finally dragged ourselves out of the forest and reached the road that led to Lebak. I found someone who had a jeep, and he agreed to take Len and me into town, while my Teduray friends rested a few hours before starting back to Figel. At the plywood factory, the doctor checked Len carefully and told me that my son was not really all that critical, that he had a kind of viral flu that produced nasty symptoms but was not actually life-threatening. My feeling of relief at that welcome news soaked into every cell of my weary mind and body. I remember the moment clearly still today.

But what especially sticks in my mind, and continues now, many years later, to cause me wonder and even awe, is the gift that those Teduray men gave me and my boy by rallying around us and risking themselves so willingly to do what I felt Len needed. It was a true gift, given simply; a gift of life, and of themselves. It was a gift of love.

* * *

In February 1972, five years after my Figel friends carried Len along the banks of the Dakel Teran, I was standing in one of the main lecture halls at the University of California, Santa Cruz. The day was lovely, sunny yet crisply cool. From behind the lectern in that familiar room where I had so often taught I looked at my students with tears in my eyes. In a few pained words I told them that the Teduray people of Figel, the community of people I had lived with in the rainforest for two years, had been massacred by a ragged band of outlaws.

My cracked voice and the horror of my message brought gasps from throughout the room. These were upper-division anthropology majors, and they had heard me speak at length about Teduray life and culture. From slide shows and many informal discussions as well as in classes, they had grown familiar with the ways and even the faces of the far-off Figel people. I believe most of my students admired the forest Teduray greatly, and they all knew that I had been personally touched by them in a way that went far beyond professional respect. They knew that I loved these people of Figel. I could not teach that morning and so merely dismissed the class. But first I asked them to stand with me for a few moments of silence in honor of those good and peaceful people, who never wanted any part of the violence that raged outside of the forest but who nonetheless had fallen before its terrible fury.

This book began to be written in my mind on that day. I believe that in their death the Figel Teduray left their story to me, that they commissioned me to be their voice to a wider world. Ever since, in formal teaching and research volumes, in conversations, in lectures and homilies to the communities where I have lived, I have told the story of the Teduray of Figel and their gracious way of life. In this book I pass on their wisdom to you. I waited a long time to write it, until I could retire from scholarly writing, until I was freed from the demands of two careers, and until a heartbreak in my family had run its course.

This is an intensely personal book, because it is not only about the Teduray; it is about me as well. I lived in Figel as an anthropologist for two years. But the story is much more personal than just an ethnographer's report from the field. In the pages that follow, I will take you into the Teduray's rainforest and deep into their understanding of reality. I will also take you into some extraordinarily sensitive times in my own life. I want to introduce you to the thinking of these people in all its beauty and elegance. But beyond that, I want to tell you about the tremendous impact their thinking had on me as a human being and the wisdom that it offers us all.

Their gracious, life-affirming, compassionate ways transformed the foundations of my life: my thinking, my feelings, my relationships, and my career. I hope a wider world will hear the voices I heard in that remote forest and realize, as I came to, that the Teduray speak eloquently to us all of tolerance, cooperation, grace, and gentlenesss, that their understanding of the world contains lessons that all of us pursuing "the good life" need to hear.

I hope that the Teduray move you in a deep and fundamental way, as they did me. Knowing and living with them was one of the greatest gifts of my life. This book is my gift of them to you.

Rick Bellows, Professed 1997

Peace that Passes Understanding: Hope and Healing for Anxious Times (2012). Review by John Brockmann

Rick and his wife Danni have been dear friends of mine in TSSF for many years. Many of us in the Northeast Convocations and at the New Orleans Provincial Convocation recall Rick and Danni with their two children, Elanna and Jacob, in tow. Rick has been known to many of us for the TSSF liturgies he has composed, including the "Eucharist for Francis and Clare" in our *Devotional Companion*, and the new liturgy for "Celebrating the Anniversary of a Profession," as well as his occasional pieces here in the *Franciscan Times* in which he integrates his nature photography with his poems and prayers. A big problem, however, with presenting his work in the *Times* is that we cannot reproduce the beauty and complexity of color. This book of his work does not have that limitation!

The Peace that Passes Understanding: Hope and Healing for Anxious Times is a collection of his nature photography with his poems and prayers. Here's the description from Amazon.com:

In August of 2008, photographer, priest, and poet, Richard Bellows, began sending cards of his photographs and written reflections to Laurel, a woman living with cancer. Because she found the cards "have the awesome power to bring peace and a tranquility that allows for healing," Richard expanded the card list to include others, including Paul and Jodi. The cards meant so much to Jodi, even though she was nearly blind, she would take her favorites pinned to a bulletin board whenever she would be admitted to the hospital. Their daughter wrote, "Rick's cards... gave us the strength we needed from God to continue on our journey. The cards were truly cherished treasures for a very difficult time leading up to and after my parents' deaths." Now collected in this book, you, too, can find hope and healing in these pages. As a Christian inspired by St. Francis, Richard sees God in the world—in creation, in people, and in community. He encourages an open-minded Christian faith that notices God sending us messages of love and wisdom—gifts wrapped in the beauty of nature. By unwrapping these gifts we find hope and healing. The author is a member of the Third Order, Society of St. Francis, an Episcopal religious Order. He started his career as a geologist, and finished as a parish priest after nearly thirteen years serving as rector of parishes. At age 42 he was diagnosed with Parkinson's disease, which forced him to retire and move at age 48. Richard, his wife, and two children (when they aren't away at college), live in Westfield, Massachusetts, where he gardens, takes pictures, and writes.

All his pictures are exquisite, ranging from the very, very close-up on nature to the wide-angle view of a horizon at dawn or dusk. His prose poems that accompany the pictures also range from just one or two lines to several pages. And yet despite the variety of text and picture, each is anchored in a very specific date and place in the church calendar (Easter, Epiphany, Advent, etc.), and the dates and pictures and prose poems take us through four years of Rick's life from 2008 to 2012. All of this arises from Rick's search for the signs of God's presence and peace in his life so that he and we may become "signs of God welcomed into our lives—living evidence of grace and healing." Rick invites the reader to join him in welcoming the mysteries of peace, hope, and trust, and it's an invitation that we all should accept.

Scott Robinson, Professed 2001

The Dark Hills, 2015

Review by Jeff Golliher (Franciscan Times, Advent 2016)

A few days ago, my wife, Asha, asked me to tell her about *The Dark Hills* and my reaction to it. She's a community-oriented librarian, so we often talk about the larger significance of books. My first response was like this: "It's not easy to describe, which amounts to high praise for the writer ... I admire what he's do-

ing … never mind that he's a Third Order Franciscan, an Episcopalian, and an interfaith minister trained at the New Seminary in New York, with which the Cathedral of St. John the Divine had a close relationship when I worked there some years ago … My personal bias is to like this book … but, setting that aside, I admire his work because he is exploring ways to recover the broken relationship between our experience, on the one hand, and the purpose of spiritual teachings and practice, on the other."

This is no ordinary book, and I have no desire to review it in the usual way. That would entirely miss the point of his contribution. In keeping with what the author has actually done, I want to tell you about the book by sharing a few thoughts on the experience of reading it. What I write here will, by its very nature, be personal. Life is personal. The spiritual path is personal, and Robinson is taking the spiritual path seriously, which makes *The Dark Hills* a very interesting and compelling book, and the writer an interesting and compelling person. He has something to say that's worth reading, not because he gives "the answers," which would diminish nearly everything that he is, in fact, doing. Rather, he's finding light within, through, and beyond the darkness of the contemporary world and revealing what he sees along the way. Robinson has many gifts, talents, and roles, but one of them is surely being a teacher. All the above, in my understanding, makes him also a spiritual pathfinder. We need a lot more people like that – not to follow him, but to follow the path.

The writer speaks, now and again, about psychological depression and his struggle through it with frequent references to the help that spiritual traditions, both Eastern and Western, have provided. In this review, I would like to comment on that, knowing that many prospective readers might stumble over both (the psychological and the interfaith dimensions of his book).

First – concerning psychological depression. I was once friends with James Hillman, the wise and sometimes controversial psychotherapist and writer. James would be among the first to say that depression is a national malady, speaking of the United States as a whole. Does that mean that every American is depressed? Well, no, but there's more going on here than meets the eye, just as there's a whole lot more going on in Robinson's book than you might think at first glance. Similarly, back in the 1930s and 1940s, American cultural anthropologists, like Ruth Benedict, sometimes spoke of American culture as "paranoid." There was some truth in that too. Yet, is every American paranoid? No, of course not; and yet, something deeply depressing and paranoid has been crystallizing within our national life (and world) for some time, and we're all involved, like it or not. So, when Robinson speaks of *his* depression or former depression, I believe him and I admire his honesty, integrity, and courage in writing about it publicly. And (this is the crucial point) it would be a huge mistake to misinterpret this fact of the writer's life – "someone who has experienced depression" – to mean that this is a "certain kind of person" and "kind of book," and draw the mistaken conclusion that if you've never experienced depression, then this book has no value or meaning for you. Let me assure you that this kind of logic illustrates precisely the broken relationship between our lived experience, on the one hand, and the purpose of spiritual teachings and practice, on the other, that the writer has so bravely taken up. *Note to the reader: I'm not actually defending Robinson here. What I'm doing is trying to remove likely obstacles for you, in the hope that you'll read what he has to say for yourself. As I said, this is an unusual, interesting, timely, and compelling book.*

Second – concerning the question of Eastern and (or *versus*) Western spiritual traditions. As some readers will probably know, I am a Franciscan, Third Order, and a recent member of Chapter, Province of the Americas. I'm an Episcopal priest. I'm also a cultural anthropologist who spent quite a bit of time living with indigenous peoples in Central America. I'm Christian; Asha is Jewish; and we have both been initiates in a yogic tradition for many years. I don't recall that we've ever seen ourselves as "being different," at least in any religious or spiritual sense. We're joined at the spiritual hip – a union of souls. So when Robinson quotes from Ramakrishna, Vivekananda, and many others of various spiritual traditions, he sees them as fellow travelers, rather than foreigners on a different path. I know what he means.

I'm bringing this to your attention because as good as the Franciscan Convocation in Minneapolis was a few years ago – an event that addressed perspectives and spiritual understandings of indigenous peoples -- my feeling is that we have a long way to go in intercultural and interfaith matters. In his own distinctive way, Robinson is a spiritual pathfinder in this regard too. I have to tell you that stories about St. Francis and Franciscan teachings play no large part in his book. Is this a problem, or should this be a reason for not reading his book or for assuming that it has limited significance for Franciscans? Definitely, no.

Let me come at this from another angle. The experience of reading *The Dark Hills* brought to mind a gift that I received, some years ago, from Lady Beverley Reeves, wife of Archbishop Sir Paul Reeves of New Zealand, who was also a leader among the Maori. A day or so after his funeral in New Zealand, Lady Reeves handed me a jade Maori pendant, called *pekapeka*, that he wore on special spiritual occasions. The *pekapeka* symbolizes the sacred bat, which, from a spiritual point of view, is understood as a superb flier through the darkness. That is what spiritual pathfinders do -- shamans, saints, and holy ones. They help us fly through the darkness. The dove is another perfectly good symbol for the same lived experience, seen from another point of view. But let's face it, as our Celtic Christian ancestors did years ago, we (in the colonial, colonized West) have always had a bad habit of interpreting the dove in ways that are way too tame. The Celts preferred the wild goose, which seems more Franciscan to me. And so does the bat. I would imagine that St. Francis was one of the best fliers through the darkness that the Christian tradition has ever known, as was

Ramakrishna in his. Are all these traditions so different? No they're not, not at a certain spiritual depth, and we need to explore that possibility soon. The darkness of the world is thick and growing thicker by the day. As the testimony of his book reveals, Robinson has some insight into what flying through the darkness involves; and for that reason alone, reading his book is important. Just don't expect a lot of dove talk – meaning no disrespect for her/him, the Spirit. Are we still stumbling over the possible gender of the Holy Spirit, rather than learning to fly spiritually? Following the Incarnation and Francis, Robinson would know that we have to get back into our bodies first, and Earth's body. This is a Brother Sun, Sister Moon place to be. So, do I see St. Francis and the spirit of Francis in Robinson's book? Definitely, yes -- not necessarily written on the pages, but between and within nearly every line.

Okay -- I've said my piece. These are difficult times, and life, God's creation and everyone and everything that's part of it are precious and sacred. That's why I hope you will read what Robinson has written. It's a very personal collection of thirty-seven relatively short chapters with titles like "Welcome to the Real World," "Make Our Lives a Blessing," "Always Be Ready to Be Surprised," and "The Pearl of Great Price." Some of the chapters have been published previously in yogic and other journals. In a way, it's a collection, but not really.

Is this a well-written book? I haven't thought of it that way, and I'll tell you why. Imagine that you're having a conversation with a friend, and it's one of those unfortunately rare, but grace-filled times when the truth of one's soul pours out like the River of Life. Darkness and light fill the room or sky with beautiful radiance. *The Dark Hills* is one of those conversations. In moments like that, we don't turn to our friend and say, "ya know, you could have said that better," as if our job is to improve (or pass judgment on) the Holy Spirit's sense of style. Episcopalians are prone to that; Franciscans, not so much. Saint Francis and especially Jesus – not a chance.

Emily Gardiner Neal, Professed 1967

Emily had a successful career as a journalist, publishing over 50 articles in popular magazines such as *Look*, *Redbook*, *McCall's*, and *Reader's Digest*. However, her life was changed dramatically after attending a healing service—an event that she described in her first book, *A Reporter Finds God through Spiritual Healing* (1956). From then on, she became a lecturer and counselor on the subject of spiritual healing. In 1961 she was appointed to the Joint Commission on the Ministry of Healing, and she wrote the commission's report to the 1964 General Convention. She always resisted the label of "healer" in reference to her work and preferred to say that she was simply an "enabler of healing" or "an instrument that is used for God's healing." In 1976 after the death of her husband, Emily moved to Cincinnati, where she lived on the grounds of the Convent of the Transfiguration. She served on the staff of St. Thomas Episcopal Church (Terrance Park, Ohio) as deacon, leading weekly healing services and counseling. At the Convent she also served as deacon leading a monthly healing

service and counseled weekly. The Episcopal Healing Ministry Foundation was founded in her honor in 1987, and she was its first president. She died in 1989. (Hein and Shattuck, 2004, p. 262)

From Hawley Todd, TSSF, Current President of the Episcopal Healing Ministry Foundation

Where Emily and I both connected was in a deep love for Jesus. I believe that is why each of us loved Francis because in him we found a kindred soul–a human who passionately loved Jesus and who followed Jesus.

Francis embodied a fallible broken human who simply wanted to follow in the footprints of his Lord—a God with a human face—known as Jesus. We love Francis because he is human—not because he is an idolized saint. I find it interesting that many who knew Emily wanted to make her into a "holy icon"—a saint in the present day. Yet like Francis, she struggled with what it means to be human. Many knew her as a "saint." I knew her as a wonderful human who at times was very transparent and a window to "divine presence," and, at times, had all the sins and weaknesses that we all have within us. I find it interesting that people confused both Francis and Emily with the ONE they loved and embodied.

I believe Emily also was attracted to Francis because he tried to be an authentic human being and still remain loyal to the Church. Personally I have extreme difficulties with "The Church" and wonder if it has not grown far removed from anything to do with the one we call Jesus. Yet she loved The Church. She also loved Mary.

Emily, as a person who works in healing, knew God as REAL and ALIVE and ACTIVE. The Holy Spirit actually touched lives and transformed people. God was not just a concept or an intellectual doctrine or a dogma of faith. God was a force that was present in our lives in the here and now. That is how both Emily and I knew/know God. And that is how Francis knew God; a real God who was and is real, incarnate, en-fleshed, active, mysterious; a God who loves and redeems us in the PRESENT.

One of the reasons Emily recommended TSSF to me is that she felt it was real. What I mean by that is that so much of Christianity is far removed from the reality of living in the moment-to-moment presence of Christ. I had no interest in being connected with any group who did not know and live a life that was fully alive in the Holy Spirit. And Francis was where I could connect with another in the tradition who had an intimate, passionate, alive connection with Jesus.

Emily also believed a Rule of Life and discipline were essential tools to staying open to God. TSSF offered an excellent way to do that in an intentional way. While I did become an Associate of the Convent of the Transfiguration, I am unsure if Emily was. She did live on the grounds though in her own apartment.

She did a healing service there every Tuesday morning and one at St. Thomas every Monday evening for many years. The "religious life" helped her to stay focused on God.

Emily and I both are/were members of TSSF. Yet we did not worship Francis. Francis was our brother –a trusted guide and example on how one might live an authentic life as a Christ follower.

Francis used creation as a ladder to reach his beloved (1 Cel 165, I believe). And I believe that for both Emily and myself, Francis has helped to be a ladder we have used to be with our beloved. Again for both us, it is not so much a matter of being a member of TSSF. It has been a process of becoming and transformation that TSSF has provided for us. And the goal was always God incarnate—the one called Jesus. Discovering who we are and living in integrity in the Holy Spirit.

As one nun said to me in India in the ashram from which the original SSF Third Order Rule was taken: "If you don't experience Christ daily, why bother to call yourself a Christian?" While that seems or can be a bit harsh if used the wrong way, it does get at a truth. God is real and as accessible as each breath we take. Why settle for anything less? Why expect anything less?

The Healing Ministry: A Personal Journal (1982)

Dora Chaplin Review from the Living Church (reprinted in Franciscan Times, June 1983)

This splendid hook has been written out of the experience of many years of healing and counseling, which are still in progress. Although it is a profound work with a deep biblical foundation, and is theologically sound, it reads like an adventure story. The author says it is "the continuation of the most exciting adventure any of us can undertake–the journey of a Christian pilgrim."

Emily Gardiner Neal lives on the grounds of an Episcopal convent and takes part in their daily Offices. The Church Year gives her journal an ordered background. At the weekly healing services in her parish church, all is done in the context of the Eucharist which approach is both catholic and evangelical. The author works among many denominations. She was ordained to the diaconate of the Episcopal Church in 1978 and has no intentions of being ordained to the priesthood.

Prayer is inextricably bound up with healing, and it is stressed that God heals by prayer alone. We are also reminded that "salvation and healing are the same word in Greek: the entire Gospel is a healing Gospel, and the healing ministry is the Gospel in action." Because of this, it is natural to find much teaching on the life of worship and prayer, given so well that I believe the book will become a prayer manual for many.

Spiritual direction is given through the saints and scholars of the past, and through reference to modern saints. The relationship of modern medical understanding and psychology to prayer is also shown, but no flip or sentimental answers are given. It is a mature work in which the experienced healer and the beginner will find help.

This is a joyful book, not because complete physical healing is always the result, but because the movement of the spirit in changed lives and relationships, although sometimes very slow, is a great reality A beautiful balance is given by the quotation on page 48: "He cannot heal who has not suffered much, for only sorrow, sorrow understands."

Review by Joanne Maynard (Franciscan Times)

Now I can tell you about this marvelous book from my own experience! I have found it to be a real "shot in the arm" for my spirit, as well as an interesting story of a period in Mrs. Neal's life, and an instruction in the area of spiritual healing. These are actual entries from Emily's personal journal, telling about her life, her ministry, her contacts with others, her worship, her prayer, as well as her frustrations and fears. Fears? Yes, in telling about her daughter's frightening diagnosis (which turned out to be an error) she was afraid and struggled with it, which gave me heart, because I also have done this where my children are concerned. She tells about wonderful instant healings, and healings that took a long time and much prayer. She stresses that the most important healing is the inner healing of one's relationships with God and other people. Do read this book, by a Franciscan tertiary. It will be a blessing to you.

From Chapter 16 in *The Healing Ministry: A Personal Journal*

October 4, Saint Francis of Assisi

This day has very special meaning for me as it is the one on which I customarily renew my annual vows as a Third Order Franciscan. The chaplain received my vows this morning at mass, and the blessing of Saint Francis, prayed over me, still rings in my ears: "The Lord bless thee and keep thee. May He show His face to thee and have mercy on thee. May He turn His countenance to thee and give thee peace. The Lord bless thee!" And so He has beyond all my deserts.

I was life-professed as a tertiary 15 years ago, as it seemed the closest I could come to the religious life to which I then felt called. Within the Franciscan "family" founded by Saint Francis in the thirteenth century, there are three Orders: the first, comprised of brothers (friars) and sisters; the second, the Poor Clares of Reparation and Adoration. These are religious, living in their respective houses under the traditional vows of poverty, chastity, and obedience. The Third Order, originally known as Brothers and Sisters of Penance, now simply as "tertiaries," is composed of laypeople and clergy, married and unmarried, living in the world in the spirit of the counsels and under rule. The three Orders are bound together by their common aim to make Jesus Christ known and loved everywhere, the same aim as their founder had so many centuries ago. The outstanding characteristics of all Franciscans are those preeminently exemplified by the life of Francis himself: joy, humility, and love.

Saint Francis, the *poverello* (little poor man) of Assisi, is one of the best-loved of all the saints and probably one of the least emulated. Few of us in the world today share his fervent love of Lady Poverty. We who are tertiaries are bound only to live simply and without undue extravagance.

I have derived much satisfaction in living here in what, for me, is a very

Franciscan manner. However, I must admit it is not as Franciscan now as it was when I first came. The community, considering that it fit into the category of "permanent improvement," has put in the most glorious bedroom closet for me, which runs the length of one whole wall. Curious how one's sense of values change: no longer do I take for granted a large closet. Having been without any closet in my bedroom for so long, I now feel I am living in the lap of luxury, and am unashamedly ecstatic!

Actually, I am afraid I am not a very good Franciscan as far as poverty goes. I have one seemingly uncontrollable extravagance–buying books. There is really no excuse for this, as the convent has a large and excellent library. The trouble is, that if I like a book want to be free to mark and underline passages in it. Obviously this means I must own it.

I often think (but most especially when a newly ordered book arrives as one did today) of how, a long time ago, Father Paul told me that at the friary the brothers changed their cells (rooms) frequently. They could take with them to their new quarters only what they could carry in both hands. Anything more than this had to be disposed of. I look around a bit guiltily, as I realize that it would take a large van to move just my books! I rationalize this by calling my books the tools with which I work. In a sense this is true, but do I need so many tools?

Saint Francis, like the majority of the great saints, was both a contemplative and an activist, a combination of gifts I wish more of us possessed. We tend to be either-or people.

Francis spent his life preaching the Gospel, making known the Lord Jesus Christ and His love, spreading the spirit of brotherhood, and serving others wherever there was a need. At the same time, he spent entire nights in contemplative prayer, the silence only occasionally broken by his cry, "My God and my all." He lived out the words of Saint Augustine, "Without God, I cannot; without me, God will not."

The key words of our lives as Christians today, as they were of Saint Francis, might well be, "I will give..," and not only of our worldly goods, but perhaps even more importantly, "of ourselves."

I often reflect on all the times I could have given more and wish that I had. And then, lest I embark on a guilt trip from which there is no return, I remember those times when I was dead-tired, and a call would come, which meant getting out of bed, dressing and driving, perhaps many miles. (Everywhere I go seems to be twenty-five miles from where I am!) I recall faces bright with gratitude, and I offer thanksgiving to God that He got me out of bed and let me go in the strength of Christ. I pray that perhaps some good was accomplished in His name and for His sake. "I will give. This is a vital part of the Gospel message and as such, of the healing ministry.

With Saint Francis, I pray this day his prayer: "Lord make me an instrument of Thy peace; where there is hate that I may bring love; where there is offence that I may bring pardon; where there is discord that I may bring union; where there is error that I may bring truth; where there is doubt that I may bring faith; where there is despair that I may bring hope; where there is darkness that I may bring light; where there is sadness that I may bring joy. O Master, make me not so much to be consoled as to console; not much to be loved as to love; not so much to be understood as understand. For it is in giving that one receives; it is in self-forgetfulness that one finds; it is in pardoning that one is pardoned; it is in dying that one finds eternal life."

Evening

Following the age-long custom of the Church, we had the blessing of animals in the chapel this afternoon. Frances, the all-American dog who belongs to one of the sisters but is in effect the "convent" dog, was first in line. Of course she has lived here a time, and knows the ropes. In fact, she often comes to the summer services in the chapel, walking through the open door and lying quietly in the sanctuary, sometimes across the feet of the chaplain. On more than one occasion, I have had to step over her to get to the altar rail. As I love dogs, it delights my heart that the sisters do not even look up when Frances comes to mass; they take it for granted.

Next in line for her blessing was Jay-Jay, a beautiful Dalmatian belonging to another of the sisters. Then came several cats followed by various and sundry other animals (including goldfish) brought by the village children. They all behaved with splendid decorum.

"Praised be my Lord by all His creatures." "Let every creature in heaven, on earth, and under the earth, and land and sea and all that is in them, Praise and exalt Him above all forever" (Saint Francis).

The Healing Power of Christ. New York (1972)

Review (Franciscan Times, December 1972)

Although the title of the book announces that it is about healing, it also deals with how to handle suffering. This is more than just another book. Here are a few snatches of our Third Order sister's words:

"As we discover with impelling impact through the healing ministry that Christ does indeed live today, we find in Him the meaning of our lives. In our subsequent commitment to Him we find new purpose, for we know at last the reason for our being. When we say and mean, 'Thou art the Christ' we open our hearts to the love and enabling power of the living God within us. We open our hearts to the transcendent God, Who directs and rules our lives. We see His hand in all the blessings of this life, both great and small."

Her other books include: *Let Go and Let God: God Can Heal You Now* (1951), *In the Midst of Life, A Reporter Finds God through Spiritual Healing* (1963), *Father Bob and His Boys* (1963), *Where There's Smoke: The Mystery of Christian Healing. With a Foreword to the Skeptic* (1967) *The Lord is Our Healer* (1968), *The Healing power of Christ/ Dare to Live Now* (1972), *Healing Ministry* (1982), and *Celebration of Healing* (1992).

References

Bellows, Rick. *Peace that Passes Understanding: Hope and Healing for Anxious Times.* CreateSpace Independent Publishing Platform, 2012.

Blount, Lucy. *Lenten Love Letters.* Maryville, Tenn.: Lightbearers Publishers, 1998.

_______ & Mary Barwick. *I Love You Greater Than Space!* Bloomington, IN: AuthorHouse, 2013.

_______ &_________. *"Lamkins J. Flock, get off that heap!": an adult fable.* Maryville, Tenn.: Lightbearers Publishers, 1997.

________&_________. *Letters from a candidate's wife: it looks like a rough ride, but there's a. rainbow in sight.* Montgomery, Ala: Lightbearers, 1994.

________&_________. *Letters to the Precious Group.* Montgomery, Ala: Light-bearers Publishers, 1990.

________&_________ & Woodie Long. *The Story of Lucy What's-Her-Name!: And Your Name Too!* Montgomery, Ala.: Lightbearers Publishers, 1990.

Golliher, Jeff. *A Deeper Faith: A Journey into Spirituality.* New York: Jeremy P. Tarcher, 2008.

________ *Moving Through Fear: Cultivating the 7 Spiritual Instincts for a Fearless Life.* New York: Jeremy P. Tarcher, 2011.

Haynes, William. *A Physician's Witness to the Power of Shared Prayer.* Chicago: Loyola University Press, 1990);

_________. *Minding the Whole Person: Cultivating a Healthy Lifestyle from Youth Through the Senior Years.* Chicago: Loyola University Press, 1994.

_________.and Geffrey B. Kelly. *Is There a God in Health Care?: Toward a New Spirituality of Medicine.* New York: Haworth Pastoral Press, 2006.

Hein, David, and Gardiner H. Shattuck. *The Episcopalians*. Westport, Conn: Praeger Publishers, 2004.

Neal, Emily Gradiner. *A Reporter Finds God through Spiritual Healing.* New York: Morehouse-Gorham Co, 1956.

______. *Father Bob and His Boys.* Indianapolis: Bobbs-Merrill, 1963.

______. *In the Midst of Life, A Reporter Finds God through Spiritual Healing.* New York: Morehouse-Barlow, 1963.

______. *Let Go and Let God.* Carmel, N.Y: Guideposts Associates, 1951.

______.*God Can Heal You Now*. Englewood Cliffs, N.J: Prentice-Hall, 1958.

______. *The Healing Ministry: A Personal Journal*. New York: Crossroad, 1982.

______. *The Healing power of Christ* New York: Hawthorn Books, 1972.

______. *Dare to Live Now* (New York: Hawthorn Books, 1972)

_____ . *The Lord is Our Healer* Englewood Cliffs, N.J: Prentice-Hall, 1961.

______. *Where There's Smoke: The Mystery of Christian Healing. With a Fore word to the Skeptic.* New York: Morehouse-Barlow Co, 1967.

_______ , and Anne Cassel. *Celebration of Healing*. Cambridge, Mass: Cowley Publications, 1992.

(About Emily Gradiner Neal) Cassel, Anne. *The Reluctant Healer: One Woman's Journey of Faith.* Colorado Springs, Colo: Shaw, 2000.

Pitchford, Susan. *Following Francis: The Franciscan Way for Everyone.* Harrisburg, Pa: Morehouse Pub, 2006.

________. *God in the Dark: Suffering and Desire in the Spiritual Life.* Collegeville, Minn: Liturgical Press, 2011.

________. *The Sacred Gaze.* Collegeville, Minnesota : Liturgical Press, 2014.

Robinson, Scott. *The Dark Hills*. Sacred Feet, The Interfaith/Interpersonal Intra-Tantric Publishing Imprint of Slate Branch Ashram, 2015.

Schlegal, Stuart. *Wisdom from a Rainforest: The Spiritual Journey of an Anthropologist.* Athens, GA: University of Georgia Press, 1998.

Sölle, Dorothee. *The Silent Cry: Mysticism and Resistance*. Minneapolis: Fortress Press, 2001.

Discover More On TSSF.ORG (Home–Resources–**History of the Province of the Americas** or **Historical Documents** There is also the indexed collection of **Franciscan Times newsletters 1971-2017**)

Chapter 1

Changing Makeup of the American Province: Relative Percentage of Professed, Novices, and Postulants From 1926 to 2012

Overall Description of the Macro-movements of the Province of the Americas (including table of the shifting 21 centers of TSSF activity)

Chapter 2

Bundle of Myrrh (1924) complete in Historical Documents on the website

1925 TSF Roster complete in Historical Documents on the website

Little Book of the Rule (1929) complete in Historical Documents on the website

Tertiary Tidings: Newsletters from the Battle of Britain, 1938-1941 complete in Historical Documents on the website

Introductory Material to the *May 1935 Roster of the Third Order*: Provincial Organization; Recruiting for the Third Order; The Common Fund; Community of Prayer

The Philadelphia Custodia

H. Baxter Liebler, January 1956 St. Christopher's Newsletter

Recollections of the Father Joseph Era: Caroline Banks of Fayetteville Arkansas

Chapter 3

Br. Paul's *Address to the Third Order Committee* (1968)

Peter Funk complete *Formation Letters*, 1968-70, in Historical Documents on the website

Complete text of the three position papers presented at International Third Order Chap ter (1973):

C. David Burt–"How may we best understand the Third Order today as an Order? What are those things, which constitute an Order? What is the nature of our Profession and Vow? In what sense is the Third Order a Community?"

Judith Robinson–"What is contemporary Franciscan spirituality? What do the traditional terms like Poverty/Chastity/Obedience or Humility/Love/Joy mean for Tertiaries today?"

John Scott–"What should be the public stance of the Third Order today in its witness and outreach to an alien world that is increasingly secular and post-Christian?"

Chapter 4

Reports from the 1st and 2nd Interprovincial Ministers Meetings (1973 and 1976)

Racine Wisconsin General Chapter (1975) Complete Text of Position Papers:

E. Will Drake–"Poverty and Social Policy: The Mirror of Society's Virtue"

Judith Robinson–"Weird random thoughts in answer to a serious request"

Michael Hollingshead–"In Search of Poverty"

Fayetteville, Arkansas Provincial Convocation (1977)

Brother Geoffrey, SSF Minister General, Keynote Talk, "Essential Franciscan Values"

Miami Provincial Convocation 1979

Fr. Jim Jones "Visit to Concept House Narcotics Rehabilitation"

Hugo Muller's "I Wish You Knew Suzanne" from *Why Don't You* (1975)

"Play Little Lilly," "My heart was at peace," poems

Casting call for a play put on by John Scott's Campus Ministries of Temple University and University of Pennsylvania in 1979: *Buckskin and Burlap: The Life of Christ According to Francis of Assisi Performed for Buffalo Bill Cody's Wild West Show*

Chapter 5

More responses to Kale King's resignation as Minister Provincial from Br. Geoffrey, Minister General SSF, Robert Goode, and Lynn Bowdish

Chapter 6

Another article from Robert Goode, "Imitation of St. Francis" (1981)

Information Sheet newsletter collection (1980-1998)

Chapter 7

"TSSF Questionnaire Results" (1983) performed in response to second largest exodus from the Province in 1992-3

From Alden Whitney's Last Minister Provincial Report to Chapter, October 1996

Information Sheet newsletter collection (1980-1998)

Chapter 8

"Impressions of New Orleans Provincial Convocation" (1997) by John Brockmann

From Alden Whitney's Last Minister Provincial Report to Chapter, October 1996

Response to Santa Barbara Convocation (2002) From Suzanne Harrison on the Internet Discussion Group

Hero of the Order: Ralph Shower Honored by Diocese for His Ministries (1998)

TSSF, SSF, CSF Preaching Trips to Mexico: 1999 and 2000

More Reflections by the American Province Representatives to Interprovincial Third Order Chapter (IPTOC) 1999 by Joan Verret and David Burgdorf

The Norms are Published For the First Time (2000)

Chapter 8 (cont.)

"Francis the Romantic" by Br. Robert Hugh, in *The Religious Life (A Franciscan View point)* (1979)

Information Sheet newsletter collection (1980-1998)

Chapter 9

"Criteria for the selection of a Bishop Protector" (2002)

Request that the Order's official recognition by ECUSA be withdrawn because of the impossibility of properly fulfilling the requirements of the House of Bishop's Standing Committee on Religious Communities (2006)

Safe Community and Conflict Transformation Policy October 2006

Chapter 11

Complete collection of *Franciscans Canada* and THAW! newsletters (indexed)

Chapter 12

Review of the Medical Mission To Guyana by Milan Schmidt and Brenda Stewart (2004)

Chapter 13

"Jane Ellen Traugott (Professed 1978, Died November 2005)"

STATEMENT TO THE COURT United States District Court, Washington, DC by Father Emmett Jarrett, TSSF

Poems by Emmett Jarrett: "Fireflies in Winter: Imagine Peace," "September 15, 2001"

Index

* indicates photograph

*"I have done what was mine to do,
may Christ now teach you what you are to do."*

*Tertiaries serving their communities
not captured in the pages of this book.*

Puts on Laurence Houseman's *Little Plays of St. Francis.*
New York Custodia, 1933

Serves with the Army in the Korean War. *Chaplain Russell O. Kirsch, 1950-51*

Founds Chicago's St. Leonard's Halfway House for parolees.
Father James Jones, 1954

Establishes the Long Island Cathedral Recording Unit
of the Episcopal Guild for the Blind. *Faith Booth, 1961*

Purchase a 337-year-old inn in Norwich to serve as a mission house
to care for the poor and needy.
Our Province's Third Order British nuns, 1963

Transcribes religious books of the Episcopal Church into braille.
Helen Struett, 1963

Builds Brotherhood House for teen runaways in Fort Wayne, Indiana.
Robert Bollman, 1971

Offers her house as a retreat facility. *Marie Hayes, 1973*

Leads a Korean Mission in Hawaii. *Noah Cho, 1978*

Helps alcoholics and drug abusers to rehabilitate.
Jim Jones, Concept House, 1979

Directs an Episcopal Home for the Elderly. *Henry Englund, 1980*

Is present with HIV/AIDS homeless persons
under downtown freeway overpasses in Los Angeles. *Ralph Shower, 1998*

Work with at-risk teens at Casa Franciscana in Rio de Janeiro.
Many Brazilian Tertiaries, 2009

Is a peacemaker with the World Council of Churches on the West Bank.
Chris Cowan, 2012